Cases on Usability Engineering:

Design and Development of Digital Products

Miguel A. Garcia-Ruiz
Algoma University, Canada

A volume in the Advances in
Human and Social Aspects of
Technology (AHSAT) Book Series

Managing Director:	Lindsay Johnston
Editorial Director:	Joel Gamon
Book Production Manager:	Jennifer Yoder
Publishing Systems Analyst:	Adrienne Freeland
Development Editor:	Austin DeMarco
Assistant Acquisitions Editor:	Kayla Wolfe
Typesetter:	Erin O'Dea
Cover Design:	Jason Mull

Published in the United States of America by
Information Science Reference (an imprint of IGI Global)
701 E. Chocolate Avenue
Hershey PA 17033
Tel: 717-533-8845
Fax: 717-533-8661
E-mail: cust@igi-global.com
Web site: http://www.igi-global.com

Library of Congress Cataloging-in-Publication Data

Cases on usability engineering : design and development of digital products / Michael A. Garcia-Ruiz, editor.
    pages cm
  Includes bibliographical references and index.
  Summary: "This book provides readers with case studies and real-life examples on usability methods and techniques to test the design and development of digital products, such as web pages, video games, and mobile computer applications"-- Provided by publisher.
   ISBN 978-1-4666-4046-7 (hardcover) -- ISBN 978-1-4666-4048-1 (print & perpetual access) -- ISBN 978-1-4666-4047-4 (ebook) 1. Computer software-- Human factors--Case studies. 2. User-centered system design--Case studies. I. Garcia-Ruiz, Miguel A., 1970-
  QA76.76.H85C37 2013
  004.2'1--dc23
                                    2013001599

This book is published in the IGI Global book series Advances in Human and Social Aspects of Technology Book Series (AHSAT) (ISSN: Pending; eISSN: Pending)

British Cataloguing in Publication Data
A Cataloguing in Publication record for this book is available from the British Library.

Advances in Human and Social Aspects of Technology (AHSAT) Book Series

Ashish Dwivedi (The University of Hull, UK)

ISSN: Pending
EISSN: Pending

MISSION

In recent years, the societal impact of technology has been noted as we become increasingly more connected and are presented with more digital tools and devices. With the popularity of digital devices such as cell phones and tablets, it is crucial to consider the implications of our digital dependence and the presence of technology in our everyday lives.

The **Advances in Human and Social Aspects of Technology (AHSAT) Book Series** seeks to explore the ways in which society and human beings have been affected by technology and how the technological revolution has changed the way we conduct our lives as well as our behavior. The AHSAT book series aims to publish the most cutting-edge research on human behavior and interaction with technology and the ways in which the digital age is changing society.

COVERAGE

- Activism & ICTs
- Computer-Mediated Communication
- Cultural Influence of ICTs
- Cyber Behavior
- End-User Computing
- Gender & Technology
- Human-Computer Interaction
- Information Ethics
- Public Access to ICTs
- Technoself

IGI Global is currently accepting manuscripts for publication within this series. To submit a proposal for a volume in this series, please contact our Acquisition Editors at Acquisitions@igi-global.com or visit: http://www.igi-global.com/publish/.

Titles in this Series

For a list of additional titles in this series, please visit: www.igi-global.com

Cases on Usability Engineering Design and Development of Digital Products
Miguel A. Garcia-Ruiz (Algoma University, Canada)
Information Science Reference • copyright 2013 • 362pp • H/C (ISBN: 9781466640467)
• US $175.00 (our price)

*Human Rights and Information Communication Technologies Trends and Consequences
of Use*
John Lannon (University of Limerick, Ireland) and Edward Halpin (Leeds Metropolitan
University, UK)
Information Science Reference • copyright 2013 • 324pp • H/C (ISBN: 9781466619180)
• US $175.00 (our price)

*Collaboration and the Semantic Web Social Networks, Knowledge Networks, and Knowl-
edge Resources*
Stefan Brüggemann (Astrium Space Transportation, Germany) and Claudia d'Amato (Uni-
versity of Bari, Italy)
Information Science Reference • copyright 2012 • 387pp • H/C (ISBN: 9781466608948)
• US $175.00 (our price)

*Human Rights and Risks in the Digital Era Globalization and the Effects of Information
Technologies*
Christina M. Akrivopoulou (Democritus University of Thrace, Greece) and Nicolaos Gari-
pidis (Aristotle University of Thessaloniki, Greece)
Information Science Reference • copyright 2012 • 363pp • H/C (ISBN: 9781466608917)
• US $180.00 (our price)

Technology for Creativity and Innovation Tools, Techniques and Applications
Anabela Mesquita (ISCAP/IPP and Algoritmi Centre, University of Minho, Portugal)
Information Science Reference • copyright 2011 • 426pp • H/C (ISBN: 9781609605193)
• US $180.00 (our price)

www.igi-global.com

701 E. Chocolate Ave., Hershey, PA 17033
Order online at www.igi-global.com or call 717-533-8845 x100
To place a standing order for titles released in this series,
contact: cust@igi-global.com
Mon-Fri 8:00 am - 5:00 pm (est) or fax 24 hours a day 717-533-8661

This book is dedicated to my wife Selene, who strongly supported me since day one of the book edition and has been an example of perseverance to follow. I also dedicate this book to our son Miguel, who is the spice of our life. I love them both. This book is also dedicated to my parents, Rosalia and Miguel, who both lived their lives intensely and to whom I owe the pleasure of learning and the motivation to work hard. I miss them both so much.

Table of Contents

Section 1
Usability of Web Products

Section 2
Usability of Mobile Applications

Section 3
Usability of Critical Systems

Section 4
Usability of Virtual Environments, Simulations, and Video Games

Detailed Table of Contents

Section 1
Usability of Web Products

For many people of all ages, Web products and online services have become important tools to support their work, education, communication, collaboration and entertainment. As such, a number of evaluation techniques and methodologies need to be developed and employed to study the usability of diverse aspects on the user experience and satisfaction of use, as well as to analyze the efficiency and efficacy of those Web products from the users' perspective.

Conducting usability sessions with children is always challenging due to their cognitive skills and vocabulary comprehension, among other issues. These characteristics make it difficult to assess the tasks children need to perform when evaluating a digital product. Chapter 1 describes usability testing of a science Web site with children and lessons learned from the experience.

As described in Chapter 2, user participation and involvement are very important when carrying out usability studies. In addition, social and technical "negotiations" between users and designers play a fundamental role in studying Web site usability. This chapter shows that early user engagement in the design of the Web site using prototypes should support socio-technical negotiations.

A user profile is a characterization of a digital product's target users, which provides condensed and representative information about users. This tool can help usability designers better understand the target population. Chapter 3 describes an exercise with graduate students who created user profiles for online products, showing that people who develop effective user profiles should have previous experience and skills to administer and interpret user demographic questionnaires.

Chapter 4 explains a compelling case study on the usability testing of an online university reporting system developed by the University of Colima, Mexico. This system shows institutional management statistics, such as undergraduate and graduate statistics. Three usability tools were used in a two-phase usability study of the system: a heuristic evaluation, the System Usability Scale questionnaire, and the Technology Acceptance Model.

Chapter 5

Chapter 5 provides a case study involving the application of important usability principles to improve the use of an online corporate collaborative environment, taking into account business goals, user engagement, and the collaborative nature of a company.

Chapter 6

The author of this chapter describes how usability testing and usability methods can be integrated into the development life cycle of public sector Web sites, a necessary step that few public institutions have implemented. Chapter 6 goes on to explain that most public sector Web sites are launched without public (final users) consultation, a bad practice that needs to be avoided. Thus, this chapter describes a methodology that includes collaborative usability testing, the inclusion of subject matter experts, IT professionals, stakeholders, and, of course, potential users of the Web sites.

Chapter 7

The case study described in Chapter 7 demonstrates the importance of semiotics in the assessment of visual objects employed in Web pages, such as links and icons. According to the chapter authors, semiotics can improve intuitiveness of the computer interface, and semiotic analysis can be useful for identifying usability problems, which represents a cost-effective methodology to support usability testing.

Section 2
Usability of Mobile Applications

Mobile computer devices, such as tablets, smart phones and e-readers are becoming ubiquitous in today's modern society. Many people of almost all ages, backgrounds, nationalities, and cultures use them every day in many diverse contexts; for example, at the park, school, home, etc. Thus, the human-computer interfaces of these devices need to be carefully designed to take into account people's individual differences and contexts of use. In addition, these devices pose special challenges regarding interface design which must take into account the reduced screen space, among other important considerations.

Chapter 8 shows the development and usability testing of a commercial application intended for sharing digital photographs among smart phones, PCs, and tablets called Intel® Pair & Share. This cross-platform application was developed based on an interdisciplinary approach and takes into account the wide variety, benefits and challenges of current mobile devices.

Chapter 9 explains a thorough usability study that tests three social network applications running on mobile devices. The usability testing was carried out using an adapted version of the System Usability Scale (SUS) questionnaire. Based on the usability testing results, the authors propose the creation of a set of heuristics to improve the interface design of mobile social networks.

Section 3
Usability of Critical Systems

Critical systems are digital systems whose defects ("bugs") can greatly affect humans, animals, the environment or other systems, often with fatal consequences. As such, usability specialists must create and follow special usability methodologies and guidelines, paying special and extreme care to the analysis and application of the results of usability tests to improve the design and development of these important systems.

The case study of chapter 10 conveys an important formative usability study performed on an electronic health care record, a critical system used at maternity wards in European hospitals. The authors of this case study used a number of usability tools for their studies, including low-fidelity prototypes (mock-ups) and high-fidelity prototypes (the pilot system). The chapter goes on to explain usability engineering issues, the iterative process and lessons learned.

Chapter 11
Barbara Millet, Texas Tech University, USA

Chapter 11 describes an interesting case study on the development and usability testing of an online error-reporting system for a rural nursing home. Underreporting of error events in the workplace, a common occurrence in nursing homes, can result in serious complications. The developed online system was compared to a traditional paper-based reporting approach. Results from the evaluations showed no significant difference in performance with regard to the online system. According to the chapter authors, this is mainly due to the users' overwhelming familiarity with the paper-based reporting system, although the usability study showed that users preferred the digital interface.

Chapter 12
Stefano Bonelli, Deep Blue Srl, Italy
Linda Napoletano, Deep Blue Srl, Italy

Chapter 12 offers a case study on the usability testing of a flight deck touch-screen prototype. Safety and other issues of this prototype were analyzed using multidisciplinary and iterative testing approaches. The chapter also stresses the importance of understanding and knowing the context in which the technology is to be used. Especially important is considering the crucial constraints that may affect the design of the system, which in this case is the airliner flight deck touch screen simulator.

Section 4
Usability of Virtual Environments, Simulations, and Video Games

Virtual environments, simulations and video games often share a number of characteristics, including graphics, colors, 2D and 3D perception and sound to keep the user engaged in particular interactions. These types of interfaces pose special usability challenges that specialists need to address.

Chapter 13

Valeria Carofiglio, Università degli Studi, Bari, Italy
Fabio Abbattista, Università degli Studi, Bari, Italy

Chapter 13 illustrates the importance of using physiological data in usability testing. The authors devised a special methodology called user-centered evaluation (UCE), which as applied to the design of interactive and adaptable virtual environments. This case study describes the use of a brain-computer interface (BCI) that obtains important data about the user's emotional levels while interacting with the virtual environment. A BCI is a digital interface that establishes a communication pathway between a brain and a digital device that enables signals from the brain to direct some external activity, such as steering an avatar in a 3D virtual environment.

Chapter 14

Stella Sylaiou, Hellenic Open University, Greece
Martin White, University of Sussex, UK
Fotis Liarokapis, Coventry University, UK

Chapter 14 explores a number of quantitative and qualitative usability methods to evaluate the usability of an augmented reality system that displays an interactive virtual museum. The case study describes how usability methodologies can improve engagement and interaction of a virtual museum, taking into account users' subjective presence and learning.

Chapter 15

Roberto K. Champney, Design Interactive, Inc., USA
Christina M. Kokini, Design Interactive, Inc., USA
Kay M. Stanney, Design Interactive, Inc., USA
Stephanie Lackey, University of Central Florida, Institute for Simulation and Training, USA

The case study described in Chapter 15 is compelling. It is about how to improve the design of a military training system where highly-important and demanding key requirements and challenges need to be addressed. To analyze this, it was necessary to design and develop a useful training system to help instructors to apply training lessons to members of the armed forces. This case study also comprises a number of formative and summative usability methodologies that were used to identify the key requirements and improve system performance.

Chapter 16

Rochelle Edwards, Electronic Arts Inc., USA

This chapter presents a case study that analyzes the usability of a chat window added to a number of online video games that belong to a Web portal called Pogo. The chat feature was eagerly wanted by many Pogo users. In response, the authors analyzed whether this requested option was feasible or not, since the Pogo game developers did not want the chat window to interfere with the game play. The case study describes a number of chat solutions tested and usability testing methods used for the Pogo games.

Preface

Usability is defined by the International Organization for Standardization (ISO) norm 9241 as "the extent to which a product can be used by specified users to achieve specified goals with effectiveness, efficiency, and satisfaction in a specified context of use." Usability is about making systems and digital products (e.g. computer systems, video games, digital toys, Web pages, etc.) easier to use, and matching them closely to user requirements, needs and desires. Digital products and computer systems that have high usability should be used more efficiently and frequently, and they often are sold more (in the case of commercial applications). Thus, people's productivity is incremented. However, products with bad usability make people waste their time trying to figure out how they work. It is possible to improve the design of digital products by carrying out usability testing of those products. Usability evaluation is an important part of the development life cycle of any software and hardware to be used by people, and all software and hardware developers should take into account usability testing of their products. There are special cases where usability is a very important part of the product design, for example, in the design of critical systems (systems that can threat human or animal life or the environment when they experience functional problems) and mobile products (such as smart phone applications). Both require special usability methodologies and techniques.

Cases on Usability Engineering: Design and Development of Digital Products presents academic and practicing hands-on experience on usability methods, tests and techniques to improve the human-computer interaction during the design and development of digital products. These products include Web pages, information systems, and interfaces found in mobile computing, among others, to be used for work, entertainment, learning, and for other applications. The usability experiences are presented in this book as comprehensive case studies to be used as learning and teaching materials in usability, human-computer interaction, human factors, software engineering, software systems, and related undergraduate and graduate courses. In this book, I included new perspectives from top practitioners, lecturers, and researchers around the world from the areas of computer science, human-computer interaction, cognitive science, psychology, human factors, and other areas that contribute to usability engineering, human-computer interaction, and software engineering.

Case studies can help computer science and information technology (IT) students prepare for real-world situations and problems by providing an approximation of various professional environments. Through the discussion and examination of specific cases on the usability of digital products, students are given the opportunity to work out their own professional issues through the trials, "war stories," experiences, and research findings of usability researchers, specialists, lecturers, and practitioners. One of the advantages of using case studies as a mode of instruction is that it allows computing students the exposure to contexts and settings that they might not otherwise experience in educational settings, acquiring the necessary competences.

Writing case studies on usability should require the "coming together" of science, technology, and social knowledge, among others, working in an interdisciplinary fashion, since the field of usability is supported by a number of knowledge areas. This "coming together" happened in this book. New perspectives from top researchers and practitioners around the world are also included. A number of chapters already answer the questions on how and why usability can support the design and development of digital products, such as Web pages and information systems, among others. Cases on Usability Engineering comprise a comprehensive –yet specialized– state-of-the-art compendium of case studies of usability in socio-technical approaches.

This book is one of my projects I always wanted to make since I started studying my PhD in Computer Science and Artificial Intelligence in late nineties. The idea for this book began when I saw how important usability testing was when it was applied to the design and development of computer programs to be used by people, as watching how my dissertation adviser carried out many usability studies.

Something that also motivated me to write this book is that in many Latin American countries there is a strong need to improve many of the Web pages, computer systems and digital products developed there. I felt that one way to do this is to edit a book that should describe the importance and methods of usability evaluation to improve the usability of such digital products. It is necessary to improve the quality and ease of use of many software products (and sometimes hardware) that are generated in many countries. Over the years, I would say decades, I have seen many computer systems and Web pages created in universities and in private companies that have many problems in its interface design. There are not only graphic design problems, but also functional problems. Many people using those pieces of software or Web pages cannot do their work or other activities properly due to usability errors, and in many cases they must use them because they have no other choice. Some managers of companies and institutions (and some professionals from the software industry) still think that conducting usability testing is prohibitively expensive. Usability definitely is not a luxury. That is quite the opposite. It is an important activity that companies and institutions that develop software and hardware applications should invest in.

This book will serve as a supporting material in academic courses and workshops such as usability, human-computer interaction, ergonomics, engineering and related software which addresses the issue of usability and user experience (UX). I hope this book will be useful for new (and not so new) generations of software developers, students, teachers and technologists that wish to improve their knowledge on usability testing with practical cases such as the ones presented in this book.

The main objective *Cases on Usability Engineering: Design and Development of Digital Products* is to provide a technical rationale for computing practice in the area of usability, providing engaging and thought-provoking case discussions, which will serve to to support the comprehension of usability methods and techniques applied to the design and development of digital products and software systems.

The book aims to provide software developers, as well as students and professors of higher education, an introduction to the subject of usability and a compendium of methods and techniques used to apply usability in the design and development digital products, such as Web pages, information systems, mobile applications, video games and more.

The volume will serve as a comprehensive reference for students, lecturers and specialists wishing to learn from and contribute to the area of usability, who require information as to how usability methods and techniques can be potentially applied to the design and development of human-computer interfaces.

Cases on Usability Engineering: Design and Development of Digital Products will impact its different audiences by providing information about how and why usability can improve digital technology. This book will provide feedback to is readership by offering diverse technological solutions that many academics have somewhat failed to disseminate. This book will provide a space for its readership to be introduced to topics students ignore or are unaware of, in order to discuss and promote usability. *Cases on Usability Engineering: Design and Development of Digital Products* will impact students, lectures, researchers and practitioners that already study, conduct research, and develop computer applications on the book topic. This book will become an important source of new knowledge, and will pave the way for further computing developments and applications for usability.

This volume will represent potential contribution to the development of usability and human-computer interaction and their applications in computing education. Exploring the practical and theoretical issues of both areas of knowledge, the book will contribute to expand the applications on methods, models, approaches, design guidelines, frameworks, and tools developed in the area of usability towards a dynamic understanding and hands-on experience described in the form of case studies written by usability researchers and practitioners.

There are many technical books about the theory, principles, and the general impact of usability and human-computer interaction and books, but this is not particularly the case with this book. Some of those usability books do not include important and recent topics, such as mobile computing, and brain-computer interfaces. Thus, this book will be distinguished from existing titles on usability. Moreover, this book will serve as an ideal reference for computer science, and other areas where the topic of usability is addressed and researched.

The target audience of this book will be composed of computer science students, lecturers, instructors, and academics from other related areas. In addition, this book will capture the attention of all those engaged in fields such as knowledge management, information technologies, computer networks, and human factors.

The case studies from this book will serve as supporting learning material for computer science and IT courses on the topic of usability, with the support of other related areas. The book will also serve as library reference and bibliographic supplement for IT, Computing, Human-Computer Interaction, Networking, Web page, graphic design and other Computer Science and technology courses for undergraduate and graduate students, as well as researchers and practitioners interested in the topic. In addition, the case studies from the book will also serve to usability practitioners that would like to put usability knowledge into practice.

Practitioners will also benefit from the pragmatic techniques, implementation guidelines, and case discussions. In addition, undergraduate-level and graduate-level students will find the case studies useful in their course work and research. This book will also be a welcome addition to academic libraries' research collections for further consult in this particular topic. Ultimately, this book will provide the latest research and applications on usability in order to provide students, researchers, lecturers and practitioners the necessary background in theory and practice to pursue this endeavor.

The book is organized into four sections according to the types of digital products that were analyzed in each chapter: Usability of Web Products (chapters 1 to 7), Usability of Mobile Applications (chapters 8 and 9), Usability of Critical Systems (chapters 10 to 12), and Usability of Virtual Environments, Simulations and Video Games (chapters 13 to 16). Students and/or practitioners may want to read and study the chapters according to the type of digital product wishing to analyze, design or improve. The sixteen chapters are described as follows:

Conducting usability sessions with children is always challenging due to their cognitive skills and vocabulary comprehension, among other issues. These characteristics make it difficult to assess the tasks children need to perform when evaluating a digital product. Chapter 1 (*Exploring Evaluation Techniques for Children's Websites*) describes usability testing of a science Web site with children and lessons learned from the experience.

As described in Chapter 2 (*Social Negotiations in Web Usability Engineering*), user participation and involvement are very important when carrying out usability studies. In addition, social and technical "negotiations" between users and designers play a fundamental role in studying Web site usability. This chapter shows that early user engagement in the design of the Web site using prototypes should support socio-technical negotiations.

A user profile is a characterization of a digital product's target users, which provides condensed and representative information about users. This tool can help usability designers better understand the target population. Chapter 3 (*Developing User Profiles for Interactive Online Products in Practice*) describes an exercise with graduate students who created user profiles for online products, showing that people who develop effective user profiles should have previous experience and skills to administer and interpret user demographic questionnaires.

Chapter 4 (*Usability Testing of an Education Management Information System: the Case of the University of Colima*) explains a compelling case study on the usability testing of an online university reporting system developed by the University of Colima, Mexico. This system shows institutional management statistics, such as undergraduate and graduate statistics. Three usability tools were used in a two-phase usability study of the system: a heuristic evaluation, the System Usability Scale questionnaire, and the Technology Acceptance Model.

Chapter 5 (*Usability Impact Analysis of Collaborative Environments*) provides a case study involving the application of important usability principles to improve the use of an online corporate collaborative environment, taking into account business goals, user engagement, and the collaborative nature of a company.

The author of Chapter 6 (*A Practitioner's Approach to Collaborative Usability Testing*) describes how usability testing and usability methods can be integrated into the development life cycle of public sector Web sites, a necessary step that few public institutions have implemented. Chapter 6 goes on to explain that most public sector Web sites are launched without public (final users) consultation, a bad practice that needs to be avoided. Thus, this chapter describes a methodology that includes collaborative usability testing, the inclusion of subject matter experts, IT professionals, stakeholders, and, of course, potential users of the Web sites.

The case study described in Chapter 7 (*Integrating Semiotics Perception in Usability Testing to Improve Usability Evaluation*) demonstrates the importance of semiotics in the assessment of visual objects employed in Web pages, such as links and icons. According to the chapter authors, semiotics can improve intuitiveness of the computer interface, and semiotic analysis can be useful for identifying usability problems, which represents a cost-effective methodology to support usability testing.

Chapter 8 (*Developing the Intel® Pair & Share Experience*) shows the development and usability testing of a commercial application intended for sharing digital photographs among smart phones, PCs, and tablets called Intel® Pair & Share. This cross-platform application was developed based on an interdisciplinary approach and takes into account the wide variety, benefits and challenges of current mobile devices.

Chapter 9 (*A Usability Study of Mobile Text Based Social Applications: Towards a Reliable Strategy for Design Evaluation*) explains a thorough usability study that tests three social network applications running on mobile devices. The usability testing was carried out using an adapted version of the System Usability Scale (SUS) questionnaire. Based on the usability testing results, the authors propose the creation of a set of heuristics to improve the interface design of mobile social networks.

The case study of chapter 10 (Pilot implementation Driven by Effects Specifications and Formative Usability Evaluation) conveys an important formative usability study performed on an electronic health care record, a critical system used at maternity wards in European hospitals. The authors of this case study used a number of usability tools for their studies, including low-fidelity prototypes (mock-ups) and high-fidelity prototypes (the pilot system). The chapter goes on to explain usability engineering issues, the iterative process and lessons learned.

Chapter 11 (*Design and Development of a Digital Error Reporting System for a Rural Nursing Home*) describes an interesting case study on the development and usability testing of an online error-reporting system for a rural nursing home. Under-reporting of error events in the workplace, a common occurrence in nursing homes, can result in serious complications. The developed online system was compared to a traditional paper-based reporting approach. Results from the evaluations showed no significant difference in performance with regard to the online system. According to the chapter authors, this is mainly due to the users' overwhelming familiarity with the paper-based reporting system, although the usability study showed that users preferred the digital interface.

Chapter 12 (*The Usability Evaluation of a Touch Screen in the Flight Deck*) offers a case study on the usability testing of a flight deck touch-screen prototype. Safety and other issues of this prototype were analyzed using multidisciplinary and iterative testing approaches. The chapter also stresses the importance of understanding and knowing the context in which the technology is to be used. Especially important is considering the crucial constraints that may affect the design of the system, which in this case is the airliner flight deck touch screen simulator.

Chapter 13 (*BCI-Based User-Centered Design for Emotionally-Driven User Experience*) illustrates the importance of using physiological data in usability testing. The authors devised a special methodology called user-centered evaluation (UCE), which as applied to the design of interactive and adaptable virtual environments. This case study describes the use of a brain-computer interface (BCI) that obtains important data about the user's emotional levels while interacting with the virtual environment. A BCI is a digital human-computer interface that establishes a communication pathway between a brain and a digital device that enables signals from the brain to direct some external activity, such as steering an avatar in a 3D virtual environment.

Chapter 14 (*Digital Heritage Systems: The ARCO Evaluation*) explores a number of quantitative and qualitative usability methods to evaluate the usability of an augmented reality system that displays an interactive virtual museum. The case study describes how usability methodologies can improve engagement and interaction of a virtual museum, taking into account users' subjective presence and learning.

The case study described in Chapter 15 (Usability Optimization of a Military Training System) is compelling. It is about how to improve the design of a military training system where highly-important and demanding key requirements and challenges need to be addressed. To analyze this, it was necessary to design and develop a useful training system to help instructors to apply training lessons to members of the armed forces. This case study also comprises a number of formative and summative usability methodologies that were used to identify the key requirements and improve system performance.

Chapter 16 (*Pogo Chat*) presents a case study that analyzes the usability of a chat window added to a number of online video games that belong to a Web portal called Pogo. The chat feature was eagerly wanted by many Pogo users. In response, the authors analyzed whether this requested option was feasible or not, since the Pogo game developers did not want the chat window to interfere with the game play. The case study describes a number of chat solutions tested and usability testing methods used for the Pogo games.

The chapters were selected following a thorough analysis based on many factors, including the appropriateness for this book, the depth on which the chapter was written, the practical issues presented in the chapters, the educational value of the case study described in the chapters, the type of the usability methodologies employed, the clarity and structure of the chapters, and the importance of the results from the usability testing, among other issues. To improve the standards of scientific rigor of this book, each chapter was double-blind peer-reviewed by at least two usability, human-computer interaction and software engineering experts from around the globe. This book would not have been possible without the valuable support of the Editorial Advisory Board (EAB).

I sincerely hope this book will help current and future generations of computer science and IT students, practitioners and researchers comprehend the importance and practicality of usability evaluations. These generations are and will be the designers and developers of digital products that many people will use, rely on and enjoy, provided that those products will be developed following adequate usability studies and methodologies. It is now more than ever that case studies on usability engineering can be a great support to those generations.

Miguel A. Garcia-Ruiz
Algoma University, Canada

Acknowledgment

I wish to express my deepest gratitude and appreciation to Dr. Silvia Gabrielli, Dr. Simon Xu, Dr. Christian Sturm, Dr. Victor M. Gonzalez, Prof. Arthur Edwards, Prof. Pedro Santana, and Dr. Genaro Rebolledo-Mendez.

Miguel A. Garcia-Ruiz
Algoma University, Canada

Section 1
Usability of Web Products

Chapter 1

Exploring Evaluation Techniques for Children's Websites

Colleen Kaiser
Melio Lab, USA

Ginger Butcher
Sigma Space Corporation, USA

EXECUTIVE SUMMARY

Children are an important target group on the web and assessing their user experience presents a unique challenge. Special consideration when conducting sessions with children includes: their difficulty articulating their thoughts, getting shy children to open up, keeping their attention focused on the test activities, understanding their non-verbal cues, and providing enough encouragement without "leading" the participant. Additionally, children have a broad range of cognitive skills, reading skills, and vocabulary comprehension, which makes it difficult to ascertain whether they understand the given task and difficult to ensure their responses are valid. Usability tests for children not only need to be designed to effectively solicit subjective preferences and objective content comprehension, but also to assess how well they are able to use the site. Verifying their understanding of the task activities (to ensure the efficacy of their response) is critical for the validity of the data. This study reports on a two-phased testing approach and the lessons learned in redesigning an agency's web portal for science content targeting 5-12 year olds.

DOI: 10.4018/978-1-4666-4046-7.ch001

ORGANIZATION BACKGROUND

The organization for this study was a federal government agency that develops web content for children as part of its overall education and public outreach strategy. This agency (like many agencies within the United States federal government) has a complex organizational structure with multiple branches, divisions, and departments. Efforts to develop web content, particularly for unique audiences such as children in primary grades (ages 5-12), are executed at the department or individual project level, and less at the agency-level. As a result, these projects are spread across multiple websites throughout the agency with different navigation styles, look-and-feel, and content – which makes it difficult for younger children to navigate and locate content.

The type of web content developed for children spans a variety of physical science topics and includes games, image galleries, videos, printable activities, and stories. Accessing these different products requires wading through various departmental websites with navigation more focused on the organizational structure than content. Additionally, assessing the success of these products is also difficult without a single location to highlight and promote the content. Thus, the development of a portal specifically designed for children could increase the organization's return on their investment in educational web content.

SETTING THE STAGE

The challenge for this organization has been to develop a web portal that would help school-aged children (as well as adults) locate content developed for children by different organizations within the larger agency. Prior to this project, agency-level websites were developed to provide access to content for all audiences from one location. The team that developed these sites consisted of designers, web developers, an information architect, and a usability expert. The testing effort employed a variety of methods and included funding for testing in a usability lab. While these sites had sections specifically designed for kids, the testing tools were primarily targeted for the adult audience and as a result were tested on just a handful of children.

The ultimate goal of the project was to design and develop a website focused on earth and space science content that appealed to the broadest scope of the target audience -- without alienating any one segment of that audience. Children respond similarly to adults, in that they leave a site if it does not immediately meet their needs or expectations (Kamishlian & Albert, 2011). This science site needed to appeal visually and engage children in the science content, but also must allow children to easily search and navigate the various science content from across the agency. However, designing a site for young children (early readers) and older children (teens) is difficult because they are two very different audiences (Nielsen, 2010). Older children are 'turned-off' by content designed for a young audience (Hanna, Risden, Czerwinski, & Alexander, 1998), while younger children find it difficult to read and navigate content developed for an older audience. Agency management decided to proceed with two separate sites, and the following study was implemented for the section of the site for a younger audience of children ages 5-12.

A review of literature reveals several usability tools and techniques that can be adapted to evaluate this young audience including card sorts, participatory design workshops, paper prototyping, website visits, and surveys (Druin et al., 1999; Bar-Ilan & Belous, 2007; Hanna, Risden, Czerwinski, & Alexander, 1998). The adapted tools incorporate more visual media (both on screen and off) to meet the needs of children with a wide range of cognitive skills, reading comprehension, and vocabulary (Joly, Pemberton, & Griffiths, 2009). When testing with children, other concerns need to be addressed. Markopoulos and Bekker (2003) explain when children are involved in usability testing they are required to do much more than use the technology under evaluation: "They have to adapt to a testing environment, interact with the facilitator, follow some processes and, usually, contribute to the evaluation by reporting on their experiences." Thus, techniques also need to take into account the difficulty in getting children to convey their thoughts (Hanna, Risden, & Alexander, 1997) and promote a comfortable environment. There has been success in encouraging feedback from indicative questions by testing children in groups (Bar-Ilan & Belous, 2007) or using friendship pairs (Naranjo-Bock, 2011), also called "co-discovery." The intention of this study was to test participants in the most accurate way, without their best friend next to them, which is how they typically use the computer and visit websites (Gilutz & Nielsen, 2002). Additionally, there is the risk of peer pressure and one participant dominating or influencing the other. This behavior would have negated the purpose of the study's first phase where the product team was collecting first impressions, preferences, and emotional responses to a variety of design options. Co-discovery sessions do have benefits, however, in that they naturally result in the participants talking about their thoughts, expectations and decisions, which could yield useful information.

The decision to test children in a one-on-one setting as opposed to co-discovery sessions for this study was to ensure that each child voiced their own unique opinions about the websites without being influenced by another child. This was based on the goal of the study which was primarily focused on soliciting emotional and personal responses to the websites as opposed to ease of use and success scores where the collaboration aspects of co-discovery might have been useful. Also, by employing multiple tools within each session, the product team hoped to solicit insightful feedback needed to design and develop an engaging website for this target audience.

CASE DESCRIPTION

To gain insight into the target audience of children ages 5-12, a two-phased test plan was established to observe the children and gather their feedback. The first phase was a design comparison study that focused on collecting qualitative feedback about the visual appeal of the website design; a survey was developed to collect early opinions on design concepts and a usability study was conducted using functional prototypes. This was followed-up with a second phase which consisted of a validation study of the final website and focused more on the navigation and functionality of the design.

Technology Components

Before choosing the testing environment different settings were considered: a standard usability lab, a classroom, a library and children's homes. Because the study was conducted in the summer while children were on vacation from school the classroom setting was not an option. A library environment was eliminated as an option because the moderator did not have access to mobile testing equipment. Additionally, it would not have been possible to set up an observation room for the product team and having them participate in the studies was a high priority. While testing in the home environment would offer the most natural and comfortable setting (Gilutz & Nielsen, 2002) it was quickly ruled out as an option because in addition to the same disadvantages of testing in a library, the government agency would not have been granted permission to conduct the sessions in private homes.

All of the usability studies were conducted in a standard usability lab. One room was set up with a computer, desk, activity table and chairs for the participant and moderator. The other room was for the observers who watched the sessions behind one-way glass.

All one-on-one testing took place in a usability lab. There was a camera recording both the participant expressions and their actions on the table. Screen capture software was employed to record the movement of the cursor and click-throughs on the computer. A note-taker was present behind a one-way mirror to free up the moderator to focus on the participant and ask questions. Additionally, the moderator did not take notes; as such activity can be distracting to participants (Druin et al., 1999).

Methodology

Phase 1: Design Comparison Study

For the first phase, three different designers were each tasked with creating a homepage design concept for the website. Each concept was designed around the same core content and information architecture. Designers were instructed to use the same navigation labels, title and footer links, but had the flexibility to add featured content and navigation aids such as descriptive text on hover. Designs varied in navigation style, interactions, and look-and-feel.

To ensure enough diversity in the three designs, the designers shared wireframes and concept sketches early in the process. Through an iterative design process, each design underwent periodic expert reviews to avoid any obvious usability issues that might distract from the main goal of evaluating the designs based on visual appeal. The designers and developers all attended at least some of the usability test sessions to witness the children's experiences and hear their feedback first-hand. The results and findings from each study were reported to the entire product team with a list of recommendations.

The design comparison phase had two checkpoints. The first was an anonymous online survey to collect qualitative feedback from the target audience early in the design process. It was an early-pulse check to confirm that the designs were generally appealing and engaging. Forty-six children participated in the survey, 19 girls and 27 boys. The survey respondents were segmented into the following age groups:

- Ages 5-6 (15 kids)
- Ages 7-8 (10 kids)
- Ages 9-10 (12 kids)
- Ages 11-12 (9 kids)

The survey was hosted online using a third-party service. Email announcements were sent to the parents of the invited participants explaining the project and providing participation instructions. It was recommended that parents assist younger children to ensure they understood each question and help them interact with the survey application. The survey sessions were not moderated, so parental influence on the responses is unknown[1].

The survey was designed so respondents could see scaled-down screenshots of each design while reading and answering the survey questions. They could also launch full-size screenshots in new browser tabs for a more detailed view. Parents were instructed to help their children with this interaction to ensure the children were able to navigate between the survey and full-size screenshots so they could look closely at the design details, navigation links, and content.

The survey consisted of the following types of questions:

- Age group and gender demographics using radio button controls;
- Seven questions using radio button controls to choose their favorite design based on personal preference for things like color, educational value, entertainment value, and visual appeal;
- Selecting overall most-favorite and least-favorite designs using radio button controls with an optional text field for an explanation; and
- **Three additional questions:** Selecting positive and negative words from a list to describe how the respondent feels about each design; rating each design as "too old," "too young, " or "just right" for somebody their age, and an optional text field to add any additional comments about each of the designs.

The survey results from all 46 respondents were compiled and analyzed in aggregate, as well as by audience segments (based on age groups and gender). The key findings indicated one of the three designs was strongly favored for five of the seven subjective criteria. One design was easily identified as the least favored with the lowest rankings for six of the seven subjective criteria. The third design was firmly ranked in the middle, favored for two criteria and least favored for one criterion.

The data and feedback collected from the survey were reported to the product team and government officials. The findings served as the basis for recommendations for refining each design and building functional prototypes with secondary and tertiary levels.

The second checkpoint in the design comparison phase was putting all three of the functional prototypes through one-on-one usability testing. The primary goal was essentially the same as that of the survey, to determine which design appealed to the broadest scope of the target audience. Unlike the survey, which only presented the children with a static view of each homepage design, this study was based on a more developed user experience. Each design consisted of a homepage, all second-tier pages, and select content detail pages at the third tier. Test participants could interact with the designs in ways such as revealing sounds and animations on hover, clicking to navigate select paths, reading content, and browsing lists of games and activities on the website. The design team was again instructed to use the same information architecture for the new levels, but the page layouts, style of content lists, and interactions varied between the design prototypes. Exploring and interacting with each prototype gave participants the ability to assess each design based on an actual experience.

A total of twelve children, six girls and six boys ages five to twelve, were screened and recruited to participate in this round of testing. These were not the same children that participated in the survey administered during the first checkpoint. Three children were tested in each of the following age groups:

- Ages 5-6
- Ages 7-8
- Ages 9-10
- Ages 11-12

Each session began with the moderator meeting the guardian and child in the reception lobby. The moderator gave the guardian the option to sit in the test room with the child, for the child's comfort, if they thought it was necessary. In a few cases with the younger participants the guardian joined and was seated at a table behind the child, out of their line of sight.

The test script for the design comparison study was developed with an initial briefing and seven activities designed to keep the children focused and engaged while also providing multiple opportunities to convey their opinions. The variety of activities required participants to move back and forth between an activity desk and a computer. The two stations were next to each other, and only required to swivel their chair, but the change of environment (even if only slight) was used to reset the participant's focus. Some activities included a demonstration by the moderator that was intended to verify the participant understood what they were supposed to do.

Initial Briefing

Participants were first seated at an activity desk and the moderator asked if they were comfortable in the chair and at the desk. Reading from a script, the moderator explained they had been invited to help an agency with a new science website and gave an overview of what they would be doing throughout the session. To set the tone and attempt to put the children at ease, they were assured this was not a test, and they couldn't make any mistakes because there weren't any right or wrong answers -- their most important job was to help the agency designing the website by sharing their opinions and talking openly about what they liked, disliked, or found hard to understand.

The moderator pointed out the video camera mounts used for recording. The one-way mirror was explained, and participants warned there might be people from the product team behind it watching. Some children were excited about the mirror and waved to it, others looked into it trying to see people on the other side and still others tended to ignore it for the most part but occasionally caught glimpses of themselves. The mirror was an occasional distraction for some children but they did not appear bothered by it. One child asked to see what was behind the mirror after her session wrapped up and the moderator obliged.

To assess knowledge of or familiarity with the government agency behind the study, the moderator asked each participant what they knew of it, and if they had ever visited their website before[2].

Closed Card Sort

Participants remained seated at the activity desk for the closed card sort. Closed card sorts are a common technique used to validate the information architecture and terminology of a website (Joly, Pemberton, & Griffiths, 2009). The participant is given a stack of index cards, each one describes an individual piece of content or functionality that can be found on the website and is instructed to put each card under the label in which they think it belongs.

It was apparent that this activity might be difficult for children to grasp conceptually, especially those younger than eight years old (Hanna, Risden, Czerwinski, Alexander, 1998), so it was adapted for a younger audience. A demonstration was added to show participants how to perform the activity and verify that they understood it. An image (screenshot) of the content was added to the card to make it more visual and simplify the activity for children at lower reading levels. Finally, the number of cards was kept relatively small to prevent the participants from getting bored or discouraged. Fourteen large index cards were created using color screenshots of the website's games, activities, videos, and content along with short text description (see Figures 1 and 2).

The moderator read the activity instructions from the script before doing the demonstration. The card sort was demonstrated using a set of eight cards, each illustrating a piece of sporting equipment from four sports "categories": golf, baseball, football, and basketball. The moderator looked at one of the sport equipment cards, verbalized what it was, and then placed it in the corresponding category. In several cases participants joined in the demonstration by helping place the cards after they got the hang of it. This was an unexpected but beneficial interaction, because it verified the participant understood the activity. After the short demonstration the moderator asked the participant if they understood the activity and if they had any questions before getting started with the actual test.

The participants were not given any deadlines for completion and most were generally finished in less than ten minutes. To minimize pressure on the participant, the moderator sat at a different table and said they would be working on something else but were available if the child had questions. When the participant appeared to be done sorting the cards, the moderator went back to the participant and asked them

Figure 1. The demonstration card sort used sports equipment to illustrate the concept of grouping together cards that belong together.

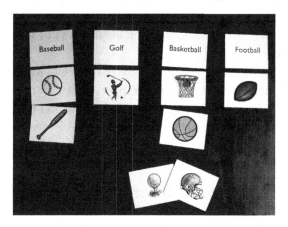

Figure 2. The card sort activity designed for the children used screenshots of the content to make them faster and easier to assess.

to explain what they had done; this verbal report not only served as an account of the participant's thought process but also provided insight into their understanding of the content.

Warm Up

The participant and moderator moved to the computer desk for this activity, and the moderator checked the participant's access to the keyboard and mouse (with regards to being left- or right-handed). The moderator asked the participant to show their favorite website and explain what they like to do there and what they like about it in general. In most cases, the participants could navigate to the website by typing the URL, but some younger participants didn't know how to get there – explaining they access the sites by bookmarks, icons on the desktop, or with the help of their parents or siblings.

The purpose of this exercise was to start the participant on the computer with an easy activity and to help encourage the participant to talk – by framing it so they feel as though they are educating the moderator. This show-and-tell activity normally lasted around five minutes.

First Impressions

The participants and the moderator were seated at the computer for this activity. Following the script, the moderator explained to the participant that he or she would be looking at three different homepages designed for the same website, and that they then will be asked a few questions about their opinions of each one. The moderator reminded the participant that there are "no right or wrong answers," and that the best way they could help is to talk about what they like and don't like – because their feedback will help make the websites even better.

The moderator brought up one website at a time in the web browser, and then provided a hard copy color print of the same design for the child to use for reference. These hard copy prints were introduced to familiarize the participant with the printed representations of the websites because they are used again during an activity later in the session. The presentation order of the websites was rotated on a schedule, to avoid any biases the order of presentation might have on the participant.

With each of the three websites, the moderator ran through the same series of questions and tasks which were targeted at assessing the participant's personal design preferences as well as some usability issues. First, participants were instructed to look at the website without clicking and respond to questions about their likes and dislikes of the design. Assessing the navigation of the site, the participants were asked to find all of the links on each website homepage, and to describe what they would expect to find if they were to click on them. This activity was designed to solicit a lot of emotional and qualitative feedback about the designs, based primarily on the look-and-feel aspects of each website. This was important to the overarching project goal of creating a website that visually appealed to the broadest possible range of the target audience.

Before moving on to the next website, the moderator asked each participant to choose one word they felt best described the website, and to also identify what link they would click on first, given the opportunity. This final question was added to find out what the most appealing or intriguing feature was on each design.

Task Scenarios

Participants and moderator remained at the computer for this activity and worked through five scripted tasks. Each participant performed the tasks only once, using the last website they were presented in the previous activity. Reading from the script, the moderator introduced the activity and asked the participant to work through the tasks on their own so the product team could learn what was easy and what was difficult for the participants to figure out. The participants were informed that they could ask questions, but that the moderator might not answer these questions until the end. Participants were instructed to think aloud and talk about their interactions and thought processes during the task; as well what they liked and disliked about the website while navigating through it. They were given permission to click on the links for some of the tasks, but other tasks only required that they indicate where they would click to find the answer. They were told that not all links worked because the website wasn't finished and if they ran into these broken links it didn't mean they did anything wrong.

As the moderator read each task out loud, the participant was given an index card with the task typed out upon it to use for reference. The cards were useful to participants when looking at specific keywords, checking spelling, and as a refresher to use, if they get stuck on a task. The tasks were asked in the same order in each session, and every participant was given all five tasks.

The participants did not do well with the think-aloud process; the moderator had to repeatedly encourage and remind them (and frequently probe by asking them) to talk about the pages displayed to them. This is the one session activity in this study that would have benefited from testing the children in pairs because their collaborative efforts would more naturally shed light on what they were thinking of doing and why.

The primary goal of this activity was to test the navigation designs in each website to ensure participants could easily find and interact with the navigation menus, and still navigate back to the homepage from deeper levels. A secondary goal was to validate the navigation labels and information architecture each design shared.

Design Ranking

This activity required the participant and moderator to move back to the activity table. The moderator read the scripted instructions, explaining to the participant that he or she was going to be given the choice to rank the three designs from "most favorite" to "least favorite, " in response to some questions about the website. The participant was then shown three faces made out of construction paper, and told the green "smiley face" represented the most-favorite design, the yellow "neutral face" with a straight mouth was for the second-favorite design, and the red frowning "sad face" was for the least favorite.

The moderator placed the color printouts of all three homepage designs on the table and demonstrated the activity by reading aloud a practice question and placing the color-coded smiley/sad faces on the designs accordingly (see Figure 3). To avoid any bias in the demonstration question, the moderator asked an objective question to rank the designs from "most" to "least" based on how much "grass" was included in the image of each: the green smiley face was used for the most grass, the yellow neutral face for the second-most, and the red sad face for the least amount of grass seen in the images. As noted in the card sort demonstration, some participants joined in the demonstration once they understood it. Again, this interaction helped verify the participants understood what to do and gave them an opportunity to help the moderator which gave them confidence. Before proceeding with the activity the moderator asked the participant if they had any questions about what they were expected to do.

Every time the participant ranked the designs based on the subjective questions, the moderator then followed up with probing questions to give the participant an opportunity to articulate why they ranked the designs in the order they did. Across all age groups, the children evaluated and ranked the designs based on the individual subjective questions; they may have favored a design for the majority of the subjective questions, but they appeared to rank the designs on the merit of the individual criteria in each subjective question. Examples of the criteria upon which the designs were ranked include: which design has the best colors, which design looks the most fun, which design looks the most educational. Ultimately, the participant was asked to rank the designs from their overall most-favorite to their least-favorite.

This exercise was designed to provide a comfortable means of communication for the shy and quieter children and a fun way to draw out more feedback after the participants had a chance to interact with all three designs online. The participants – especially the younger ones – appeared to enjoy this hands-on activity of ranking by placing the color-coded faces on each design.

Exit Interview

The moderator placed the participant's favorite design on the table and instructed them to refer to it when answering the last few questions of the session. The exit interview questions were used to confirm opinions collected throughout the session and to dig deeper to understand what makes an engaging website for the target

Figure 3. The design ranking activity has participants placing the color-coded faces on each design to designate them as "most favorite," "second favorite," and "least favorite" for each subjective question.

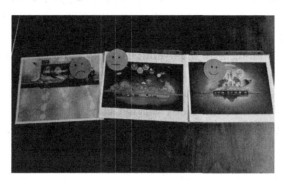

audience. Other questions were targeted to the participant's interest in the specific categories and the activities on the website, to gauge their understanding of the concepts displayed.

Name Selection Survey

The moderator announced there was "One last thing!" and then handed the participant a short survey listing six options for this website's title. The participant was asked to help select the best name for the website by circling up to three of their favorite options and placing a star sticker next to their most favorite option. The participants were also given the option to propose their own idea for a website name. Younger children appeared to enjoy the use of stickers in this activity.

The moderator instructed the participant to complete the survey and then excused herself before leaving the testing room to collect any comments or questions from the rest of the team in the observation room.

The session wrapped up after the moderator re-entered the testing room and thanked the participant for the their time and valuable feedback. After asking if the participant had any last questions, the moderator introduced a member of the product team who personally thanked the child and gave them a small thank-you gift.

The overall favored design and test findings were consistent with the results of the survey, and this was reported back to the government officials and product team. One design emerged as the strong favorite, and this design was subsequently refined based on the report's recommendations and built out into a fully functional website for the next phase, the validation study.

Phase 2: Validation Study

The second phase of the project test plan was an evaluation focused on validating the design and development decisions that resulted from the findings in the design comparison phase. This included validating the content organization, navigation and age-appropriateness along with the overall usability of the website.

This test script was built around five activities, with an emphasis on task scenarios that tested the user interface elements, the organization of content, and the level of participant engagement. This study was the same size as the design comparison study - twelve participants, 6 boys and 6 girls; 3 children were recruited for each of the following age groups:

- Ages 5-6
- Ages 7-8
- Ages 9-10
- Ages 11-12

Initial Briefing

Just as in the design comparison study, these sessions also began with the moderator meeting the participant and parent or guardian in the reception lobby and inviting the guardian to join if they felt it appropriate. The initial briefing was conducted using the same script as the one for the design comparison study. These few minutes were again used to set the stage for the test session, putting the participant at ease and making sure he or she was comfortable.

Card Sort

This card sort was conducted much the same way it was in the first round, using a limited set of cards with screenshot images representing different content on the site. Again, the moderator demonstrated the activity using the sports equipment cards, but this time the participant was invited to help complete the demonstration. The children from the first round of testing who, on their own initiative, joined in the demonstration and helped the moderator inspired this modification to the script. This proved to be an effective change to the exercise that gave participants confidence and ensured they understood the activity.

Warm Up

The warm up was conducted with the same script as used in the design comparison study. The main lesson learned from the first round of testing was to adhere more closely to the time limit allocated for this "show and tell" activity; some participants were eager to not only to share their favorite websites but also to get sidetracked by them, especially gaming websites.

Task Scenarios

Similar to the first round of testing, the emphasis when introducing this activity was to assure the participant that they were not being "tested" (the way they understood the term in school) and instead they had been invited in to help in the creation of a better website. They were encouraged to verbalize their thoughts, opinions and ideas on what was both good and bad about the website. Also, during the first round of testing most participants relied on the printed task cards to check the spelling of keywords or recall what they were supposed to be doing for some of the more challenging tasks. The cards seemed to be helpful in the first round of testing, so they were used again for this study.

There were 17 individual task scenarios created for this script to ensure there was enough test material for older students who could potentially get through the tasks fairly quickly. Most participants didn't complete all of the tasks but some older children worked through the entire set, as was predicted. As the study progressed, it was not uncommon to eliminate a task after witnessing enough repeat behavior to provide enough data, or to add new tasks if applicable.

The tasks from this study were designed to validate design and user interface decisions resulting from the first round of testing: interactions, navigation labels, iconography, and content organization. Additionally, the product team was looking for evidence of the participants' level of interest and engagement in the content topics and activities offered on the website. The content topics were tied to the science lessons that children learn in school, so the activities ranged in level of difficulty.

This portion of the test session was long and some participants exhibited verbal and/or non-verbal signs of boredom and lost focus. Some children outright said they were bored or didn't want to continue with the tasks; others indicated the same through their body language by sitting back in the chair, sighing, yawning, looking around the room, or asking to visit their favorite websites. In situations where this boredom appeared, the participant sometimes simply needed a quick break from the task activities, after which the moderator attempted to re-engage them by giving them an opportunity to play a game or explore something on the website that had caught their eye earlier, or even visit a different website.

Several of the tasks proved difficult for the younger children, especially those at lower reading levels, and these participants showed signs of frustration. In cases where the participant was visibly frustrated the moderator moved on to a different, sometimes easier, task. In one case a young participant stopped listening to the moderator all together and just sat at the desk resting her head. Her mother, who was sitting in the test room, told the child to answer the moderator, this proved less than helpful when the child completely shut down and the moderator had to end the session early.

The script was flexible with regards to the order tasks were presented. It became apparent throughout the testing sessions that certain tasks were too easy for older participants while others were too difficult for the younger ones. Once the product team was confident they had the feedback they needed on a specific task, the task was skipped for the remaining participants to make better use of their time and avoid the anticipated boredom or frustration.

Throughout the sessions the majority of participants needed to be prompted to verbalize their thoughts and actions. Some of the younger and more shy participants had a difficult time of this, which required the moderator to frequently interject questions such as: "What are you looking for now?" and "Is this what you expected...?" In addition to the non-verbal cues, the responses to these questions provided some insight into the participant's thought- and decision-making processes. They also helped validate the participant's level of understanding of the content, which was an important goal in this study.

Given the moderator's difficulty in getting participants to think aloud and verbalize their actions, co-discovery sessions most likely would have benefited this study by naturally encouraging the think-aloud process as the two children talk through their actions and expectations with each other. Additionally, the co-discovery method might have been useful in helping to prevent boredom and alleviate the stress some participants encountered when working through task activities.

Exit Interview

The exit interview questions were written to solicit summarized feedback from the participants about their experiences with, and reactions to, the website. It was their last opportunity to share their opinions and ideas for improving the website.

Before dismissing each test participant, the moderator asked if they had any questions. The children generally had no further questions with the exception of some wanting to know when the website would be finished so they could visit it. The moderator thanked the participant for helping out and then introduced a member from the product team who came into the testing room to personally offer a small thank-you gift, and a certificate with their name on it, to celebrate their participation in the study. The certificate was created for this study in response to a parent asking for one for their child who participated in the design study.

CURRENT CHALLENGES FACING THE ORGANIZATION

Designing content for children still remains a challenge, particularly with early readers. This study succeeded in developing a more-effective portal for young learners to find and access science content from a wide range of sources within a large government agency. However, while the product team had control over the user experience of this portal website, we did not have any control over the design and usability of the content contributed by multiple departments within the agency. The usability evaluation efforts were geared towards helping children successfully navigate the portal site and find content they would be interested in but could not ensure the usability or engagement level of the actual content.

While there is a mandate for all U.S. government websites to be accessible by people with disabilities as a requirement of the Americans with Disabilities Act, there is no such requirement to ensure a website meets general usability standards. Thus, while an agency can be assured their web content is developed so that it can be accessed via screen readers or other assistive devices, they cannot (at this time) ensure that web content developed for children is indeed easy enough to navigate, use, and be read by this target audience. The Health and Human Services (HHS) and General Services Administration (GSA) provide guidance and resources to help government agencies create usable, useful and enjoyable web experiences but there is currently no mandate, nor funding, to have content and websites specifically tested to meet these requirements.

SOLUTIONS AND RECOMMENDATIONS

This case study looked at the various evaluation techniques used to run an effective and productive session with children. We employed a variety of techniques that have been successful with young children in other studies and adapted traditional usability methods and tools to meet the evaluation goals. In addition to the specific tools, we found that varying the activities frequently between several short activities and moving from table to desk to table, helped keep the children focused and engaged. Because the study was divided into phases, each with its own usability test, the team had a chance to refine their evaluation and communication techniques between phases, resulting in the following findings and lessons learned. However, more research is needed to compare these techniques in different settings (home, school, or library) and longitudinal study. See Table 1 for some of the common issues encountered during evaluation.

Table 1. Common issues and recommendations for evaluating children

Issues Evaluating Children	Recommendations
Difficulty articulating their thought process	• Design hands-on activities that provide an opportunity for the child to express their opinions without relying on just talking. • Co-discovery sessions allow for natural conversation between two children as they work through tasks and activities together. • Use observational analysis, children convey a lot of non-verbal feedback and emotion through body language.
Validating feedback	• Rephrase interview questions to ask the same thing in another way to validate the child's responses and intentions. • Use a combination of tools all designed to solicit the same type of information to make sure the child is giving consistent and truthful feedback.
Diverse cognitive skills	• Demonstrate activities so children can learn by example and practice. • Invite the child to participate in the activity demonstration or explain what they are expected to do in order to verify they understand the objective.
Wide range of reading abilities	• Use visual instruments and tools that are less dependent on words. • Give the child the task activities printed out on index cards so they can use them as a reference when looking for the specified content on the website.
Shy with strangers	• Create icebreaker activities that give the child time to get comfortable with the moderator. For example, ask the child to show their favorite website or game. • Ensure the microphone and audio set up in the room is sufficient for softer-voices; repeat softly spoken statements so observers can hear.
Shorter attention spans	• Limit test sessions to an hour or less. • Design several short activities to help keep the child engaged. • Activities that move the child from one work station to another (e.g. computer desk to activity table) help to reset the child's focus. • Be aware of non-verbal signs of boredom, frustration and lost focus. If a child becomes overly frustrated with an activity move on to the next one. When a child shows signs of boredom or drifting focus give them a short break to visit another website or play a game.

Communicating with Children

Children can be shy with strangers and have difficulty articulating their thoughts. The think-aloud method did not work very well for this target audience as it is not something that comes easy, even for adults. The moderator had to continually remind or encourage participants to verbalize their thoughts. Periodically probing the participants with specific questions about their actions worked more reliably than counting on the children to think (e.g. Why did you click on that? What key words are you looking for? What did you expected to find after clicking that link?).

Likewise, children may not understand such direction as is provided by the moderator. Ask the child to rephrase or repeat what it is they are trying to do (if it appears they don't understand or a task has gone on for too long) and they may prove to be unresponsive. The co-discovery testing method can be a useful tool for facilitating conversation and getting children to talk.

Ease into It

Children generally don't like to be wrong or disappoint adults; the moderator started sessions with easy icebreaker questions and tasks and found that some children responded positively by gaining confidence and being put at ease. For example, the moderator first asked participants to show their favorite website and explain what they like about it. This activity also presented an opportunity to uncover some of the participant's motivations and preferences.

Demonstrate Activities

Children's cognitive abilities are under constant development and the evaluation activities typically used in usability test sessions can be difficult concepts for children to understand. In an effort to help children understand what was being asked of them the moderator used clear instructions written at the children's language-level and demonstrated some activities (the card sort and design ranking) before involving the child. After several sessions the moderator found some children joined in and helped complete the demonstration, which verified they understood their goal. This also gave them confidence and helped engage them in the activity itself. The validity of data relies on the participant understanding what is being asked of them, and the demonstration and hands-on practice appeared to go a long way towards making sure the sessions yield useful data.

Designing Test Instruments for Early Readers

The cognitive abilities range a great deal within this target audience, as do reading levels and vocabulary. To help ensure that every child, regardless of age and development level, could understand the materials and content, the product team explored options for creating more visual and hands-on test instruments. Children generally prefer images to text and using images in the card sort activity make it easier for them to engage and have been proven successful (Joly, Pemberton, & Griffiths, 2009). The solution was to use screenshots of activities and content for the card sort activity and emoticons for the design ranking activity. Most children enjoyed the interaction of the hands-on activities and for some it appeared to help prolong their engagement in the session.

Pay Attention to Non-Verbal Cues

Children are not as inclined and/or able to say exactly how they're feeling for several reasons: difficulty fully articulating their thoughts and emotions, possible shyness, and an inherent desire to please adults (Read, 2011). The moderator paid attention to body language and non-verbal cues such as: facial gestures (like frowning, smiling or raised brows), eye movements (like rolling eyes and/or big surprised eyes), sighs and yawns, posturing, fidgeting, or moving around in their chair. To determine whether these cues are a reaction to the product being tested, to reaction a specific task or activity requested, or an indication of how the child is feeling overall about the test session, the moderator needs to accurately read the situation and assess the cause for the non-verbal cues (Barendregt, 2006). It is the role of the moderator to decide how to best rectify the situation in real time. At times the moderator tried probing to get the child to articulate their thoughts and in other cases the moderator moved on to a new task or gave the child a break by letting them play a game or visit a different website.

Give Children Breaks and Session Limits

Children, especially younger ones, tend to have shorter attention spans and can lose focus, becoming distracted after prolonged periods of activity. This can lead to frustration, boredom, and diminishing performance. The moderator tried to limit sessions to approximately 45 minutes in an effort to minimize the risk of children becoming bored and losing focus. The test plan was designed with a mix of activities (e.g. some hands-on activities mixed with some computer activities), and the different experiences were successful in keeping some of the children engaged. When signs of boredom, lost focus or frustration showed up, the moderator found that it was helpful to give the child a short break to play a game or visit another website, before continuing on with a new task or activity. Another tactic the moderator employed was to run the test tasks in different orders, to ensure children aren't always attempting the same tasks at the end of a tiring session

Deflecting Questions and Requests for Help

Asking for help is something children are used to doing but in most cases the moderator can't intervene. At the beginning of the test the moderator explained to the child that they should complete the tasks on their own without asking for help and then reminding the child again when introducing new activities. The moderator explained to the child that it was important for the product team to see what they could do on their own. When the child did ask a question the moderator tried to deflect it by answering with another question, e.g. "What do you think you should do?" or "What would you do if you were on your own right now?" and "Is there any last thing you want to try before we move on?"

Testing Room Set Up

Children have a tendency to speak softly, even if the moderator next to them can hear them just fine – those in the observation room may struggle and the quiet voices aren't easy to hear on the recordings. The moderator had to repeatedly ask the soft-spoken children to speak up and in some cases it had the adverse effect of making them more uncomfortable. The lab technicians relocated the microphones closer to the participant and retested the audio quality in the observation room and on recordings to try to get the best quality possible. The moderator tried to account for the soft voices by repeating quiet statements back to the child for confirmation so the observers could hear and the recordings were audible.

The chair and desk were too big for smaller children but the moderator did their best to make sure the child was sitting comfortably in the chair and at the desk, with easy access to the computer keyboard and mouse. The moderator asked the child if they were right- or left-handed, and positioned the mouse accordingly

Some younger children may be more comfortable if their parents or guardian sit in the testing room during the session. The moderator offered the parent or guardian the option to sit in the testing room if they felt it would be better for the child but ideally it is best if the child is alone. In one case the parent was a major distraction for not only the child but the moderator as well. However, there were a few other sessions where a parent or guardian sat in and they did not appear to be a distraction or influence on the child.

Test Environment

The most natural and comfortable setting for any test participant is going to provide the most realistic picture of the website's user experience; for most users this would be their home environment. Their physical environment, where and how they actually use their computer, is going to be familiar and comfortable. The computer they use for the study is going to be their computer. The distractions in the home are generally going to be common. The home environment was not an option for this study but it would be interesting to witness the impact the test environment has on the participants in the study. Some alternative settings appropriate for an audience of children include: a classroom, library, museum, home and usability lab. Each of these settings has their pros and cons (Gilutz & Nielsen, 2002).

Know When to Call it Quits

When the participant has gotten so discouraged or frustrated that their focus and interest can't be brought back to the tasks at hand, despite the moderator's attempts, the participant can cease to be productive and their feedback at this point will most likely not be very reliable or useful. Forcing the session to continue will leave the child with a negative experience. The moderator encountered some sessions where the participants were fading from boredom or frustration. The moderator tried to refocus and reengage the participants but in some cases the child wasn't coming back and the sessions quickly went downhill as the child became increasing frustrated. The moderator eventually decided to end sessions that couldn't be refocused. Rather than explaining why the session was ending early, the moderator suddenly warned the participant that the session was almost over and that there was just one last question that they needed help with. This soft transition provided the opportunity to end the session on a positive note. The moderator chose a single question from the exit interview, such as: "What did you find the most interesting about this website?" or "What one thing could be done to improve this website?" The moderator thanked the participant for their time and helpful input. A situation like this can be stressful and challenging for a novice moderator. Wrapping up the session early gave the moderator a little extra time to reset their focus before the next session began.

Thanking the Participant

After the design comparison study the moderator received a follow up request from a parent asking if there was any sort of certificate given for the child's participation (in addition to the cash incentive). There wasn't, but it turned out to be a great idea. For this validation study the product team designed special certificates and signed them for each participant at the end of their session. The feedback relayed from the vendor who recruited the participants was that this small gesture went a long way towards making sure the children felt appreciated for their participation.

Alternative Methods

Participatory Design: While the target audience was invited early on in the design process to provide feedback about the three different design options, they weren't actively involved in the design process. Participatory design workshops involve the children working together with the designer in hands-on activities that result in website prototypes. These workshops aim to engage the children in the process but also strike a balance between child-driven and designer-driven development

(Brodersen et al., 2005). Given that one of the study goals was to create a website that appealed to the broadest target audience, and there was a significant age gap between the target audience and the product team, it would have been an interesting methodology to consider for this project.

Co-discovery: In this case study, the moderator still had difficulty getting children to talk out loud and share their thought processes. Conversations that take place between the children in co-discovery sessions can provide insight into their thought processes; however, in the initial design comparison study, we wanted to avoid any peer pressure issues skewing their personal preferences. Indeed this was effective for the design comparison but including groups or friendship pairs for the validation study might have produced more valuable results.

Longitudinal Studies: A longitudinal study would have added rich data regarding the repeat use and evaluation of the website by the same group of participants. There were select survey respondents who did participate in the validation study to assess their reaction to the later stage design and development of the website. There were resource and timing issues that didn't make this type of study feasible for this project but the methodology is relevant, especially in beta testing and finished products, and yields different findings than first-time-visitor studies.

The validation study was the first chance children had to really interact with the full website and its content - this test was focused on finding initial discoverability and learnability problems as well as unexpected problems and issues associated with a first-time visitor. Half of the children that participated in this usability study had also participated in the design comparison survey; the other six children had never seen these designs before. Some of the survey respondents were invited back for the validation test to assess whether or not the progression of the website design matched their expectations. The survey respondents were not included in the design comparison study because the goal was to capture initial impressions and reactions to the websites. Had time and resources allowed, it would have been valuable to do a longitudinal study testing the same group of children on repeat visits to the website. This would have provided the team an opportunity to capture data related to expert user behaviors, sustained use and engagement over time.

REFERENCES

Bar-Ilan, J., & Belous, Y. (2007). Children as architects of web directories: An exploratory study. *Journal of the American Society for Information Science and Technology*, *58*(6), 895–907. doi:10.1002/asi.20566

Barendregt, W. (2006). Evaluating fun and usability in computer games with Children. In *Department of Industrial Design*. Eindhoven: Eindhoven University of Technology.

Brynskov, M., Christensen, B. G., Ludvigsen, M., Collins, A., & Grønbæk, K. (2005). Designing for nomadic play: A case study of participatory design with children. In *Proceedings of the 4th International Conference for Interaction Design and Children*.

Druin, A., Bederson, B., Boltman, A., Miura, A., Knotts-Callahan, D., & Platt, M. (1999). Children as our technology design partners. In Druin, A. (Ed.), *The design of children's technology* (pp. 51–72). San Francisco, CA: Morgan Kaufmann Publishers.

Gilutz, S., & Bekker, M. (2003). Children's online interfaces: Is usability testing worthwhile? *IDC, 7*(3), 143–145.

Gilutz, S., & Nielsen, J. (2002). Usability of websites for children: 70 design guidelines. *Nielsen Norman Group*, pp. 117-121. Retrieved from http://www.nngroup.com/reports/kids/

Hanna, L., Risden, K., & Alexander, K. (1997). Guidelines for usability testing with children. *Interaction, 4*(5), 9–14. doi:10.1145/264044.264045

Hanna, L., Risden, K., Czerwinski, K., & Alexander, K. (1998). The role of usability research in designing children's computer products. In Druin, A. (Ed.), *The design of children's technology*. San Francisco, CA: Morgan Kaufmann Publishers.

Joly, A. V., Pemberton, L., & Griffiths, R. (2009). *Card sorting activates with preschool children* (pp. 204–213). HCL.

Kamishlian, C. C., & Albert, B. (2011). You need an outlet and a browser: How children understand and use the Internet. *User Experience, 10*(1), 12–15.

Markopoulos, P., & Bekker, M. (2003). On the assessment of usability testing methods for children. *Interacting with Computers, 15*, 227–243. doi:10.1016/S0953-5438(03)00009-2

Naranjo-bock, C. (2011, March 7). Approaches to user research when designing for children. *UXmatters*. Retrieved from http://www.uxmatters.com/mt/archives/2011/03/approaches-to-user-research-when-designing-for-children.php

Nielsen, J. (2010, September 13). *Children's websites: Usability issues in designing for kids*. Retrieved from http://www.useit.com/alertbox/children.html

Read, J. C. (2011). Mess days: Working with children to design and deliver worthwhile mobile experiences. *User Experience, 10*(1), 4–6.

KEY TERMS AND DEFINITIONS

Closed Card Sort: Participants are given cards showing site content with an established set of categories. Participants are instructed to place the cards into these pre-established categories based on where they think each one fits best. Closed card sorting is useful when adding new content to an existing structure, or for gaining additional feedback after an open card sort.

Co-Discovery Method: This is a usability testing technique where pairs of users work collaboratively through tasks and activities. The co-discovery technique offers an advantage over single-participant testing in that pairs of users working together will naturally discuss their thought process, expectations and intentions as opposed to a moderator trying to elicit this same information via the think aloud method.

Cognitive Skills: The mental capabilities that allow a person to efficiently and easily read, think, prioritize, understand, plan, remember and solve problems.

Expert Reviews: A general method of usability testing that relies on experts with experience in the field of usability to evaluate the usability of a website.

Information Architecture: Information architecture refers to how content is structured and organized on the website. This field studies how to organize information so it is easy for people to find and use. It also refers to how the pages relate to one another.

Iterative Design: The process by which a website is progressively developed in a repeated cycle. Iteration is repeated revisions.

Think Aloud: A technique that involves the user talking out loud while performing a task. By thinking aloud while attempting to complete a task the user narrates their approach to solving the task and therefore illuminating the difficulties or pleasantries they encounter.

Wireframe: A line drawing or sketch of a website design that depicts navigational concepts, general layout and prioritization of information and functional elements. It does not take into account the visual design or actual content.

ENDNOTES

[1.] Parental influence on the survey data is unknown but it is important to point out that the trending responses in the surveys were very similar to the findings from the one-on-one test sessions, so the assumption remains that there was little parental influence during the survey.

[2.] It is interesting to note that some children said they been to the website just before coming to the study because their parents told them to. Before getting started on the first test activity, the participants were asked if they had any questions.

Chapter 2
Social Negotiations in Web Usability Engineering

Ian Martin
Leeds Metropolitan University, UK

Neil Simpkins
Open University, UK

Karen Kear
Open University, UK

John Busvine
Open University, UK

EXECUTIVE SUMMARY

This study of a website development project for a university athletic club illustrates how negotiations between designers and users play a fundamental role in defining website usability. Whilst usability can be 'objectively' measured using formal scales (number of clicks required, user effort or error rate to achieve an aim etc.), it may also be subjectively defined as the extent to which a website serves its intended audience. Usability engineering is therefore a social process involving interactions between users and designers that determine what is appropriate for a given context. This case demonstrates the value of a 'heterogeneous' approach to website usability that involves engineering this context by negotiating the social alongside the technical. A strong stepwise website methodology that promotes early and continual user engagement – including sign-off of staged prototypes – is seen to be an important facilitating structure that carries these social negotiations forward through the web usability engineering lifecycle to successful project conclusion.

DOI: 10.4018/978-1-4666-4046-7.ch002

INTRODUCTION

Usability can be defined in terms of three aspects: effectiveness; efficiency; and satisfaction, which occur in a specified context of use (Spilotopolous et al., 2010, p. xvii). Activities aimed at improving the usability of a product or system have been described as 'usability engineering' (Faulkner, 2000). Different techniques can be used at different stages in the usability engineering process. To generate design ideas at an early stage, designers can undertake various activities with users, for example: product reviews, observations, interviews, questionnaires, 'brainstorming' or other types of participatory workshops. Then, in later stages, prototypes can be developed and evaluated by users. These kinds of approaches, which involve active participation by users, are characterised as user-centred design (Marti & Bannon, 2009).

Prototyping is a well-known method for involving users in the development of a system (Ford & Wood, 1996, p. 275) but it can be poorly understood by usability engineering students (Carroll & Rosson, 2005, p. 13). A prototype is a rapidly-developed product which looks and behaves somewhat like the proposed system. Users are asked to try out the prototype and suggest amendments, which can then be quickly implemented and re-evaluated. Prototypes can be categorised as low-fidelity or high fidelity (Rosson & Carroll, 2002, p. 206). A low-fidelity prototype may even be a paper prototype consisting of sketches of screens on pieces of paper which can be manipulated to imitate system behaviour (Holtzblatt & Jones, 1993). Low fidelity prototypes are quick to produce, and allow alternative designs to be explored quickly and at low cost with prospective users. Alternatively, or subsequently, high fidelity prototypes can be built in software and tried out by users. This is helpful in the later stages of the design process, so that users can explore proposed system features and user interface elements. Prototypes test out designers' understanding of user requirements and allow users to further articulate their requirements. Prototypes may also be 'throwaway' or 'evolutionary'. Throwaway prototypes are prototypes that are discarded, whereas evolutionary prototypes are prototypes refined in response to user feedback and subsequently developed into a fully-functional finished system (Vidgen et al, 2002, p. 7).

Prototyping and usability engineering are social processes that involve discussions and negotiations between designers and users (Sefyrin & Mortberg, 2010) throughout the systems development life cycle. However, most website usability case studies focus on website evaluation post-implementation, rather than showing the ways in which usability engineering is incorporated into the analysis and design stages of a project. Of the few case studies that deal with usability engineering early in the systems development life cycle, two are worth noting here. Laster et al. (2011) stress the necessity of gathering user requirements carefully and correctly, exposing the importance of designer-client interaction in determining the usability of a library website. In their study a lack of appropriate interaction with all stakeholders resulted in a website which was unusable by students in the library. It had to be redeveloped using prototyping and staged sign off. Clutterbuck et al. (2009) report on the development of a website for a small business. They contrast the waterfall approach (Guntamukkala et al., 2006) with the agile approach (Barlow et al., 2011) and propose that the agile approach offers greater flexibility and productivity for designers and developers. The waterfall approach is judged to have imposed overheads and constraints on change as development proceeded. However, the agile approach was not without risks. In particular, there remained a concern that concomitant with increased agility was a loss of control over client-requested changes.

In the website development project reported in this chapter the designers employ a hybrid of the waterfall and evolutionary approaches to website development. A stepwise waterfall methodology helps plan, manage and control the web development project while throwaway and evolutionary prototypes draw out user requirements. We investigate and illustrate how social negotiations between web designers and users, structured by the web development methodology and various prototypes, define website usability. In practice, we show how these negotiations involve not only drawing out user requirements through brainstorming and prototyping, but also shaping them within a framework of technical, aesthetic, business, economic, legal and professional concerns.

ORGANISATIONAL BACKGROUNDS

Both the athletic club and the web design company that form the organisational context for this case study are small scale. This low level of organisation complexity affords an empathy with personal perspectives and ensures that negotiations between designers and users are clearly exposed.

The Client

The Open University Running Club (OURC) was formed in 2006, although Open University runners have gathered together informally to train and race since the university's foundation as a distance learning institution in 1969. The club organises three types of events that are open to staff and students of the Open University (OU), as well as members of the local community living and working around the university's headquarters in Milton Keynes, UK.

1.   Handicap races are organised once a month over a distance of 5 km, 10 km or 5 miles. Runners' start times in the handicaps are staggered according to their performances in previous races.
2.   A relay is run annually in late February or early March for teams of four runners which must include at least one female. The relay consists of four legs each of 1.1 miles.
3.   The 'OURC tour' takes place every year in October, and consists of three races (5 miles, 5 km and 10 km) contested over five days. There are no handicaps and the overall winner is the person who completes all three distances in the shortest cumulative time.

The club has approximately 200 members with events typically featuring fifty participants or teams.

The Designers

Online Solutions (OS) is a London-based web design and development firm. The company was commissioned to develop a custom website for the OURC with two objectives in mind: (i) to deliver a user-centred web presence for the club (ii) to provide case study material for a new Open University second-level undergraduate module entitled 'Web Technologies.' To fulfil this second purpose a number of video recordings were made of the web development process. Extracts from transcripts of these recordings together with other artefacts from the process are used throughout the chapter for illustrative purposes.

Online Solutions had previously worked with the Open University, having created the OU's Postgraduate Computing website, the Faculty of Mathematics and Computing website, and the Vice Chancellor's website.

SETTING THE STAGE

Prior to the project, OURC event start times, results, records and a calendar were held in spreadsheets and administered variously by the club organiser, timekeeper and chair. An email distribution list was used to communicate these spreadsheets to club members. News items were also sent via email. The club did not have its own web presence other than a small entry on the Open University website created for its affiliated clubs (OU Club).[1] This entry contained a brief description of the OURC and provided contact email addresses for interested runners.

OURC representatives with an interest in the website development project (the stakeholders) were:

- Nicky Moss, OURC event organiser. Nicky was the website development champion responsible for signing off each stage of the project. He was also charged with creating initial content for the site.
- John Gillespie, OURC event organiser from 1987-2008. John is retired from the Open University but still runs with the club. He has many years' experience of organising OURC events.
- Mick Bromilow, OURC chair. Mick also administers a website for the Milton Keynes athletic club.
- Dave Phillips, OURC timekeeper and photographer. Dave is an official timekeeper at OURC events and others around the UK.
- Karen Kear, OURC member. Karen represented the interests of the club runners.
- David Clover, OU Infrastructure and Development Manager. David was responsible for hosting the finished website and ensuring that it complied with Open University regulations.

The stakeholders shared a variety of computing experience from general office use to several years' programming and operations experience. David Clover had worked with Paul Woodford and Jon Wade from Online Solutions on previous Open University projects and they suggested David also form part of the stakeholder team for this project.

Online Solutions' web design and development team was made up of the following people:

- Paul Woodford, Creative Director. Paul was responsible for website usability and accessibility, its design and its brand. He was the OURC's primary point of liaison for the analysis and design stages of the project.
- Jon Wade, Development Director. Jon was responsible for project managing website development, website functionality and web technologies.
- Colin Gilder, Technical Director. Colin was responsible for developing, testing and delivering the website.

Online Solutions has its own web development methodology that it has improved and refined over several years. This methodology is detailed in Figure 1.

Usability engineering is intertwined throughout each stage of Online Solutions' methodology. There is an early emphasis on the best practice of meeting and un-

Figure 1. Online Solutions' web development methodology

DESCRIPTION	FURTHER DETAILS	LOCATION OF TASK
1. DEFINING THE PROJECT (ANALYSIS PART 1)		
Information Gathering Brainstorm (External meeting with client)	Brainstorming session carried out between Online Solutions and key stakeholders at The Open University	
Understanding The Audience		Open University
Identify Back-end Programming Requirements		Open University
Functionality List		Open University
Content Audit		Open University
Establish Mandatory Inclusions		Open University
Minimum Browser Requirements		Open University
Accessibility Guidelines		Open University
Workflow Requirements		
Hosting Requirements		Open University
Determining Overall Goals		Open University
Determine Success Criteria		
Privacy Requirements		
Establishing a Creative Brief	Branding requirements/restrictions - specifically the running club's relationship to the over Open University brand. Availability of source imagery (Stock Photography?, existing library?, Illustrations or diagrams?) Perception/Tone/Guidelines. Competitive positioning, Targeted message?	Open University
2. DEVELOPING SITE STRUCTURE (ANALYSIS PART 2)		
Information Architecture, Site mapping and Wireframing		
Scheduling and Project Plan	Written and delivered for feedback	Online Solutions
Visual Design Brief Authoring	Written and delivered for feedback	Online Solutions
Visual Design Brief Sign-off		
Site Mapping		Online Solutions
Site Map Delivery		
Information Architecture and Navigation Mapping		Online Solutions
Naming and Labelling		Online Solutions
Defining Key User Tasks		Online Solutions
Draft Wireframe Production	On paper	Online Solutions
Wireframe Production	Interactive HTML/PHP	Online Solutions
Wireframe Presentation & Published Online	Feedback and modifications applied to the live site	Open University
UX Testing (Wireframes)	Test plan written - Users given specific tasks to complete on the wireframes feedback gathered	Open University
Wireframe Modifications	Feedback gathered and modifications applied to the wireframes	Open University/Online Solutions
Wireframe Sign-off		
3. VISUAL DESIGN		
Visual Concepts Development	x 2 based upon the creative brief, wireframes, site mapping and information architecture	Online Solutions
Visual Design Presentation	Feedback gathered and modifications applied	Open University
Visual Designs Published Online	Feedback gathered and modifications applied	N/A
Visual Design Sign-off		
4. DEVELOPMENT AND PRODUCTION		
Slicing and Optimizing Visual Designs		Online Solutions
Website Front End Production		Online Solutions
Content Management System Development & Integration		Online Solutions
Initial Site Population (Test Data)		Open University/Online Solutions
Site Deployed on Staging Server	Online Solutions server for testing	Online Solutions
Online Bugs Database Set-up		Open University/Online Solutions
Website & CMS Delivery & Training Session		Open University
Prioritizing & Fixing Bugs		Online Solutions
Test Site Deployed on Live Server	Open University server for further testing	Open University/Online Solutions
[Optional] UX testing (Website)	Test plan written - Users given specific tasks to complete on the wireframes feedback gathered	Open University
Conducting Final Checks & Apply any Modifications Required after UK Testing		Open University/Online Solutions
5. LAUNCH AND BEYOND		
Setup Ongoing Maintenance Plan		Open University/Online Solutions
Website Launch		Open University/Online Solutions

derstanding prospective users (Gould & Lewis, 1985) and maintaining this dialogue throughout the process. Online Solutions' methodology is based on the 'waterfall model' where one stage has to be completed before the next one is begun (Sanders & Curran, 1994, pp. 80-108; Avison & Fitzgerald, 2006, p. 31-44). The waterfall approach provides a structure for moving the web development project forward, but Online Solutions retain a necessary degree of flexibility by allowing some iteration between stages within a phase.

As detailed in Figure 1, the methodology separates website development into five phases. The usability case study related here focuses on phases 1 and 2 (the analysis phases):

1. Project definition (analysis part 1)
2. Developing site structure (analysis part 2)

CASE DESCRIPTION

The first 'definition' stage of the project took the form of an information gathering and brainstorm analysis session between the OURC and Online Solutions. This was held at the Open University's campus in Milton Keynes, UK. In attendance were Paul Woodford and Jon Wade from Online Solutions, and John Gillespie, Dave Phillips, David Clover, Mick Bromilow and Karen Kear from the OURC.

This first session lasted two hours and broadly followed an agenda supplied via email by Paul from Online Solutions:

```
Agenda: Brainstorm analysis
Introduction
-Introductions of people present, roles
-Introduction to the brainstorm process
Design
-Branding (relationship to The Open University)
-Understanding the audience
-Overall goals
-Success criteria
Technology
-Minimum browser requirements
-Mobile compatibility
-Accessibility guidelines
-Content management & security
-Hosting requirements/staging servers
Content
-Content audit
-Content grouping
-Architecture
-Content privacy
Functionality
-Required functionality/feature list
```

The agenda was a signifier that this brainstorm was to be carried out along the lines of a formal meeting rather than an unstructured discussion. At the start of the meeting Paul and Jon were seated at the head of a table in front of two A0 flip charts and an assortment of marker pens and sticky notes. Paul assumed control and specified how he would like the session to proceed:

Paul [OS]: Firstly thank you for coming along. Today we are going to be analysing the requirements for the Open University running club website. As part of that process in this brainstorming session, we will be writing up on boards, jotting things down and trying to establish basically everything that is required for the website.

So it kind of breaks down into four major areas. We will talk about design first and the branding relationship to the Open University if there is one. Also understanding the audience, the overall goals and success criteria of the website, technology, minimum browser requirements, accessibility, whether it needs to work on a mobile device or not, the content management system involved and the hosting requirements.

The main bulk of the brainstorming is the next phase which is talking about the actual content which is required for the site, listing and auditing that content, then arranging that into some semblance of architecture. Making some sense of it basically and putting it into a labelled structure.

So if we can start by introducing ourselves – round the table – and also maybe discuss the reason for your presence here and your relationship to the potential website at the end.

By setting the agenda and taking the lead in the meeting Paul set the scene for making progress on aspects of the development that Online Solutions had already identified as priorities. These priorities were drawn from the first stage of the company's web development methodology. The focus of the first part of the meeting, before content was discussed, was set upon 'understanding the audience', eliciting 'goals and success criteria', 'minimum browser requirements', 'accessibility' and 'support for mobile devices'. These were the aspects that would define the usability of the website.

After introductions, Paul and Jon began to ask questions and record ideas generated by the OURC stakeholders using the marker pens, sticky notes and flipchart. The small size of sticky notes encouraged the recording of concise single ideas (Saddler, 2001) which could easily be grouped and rearranged on sheets of flipchart paper. These sheets were torn off and pinned up on the walls of the meeting room as the analysis progressed. The first area to be discussed, in keeping with the agenda, was 'branding'.

Branding Considerations

The significance of wider corporate considerations was highlighted when the discussion began in earnest with talk of whether the OURC website would have to comply with university branding requirements. This also served to underline the importance of prior knowledge and pre-existing relationships between the designers and the client. Remember, David Clover had worked with Online Solutions on previous Open University projects:

Jon [OS]: OK so if we go straight into the design requirements of the website first. What I would like to establish because we have worked before with the OU we have some idea of the branding and I know that it has kind of altered a little bit of extra bits of pieces, it has kind of evolved a little bit now there is another site I believe which is OU ICE?

David [OURC]: The current kit of parts, if you like from the university has got a code name where we use the words OU ICE for the code name but it is essentially a series of design concepts. It doesn't assume any particular technical stuff behind the scenes but it is a look and feel concept.

Jon [OS]: And would the running club website have to fit to that brand or will it sit outside of that as separate?

David [OURC]: Well, that is a very, very good question. Obviously sites that are angled towards student use or public in various different ways are asked to comply with brand requirements. In the case of a site like this, it's a more open question, I suspect. It depends very much on the audience it has to serve.

Mick [OURC]: We are affiliated to the OU Club. It's a fairly loose affiliation and I suspect our target is just the people that run at lunchtime and take part in the running club events.

Dave [OURC]: That does mean, in fact that we will need to be partly branded, especially with the OU Club brand.

OU ICE is an online style guide which provides a layout, fonts and colour palette for a consistent look and feel across all Open University websites. It also includes template style sheets that facilitate effective default rendering on mobile as well as desktop devices. The OU ICE online style guide had proved a useful resource for Online Solutions in the past and the designers were keen to make use of it again.[2]

Audience

The availability of OU ICE meant that styling aspects were discussed much less than might be expected. The discussion turned quickly to focus on the potential audience. The first step in the usability engineering lifecycle model is 'know the user' (Neilsen, 1993, p. 72; Faulkner, 2000, p. 15). Paul from Online Solutions tried to build up profiles of likely users:

Paul [OS]: And the audience, would that be runners within the club? Would it be - would it need to be browsed by people sitting outside? Would they have any vested interest? It is obviously a website so it is open to everybody. Is it students, or just staff, or...?

John Gillespie [OURC]: It is principally staff that take part in the events. There are no students taking part because they don't generally have any connection here with the campus. In addition to staff there are a number of people from local companies and organisations that do come in on to the campus to take part in the events with the blessing of the OU running club.

Karen [OURC]: We do have some graduate students here, so there are quite a few of them who run actually but people who are here - that's the feel of the place - people who are here.

Paul [OS]: Is there an age range at all?

Karen [OURC]: Very broad.

John [OURC]: In the events we have been running this week, we had the youngest who took part was 12 and the oldest was over 75.

Paul [OS]: The average?

John Gillespie [OURC]: The average age of participants I would say would be about 50. I think we would like to see that reduced but that is the way it is.

Success Criteria

As the discussion started to warm up with talk of branding and understanding the audience, OURC stakeholders became eager to talk about website content.

Mick [OURC]: You want things like photographs of people running at lunchtime. You want to know if you want to run at lunchtime, when are the best times to turn up at the pavilion, you know, the changing rooms on site, maybe even maps of the best routes that they could use so that they don't feel they are coming to something totally new when they go...

However, it was important for Online Solutions to regain control and steer the conversation back towards determining some overall goals and success criteria for the website according to the agenda. Eliciting and recording the criteria that would constitute a successful – and by extension usable – website was the designers' main concern.

Jon made a suggestion to Mick as to what one criterion might be, which was affirmed by Mick:

Jon [OS]: *But looking from the perspective of success criteria: you develop a new website, it's up there, it's live, people are looking at it and if you were to say, yes, we tick that box by doing that website, what would it be? Would it be fair to say that one of those things would be gaining more participants?*
Mick [OURC]: *Gaining more participants, yes.*

OURC stakeholders took some time to realise what the designers meant by success criteria, and why they were being asked to suggest them. An understanding between the two parties developed gradually as Jon and Paul encouraged the development of ideas which appeared to be leading towards the definition of success criteria. These criteria were then confirmed by Online Solutions in one or two words that could be written on a sticky note. For example:

Dave [OURC]: *I also think one of the other criteria for saying it is a success is that the university itself looks for an outreach to the local community, so if we have got a site where we find that there is much more people within the Milton Keynes area, seeing what we are doing, and even contacting us to get involved, that would meet the criteria that the university asks us to do when it comes to meeting and bringing other people in.*
Paul [OS]: *So sort of 'outreach'.*

Some stakeholders even went beyond determining specific success criteria and suggested ways in which they could be made measurable.

John [OURC]: *… We could in fact, have a training area so you can find out what's going on this week that you could join in with, what you might want to organise yourself.*
Jon [OS]: *Sounds good. Presumably, tied into that would be a success criteria there, because effectively if you can have better dissemination of information to those people then they can, say, better themselves and sort of encourage that training.*
John [OURC]: *And it's easy to measure that success by the number of people that turn out for that specific training session.*

Jon and Paul used active listening techniques such as paraphrasing and feedback to draw out and summarise success criteria from the stakeholders' comments. This created a shared understanding between the designers and the client, which was often built upon analogies, similes and metaphors. Familiar ideas, for example 'a poster', were used to clarify conventions that were particular to web design and its specialist vocabulary.

Mick [OURC]: *Well one measure is the number of times people visit the website, because a lot of websites where you go once and you see some information that is very static and doesn't change at all but you would never go there again, and other websites where the information is constantly changing, evolving, getting better and it is the information that you want, so you keep going back.*

Jon [OS]: *So encouraging repeat visitors.*

Paul [OS]: *So you would like the site to be 'sticky' basically.*

Mick [OURC]: *Dynamic.*

Paul [OS]: *Dynamic?*

Jon [OS]: *Well dynamic is the fact that it is ever evolving and a sticky site would be something where someone doesn't just... It has two sides to it, one where you wouldn't just go and that's it, I have got everything and bye, bye. The second one is the fact that when I go on to something to go and get the piece of information that I thought that I wanted I might actually just stick around for a little bit, and I might go over here and have a look at something else and might find a little bit more about something else over here. In fact it is a bit like changing your website so it is not effectively like a poster. You read a poster once. You read it on the wall, you have got all the information you want and then you walk away. Where the website would be a sticky website then it sparks enough interest for you to go elsewhere...*

The gathering of requirements was a fluid process and the discussion continued to move away from determining success criteria and towards generating ideas for website content. Online Solutions attempted to bring the process of developing success criteria to an end, but the Open University stakeholders were keen to keep their ideas about content flowing:

Paul [OS]: *So we have got some good success criteria there.*

Karen [OURC]: *I think another one might be... I'm thinking of the routes because there's quite a few people who join in with the races and unless they've been doing it for quite a while, they don't necessarily know what the route is, which is always a bit of a problem. So if we could provide some maps or something like that?*

John [OURC]: *I think with things like Google Earth and that these days and...*

Mick [OURC]: *There's something called Map My Run...*

Figure 2. Audience characteristics and success criteria

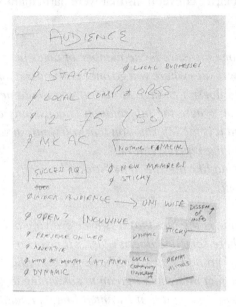

As the stakeholders bounced content ideas around, Jon from Online Solutions had to tactfully intervene in order to bring the conversation back to the definition of success criteria. Realising that the client was keen to carry on generating content ideas, Paul tentatively suggested they move the discussion formally on to content. However, Jon wanted to make sure they kept to the agenda and discussed technology requirements next.

Jon [OS]: *I think we need a success criteria, rather than just content really, as that's where we're kind of looking, but there is something to be said for what you're saying there...*

Paul [OS]: *... Shall we just keep pushing and just do the content? Because everyone is just warming up to the content.*

Jon [OS]: *Oh no I think we should take a break.*

Paul [OURC]: *And then do a quick one with technology.*

Figure 2 shows the audience characteristics and success criteria captured from this brainstorm.

Minimum Browser Requirements

The information-gathering brainstorm then moved on to the issue of minimum browser requirements. The discussion centred upon how usable the new website needed to be for users of Internet Explorer 6 (IE6). First of all, Jon from Online Solutions had to establish whether support for IE6 was a requirement:

Jon [OS]: What we need to find out is there a requirement for a lower browser version, say Internet Explorer 6.

John [OURC]: I would say yes, in the sense that there would be people viewing from home, home machines. I mean the OU do have up-to-date modern machines, but a lot of our audience would not be in that situation.

Having ascertained that there was a requirement to cater for users of IE6, Online Solutions began to negotiate that requirement. IE6's support for modern web standards is poor and it is widely disparaged by web developers so Jon quickly informed the stakeholders of the implications of this requirement. He began by suggesting that IE6 was no longer supported by Microsoft, the tacit implication being that if a vendor was no longer supporting a version of its own product then web developers shouldn't either. Microsoft did still support IE6 at the time of the discussion, but many influential companies such as YouTube and Google were phasing out support:

Jon [OS]: Ok. Internet Explorer 6 is no longer supported by Microsoft any more, but you are perfectly right, there are people who still have it kicking around because they haven't upgraded or they haven't sort of... there are a lot of people who don't even download updates for Windows and will be quite happily going along with it as it was installed when they bought it.

Jon continued by explaining that IE6 users could be supported, but their experience would not be exactly the same as users with newer browsers:

Jon [OS]: So what we have to do now, we have to make that call as to, do we want to not only support those lower browser versions, but are you happy for it not to be a perfect representation of what it would be in a newer browser version? The reason I am asking this is because you can get away, you can do a lot more with technology and a lot of newer technology, a lot of new tricks and things like that, for want of a better word that you would use in IE 7, 8 or 9 that won't work in IE6.

Mick [OURC]: It depends what you mean by not working. If it just looks a little bit different...

Paul then stepped in to clarify with an example of what one usability issue might be for users of IE6:

Paul [OS]: That's the definition basically of what we would make it, or optimise it for IE7 and above but the content can still be viewed in IE6, just some of the left hand nav might not be in the same place as it is in other browsers...

Paul and Jon found an ally in OURC stakeholder David Clover, the OU's Infrastructure and Development manager, who they had suggested join the OURC stakeholder team. David lent his technical authority to the debate:

David [OURC]: I wouldn't myself today if I was developing, even begin to regard IE6 as a target for development. I wouldn't even necessarily think of IE7 as being a main target for development. I can quite see how people would have old fashioned equipment or older equipment, but to be honest provided the site can be shown in some form, even if it is only text, at a low level then I think that would be adequate. I wouldn't want to disable development by pointing at a browser which was no longer secure, no longer sold, no longer available. That wouldn't make sense to me.

David's comments provided Jon with an opportunity to close the discussion. Jon summarised negotiations with an agreement to make information 'available and accessible' for users of IE6, but that usability engineering would concentrate on modern ('supported') browsers.

Jon [OS]: That sounds fine. OK. So we will agree to make all the information available and accessible using one of those low browser versions but we will concentrate on the ones that are supported.

Support for Mobile Devices

Users of mobile devices also needed to be considered as part of the potential OURC website audience. Jon raised the issue, but worded his question carefully. He had already considered a mobile-specific site or mobile app, but judged that it was out of scope for the current project. David Clover also knew this from his prior experiences of working with Online Solutions.

Jon [OS]: Is it something that you want to pursue, mobile development? Is it something that you are not really that bothered about at this stage, or is it something maybe you would consider later on?

Mick [OURC]: A lot more people are accessing Milton Keynes athletic club website using smart phones than certainly they used to and I suspect in a year or two it is going to be much more the way of doing things than now, so I think if we can build that in to the solution, it would advantageous.

David [OURC]: *Will we get down to the app level at this stage or just simply a web enablement that makes use of the small space?*

Paul [OS]: *The constraints of this project are that basically we are just talking about the website. But we need to get down all of your requirements just so that at a later stage we could recommend that we re-address the app.*

Developing a mobile app or a dedicated mobile site was deemed out of scope of what Online Solutions could develop for the OURC within budget. Nevertheless, requirements were gathered and ideas generated for future projects or project 'phases' that could specifically address the requirements of mobile users. It was important to collect all the client's requirements, rather than just those that were within current scope. There were two reasons for this. First, this was a brainstorm where all ideas were valid and it was important to record them. Second, documenting out of scope requirements meant that they could be categorised as aspects to be addressed in a later development phase, while crucially protecting the scope of the current project.

Accessibility

OURC stakeholders were then encouraged to talk about accessibility requirements for the new site, i.e. to consider the needs of any disabled users.

Jon [OS]: *One question we have just got to quickly ask as well will be accessibility. Is there an OU standard for accessibility?*

Karen [OURC]: *It is very important and we teach it in all our courses. It is so easily neglected.*

David [OURC]: *There certainly is, yes. [...] We call it SENDA which is the, I have forgotten what they stand for now, but anyway it is a legal requirement that we have to make our sites accessible which we have met in some cases either by providing bigger and smaller writing at the press of a button, or a text only version of the site which can be read into a reader or something like that. So we do have a statutory requirement to make our sites accessible.*

Mick [OURC]: *DA is the Disability Act, I think.*

The client was concerned to meet the legal obligations of the UK's 2001 Special Educational Needs and Disability Act (SENDA). This concern precipitated Online Solutions to propose a specific approach based on past experience:

Jon [OS]: I mean organisations like the RNIB [Royal National Institute of Blind people UK] now, their requirements or their recommendation is that sites follow the W3C's accessibility guide to a priority of 2...Yes, it is pretty much kind of the similar thing anyway as SENDA which I don't know if that is an actual thing now, sort of that the OU would say, all our websites must be W3C...

Online Solutions' approach was based on meeting priority 2 (now known as level AA conformance) of the W3C's Web Content Accessibility Guidelines (WCAG). Online Solutions suggested that the Royal National Institute of Blind people UK (RNIB) was happy with WCAG priority 2. However, concern over legal obligations remained. The OURC stakeholders began to negotiate these obligations between themselves.

David [OURC]: Well we don't have a choice now because it is a legal requirement that we have that we pay attention to what is in the Act, so if we were challenged on this, we simply have to say we have met the Act by providing this facility. So there has got to be something in there that we can respond on that with...

Mick [OURC]: Well you can satisfy the Act by saying we have looked at this issue and decided that the only solution is too expensive for us, but we have to consider it.

Online Solutions stepped in to propose its WCAG priority level 2 solution as a legitimate solution again. Its wide adoption was stressed and Jon brought in a high-profile organisation for which the company had recently done some web-development in order to lend weight to the argument. He also stressed that accessibility would not adversely affect overall usability:

Jon [OS]: I would pretty much say that if we developed at priority level 2, the United Nations, let's say for example every site that is affiliated to the United Nations has to be priority level 2, which is kind of becoming pretty much a standard now, that that fills and ticks virtually all the boxes. So it will give you things like text that can be expanded to a 200% size without mucking things up, so therefore it is perfectly legible. It's not affecting the usability, that kind of thing, so people who are harder of sight can utilise the tools, the browsers and things offer them in order to help them effectively access the information that they need.

The OURC's concerns regarding the legal aspects of accessibility led to a discussion of the needs of other categories of disabled users. Note how, in his response to Karen's concern (see below), Jon used the word 'you' rather than 'we'. He was subtly implying that the responsibility for providing transcripts of audio-visual content lay with the OURC rather than the web developers.

Karen [OURC]: *What about other kinds of requirements - say people who are deaf - so if we had some audio on the site, we would need to provide something.*

Jon [OS]: *Yes, you would provide a transcript for anything that is audio visual wise, the same thing as you should also have... a description... every audio, every video would have that written description. The thing is, as long as we can establish what the guidelines are then obviously we can work to them. If we start to work to those guidelines from the ground up then it is obviously a lot easier than to do it retrospectively.*

Again, David Clover stepped in to help the designers. Jon echoed David's comment (see below) and closed negotiations down with a reference to 'professionalism'. He suggested that accessibility was part and parcel of a professional approach to web design.

David [OURC]: *It's a way of thinking when you start.*

Jon [OS]: *You just establish that from the start, what are your accessibility limitations/requirements, so that we can just build to... it is part of the process. If you are a professional web developer you have to do it...*

Website Content

After then having quickly discussed technology requirements, Online Solutions encouraged the Open University stakeholders to consider content in earnest. Paul and Jon from Online Solutions continued to listen attentively and make use of analogies, similes and metaphors in order to create shared understanding. Ideas for website content recorded on sticky notes were grouped together on flipchart paper (see Figure 3) which would later be translated into the website's information architecture.

Online Solutions was careful to ensure that essential content for a website, such as imagery, were included in the discussion and to explore sources for images:

Jon [OS]: *Imagery for this as well is quite an important thing. There are kind of two levels. There is imagery that somebody may want to put an image of themselves... And there is also general imagery for the website and I was just wondering whether that existed. Do you have like a library of imagery that you have used before that we could have access to?*

Figure 3. Ideas for website content

Mick [OURC]: *I have a very extensive library of images that I have been using over the last 8 - 10 years and which I have very carefully coded so that if I need to get hold of a photograph of a particular person, I can find the images if I need to.*
Dave [OURC]: *I have got a selection of pictures of the OU runners.*

The brainstorm session continued with Online Solutions separating ideas for website content from website functionality. The session ended with Jon and Paul outlining the next steps in the process, which would be creation of an information architecture and site wireframing.

Developing Site Structure and Wireframing

Back at the Online Solutions office in central London, a few days after the initial brainstorming session at the OU, Paul and Jon pinned the flipchart sheets and sticky notes on the walls of their office and began to develop a structure for the new website (Figure 4).

The analysis continued to unfold using pen and paper and 'brainstorming' conversations between Jon and Paul. This involved some revisiting of the user requirements, and discussion to make sure they had a shared understanding of the users' requirements. They were also conscious that there could be issues for users in moving to a new way of doing things, via the website, and that the transition would need careful handling.

Jon and Paul discussed the usability of the 'results' section for the website. They concluded that before proceeding they would need to check with the client whether updating and presenting race results via the website would need the same functionality as the spreadsheet-based system the OURC were already using:

Figure 4. Developing a site structure

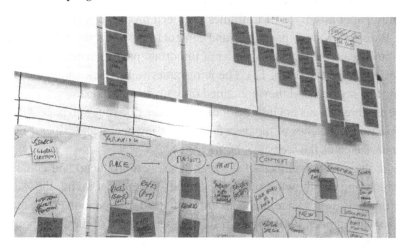

Jon [OS]: So if we move on to results...

Paul [OS]: Yes I've got the spreadsheets from those and I've had a look and none of them are particularly consistent so it's how that is presented... Can Excel spreadsheets just be put in and squirted out onto a webpage? Or do we recommend that we have a spreadsheet that we set up, they put in the relevant details and then put that in?

Jon [OS]: I'd say there's two ways of doing it though because there's also a mention of a 'nice to have' would be some kind of graphical looking at the data which is something you could do effectively, the spreadsheet is just collecting the data in – we can create a mechanism for transferring that info into a database, whether that would be importing from the spreadsheet or putting the data into an online form. And then when that information is in the database we can play with it in terms of its representation so we can have graphs or even just use simple filtering, re-sorting... But at the end of the day it is just simple data – name, race, time, whatever potential category – handicap etc. etc...

Paul [OS]: Maybe that's a conversation that we need to have with the clients about what they actually want to achieve from this data basically. I mean they may have ways of working now...so we need to gently build that in... because they might think 'I'm using an excel spreadsheet, that's all I'm going to use, I'm not going to use a web-fronted spreadsheet' we don't want them to go off and just do that anyway and then just email them regardless. Because then obviously the whole point of the website starts to become moot... So it would be good to have a conversation to see what they want to achieve and see what we can do obviously within those constraints.

After Jon and Paul's initial conversations, Paul began the process of creating low fidelity paper prototype 'wireframes' for each proposed web page in the new website. Wireframes show page form and content (e.g. see Figure 5). The emphasis in wireframes is on the layout and order of important page elements rather than the visual design (Silver, 2005, p. 12). The wireframes were black and white, with no images or font styling, and they contained only placeholder text.

There are three stages in Online Solutions' production of a web page wireframe. First, some rough sketches of the page are made using pencil and paper. Figure 5 is an example sketch of the website's home page.

Second, the most developed of these sketches is reproduced and enhanced on a computer using the drawing package, Adobe Illustrator. Finally, the Adobe Illustrator image is used as a reference point so that a developer can create an online interactive wireframe in PHP. Figure 6 shows a screen shot of the same home page as an interactive online wireframe.

The online wireframes made the designers' concepts tangible and communicable to the OURC stakeholders, while allowing them the flexibility to quickly change the design in response to feedback. The wireframes also served as a way of documenting and agreeing user requirements. Paul explained this to the authors as follows:

Figure 5. Paper wireframe for home page

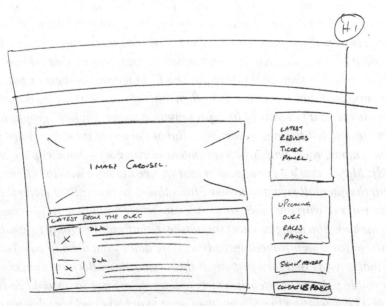

Figure 6. Screen shot of interactive online wireframe for home page

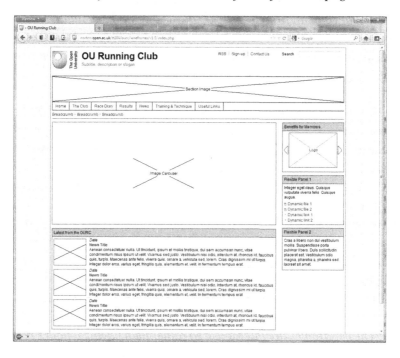

Paul [OS]: *We can alter the wireframes really quickly as opposed to going through the design process and having to actually change the entire website. What we can do is really quickly move things around, move things from the left to the right, from the right to the left. And it gets to a point where the client can then sign off, so at least you have something, and this is from our point of view, a benefit that at least we have something to always refer back to so you go 'well if you look at the wireframes you'll see that we agreed this'.*

Once the wireframes had been created in Adobe Illustrator, Paul passed them to Colin Gilder who created online and interactive versions of the wireframes using PHP. The earlier paper and Adobe Illustrator wireframes were discarded at this point as 'throwaway' prototypes, and the creation of the first online and interactive wireframes was the beginning of a series of 'evolutionary' prototypes that would be transformed into the finished system. Paul commented:

Paul [OS]: *I think it's the interactive nature of the wireframes online that makes them, gives them – a completely different dimension. So the advantage of the wireframes online would be that they can be edited very quickly and we can take various pieces of content, page aspects out quite quickly, move them*

around from left to right or into the top. Not only that, sometimes we get con-
tent, actual content, from the client so we can put the actual content into the
wireframe so we can see straight away that something isn't correct. [...] and
you can have this discussion with the client via email, over the phone, and
they can see something visual which is the wireframe.

Once PHP wireframes had been created for the whole of the OURC site they
were hosted on a web server so that the OURC stakeholders could interact with them
and provide feedback on this stage of the design process.[3] Initial feedback from the
OURC stakeholders on the interactive wireframes was collated into a single document and sent back to Online Solutions. Excerpts from this feedback document are
provided in Table 1.

Some of the OURC stakeholders, perhaps unsure as to the exact purpose of the
wireframes, made comments on the website's visual design or the web technologies
to be used rather than the site structure. On a visit to the Open University to give a
presentation of the wireframes to OURC stakeholders, Jon provided clarification
of the purpose of the wireframes from Online Solutions' perspective.

Jon [OS]: *The wireframes are interactive so rather than having a paper representa-*
tion they give you that feel of how content is inter-related, how sections work...

Table 1. Initial OURC wireframe feedback

Perhaps the start times could be displayed via link within 'Race Diary'? Otherwise looking good.
Looks good. The only thing I could not see was where we put up the handicap start times.
Looks nice. Will there be colours?
I like the fact that you can click on anyone's name to get a summary of their race results. But can I go directly to my own results? ... ah ... just spotted that you can type a name into a search field.
For the website, I'd like some indication on the front page of the core training times - 12:20pm every lunchtime from the pavilion.
For the results of races I would prefer a link to the results from the front page (with something in the news section to mention the winner and the fastest times). Otherwise the front page might look a bit odd with 30-40 times and anything underneath it would only be accessible if you scroll down. Alternatively, put the race results as the bottom item on the right hand side so you can see the first few and can scroll down for the rest.
The benefits for members should be linked to on the front page rather than hidden in the about us section.
Contact us: does this need to be any more than an email link? We are in danger of creating too much friction with this form.
Withdrawal form: requires too much info - don't need DOB or gender surely just freeform text and name. In this form race name should pre-populate from current page.
One thought is that the main logo or slogan should be clickable to return to the main home page (which is, kind of, a convention that I'm used to).

> *[They] almost give you that full user feeling of using the site without any kind of graphical elements or any real text or things like that. So divided up into the sections of the club, race, diary, results, news, training and technique and useful links are the primary, which we worked through from the original brainstorm what we determined the sections to be. There's obviously been a few naming changes since that time that we're proposing in these wireframes.*

The naming changes and the layout of the website were all agreed by the OURC stakeholders. Nicky (the OURC stakeholder responsible for signing off each stage of the project) emphasised the wireframes' utility as an interactive tangible representation of the form of the proposed website. However, he also raised a concern about the unseen back-end mechanisms for content creation and management which would be required for site administration:

> ***Nicky [OURC]:*** *The wireframe gave you a feel of what it's going to feel like, which I thought it was quite a reasonable presentation because people that will be using it are just general users they're not necessarily specialists in it or anything, so in that respect I thought it was quite friendly. So from a usability point of view I got a good feel for what it's going to look like and various aspects of content. Obviously we had some detailed feedback about how we might do some of the technical stuff like getting the race times up and editing those and that sort of stuff so it's the stuff that goes on in the background that obviously we need to prep, like mechanics of how we're going to use it if you like...*

Paul fended off the question by explaining that back-end considerations would come later in the development lifecycle.

After the presentation, Online Solutions asked that the previously gathered wireframe feedback and new issues arising from the meeting were distilled into a concise list of required changes in order to produce a version 2 of the wireframes. This would help manage the stakeholders' opinions as a single voice. Jon, confident that most of the OURC's requirements had already been met, didn't anticipate version 2 of the wireframes being very different from version 1.

> ***Jon [OS]:*** *We'll then work through those, present them back to you guys with a new version. I doubt there'll be a lot of changes but with an itemised list of what has changed so therefore you can work through it again and then go through that sort of review process again so then you can collect any more comments that maybe come in from that and then again we'll update the wireframes accordingly. [...]If we're all very happy then we'll move to sign them off and use those as effectively the blueprints, the plan, for the developers to build a new building.*

Email conversations continued between Nicky and Paul from Online Solutions. As a consequence, a number of further minor modifications were made to the wireframes.[4]

Each stage of the wireframing process solidified user requirements. The overhead of formal requirements documentation was deemed too great for a small-scale project such as this, so signoff of the wireframes provided acceptance of the requirements encapsulated in the wireframes.

THE CHALLENGE OF MANAGING SOCIAL NEGOTIATIONS

In order to further understand the role social negotiations play in website usability engineering, the authors conducted an interview with the designers in which they were encouraged to talk about the social aspects of the OURC website development process.

Jon and Paul from Online Solutions stressed the potentially open-ended and messy nature of client-designer relations and stressed the important roles their web development methodology and prototypes (wireframes) played in structuring negotiations with the client.

Jon [OS]: ... You have to make sure that the projects are... rigid isn't the right word, but they have to be very well structured. So having been – I wouldn't say burned at the beginning – but we did notice that it was very easy for a client to increase the scope of a project unless they were well reined in. And what we didn't want to do was turn into a company that was effectively telling clients what they need to do. Because it is the client who's effectively paying our wages but who is coming to us to deliver it so we shouldn't be in this position saying, 'no no no', we should be the ones saying 'yes yes yes'. So we had to kind of develop a way that we could keep the project on a good schedule but with some clear boundaries but at the same time be their yes kind of company... And the best way of doing that was to have very visual things that the client can relate to themselves... We really want to focus on something physical, something real, something people can relate to, it's not full of jargon...

Paul [OS]: So what we did was develop an online wireframe system which was previously only on paper where we put the website online just in outline form and they could see the structure as we built it and add various sections and content. And that way what happened was we created dialogue between ourselves and the client...

The online wireframes were an important user-designer medium of communication. They not only allowed for quick feedback, experimentation and reflection but also limited the issues that could be addressed at any one time. Within Online Solutions' waterfall methodology, the wireframes also encapsulated a subset of usability requirements that could be signed off at the end of the analysis stages. The prototypes were a way of getting around the communication problems associated with purely paper-based specifications and had the advantage of being self-documenting.

Paul [OS]: It gives you a point of reference, that's the other important thing. So there's a definite, there's a clear point where something is signed off so the wireframes are signed off at a certain point and the designs are signed off at a certain point so each and beyond that, well a client can say oh I've had this new idea where I would like to, I want it to open up certain things and do certain bits of animation or whatever and you go well I'm sorry it's been signed off that's going to be extra, it's going to be x more because it's further development, but it does give them the opportunity to – there's still the dialogue there – we can still add bits and pieces – but at least we have a point of reference from which everything is sort of based and stopped. I mean that, there is certain restrictions within that because that's also based on, say a proposal for a particular project before that and then also obviously budgetary restrictions and time.

Jon emphasised the tangible nature of the wireframes and the advantages they held for the designers over a written requirements document.

Jon [OS]: It is nice though to be able to still be in that position to say 'yes you can have that' but the client already knows that yeah that wasn't a part of an agreed thing because everything that is agreed in the project is very clear. It's not buried inside a document somewhere that got lost or shoved on a server somewhere.

The wireframes and methodology were embedded within wider social negotiations that took place in the face-to-face meetings and via emails and phone calls. An understanding of the client's requirements became clearer as the negotiations progressed through the various stages of analysis.

Paul [OS]: Sometimes that takes a fair amount of teasing, teasing out because a client can say one thing and say this is our requirement, but actually it's something else and sometimes it takes a few rounds to kind of get to that point where you completely understand what the requirements are.

However, designer-user interactions in the early stages of usability engineering are not just about getting to know the user by eliciting user requirements. They are also used to motivate stakeholders, generate commitment to a project, and to set expectations as to which requirements will fall within project scope. Online Solutions began purposefully managing client expectations of website usability from the outset of the project. Jon and Paul commented on the purpose of the first project definition meeting ('brainstorm').

Jon [OS]: The brainstorm... serves two purposes. (1) It has to collate all the information; and (2) to brainstorm ideas in a room effectively so that the solution that you do come up with at the end of the day is the right solution and covers all angles. But the other side of it is to manage the user's expectations of the project – how it's going to go, what it's going to be like. Getting them on board and tied into the project, selling the advantages of it.

Paul [OS]: It's really important to get their buy in straight away but also to manage that analysis. So, when it's delivered or you get to a certain point, which is wireframes or the designs put up for everyone to see, all of a sudden out of nowhere they go well that's completely wrong, it has to have this whole new section which is going to be costly and takes a lot of time... We're normally aware of what the budget is so we kind of angle the whole project or the whole analysis around a certain limitation so we know what's going to be quick to build what's going to be slow. You know creating a whole new mobile site for something that is mainly developed for desktop for instance is going to be quite costly so we always mention that maybe that could be phase 2. Phase 2 is often a phrase we use quite often to keep... keep it within budget.

Project scope is determined by a number of constraints which must be balanced against the need to satisfy user requirements. Paul's articulation of the economic constraints was couched in language that carefully positioned requirements deemed too costly as something to include in 'phase 2' of the project. Jon also raised the issue of business concerns when managing multiple projects for multiple clients.

Jon [OS]: ... In the real world, you can't rely on simply one project. You have to run several projects concurrently, especially when you run a methodology which enables you to deliver let's say designs for example, there will be a period of dead time during that before the designs are either finalised or signed off, where you can be doing some things but you can't afford to waste the money by developing something that might need to be rewritten. So therefore what you need to do is carefully balance projects over the top of each other.

Together with business and economic concerns, the designers had to take into consideration legal obligations such as compliance with accessibility regulations and adherence to wider corporate and professional norms as they managed negotiations with the client. Careful negotiation was required to ensure user requirements were gathered and met within this framework of concerns.

The authors are conscious that even with excerpts from meeting transcripts it is difficult to fully illustrate the soft skills that designers require to manage and shape these social negotiations. We encourage you to watch the videos that capture in more detail the dynamics between the designers and users at these early analysis meetings.[5]

CONCLUSION AND RECOMMENDATIONS

The authors consider the work that designers do in managing and shaping user requirements to be a form of 'heterogeneous engineering' (Law, 1987). In order to build usable products, designers must make connections between the social and the technical. The social negotiations in the early analysis stages of the usability engineering life cycle define the technical solution that is delivered in the end.

Usability engineering originally focused on evaluating and improving existing systems, particularly in terms of their user interfaces (Bringula & Basa, 2011; Persson Långh & Nilsson, 2010). Attention was principally paid to how easy a system was to use and to learn. However, the discipline has broadened to include consideration of the functionality needed within a system, particularly requirements analysis (Rosson & Carroll, 2002, p. 14). Designers of web-based systems have increasingly adopted user-centred or participatory design approaches. These approaches are based on close involvement with users or potential users at an early stage in order to ensure that resulting products are grounded in the needs and characteristics of users (Schuler & Namioka, 1993). This user-centred approach contrasts with earlier design approaches where users were largely ignored by product designers, resulting in frustrating or unusable systems (Norman, 1998).

Processes for the design of interactive products, described by Preece et al. (2002, p.12) as 'interaction design,' can be broken down into four steps: '1. Identifying needs and establishing requirements. 2. Developing alternative designs that meet those requirements. 3. Building interactive versions of the designs so that they can be communicated and assessed. 4. Evaluating what is being built throughout the process.'

Ensuring that substantive usability activities are included in step 1, before design is started, is the least expensive way of ensuring overall product usability (Nielsen, 1993, p. 72). Gathering requirements is not a one-way process. It involves designers not only getting to 'know the user' by drawing out requirements through brainstorming and prototyping but also engineering a project's socio-technical context in order to negotiate these requirements against economic, business, legal, technical and professional concerns.

These negotiations, which begin at project definition and are refined in subsequent phases of the web development lifecycle, have significant impact. In this case study, almost all aspects of the website were directly derived from discussions in the first two meetings. These meetings were structured around an agenda that was designed to promote discussion of the issues that the designers considered to be important. When stakeholders strayed from the agenda the designers had to gently bring conversations back on track. Later in the process, wireframe prototypes served to move forward and narrow these discussions to provide a necessary focus that made the activities of design and development manageable.

Website usability engineering is a complex socio-technical process. This case study has made visible the social negotiations that take place in the analysis stages of the web development life cycle in order to highlight the often-neglected part they have to play in usability engineering. It is our firm belief that usability engineers must be heterogeneous engineers if they are to succeed in building usable products.

REFERENCES

Avison, D., & Fitzgerald, G. (2006). *Information systems development: Methodologies, techniques and tools* (4th ed.). Maidenhead: McGraw-Hill.

Barlow, J., Keith, M. J., Wilson, D. W., Schuetzler, R. M., Lowry, P. B., Vance, A., & Giboney, J. S. (2011). Overview and guidance on agile development in large organizations. *Communications of AIS, 29*, 25–44.

Carroll, J. M., & Rosson, M. B. (2005). A case library for teaching usability engineering: Design rationale, development, and classroom experience. *Journal on Educational Resources in Computing, 5*(1), pp. 1–22.

Bringula, R. P., & Basa, R. S. (2011). Factors affecting faculty web portal usability. *Journal of Educational Technology & Society, 14*(4), 253–265.

Clutterbuck, P., Rowlands, T., & Seamons, O. (2009). A case study of SME web application development effectiveness via agile methods. *Electronic Journal of Information Systems Evaluation, 12*(1), 13–26.

Faulkner, X. (2000). *Usability engineering*. Basingstoke: Macmillan Press.

Ford, J. M., & Wood, L. E. (1996). An overview of ethnography and system design. In Wixon, D. & Ramey, J. (Eds.) *Field methods casebook for software design* (pp. 269-282). New York: Wiley.

Gould, J. D., & Lewis, C. H. (1985). Designing for usability: Key principles and what designers think. *Communications of the ACM, 28*(3), 300–311. doi:10.1145/3166.3170

Guntamukkala, V., Wen, H. J., & Tarn, J. M. (2006). An empirical study of selecting software development life cycle models. *Human Systems Management, 25*(4), 265–278.

Holtzblatt, K., & Jones, S. (1993). Contextual inquiry: Aa participatory technique for system design. In Schuler, D., & Namioka, A. (Eds.), *Participatory design: Principles and practices* (pp. 177–210). Mahwah, NJ: Lawrence Erlbaum.

Laster, S., Stitz, T., Bove, F. J., & Wise, C. (2011). Transitioning from marketing-oriented design to user-oriented design: A case study. *Journal of Web Librarianship, 5*(4), 299–321. doi:10.1080/19322909.2011.623517

Law, J. (1987). On the social explanation of technical change: The case of Portuguese maritime expansion. *Technology and Culture, 28*, 227–252. doi:10.2307/3105566

Marti, P., & Bannon, L. J. (2009). Exploring user-centred design in practice: Some caveats. *Knowledge, Technology & Policy, 22*(1), pp. 7-15.

Neilson, J. (1993). *Usability engineering*. San Diego: Academic Press.

Norman, D. A. (1998). *The design of everyday things*. Cambridge, MA: MIT Press.

Persson, A., Långh, M., & Nilsson, J. (2010). Usability testing and redesign of library web pages at Lund University, Faculty of Engineering: A case study applying a two-phase, systematic quality approach. *Information Research, 15*(2).

Preece, J., Rogers, Y., & Sharp, H. (2002). *Interaction design: Beyond human-computer interaction*. New York: John Wiley & Sons.

Rosson, M. B., & Carroll, J. M. (2002). *Usability engineering: Scenario-based development of human-computer interaction*. San Francisco: Morgan Kaufmann.

Saddler, H. J. (2001). Design: Understanding design representations. *Interaction, 8*(4), 17–24. doi:10.1145/379537.379542

Sanders, J., & Curran, E. (1994). *Software quality*. Addison-Wesley.

Schuler, D., & Namioka, A. (Eds.). (1993). *Participatory design: Principles and practices*. Mahwah, NJ: Lawrence Erlbaum.

Sefyrin, J., & Mörtberg, C. (2010). 'But that is a systems solution to me' – negotiations in IT design. *CoDesign 6*(1), 25–41. doi:10.1080/15710881003671882

Silver, M. (2005). *Exploring interface design*. Clifton Park, NY: Delmar Learning.

Spiliotopoulos, T., Papadopoulou, P. & Kouroupetro, G. (Eds.) (2010). *Integrating usability engineering for designing the web experience: Methodologies and principles*. Hershey, PA: IGI Global.

Vidgen, R., Avison, D., Wood, B., & Wood-Harper, T. (2002). *Developing web information systems: From strategy to implementation*. London: Butterworth-Heinemann.

ENDNOTES

[1]   The URL for the OU Club website is http://www8.open.ac.uk/ouclub/main/

[2]   Version 3.0 of OU ICE is available from: http://www.open.ac.uk/webstandards/v3.0/index.php

[3]   Version 1 of the interactive wireframes can be found at: http://norton.open.ac.uk/igi/index.html

[4]   Version 2 of the interactive wireframes can be found at: http://norton.open.ac.uk/igi/index.html

[5]   The case study videos are available from: http://norton.open.ac.uk/igi/index.html

Chapter 3

Developing User Profiles for Interactive Online Products in Practice

Hana Al-Nuaim
King Abdulaziz University, Saudi Arabia

EXECUTIVE SUMMARY

The user profile is one of the tools that usability engineering designers use to focus their design efforts on a particular target population. This chapter presents a qualitative case study on the effectiveness of creating user profiles from data collected through questionnaires administered to target users as a basis for design. During a three-year period, computer science students in the final year of their undergraduate program who had an extensive background in programming and software engineering were asked to create user profiles for their graduating software development projects. This research found that designers must have the skills and experience to develop, administer, and interpret questionnaires that collected accurate data from respondents. A high investment in user profile questionnaire development only produced general usability requirements, which should be the goal of designers for every user interface. Therefore, these requirements were not effective and failed to provide the students (designers) with ideas on which to base their user interface designs. In his book, The Inmates Are Running the Asylum, Cooper (1999) argued that programmers and engineers actually in charge of software development create products and processes that waste significant amounts of money, squander customers' loyalty, and erode competitive advantages—a process that allows talented people to continuously design bad software-based products. Software engineers have their own techniques and tools for managing the software development process instead of integrating usability and its related engineering techniques into existing software engineering (SE) methods to maximize the benefits gained (Seffah et al., 2005).

DOI: 10.4018/978-1-4666-4046-7.ch003

SETTING THE STAGE

In standard SE lifecycle models, which are system-centered, each activity leads naturally to the next; the requirements are collected at the beginning and each subsequent phase is coded, integrated, and tested at the end of the cycle. According to Costabile (2001), the problems with traditional SE lifecycles are as follows:

- Usability is not addressed;
- Testing is conducted too late to enact radical design modifications to cope with possible discrepancies with the requirements; and
- Requirements are collected from customers who negotiate with designers about the features of the intended system and often differ from those who will actually use the designed systems.

Usability engineering (UE) is a discipline that provides structured methods for achieving usability in interactive computer products during the development lifecycle (Mayhew, 1999). Whereas traditional SE phases include goal-oriented requirement gathering, coding, testing, and maintenance, UE is more concerned with user analysis, task analysis, and testing the design through a series of prototypes.

In a survey of 8,000 software development projects, the Standish Group found that one third of the projects were never completed and one half succeeded only partially; the number one reason that projects succeed is because of user involvement during the development process. About half of the managers interviewed acknowledged poorly identified requirements as a major source of problems (Aurum & Wohlin, 2005).

To capture a comparative view of the maturity of UE around the world, the HFI UX Maturity Survey (2009) found that the most common challenges faced when developing usability practices today are as follows:

- No real executive champion, resulting in a lack of organizational recognition and funding;
- No centralized function in organizations and a lack of visible recognition that the usability/user experience represents a discrete skill set reinforce the myth that usability is just common sense; and
- No clear charter, governance, or accountability operated by established usability groups for an unanticipated number of organizations.

As a discipline, UE has come a long way since the 1990s because of the fierce competition among software vendors and the migration of most applications and services, whether commercial, educational, or governmental, to the Internet. A shift has occurred from developing system-centered products to human-centered products focused on the interaction between computers and humans using user-centered design (UCD) tools and methods. SE is a tedious but necessary process that deals with the capabilities of the machines. UE is an even more tedious set of methods and tools that focuses on user involvement throughout the design process. UE ultimately develops products to accommodate the needs of diverse users by conducting analyses of users in terms of age, gender, expertise with technology, educational background, attitude toward the technology, and linguistic ability, because such characteristics can influence the product's use (Liu et al., 2010).

According to Norman (2005), for those in the field of user-interface design and human-computer interaction, "know your user" is sacred. The plethora of bad designs in the world are excellent demonstrations of the perils of ignoring the people for whom the design is intended. However, by continuously emphasizing the needs and abilities of software's target users, usability and understandability of products have improved, yet complex and confusing products are still being developed (Norman, 2005).

"The user" is the human being engaged in an activity with the product. A user can be defined as any individual who, for a certain purpose, interacts with the product or any realized element of the system manifested in the product during any phase of the product lifecycle (Warell, 2001). Janhager (2005) classified "the user" in relation to his or her use of the products by investigating such individuals through the following categories:

- Users' experience with the product, which depends on their length of use, education, and frequency of use;
- Influence on and responsibility for use according to their influence on the choice of product they will use, influence on the use situation, and responsibility for use of a product;
- Emotional relationship with the product, which is comprised of the special feelings that users may have for a product in terms of ownership, social aspects, exclusiveness or group affiliation, feelings, impressions, and opinions; and
- Degree of interaction with the product according to users' mental and cognitive interaction and their physical contact with the product.

The user profile is a tool available to usability engineers. Gabbard et al. (2002) suggested that to effectively narrow the scope of the potential design space, usability and software system engineers can focus their design efforts on a particular target population through user profiles, which provide a characterization of an interactive system's target population. Kuniavsky (2003) suggested that user profiles allow designers to focus on a specific image of users that everyone on the design team can reference when generating design ideas. Many qualitative and quantitative methods exist to solicit data from users, such as interviews, questionnaires or surveys, focus groups, and case studies, each with its own set of strengths and limitations. Selecting the method to use depends on a number of factors, such as the number of users required, accessibility to users, cost to develop the method and its administration, and interpretation of the data.

The requirement analysis phase of UE, which begins the design process, involves: (a) a user profile, which helps identify user characteristics that could be cognitive or non-cognitive in nature; (b) contextual task analysis (CTA) to execute typical use cases and identify the problems faced by users in executing the scenarios; (c) usability goals, which include ease of use, ease of learning, and performance; and (d) identification of preferences and satisfaction goals based on user profiles and CTA (Durrani & Qureshi, 2012). Mayhew (1999) also considered the development of user profiles as the first step in requirement analysis—the first phase in the UE lifecycle model; an entire chapter of her book is dedicated to user profile development, provides examples of data-gathering techniques, and describes how to interpret the data to form user characteristics, which in turn can be transformed into usability requirements. Importantly, note that user involvement during the requirement phase of SE, as opposed to UE, is limited to requirement gathering for the functionality of the system, not for the design of the user interface (UI).

Durrani and Qureshi (2012) posed a question to employees of 26 software organizations on their usability activities during the requirement phase, which helps to identify and categorize user profiles. Eighty percent of the 35 responses indicated that the companies do not create user profiles. Ninety-four percent of the organizations are more concerned with job and task characteristics, and the organizations that collect data for user characteristics do not use them for user profiling.

Case Study Objective

This chapter presents a qualitative case study on the effectiveness of creating user profiles from data collected using questionnaires administered to target users as a basis for design. Over a three-year period, computer science students in the final year of their undergraduate program who had an extensive background in programming and SE were asked to create user profiles for their graduating software development projects as part of the only undergraduate human–computer interaction (HCI) class offered by the department. The students were asked to create a draft questionnaire based on Mayhew's (1999) user profile technique, choosing from the relevant list of attributes by Kuniavsky (2003). They were asked to state the reason for including each item on the questionnaire, pilot the questionnaire, and administer it with real target users.

This chapter presents the challenges that the students faced while developing the user profile questionnaire and their interpretation of the results. The chapter concludes with the researcher's findings on the effectiveness of user profile development and use, especially for geographically distributed users for Web-based applications.

Note that for the purpose of this chapter, the user profiles discussed are those used to initiate design ideas. They are not user profiles used at the end of the development process during the usability testing phase. The advantages of using user profiles during testing is that they provide information on a particular user to explain outliers in the data and trends in user behavior that could explain problems faced by users that may not be from a problem with the product itself.

ORGANIZATION BACKGROUND

The computer science (CS) department is one of three departments in the School of Computer and Information Technology at King Abdulaziz University in the coastal city of Jeddah, Saudi Arabia. As part of the curriculum of the CS department, students must submit a senior graduation software development project. The interactive software products chosen by the students range from simple educational software to artificial intelligence systems; by far, the projects of choice are interactive Websites for different purposes. The students enrolled in the graduation project course must also register for the introductory HCI course. The topics listed in the course syllabus include UE, UCD, data collection methods, and usability testing. As part of their HCI homework, students are required to create a user profile for their software projects and work in groups that range in size from two to six.

References Used

As part of the UCD and UE lectures, the following references for user profiles were used:

1. *Observing the User Experience* by Kuniavsky (2003) is a general how-to handbook on user research with a complete toolbox of techniques to help designers and developers see through the eyes of their users. The dedicated chapter on user profiles explains when and how to create them, providing a detailed list of attributes that serves as seeds when thinking about such attributes. The following is a list of Kuniavsky's (2003) user profile categories with some of their attributes:

    a.   *Demographic*
- i.   Age
- ii.   Gender
- iii.   Income and purchasing power
- iv.   **Location:** Are users urban, suburban, or rural? Do they come from certain regions, a certain country, or they are worldwide?
- v.   **Language:** What is their primary language?
- vi.   **Culture:** Does culture affect the way they use the product?
- vii.   **Title:** What job titles do they hold?
- viii.   Company size (if the product is for people who are working in a company)

    b.   *Technological*
- i.   **Computer:** What kind of computer does the typical user have and how long has he or she had it?
- ii.   Monitor resolution
- iii.   Type of Internet connection and its speed
- iv.   **Experience:** How have they been using their hardware? What kind of things do they use it for?
- v.   Browser and version
- vi.   Operating system

    c.   *Web Use*
- i.   **Experience:** How long have they been using it? How often do they use it? How often do they use it for business or pleasure?
- ii.   **Typical tasks:** What do they do on the Web?

    d.   *Environment*
- i.   **Use location:** Will the service be used from home or from an office?
- ii.   **Time:** Will they be using the product during work or during off hours?
- iii.   **Tool context:** What other tools do they need when using the product?

    e.   *Lifestyle/ psychographic*
- i.   **Values and attitudes:** What is important in their lives? Thrift? Speed? Ease? Fun? Comfort?
- ii.   **Media:** What media do they use to learn about products, services, and ideas?
- iii.   **Activities:** What else do users do in their lives? What do they do for entertainment?

    f.   *Roles*
- i.   Titles and responsibilities
- ii.   **Training:** What training have they received at work?
- iii.   **Power:** What is their responsibility for the product?

        iv. **Relationships:** Whom do they work with? Whom do they consult with when making a choice?

        v. **Interactions:** What is the nature of the interactions with others? Informational? Regulatory? Commercial?

g. *Goals*

        i. **Short term:** What problems are your users trying to solve?

        ii. **Long term:** What effect does using the product have on the business as a whole?

        iii. **Motivation:** Why are they using your product? What is driving them? Are these goals personal? Professional? What is the relationship of the goals to a user's job or life?

        iv. **Outcome:** What does the successful completion of each goal mean? How is success defined? Is there an ultimate goal?

        v. **Pain:** What is keeping users from solving their problems with their current tools? How severe is the pain?

h. *Needs*

        i. **Functional:** What has to happen for the problem to be solved? For the goal to be reached? Emotional: What do they need to enjoy using the product?

        ii. **Reasons:** What are their reasons for using the product?

i *Desires*

        i. **Stated desires:** What do users say they want?

        ii. **Unstated desires:** What do they really want?

j. *Knowledge*

        i. **Domain knowledge:** How much do users know about what they are trying to do?

        ii. **Product knowledge:** How much do users know about your product or service?

k. *Usage Trends*

        i. Frequency of use

        ii. **Considerations:** What will they be asked to know about the product before using it?

        iii. **Loyalty:** How loyal are they to their chosen product?

l. *Tasks*

        i. **Reason:** Why do they want to do these tasks?

        ii. **Duration:** How long do they do it for?

        iii. **Order:** What is the sequence of tasks and does it matter?

        iv. **Criticality:** How important are the tasks?

        v. **Method:** How do they want to accomplish the task?

       vi.   **Model:** Is there some way they are doing this already? What tools are they using and how are they using them?

2.   *Usability Engineering* by Deborah Mayhew (1999) is a book on a series of product lifecycle techniques for UE. The book presents highly structured iterative design and development tasks guided by user feedback that results in easy-to-learn and easy-to-use software. This book was chosen because its chapter on user profiles provides a detailed step-by-step guide on how to construct user profile questionnaires. The chapter provides good examples of how to elicit user feedback by asking the question correctly; providing appropriate options that are not open to interpretation; and avoiding leading, loaded, or emotional phrasing of the questions. For example, many questionnaires ask users about their level of expertise, including "beginner," "novice," or "expert" as answer options, whereas "expert" means for many users only browsing online and checking email. However, for designers, expertise means much more than that. Therefore, the questions posed for users need to define their terminology. The following are typical questions for a few user profile categories provided in the sample questionnaire by Mayhew (1999, p. 50):

   a.   *Attitude and motivation*

       i.   In general, how do you feel about working with computers?

         ..... I don't like working with computers.

         ..... I have no strong like or dislike of working with computers.

         ..... I like working with computers.

         ..... Other (please explain) ....

       ii.   Do you enjoy learning how to use new software applications?

         ....Yes, it's usually challenging and interesting.

         ....Sometimes, depending on the application.

         ....No, it's usually tedious and frustrating.

         ....Other (please explain)..........................

   b.   *Knowledge and Experience*

       i.   What is your level of typing skill?

         ...."Hunt and peck" typist (less than 15 words per minute)

         .....Moderately skilled touch typist (between 15 to 50 words per minute)

         .....Highly skilled touch typist (greater than 50 words per minute)

       ii.   How would you describe your experience level in your current job title?

         .....Novice (less than 1 year)

         .....Experienced (1–3 years)

         .....Expert (more than 3 years)

         .....Other (please describe) ....

  c. Physical Characteristics
    i. Do you wear glasses or contact lenses?
      .... No
      .... Yes (please describe your vision problem and correction method; for example, nearsighted, farsighted, bifocals, contact lenses.)

CASE DESCRIPTION

Each semester, students receive the requirements and guidelines for the user profile homework as part of the HCI course. The main steps for creating a user profile are explained in detail as follows.

Step 1: Selection of a User Group

Each student group has a certain interface they are designing for their product. They are requested to identify the target user groups and select seven to ten users to profile.

Step 2: Preparation of a Draft Questionnaire

Students are lectured on developing questionnaires, with an emphasis on avoiding common pitfalls by following the principles and guidelines of questionnaire design and construction, such as those listed by Borgatti (1998):

1. Target the vocabulary and grammar to the population be surveyed;
2. Avoid ambiguity, confusion, and vagueness;
3. Avoid emotional language, prestige bias, and leading questions;
4. Avoid double-barreled questions;
5. Avoid false premises;
6. Avoid asking about future intentions;
7. Avoid negatives, especially double negatives;
8. Avoid asking questions beyond a respondent's capabilities, and never assume the respondent is an expert;
9. Sequence and lay out the questions in such a way that does not cause one item to influence the response to another;
10. Filter "Don't Know;" and
11. Choose between open-ended versus closed-ended questions.

Other issues relating to questionnaire construction are also explained, such as ratings scales, rank ordering, and paired comparisons, in addition to confidentiality and other ethical considerations related to administrating the questionnaire.

Students were also lectured on the user characteristics needed to develop a persona or user profile using the chapter on user profiles by Kuniavsky (2003) as a reference. The chapter served as a guide for the complete set of user characteristic categories presented in the previous section. Students were then instructed to create a draft questionnaire that included the categories in which they needed information on their users, including the appropriate parameters for their selected interface to be developed. At the same time, they considered the ultimate goal of their product.

During this phase, the confusion develops and the questions begin for those whose software projects lack clear, specific goals and that are not within the reach of target users. Example projects include creating an archiving system for a local library, classroom allocation systems for a certain college, and different programs for special needs children in a certain organization. Users in these projects are limited in number and are known—some by name—to the students; hence, creating their profiles is just a matter of asking the questions correctly because the requirements are clearly given by upper management. In such cases, the number of users profiled represented a true sample of the target population. Although limited in number, these students had some concerns regarding some of the user profile attributes, and included the following example questions:

1. If designers have been asked to develop the software by upper management, why do they care what users' motivations and attitudes are about use? The software will be developed even if their motivations and attitudes around the product used are poor.
2. If the product is work-related, why should designers ask users about their monitors and browsers when a more accurate reply can be obtained from upper management or tech support, and what they have at home is of no relevance?

However, students who had Web-based systems and general systems for widespread use that could be used by anyone worldwide faced more significant challenges in creating user profiles. For those students, some of the questions they asked included:

- How many users should fill in the questionnaire if the target user population could reach millions of people from all walks of life?
- What if we obtain results for a certain item that are 50% in one extreme and 50% in the other extreme? Which 50% should we consider for design?

After the instructor addressed the concerns raised by the students, they were asked to use their knowledge about the project's goals and requirements, principles of questionnaire construction, and the two chapters on user profiles as a guide to create their own user profiles for their interfaces. The drafts of the user profile questionnaire included the reason for including every item on the questionnaire to ensure that they were not just added indiscriminately without focusing on the goal of the user profile or of the product.

Step 3: Piloting the Draft Questionnaire

To assess the quality of their work, the students were asked to pilot the questionnaire with at least two reviewers (who might have represented a sample of the respondents targeted) to elicit their feedback on how well they understood the questions and whether they were able to answer them. The pilot also ensured that the questions were not misinterpreted. The students acted as observers and each of the reviewers responded to the questionnaire, addressing areas of confusion and taking notes on problematic areas, in addition to calculating the average time that each respondent took to complete each item.

Step 4: Preparation of a Final Questionnaire

The draft questionnaire was revised and adjusted to reflect the concerns found during the pilot process. The final questionnaire was submitted with the pilot results and documented any changes to the original questionnaire, which were explained to ensure that students fully understood the need for adjustments.

Step 5: Administration of the Final Questionnaire (the User Profile)

Students prepared the user profile with a cover page as a consent form that explained vaguely that the purpose of the questionnaire was to gather information on potential users for a software product. To avoid bias, it did not mention any product details. The user profile was then administered to seven to ten users, mostly on an individual basis.

Step 6: Analysis of the Results

The students were instructed to analyze their results using any simple descriptive statistical method they deemed necessary and to provide a summary of their data analysis using Mayhew's (1999) chapter as a guide.

Step 7: Development of Usability Characteristics and Usability Requirements

The students interpreted the data to develop user characteristics and, consequently, usability requirements for the design of their UI according to the following example from Mayhew (1999) for production workers:

User Characteristics

Of this user category, 67% are over forty years of age. Attitude and motivation toward computers are fairly high. However, nearly 73% of these users do not perceive computers to be important to their job. Their educational level is a general high school degree or lower. By inference, reading skills probably average around the eighth-grade level. Job experience levels are quite high, yet turnover is low. In contrast, computer experience is quite low and the frequency of computer use is also quite low. A majority of users have no typing skills, and only a small number are experienced typists. A majority of these users are male. By inference, slightly more than 7% have some form of color vision deficiency. A substantial majority wears corrective lenses and virtually 100% wear protective eyeglasses on the job.

Usability Requirements

These users have a high need for ease of learning because of their lower educational levels, low computer experience, low frequency of use, discretionary use, minimal training support, and the perception that computers are currently not particularly important to their jobs.

However, they are very experienced on the job, their attitude and motivation regarding computer usage is high, and their turnover rate is low. These characteristics suggest that power without complexity (i.e., simplicity) is also important. That is, the power ought to be immediately perceivable, not hidden by a complex and difficult-to-learn user interface.

Very low typing skills and the prevalence of corrective lenses suggest that icons and visual displays (rather than verbal ones) will be useful. Any text that is displayed should be written at about the fifth-grade reading level. The prevalence of corrective lenses and the generally older age of these users also suggest that text and symbols should be adequately large. That most users are male suggests that the use of color must be taken into consideration because of color blindness.

CHALLENGES FACING DESIGNERS

Within the three-year period, only 57 out of 68 user profiles were developed correctly. Each semester, the instructor analyzed the user profiles that the students developed correctly and found that, in general and regardless of the projects, the attributes they described were nearly the same, with minor exceptions and slightly different phrasings. The questions that solicited this information were intended to gather straightforward, easy-to-phrase, concrete, and unambiguous answers that the students could use to make a design decision. The following attributes appeared most frequently on student-developed user profile questionnaires, including the reasons for including them:

- **Age:** If the product is targeted toward children, it should be fun and grab users' attention. If the product is for seniors, the text needs to be relatively large;
- **Gender:** To help with color choices and to use terminology familiar to a specific gender;
- **Language:** To decide on the main language of the interface;
- **Type of Internet connection and its speed:** To determine the volume of media to include within the interface;
- **Experience:** To determine the interfaces that users are familiar with to maintain the look and feel of such interfaces;
- **Operating system:** To decide on the scripting code to use to be rendered correctly by the browser;
- **Web experience:** To determine the Website interfaces and terminology that users are familiar with to maintain the look and feel of such interfaces;
- **Typical tasks:** To conclude whether users are shopping online, banking, playing games, networking, or just using email to determine navigation element familiarity; and
- **Frequency of use:** To judge users' level of expertise with respect to their normal online activities.

Every semester, the instructor found that students committed the following two common mistakes on their user profile questionnaires:

1. The purpose of user profile questionnaires is to elicit information about the users, not the product, to make design decisions. However, students often asked users directly about design ideas in terms of their preferences for interface widgets, preferred colors, and other interface preferences.
2. Students asked users about system requirements, which should be done during the requirement gathering phase of the SE lifecycle. They asked users about

the limitations of their old systems or manual methods, and the type of functionality that they wanted to see in the product, thereby exposing the type of system that the students are designing when users should not be aware of such knowledge to avoid biasing the results when responding to the user profile. For example, students asked users if they preferred "contact us" to filling out a form or to clicking an email link that launches an email program such as Microsoft Office's Outlook.

When asked why they included such items, students responded that they felt that the questions they included in the user profile did not provide them with concrete guidance for design. Therefore, they had to include questions that gave them answers that provided information they could actually use to jump-start the design of their interfaces.

Feedback Session with Students

Each semester, the graded user profile homework projects were returned to the students. The instructor opened a discussion in a focus group type session to discuss the problems discovered and the problems that students may have encountered during questionnaire design, construction, administration, or data interpretation. The instructor found that the 57 user profiles created correctly by the students during the three-year period never included certain user characteristic attributes. Table 1 provides some of the student responses as to why they excluded such items from their user profiles.

Context Design

Dourish (2004) stated that translating ideas between different intellectual domains can be both exceptionally valuable and unexpectedly difficult; one reason is because the ideas need to be understood within the intellectual frames that give them meaning, and we need to be aware of the problems of translation between these frames. Dey and Abowd (2000) defined context as any information that can be used to characterize the situation among entities whether people, places, or objects, and including a user and an application that is considered relevant to the interaction between a user and an application. Context design plays a central role in many areas of design, especially when computation is moved "off the desktop" to the mobile environment, which contextualizes and disambiguates forms of activity and information (Dourish, 2004).

Researchers have attempted to define context in terms of dimensions or categories such as a time context, location context, activity context, physical context, computing

Table 1. Excluded User Attributes

User attribute	Reasons for exclusion from the questionnaire
Company size and location	Most users do not know the size of their company; in addition, company size and location have no design ramifications, especially when a company commissioned the development of the product. Management should consider the company's size when deciding whether the investment in the software product requested is cost effective.
Income and purchasing power	Users' upper management will decide on whether to have the software developed regardless of users' income; moreover, if the product is an interactive Website, users' income is meaningless with respect to use and has no design consequences.
Values and attitudes, needs and desires	Students have a problem asking questions relating to these attributes because they are psychological in nature and the questions need to be in-depth for the answers to affect the design.
Computer and monitor resolution	Users are not necessarily aware of such attributes if the product is being used in the office. If the product will be used online, then such issues may be resolved by changing user preferences regarding the platform they use. Although some students asked about these attributes, they found the results useless and users' responses inaccurate.
Reasons	Available from management.
Culture	This attribute is extremely difficult to discuss with users. Many questions need to be asked to draw meaningful conclusions about culture for it to have an effect on design ideas. Culture or internationalization can be researched and design ideas may be tested with the target user group to obtain feedback if users are from the same culture. However, the design of an interactive Website for worldwide use should easily adapt to various linguistic and cultural differences by separating such data from the source code. Therefore, this attribute is a programming concern and not a design one. For example, in Western countries, green is the color for hope, whereas in Indonesia, it is the color of danger and in India it is the color of sadness and sorrow. Yet, in Western countries, the color of sadness and sorrow is black (Thurnher, 2004). Another example of a common cultural difference among the youth are the symbols for smiling, winking, and crying, which are ":-)," ";-)," and "'-(," whereas in Japan the symbols are "^_^," "^_^," and ";_;," respectively (Thurnher, 2004).
Browser and its version	Most browsers can display all pages, although some forms may be activated only on certain browsers. If the software is for a specific organization, then questions on the browser used should be asked of the relevant technical support personnel and not of users. However, if different users will use the software or if the product is a Website and 50% use Internet Explorer (IE) and 50% use Google Chrome (GC), how can such data help designers? Moreover, 90% of users may use IE during design but may switch to GC if a new version of IE is launched with which they are unhappy; therefore, basing the design on a certain browser is counterproductive.
Media	Today, media are everywhere, and finding users who are so isolated that it is worth asking them about the media they use is difficult.
Activities	Users are diverse in their activities; the responses to such a question would never be conclusive enough to determine a design guideline.
Roles	Information about titles, responsibilities, training, relationships, interactions, short- and long-term goals, motivation, and outcome are only necessary if the product to be designed is organization-specific.
Domain knowledge	Should be asked during the system analysis phase of SE.

continued on following page

Table 1. Continued

User attribute	Reasons for exclusion from the questionnaire
Use location and time	The information with respect to where and when users will use the product, such as when or whether at a certain office of an administration entity, may be obtained from management. If the product is an interactive Website, location and time are irrelevant because the Website should be accessible at anytime and from anywhere, including through wireless devices.
Tasks	The tasks that users will perform, in what order, for what length of time, and for what reason should be another part of the requirement gathering phase of the UE lifecycle.
Context	With the prevalence of mobile technology and the widespread use of mobile phones, designers must create richer multimedia experiences for mobile users. Context is an extremely important new area of research within the HCI community, yet students argued against directly asking users about this attribute on their user profiles because they found doing so particularly puzzling. To fully understand the source of student confusion, the following section provides a simple overview of context design.

context (such as net connectivity, communication costs, and bandwidth), and physical context (lighting, noise levels) (Ariza Avila, 2006). These concepts help to clarify the nature of context, but they do not really address the issue of how to represent it.

Users often find unexpected or unanticipated ways of using technology, and the notion of context offers system developers new ways to conceptualize human actions, the relationship between those actions, and the computational systems to support them (Dourish, 2004). Context also draws from social science, placing analytic attention on certain aspects of social settings (Dourish, 2004).

Häkkilä and Mäntyjärvi (2006) concluded that because the UI design and technical development of context-aware applications tend to be quite far apart, a need exists for practical tools that can bridge the gap and improve the design outcome. They also proposed—what they consider especially important—something tangible for helping UI designers in developing context-aware mobile applications because these designers may not be familiar with the concept of context-awareness and do not necessarily understand the underlying complexity that can affect system functionality and, thus, user interactions. Furthermore, small software development companies may not have dedicated personnel responsible only for UI design; therefore, for real-life usage, providing practical design tools and guidelines that can help achieve better and more usable products is important (Häkkilä & Mäntyjärvi, 2006).

Therefore, when developing user profiles during the initial design phase, asking users where and when they use the product is irrelevant unless users have complete knowledge of what the product actually does. However, such information is certainly not provided when collecting data for user profiles.

DISCUSSION

The usability requirements that students developed from their interpretation of their user profile data included having an interface that is easy to use, easy to learn, and simple, with limited colors and user-entered data, and so on. A close review of an example of usability requirements by Mayhew (1999) showed that the requirements mentioned included "high need for ease of learning," "power without complexity (i.e., simplicity)," "visual displays (rather than verbal ones) will be useful," "text and symbols should be adequately large," and "color must be taken into consideration." However, these requirements are merely general principles and guidelines for UI design. The students' conclusions were quite similar to the usability requirements example by Mayhew (1999), which provides a specific result for a specific group of people from a pool of known targets with whom user group designers can meet and talk.

The students were asked whether the usability requirements that they determined from their user characteristics results formed a basis for their design. Each semester, the answer was an overwhelming "no." They were initially hesitant to answer because they believed that a negative answer was wrong and that it might affect their overall grade. The discussion with the students about why they found user profiles not useful as a basis for design revealed that the attributes most commonly elicited from users by the students were of no consequence for the following reasons:

1. **Age:** Aging has been found to result in a decline in the physiology and neurophysiology of the eye through physical, sensory, and cognitive factors in higher-order cognitive processes such as attention, and through a slower speed in almost all tasks that stress rapid performance (Liu et al., 2010).

    That any company would design for elderly employees is highly questionable; however, if a product is targeted toward the elderly alone, asking their age is meaningless because text and icons should be visible and the design should be simple and use touch-screen items or virtual keyboards large enough to be focused on and tapped. Therefore, designers need to know whether the design is for the elderly to be able to enlarge the text using the options provided by the browser or using the screen settings. If the product is targeted toward children, asking the children their age is also irrelevant. Designs for children should be based on age group because each group has different usage behavior and preferences. However, this information can be researched because eliciting user profiles from children themselves is challenging. According to Ibrahim and Salim (2004), when developing software for children, the following questions need to be considered. None can be asked directly of children but rather must be observed or researched during the initial analysis phase or during testing:

a. How will the children understand the software being developed?
b. How will software reflect the children?
c. How will the children learn?
d. What problems do children face that are not usually addressed?
e. How can we measure their ability to interact with the interface and manipulate an item on screen?
f. How do gender issues influence the interface design?
g. How do children differ from adults in terms of development level and the way they use the tool?
h. What are the influences of hardware and tool technology on their interface requirements?
i. How will the children interpret the size and location of icons on the screen?
j. What is the limit of sound to support the design of a user interface?

2. **Gender:** Researchers have long recognized the relevance of gender in affecting computer skills and computer design issues, and have related this issue to the decision-making process, different perceptions, and preferences with respect to the use of and satisfaction with different Website features (Hubona & Shirah, 2004). Other studies proposed that males behave more actively, focus on perceptual aids, tend to be more abstract learners, and are more intuitive and undirected, whereas females are more anxious about results, more analytical and organized, and focus on haptic aids (Liu et al., 2010). For example, if the Website is targeted toward women, such an audience should be reflected in the design, and asking about gender may help in color choices and terminology familiar to a specific gender. Additionally, the majority of users in an organization may be women at a certain point in time, for example, but this majority may change to being male at different levels of employment; therefore, no company should limit its product's interface design to a specific gender.

3. **Language:** Today, browsers can easily translate webpages into several languages. Through internationalization, a site should be available in several major languages. However, if the software is to be developed for a certain group of people, management can provide the language in which the interfaces should be developed.

4. **Type of Internet connection and its speed:** Knowledge of this item was once valuable when slower speeds meant decreasing media elements in the design to avoid delaying the display of elements on a Webpage. Today, Internet connections are fast, and most users are unaware of their type of connection or its speed, even in their homes. Given the ubiquitous nature of wireless technology, for designers to know the type of connection and its speed is irrelevant.

5. **Operating system:** The operating system should be part of the platform capabilities and constraints of the requirement phase of the UE lifecycle, and upper management should be asked whether the product is for a specific purpose. Most Websites render well with the commonly used browsers, such as IE, GC, and Firefox.

Finally, knowledge of users' computer experience, Web experience, typical tasks, and frequency of use all help designers understand the type of interfaces, interactions, and navigation with which users are familiar. However, distinguishing users using exact date/time or exact amount of practice or skill level is almost impossible (Liu et al., 2010)

SOLUTIONS AND RECOMMENDATIONS

After reviewing 57 correctly developed user profiles from a three-year period, documented reasons for including and excluding certain items on a user profile questionnaire, and comments from students on their experiences, the researcher concluded that developing a user profile at the beginning of the design phase of the UE lifecycle is of value in only one situation, which is when a product is to be developed by a certain company or organization with a limited number of known users that have certain qualifications. Developing user profiles to create a persona or model of such users can form a basis for the design of the UIs of the interactive product by focusing design efforts on providing a characterization of an interactive system's target population. The results concluded by the designers are general guidelines that apply to a small set of target users. However, this researcher's opinion is that even then, the process of developing, analyzing, and interpreting a questionnaire for the purpose of concluding general guidelines is not cost effective when such guidelines can be easily reached by assuming or researching employee information, which differs when different employees assume the job or are rotated among departments.

Based on instructor and student experiences for interactive online products, creating the type of structured user profiles suggested by Mayhew (1999) and Kuniavsky (2003) during the initial design phase is not effective for the following reasons: (a) for user profiles to be done correctly, designers must be skilled in asking the correct questions and providing the correct answer options; furthermore, creating a well-written and well-designed questionnaire with questions posed accurately with no risk of misinterpretation by respondents is not an easy task and requires skill and experience to develop, administer, and interpret; (b) users are diverse and dispersed;

therefore, user profiles do not necessarily mirror or present a true model of those users to sway design ideas one way or the other.

Pruitt and Adlin (2006) made the core assertion that "building personas from assumptions is good; building personas from data is much, much better." However, this research found that user profile questionnaires developed to elicit users' personal attributes generated only general usability requirements that should be the goal of every designer for every user interface. This result was not effective and did not provide the students (designers) with any ideas on which to base their UI designs. Following well-researched and tested design guidelines such as Shneiderman's (2000) "Eight Golden Rules of Interface Design," Nielsen's "113 Guidelines for Homepage Usability" (Nielsen & Tahir, 2002), Smith and Mosier's (1986) "Guidelines for User Interface Software," Patrick and Horton's (2009) "Web Style Guide," and Usability.gov guidelines may produce the same outcome but without wasting the time, cost, and effort on user profile questionnaire development during the initial stage of the requirement analysis of the UE lifecycle. Even if user profiles are developed successfully and usability requirements are concluded, a necessary part of UCD is using paper prototypes to communicate and test design requirements with target users. Therefore, this researcher suggests that a more effective approach may be to characterize, through research, users in terms of personal attributes and then allow a sample of those users to evaluate initial usability requirements rather than profiling a sample of the target users individually at the very beginning of the UE lifecycle. This recommendation does not suggest that students should not be taught the value of user profiles to "know the user" or the skills for developing qualitative and quantitative methods for soliciting data from users. On the contrary, this research only questions the effectiveness of the structured methods used for profiling users for Web-based products, such as those suggested by Mayhew (1999) and Kuniavsky (2003).

REFERENCES

Ariza Avila, C. (2006). *Application of a context model in context-aware mobile government services* (Unpublished doctoral dissertation). Universidade do Minho, Guimaraes, Portugal.

Aurum, A., & Wohlin, C. (2005). Requirements engineering: Setting the context. In Aurum, A., & Wohlin, C. (Eds.), *Engineering and managing software requirements* (pp. 1–15). Heidelberg, Germany: Springer-Verlag. doi:10.1007/3-540-28244-0_1

Borgatti, P. (1998). Principles of questionnaire construction. *Analytic technologies.* Retrieved from http://www.analytictech.com/mb313/principl.htm

Cooper, A. (1999). *The inmates are running the asylum.* Indianapolis, IN: SAMS.

Costabile, M. (2001). Usability in the software life cycle. In Chang, S. K. (Ed.), *Handbook of software engineering and knowledge engineering* (pp. 179–192). City, NJ: World Scientific.

Dey, A., & Abowd, G. (2000). Towards a better understanding of context and context awareness. In *Proceedings of the Workshop on the What, Who, Where, When and How of Context-Awareness, Affiliated with the CHI 2000 Conference on Human Factors in Computer Systems.* New York, NY: ACM Press.

Dourish, P. (2004). What we talk about when we talk about context. *Personal and Ubiquitous Computing, 8*(1), 19–30. doi:10.1007/s00779-003-0253-8

Durrani, Q., & Qureshi, S. (2012). Usability engineering practices in SDLC. *ICCIT: 1st Taibah University International Conference on Computing and Information Technology.* Al-Madinah Al-Munawwarah, Saudi Arabia. Retrieved from http://www.taibahu.edu.sa/ iccit/allICCITpapers/pdf/p319-durrani.pdf

Gabbard, J., Swan, J., Hix, D., Lanzagorta, M., Livingston, M., Brown, D., & Julier, S. (2002). Usability engineering: Domain analysis activities for augmented reality systems. In A. J. Woods, J. O. Merritt, S. A. Benton, & M. T. Bolas (Eds.) *Stereoscopic displays and virtual reality systems IX* (pp. 445–457). San Jose, CA: Photonics West, Electronic Imaging conference.

Häkkilä, J., & Mäntyjärvi, J. (2005). Collaboration in context-aware mobile phone applications. In *Proceedings of the 38th Hawaii International Conference on System Sciences.* HI, USA.

Häkkilä, J., & Mäntyjärvi, J. (2006, October 25–27) Developing design guidelines for context-aware mobile applications. In *Proceedings of the 3rd International Conference on Mobile Technology, Applications & Systems (Bangkok, Thailand, October 25 - 27, 2006). Mobility '06, vol. 270.* ACM, New York, NY.

Hubona, G., & Shirah, G. (2004). The gender factor performing visualization tasks on computer media. In *Proceedings of the 37th Hawaii International Conference on System Sciences.* HI, USA.

Ibrahim, A., & Salim, S. (2004). Designing software for child users: A case study of a web page construction kit for children. *Malaysian Journal of Computer Science, 17*(1), 32–41.

Janhager, J. (2005). *User consideration in early stages of product development: Theories and methods* (Unpublished doctoral dissertation). Royal Institute of Technology, Stockholm, Sweden.

Kuniavsky, M. *Observing the user experience: A practitioner's guide to user research*. San Francisco, CA: Morgan Kaufmann.

Liu, Y., Osvalder, A., & Karlsson, M. (2010). Considering the importance of user profiles in interface design. In Matrai, R. (Ed.), *User interfaces* (pp. 61–80). Vukovar, Croatia: InTech Publishing. doi:10.5772/8903

Lynch, P., & Horton, S. (2009). *Web style guide: Basic design principles for creating web sites* (3rd ed.). New Haven, CT: Yale University Press.

Mayhew, D. (1992). *Principles and guidelines in user interface design*. Englewood Cliffs, NJ: Prentice-Hall.

Mayhew, D. (1999). *The usability engineering lifecycle: A practitioner's handbook for user interface design*. San Francisco, CA: Morgan Kauffman.

Mostéfaoui, G., Pasquier-Rocha, J., & Brézillon, P. (2004). Context-aware computing: A guide for pervasive computing community. *IEEE/ACS Proceedings of the International Conference on Pervasive Services,* Beirut, Lebanon, 39–48.

Nielsen, J., & Tahir, M. (2002). *Homepage usability: 50 sites deconstructed*. Indianapolis, IN: New Riders Publishing.

Norman, D. (2005). Human-centered design considered harmful. *Interactions. Communications of the ACM, 12*(4), 14–19.

Pruitt, J., & Adlin, T. (2006). *The persona lifecycle: Keeping people in mind throughout product design*. San Francisco, CA: Morgan Kaufmann.

Seffah, A., Gulliksen, J., & Desmarais, A. (2005). An introduction to human-centered software engineering: Integrating usability in the development process. In Seffah, A., Gulliksen, J., & Desmarais, A. (Eds.), *Human-centered software engineering: Integrating usability in the software development lifecycle* (pp. 3–14). Dordrecht, The Netherlands: Springer. doi:10.1007/1-4020-4113-6_1

Shneiderman, B. (2000). Universal usability. *Communications of the ACM, 43*(5), 84–89. doi:10.1145/332833.332843

Smith, S., & Mosicr, J. (1986). *Guidelines for designing user interface software*. Bedford, MA: MITRE Corporation.

Thurnher, B. (2004). *Usability engineering*. TU Wien, Institute of Software Technology and Interactive Systems (IFS). Retrieved from http://qse.ifs.tuwien.ac.at/courses/Usability/downloads_05/Usability_Engineering_20040920b.pdf

Warell, A. (2001). *Design syntactics: A functional approach to visual product form – Theory, models, and methods* (Unpublished doctoral dissertation). Chalmers University of Technology, Gothenburg, Sweden.

KEY TERMS AND DEFINITIONS

Context Design: Any information that can be used to characterize the situation of entities whether a person, place, or object is considered relevant to the interaction between a user and an application, including the user and the application.

Persona: A model of a person (fictional) that describes the target users of a product and what he/she seeks to accomplish.

Software Engineering: A software development lifecycle methodology with a goal-oriented requirement gathering, coding, testing, and maintenance process.

Usability Engineering: A discipline that provides structured methods for achieving usability in interactive computer products during the development lifecycle.

User Centered Design: A usability engineering approach to design that focus on users—the people who will use the product—during analysis, design, and development of a product.

User Profile: A characterization of an interactive system's target population that allows designers to focus on a specific image of users that everyone on the design team can reference when generating design ideas.

Users: A human being who, for a certain purpose, interacts with the product or any realized element manifested in the product at any phase of the product lifecycle and uses the final product.

Chapter 4
Usability Testing of an Education Management Information System:
The Case of the University of Colima

Pedro C. Santana
University of Colima, Mexico

Ana C. Ahumada
University of Colima, Mexico

Martha A. Magaña
University of Colima, Mexico

EXECUTIVE SUMMARY

A usability study of the platform e-planea from the University of Colima in Mexico is presented. This system allows the gathering of relevant information regarding the institutional management indicators. The usability evaluation focuses on three modules of the platform: Annual Reports, Undergraduate Statistics and High School Statistics. The study consists of two evaluation phases: the first one used a heuristic evaluation, and the second one applied the System Usability Scale (SUS) and the Technology Acceptance Model (TAM). The results showed high user satisfaction.

DOI: 10.4018/978-1-4666-4046-7.ch004

CONTEXT

The University of Colima (http://www.ucol.mx) is an Institution of Higher Education with 72 years of history and is formed by 128 departments, 29 undergraduate schools with 14,244 students and 34 high schools with 11,801 students. It also offers 30 graduate programs serving 592 students.

The university has established throughout its existence various mechanisms for institutional evaluation and transparency. The main mechanism is to collect and analyze management indicators regarding education and management sectors, and aims to support the processes of strategic planning, resource assignation, monitoring, policy formulation and decision making.

This process is performed by the Department of Institutional Planning and Development (DGPDI for its acronym in Spanish). The DGPDI is composed by 1 department head and 13 planning advisors. Currently, the DGPDI carries out this task with the use of an Education Management Information System (EMIS) called *e-planea* (Magaña Echeverría, Santana-Mancilla, & Rocha, 2012) in order to allow fast and well-organized information visualization.

SETTING THE STAGE

Many efforts to optimize the quality of data and available information to improve the educational system and support decision-making have occurred for a long time in the University of Colima. The EMIS began with the rise of systems programming in the 80's with projects in many countries to compute the annual school census and other administrative routines (Cassidy, 2006).

There are evidences that the education planning allows a solid structure to expedite the establishment of goals and priorities, facilitates the creation of guidelines for the expansion of the educational system and prevents the neglect or misuse of resources (International Institute for Educational Planning, 2010).

The development of an EMIS has benefited the DGPDI, allowing this department to achieve the educational targets such as increase enrollment, decrease dropout rate and increase student academic performance with a rigorous monitoring and evaluation system. Like any software, the platform needs to follow the usability guidelines and have a high acceptance of use in order to avoid errors and changes with high cost in time and money.

Usability testing involves observing users as they perform a series of tasks intended to address specific functions or portions of a system in order to determine strengths and problems with the software. Another kind of usability test is the heuristic evaluation; this test was designed to find interface design problems and is performed by experts on usability who tested and judged the interface with the 10 heuristics of Nielsen (Nielsen & Molich, 1990). On the other hand, acceptance of use is responsible for evaluating the characteristics that affect the possibility that users prefer to use our software to perform their task or otherwise.

This research work was conducted by researchers at the Schools of Telematics and Pedagogy of the University of Colima, with research experience concerning learning technology, with a focus on human factors, and one undergraduate student doing her BA dissertation on the human-computer interaction laboratory of the School of Telematics (IHCLab).

CASE DESCRIPTION

Technology Components

e-planea is a cloud Web application developed and implemented in a LAMP platform (Dougherty, 2001). LAMP refers to the first letters of Linux (operating system), Apache HTTP Server, MySQL database and PHP. As the application resides in the cloud, the users (planning advisors, head of departments and administrators) can access the system from any computer with a Web browser and Internet connection.

Analysis

Use cases represent a typical interaction between a user and a computer system (Fowler & Kendall, 1999). Such diagrams are a primary element of software development, and part of the Unified Modeling Language (UML).

For the *e-planea* platform the actors are the user previously defined: planning advisors, head of departments and administrators. The Figure 1 shows the use case diagram for the proposed EMIS.

Software Design

As illustrated in Figure 2 for the development of the *e-planea* platform a cloud Web configuration is used, in order to allow Access to the users from a Web browser (e.g. Firefox, Chrome or Safari).

Once the data is collected by the platform we can get the following outputs: reports, tables, charts and research productivity of the professors.

This information is available for information dissemination by three ways: printed, a word processor file generated in real time, and through the website of the Department of Institutional Planning.

Figure 1. Use-case diagram

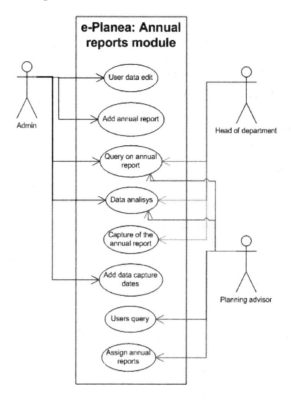

Figure 2. System architecture

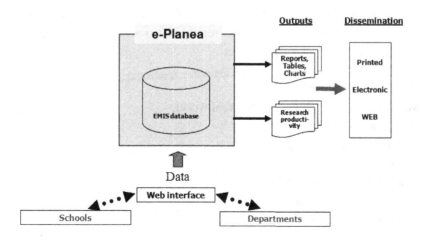

Implementation

The next step is the software implementation; which should provide a user friendly interface. A fully-functional system was developed, in which each user of the application should fill in identification requirements in order to login in its personalized interface and start using the system.

Study Concerns

As previously mentioned, three modules of the *e-planea* platform were evaluated, the ones which were in use at the time of this study. The evaluated modules were: Annual Reports, Undergraduate Statistics and High School Statistics.

The study was divided into two parts. The first part consisted in a heuristic evaluation, which must be performed by usability experts and focuses into find specific aspects of the usability of the user interface. The second part was conducted an evaluation with the users of the platform, which are heads of schools and planning advisors.

The combination of these two parts is expected to result in an effective way to get as much information as possible and that the information is useful and meaningful, in such a way that will create a sense of the usability of the platform by obtaining the outcomes of the evaluation. These two methods were used to perform a fair comparison and support our arguments on quantitative and qualitative data.

Heuristic Evaluation

The heuristic evaluation was conducted in the laboratory of Human-Computer Interaction of the School of Telematics (IHCLab) of the University of Colima. This test was applied to five experts in the field of usability. They answered a questionnaire consisting of thirty-six questions based on the heuristics of Jakob Nielsen. We used a Likert scale of 1 to 5, where 1 is "totally disagree" and 5 is "totally agree."

The general principles evaluated are:

1. Visibility of platform status,
2. Match between platform and the real world,
3. User control and freedom,
4. Consistency and standards,
5. Error prevention,
6. Recognition rather than recall,
7. Flexibility and efficiency of use,
8. Aesthetic and minimalist design,

9.   Support users recognize, diagnose and recover from errors,
10. Support and documentation.

Usability Evaluation

For the evaluation with users the System Usability Scale (SUS) and the Technology Acceptance Model (TAM) were used and comments of the users were also collected. This evaluation was conducted online, with an electronic evaluation instrument.

The (SUS) is a simple, ten-scale questionnaire giving a global view of subjective assessments of usability (Brooke, 1996). It has proved to be a robust and reliable evaluation and correlates well with the usability metrics. The scale list is as follows:

1.   I think that I would like to use this system frequently.
2.   I found the system unnecessarily complex.
3.   I thought the system was easy to use.
4.   I think that I would need the support of a technical person to be able to use this system.
5.   I found various functions in this system well integrated.
6.   I thought there was too much inconsistency in this system.
7.   I imagine that most people would learn to use this system very quickly.
8.   I found the system very cumbersome to use.
9.   I felt very confident using the system.
10. I needed to learn a lot of things before I could get going with this system.

Once filled the ten items, the questionnaire is scored as next: first sum the score contributions from each item; for the odd items (1, 3, 5, 7 and 9) the score contribution is the scale position minus 1. For even items (2, 4, 6, 8 and 10) the score contribution is the scale position minus 1. Multiply the sum of the scores by 2.5 to obtain the overall value of usability. SUS scores have a range of 0 (no usability) to 100 (excellent usability). The SUS questionnaire where applied to all the heads of schools in the University.

To measure the acceptance of the platform, the Technology Acceptance Model (TAM) was used. Developed by Davis, (1989), because it is a highly effective model tested on predicting the use of the technology. The purpose of TAM is to explain the causes of the users' acceptance of this technology. The TAM proposes that perceptions of usefulness and ease of use by an individual in an information system are conclusive in determining their intention to use the system. The TAM evaluation was performed with two groups: the first group was the heads of schools and the second group was 13 users of type "Planning advisors," which means 100% of the

DGPDI's staff of advising. We included this group since they are the direct links between DGPDI and all the departments and schools of the University. Besides, they are the ones who review the annual reports and train the directors in order to use the EMIS.

Results

Heuristics Evaluation

Table 1 describes the results of the heuristic evaluation. The Annual Reports module had a geometric mean of 3.4258 from a maximum of 5 and a standard deviation of 0.8555. Meanwhile, in the Graduate Statistics module, the geometric mean was

Table 1. Results of the heuristic evaluation

Heuristic	Annual Reports		Graduate Statistics		High School Statistics			
	Geometric mean	Standard deviation	Geometric mean	Standard deviation	Geometric mean	Standard deviation		
Visibility of platform status	3.508506	1.1	3.597843	1.1225	3.630101	0.9883		
Match between platform and the real world	4.366539	0.8338	4.366539	0.488	4.431982	0.4577		
User control and freedom	2.63703	1.2799	2.688093	1.1751	2.566703	1.1751		
Consistency and standards	4.624359	0.4894	4.728708	0.4443	4.781762	0.5026		
Error prevention	2.761174	1.2763	2.890618	1.2763	3.069974	1.268		
Recognition rather than recall	4.17265	0.9234	4.319799	0.7906	4.319799	1.04		
Flexibility and efficiency of use	3.437544	1.075	3.266355	0.9244	3.266355	0.9487		
Aesthetic and minimalist design	4.408269	0.6048	4.522312	0.7539	4.368265	0.513		
Support user recognizes, diagnose and recover from errors	2.107436	1.1425	2.150597	0.9333	2.251417	0.9333		
Support and documentation	3.239483	1.429	3.569091	1.0669	3.529491	1.1653		

Figure 3. Results of the heuristic evaluation by scale

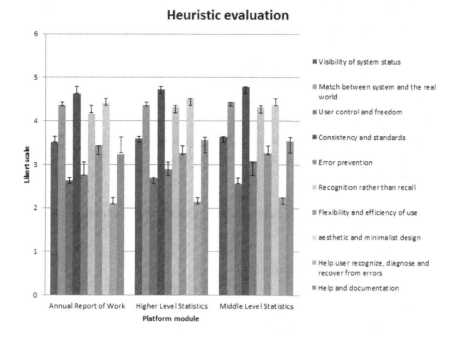

3.5086 from a maximum of 5 and with a standard deviation of 0.8678. Finally, the High School Statistics module has a geometric mean of 3.5258 of a scale from 1 to 5 and a standard deviation of 0.8483.

Figure 3 shows a graphic representation of the geometric mean for every Nielsen's Heuristic.

After analyzing this information (Table 1 and Figure 3), it is evident that the heuristic evaluation results show an interesting geometric mean with strong heuristics such as consistency and standards, aesthetic and minimalist design and match between system and the real world. The results also suggest that the platform can be improved if it gives more user control and freedom and helping the user recognize, diagnose and recover from errors.

From these results it is possible to reach important conclusions, especially about the platform improvement.

Users' Evaluation

We collected from the heads of departments some comments in order to improve the platform. They were about performance and productivity improvements, not about usability. These comments indicated positive results. For instance, they felt that it needed more features instead of having more usability and issues related to user experience. This indicates that we are on the right track. And still some of the suggestions are adaptable to user experience improvements, such as:

1. Sometimes it takes too long to load.
2. Occasional saturation.
3. It is difficult to copy and paste information in it.
4. Increase the support section.
5. While working in the platform, sometimes we lose track of the section in which we are working at, and it is kind of stressful so a label to know in which section we are would be great.

A summary of the Planning Advisors suggestions about usability issues is as follows:

1. The support section is incomplete.
2. A user manual for the navigation in the platform would be great.
3. The save option not only in the bottom part, also in the upper side.
4. Use of colors to indicate if some of the inserted information is wrong.
5. Show a sand clock for indicating time expiration before it expires automatically.

Regarding the user experience improvements, the loading and saturation issues are important because they create a stressful situation for the user. The label indicating the sections where the user is working and the sand clock are also great suggestions that would improve not only user experience, but also usability.

The other suggestions are interesting and should not be discarded. However, they are not all related to usability improvements and thus are not as crucial as the ones mentioned before.

SUS Evaluation

Table 2 shows the results of the SUS evaluation with their geometric means and the interpretation of each question.

After analyzing this information from the SUS questionnaires, we can conclude that the platform is satisfying for the participants, but still needs to be more attractive.

In addition to the geometric mean of every SUS scale evaluated, the study exposed a frequency of the distribution of SUS scores shown in Figure 4 from which we can infer that the platform evaluated, at least in the System Usability Scale is going on

Table 2. Results of the SUS evaluation

Question	Geometric mean	Interpretation
1. I think that I would like to use this platform frequently	2.58	We can deduce that the users won't like to use the platform frequently
2. I found the platform unnecessarily complex	2.84	We can deduce that the users didn't find difficult to use the platform
3.I thought the platform was easy to use	3.04	We can deduce that the users find the platform easy to use
4. I think that I would need a technician support to be able to use this platform	3.24	We can deduce that the users don't think they would need any help using the platform
5. I found the various functions in this platform were well integrated	2.86	We can deduce that the users find some functions of the platform not integrated
6. I thought there was too much inconsistency in this platform	2.88	We can deduce that the users didn't find inconsistency in the platform
7. I would imagine that most people would learn to use this platform very quickly	3.20	We can deduce that the users think that people will learn to use the platform quick
8. I found the platform very cumbersome to use	2.93	We can deduce that the users didn't find the platform "complicated" while using it
9. I felt very confident using the platform	2.91	We can deduce that the users felt diffident while using the platform
10. I needed to learn a lot of things before I could get going with this platform	3.30	We can deduce that the users believe they will need to learn some things before using the platform

Figure 4. Frequency distribution of SUS scores of participants

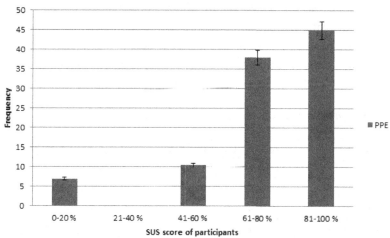

89

the right track because 44% of the participants consider their needs satisfied with this platform: between 81 and 100% of satisfaction.

TAM Evaluation

Table 3 shows the results of the TAM evaluation with their geometric means and standard deviations.

This information states that the acceptance of this platform is over the mean.

The head of departments show acceptance of use over the mean, although we cannot settle with this; it can be improved and it will if we concentrate on improvements about lower rate resulting in this study as shown in Figure 5.

Table 4 states that the planning advisors found the platform easy to use and useful, with a high level of acceptance. Figure 6 illustrates Table 4.

After analyzing the outcomes of this study outcome, we can conclude that the platform has strong points regarding the acceptance of the participants, but it can be improved with the recommendations mentioned in the users' evaluation section. In addition, the frequency distribution of TAM scores by scales establishes the belief that the platform was doing fine in this evaluation.

CURRENT CHALLENGES FACING IN THE INSTITUTION

At the University of Colima we are experiencing the following challenges:

- To achieve the educational targets, such as, increase enrollment, decrease dropout rate and increase student academic performance, it is necessary a rigorous monitoring and evaluation system.
- Our problem was an inadequate system for data gathering, managing, planning and decision making.
- The information cycle starts with an outdated data collection system with partial and inconsistent data in files of word processor software.

Table 3. Descriptive statics of TAM study with heads of schools

Variables	Geometric mean	Standard deviation
Perceived ease of use	5.4914	0.1877
Perceived usefulness	5.3058	0.2485
Attitude toward using	5.5509	0.9726
Actual platform use	5.6095	0.2986

Figure 5. Frequency distribution of TAM scores with heads of schools

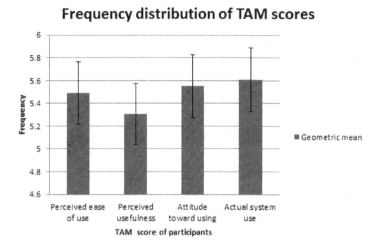

Table 4. Descriptive statics of TAM study with planning advisors

Variables	Geometric mean	Standard deviation
Perceived ease of use	6.6449	0.5912
Perceived usefulness	6.3202	0.7417
Attitude toward using	6.6996	0.789
Actual platform use	6.863	0.3387

Figure 6. Frequency distribution of TAM scores for planning advisors

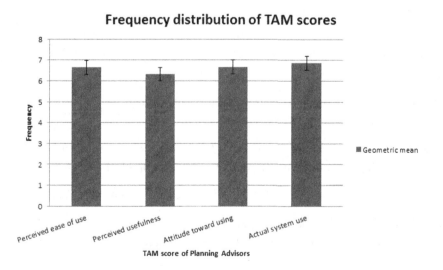

- The analysis and organization of the data is done manually, this process is time consuming, and it is labor intensive and inefficient. This gives inadequate monitoring resources.

According to the above challenges, we were unable to undertake a proper systematic process resulting in major information gaps.

SOLUTIONS AND RECOMMENDATIONS

To stop the cycle of getting, processing, and analyzing data manually, we need to change the paradigm through an evidence-based policy formulation, an implementation of a result-oriented program, and, the most important element in order to have good data, the affordability of good IT solutions and a competent and committed staff. At this point, the process involves the planning advisors who are the staff of the department of institutional planning and the heads of the dependencies of the different schools. To achieve this, it is necessary to measure the usability and the acceptance of the platform. Our study results show that the platform is useful and allows a greater performance and efficiency, and it is also considered a good idea. Thus, this motivated users to keep using it again in the future.

REFERENCES

Brooke, J. (1996). SUS: A quick and dirty usability scale. In Jordan, P. W., Thomas, B., Weerdmeester, B. A., & McClelland, A. L. (Eds.), *Usability evaluation in industry*. London: Taylor and Francis.

Cassidy, T. (2006). *Education management information systems (EMIS) in Latin America and the Caribbean: Lessons and challenges*. Inter-American Development Bank.

Davis, F. D. (1989). Perceived usefulness, perceived ease of use, and user acceptance of information technology. *MIS Quartely, 13*(3).

Dougherty, D. (2001, 26 January). *LAMP: The open source web platform*. Retrieved from http://onlamp.com/pub/a/onlamp/2001/01/25/lamp.html

Fowler, M., & Kendall, S. (1999). *UML distilled*. Addison-Wesley Professional.

International Institute for Educational Planning. (2010). *Guidebook for planning education in emergencies and reconstruction*. UNESCO.

Magaña Echeverría, M. A., Santana-Mancilla, P. C., & Rocha, V. M. (2012). An educational management information system to support. *International conference on New Horizons in Education*. Prague.

Nielsen, J., & Molich, R. (1990). Heuristic evaluation of user interfaces. In *CHI '90 Proceedings of the SIGCHI Conference on Human Factors in Computing* (pp. 249-256). New York: ACM.

KEY TERMS AND DEFINITIONS

Education Management Information System (EMIS): It integrates all the information related to educational planning and management activities which are available from various sources. The organization of EMIS involves collection, processing, storage, retrieval, analysis and dissemination of data.

Heuristic Evaluation: It is a usability inspection method for computer software that helps to identify usability problems in the user interface (UI) design. It specifically involves evaluators examining the interface and judging its compliance with recognized usability principles (the "heuristics"). These evaluation methods are now widely taught and practiced in the New Media sector, in which UIs are often designed in a short space of time on a budget that may restrict the amount of money available to provide for other types of interface testing.

Human–Computer Interaction (HCI): It involves the study, planning, and design of the interaction between people (users) and computers. It is often regarded as the intersection of computer science, behavioral sciences, design and several other fields of study.

System Usability Scale (SUS): It is a simple, ten-item attitude Likert scale giving a global view of subjective assessments of usability.

Technology Acceptance Model (TAM): It is an information systems theory that models how users come to accept and use a technology. The model suggests that when users are presented with a new technology, a number of factors influence their decision about how and when they will use it.

Usability: It is the ease of use and learnability of a human-made object. The object of use can be a software application, website, book, tool, machine, process, or anything a human interacts with.

Usability Testing: It is a technique used in user-centered interaction design to evaluate a product by testing it on users. This can be seen as an irreplaceable usability practice, since it gives direct input on how real users use the system.

Chapter 5
Usability Impact Analysis of Collaborative Environments

R. Todd Stephens
AT&T, USA

EXECUTIVE SUMMARY

This chapter will focus on the application of usability principles in a corporate collaborative environment in order to show improvements in utilization. Collaborative applications create a two-way communications structure as opposed to the one way communication method of traditional web environments. Collaboration applications can vary in the complexity from discussion forums to complex social software integration. Usability principles have been applied to web sites, but very little research has been done on the implications of usability in collaborative environments. Collaborative environments create a unique set of opportunities that create a different set of user goals. End users want a more collaborative environment that is easy to use and engaging. Organizations need to ensure the business goals stay at the forefront while improving the collaborative nature of the company.

ORGANIZATION BACKGROUND

AT&T Inc., together with its subsidiaries, provides telecommunications services to consumers, businesses, and other providers worldwide. The company's Wireless segment offers wireless voice and data communication services, such as local wireless communications services, long-distance services, and roaming services. This segment

DOI: 10.4018/978-1-4666-4046-7.ch005

also sells various handsets, wirelessly enabled computers, and personal computer wireless data cards; and accessories, including carrying cases, hands-free devices, batteries, battery chargers, and other items. This segment sells its products through its own stores, or through agents or third-party retail stores. Its Wireline segment provides data services comprising switched and dedicated transport, Internet access and network integration, U-verse services, and data equipment; businesses voice applications over IP-based networks; and digital subscriber lines, dial-up Internet access, private lines, managed Web-hosting services, packet services, enterprise networking services, and Wi-Fi services, as well as local, interstate, and international wholesale networking capacity to other service providers. This segment also offers voice services, such as local and long-distance, calling card, 1-800, conference calling, wholesale switched access, caller ID, call waiting, and voice mail services; and application management, security services, integration services, customer premises equipment, outsourcing, government-related services, and satellite video services. The company was formerly known as SBC Communications Inc. and changed its name to AT&T Inc. in November 2005. AT&T Inc. was founded in 1983 and is headquartered in Dallas, Texas.

SETTING THE STAGE

This research will look into a large scale deployment of over 80,000 collaborative sites. Each site is unique in its design, development, and business function. Therefore, many of the user tasks are also unique. We will look to discover the impact of applying usability principles to the collaborative environment and the end user experience. The basic research question revolves around the idea that if we apply usability principles to the original design then does the collaborative environment shows an increased use from the community? Much like web site metrics of page views or transactions, we will review the number of document managed, the number of members of the community, page views, and several other base measurements in order to determine the impact of usability and design. Most information technology professionals push to deploy collaborative solutions out of the box with little effort to improve the usability of the application. However, we will show that this strategy actually limits the value-add opportunities. The goal is to show that the more usability principles and early design methodologies applied to the collaborative space the greater value the company will gain from the deployment.

BACKGROUND INFORMATION

Usability Research and Frameworks

The goal of this chapter is to ask the question does usability have an impact on a collaborative environment. Can you apply usability principles to a collaborative environment and see an improvement in end user engagement? First, we need to define what usability actually is or is not. The importance of usability is well documented. Lecerof and Paterno (1998) defined usability to include the concepts of relevance, efficiency, user attitude, learnability, and safety. The ISO organization defines usability as the extent to which a product can be used by specified users to achieve goals with effectiveness, efficiency, and satisfaction within a pattern of contextual use (Karat, 1997). Usability is the broad discipline of applying sound scientific observation, measurement, and design principles to the creation and maintenance of web applications in order to bring about the greatest ease of use, ease of learnability, amount of usefulness, and least amount of discomfort for the humans who use the application (Pearrow, 2000). All of these definitions focus on the ability of the user to leverage the application for value creation.

There are various schools of thought on which design elements make a successful web site. Scanlon, Schroeder, Snyder, and Spool (1998) collected qualitative and quantitative data on key design factors, which included: searching, content, text links, images, links navigation, page layout, readability, graphics, and user's knowledge. Each of these design elements makes an important contribution to a successful website. Websites are built to provide information or sell a product or service. Experts indicate that usability is about making sure that the average person can use the site as intended. Well chosen names, layout of the page, text, graphics, and navigation structure should all come together to create instantaneous recognition (Krug, 2000). Becker and Mottay (2001) developed a usability assessment model used to measure a user's experience within a web environment. The authors defined eight usability factors, which included page layout, navigation, design consistency, information content, performance, customer service, reliability, and security. Usability and design can play an important role within the electronic commerce market. Design consistency has been defined as the key to usability (Nielsen, 1998). Karvonen (2000) reported that experienced users admitted to making intuitive and emotional decisions when shopping online. Some users simply stated, "If it looks pleasant then I trust it." Even if developing trust is not that simple, the research clearly shows how important design is in the area of trust.

There are a variety of web design elements that can have a positive impact on a website's image, effectiveness, and trustworthiness. Design elements like well-chosen images, clean and clear layout, careful typography, and a solid use of color can create an effective site. In addition, a solid navigation structure and continuity in design can provide the user with the control and access required within an electronic commerce interface (Andres, 1999). Although, design elements may take on the form of a visual cue, the true value comes from a combination presentation, structure, and interactivity. A solid website is a collaboration of design, content, usability, and a back end system that is integrated into the processes of the business (Veen, 2001). Krug (2000) defines a set of tools as location indicators, which are design elements of the site that tells the user where they are. This can be in the form of a page name, header, sitemap or page utility. The page utility should be used within a list type program, which allows the user to know where they are within the list of elements. Indicators like "Page 1 of 12" can be extremely helpful informing the user of their location. Nielsen (2000) describes the need for the user to know where they are, where they have been and where they can go.

Collaborative Environments and Technology

Knowledge Management

Knowledge management continues to be one of the most critical aspects of doing business in today's environment. Organizations are beginning to realize the importance of managing organizational knowledge in order to deliver innovation and competitive products. Sewry and Sunassee (2003) indicatesindicate that the only true source of competitive advantage is knowledge. Managing this intangible asset requires a change in mindset from a command and control to a collaborative perspective for sharing information. Knowledge management is central to improving the overall effectiveness of the organization where the growing complexity of the distributed work environment requires better utilization of knowledge. Applehans, Globe, and Laugero (1999) define knowledge as the ability to turn information and data into action. Knowledge and content management emerged as disciplines due to the needs of the business to ease the partnering aspects of the organization, manage expertise turnover, and decentralize decision making. Knowledge management includes acquiring or creating knowledge, transforming it into a reusable form, retaining it, and finding it and reusing it (Grudin, 2006). Finally, knowledge can be defined as a fluid mix of framed experiences, values, contextual information, and expert insight that provides a framework for evaluating and incorporating new experiences and information (Davenport & Prusak, 1997).

Researchers divide knowledge into two main categories: explicit and tacit. Explicit knowledge is knowledge that can be articulated, codified, and stored in various types of media. This media may be in the form of manuals, presentations, documents, spreadsheets, or database systems. Tacit knowledge is often transmitted through a combination of demonstration, illustration, annotation, stories, experiences, and discussion. This type of knowledge is usually not openly expressed or taught. This does not to imply that tacit knowledge is inaccessible to conscious awareness, unspeakable, or unteachable, but merely that it is not taught directly in the normal course of business (Wagner & Sternberg, 1985).

Web 1.0

The term Web 1.0 emerged from the research around Web 2.0. Basically, web 1.0 focused on a read only web interface while Web 2.0 focuses on a read-write interface where value emerges from the contribution of a large volume of users. The Internet as well as the Intranet initially focused on the command and control of the information itself. Information was controlled by a relative small number of resources but distributed to a large number which spawned the massive growth of the web itself. Like television, the web allowed for the broadcasting of information to a large number of users.

Inside the organization, the Intranet has changed the way organizations structure and operate their business. Specifically, the Intranet has centralized communications and corporate information as well as built a sense of community across organizational boundaries (McNay, 2000). Typical organizations will have office-based employees in various locations, telecommuting, and off-shoring staff. The traditional day by day communication landscape has changed from personal to electronic. The migration to electronic communications emerged as standards, technology and infrastructure matured. This allowed more information sharing and community building to occur without a requirement of physical location. Over the past several years Intranets have emerged as the key delivery mechanism for application and business information. Intranets may be thought of as providing the infrastructure for intra-organizational electronic commerce (Chellappa & Gupta, 2002). This allows organizations to utilize the technology to achieve its organizational goals and objectives. Web 1.0 allowed the organization to govern the information flow and focus on achieving the business goals.

Unfortunately, most technologies fail to deliver competitive advantages over an extended period of time. Investments in information technology, while profoundly important, are less and less likely to deliver a competitive edge to an individual company (Carr, 2003). This is especially true in the world of the Web 1.0 since much of the knowledge and information is disseminated all over the world as quickly as it gets published. Organizations are beginning to see that the command and control model is no longer effective at developing a high performance work force which opens the door for the next evolution in technologies as described by the Web 2.0 framework.

Web 2.0

While Web 2.0 has been debated by researchers as to who and when the concepts emerged, little argument exists that the technology and demand has arrived. Unlike Web 1.0, this new technology encourages user participation and derives its greatest value when large communities contribute content. User generated metadata, information, and designs enable a much richer environment where the value is generated by the volume of employees. Sometimes referred to as sharing, collaboration, aggregate knowledge, or community driven content, social software creates the foundation of collective intelligence (Weiss, 2005). Much of the Web 2.0 technology is difficult to nail down an exact definition,definition; the basic truth is that Web 2.0 emphasizes employee interaction, community, and openness (Millard & Ross, 2006). Along with these characteristics, Smith and Valdes (2005) added simple and lightweight technologies and decentralized processing to the mix. O'Reilly (2005) defined Web 2.0 as a platform, spanning all connected devices; Web 2.0 applications are those that make the most of the intrinsic advantages of that platform: delivering software as a continually-updated service that gets better the more people use it, consuming and remixing data from multiple sources, including individual users, while providing their own data and services in a form that allows remixing by others, creating network effects through an "architecture of participation," and going beyond the page metaphor of Web 1.0 to deliver rich user experiences. While Web 2.0 has many and often confusing definitions most include the concepts of Weblogs, Wikis, Really Simple Syndication (RSS) Functionality, social tagging, mashups, and user defined content.

Collaborative Technologies

Virtual workplace environments allow people to work separately while still experiencing a mutual sense of presence. Working collaboratively over networks is ultimately about real communication enhanced by a virtual presence. The tools for these virtual communities include threaded discussions, email, calendaring, surveying, instant messaging, customizable interfaces, document management, and real-time conferencing (Chignell, Ho, & Schraefel, 2000). Virtual workspaces provide historical reference, enhance situation awareness, and facilitate multi-channel interactions (Hinds & Baily, 2003). In addition, virtual workspaces are provided for distributed teams where the physical constraints of time and presence of removed. Distributed team can be defined as groups of people who interact through interdependent tasks guided by a common purpose, and work across space, time, and organizational boundaries primarily through electronic means (Maznevski & Chudoba, 2000). Another common area description of collaborative work includes Computer-Supported Cooperative Work (CSCW). Most researchers agree that CSCW is an interdisciplinary field that encompasses artificial intelligence, computer science, phycologypsychology, sociology, organizational theory, and anthropology (Greif, 1988).

While traditional workflow management systems have proven useful in supporting well-defined organizational processes, they are less suitable for the support of less well-defined and emergent processes. The early efforts of computing focused on the structured side of systems. Specifically, these efforts resulted in transaction processing system as well as data warehouses and data marts. Knowledge and content management emerged as disciplines due to the needs of the business to ease the partnering aspects of the organization, manage expertise turnover, and decentralize decision making (Applehans, Globe, & Laugero, 1999). Both of these two efforts focused on standardized and well defined processes. Virtual workspaces realize that speed to market and innovation are keys to the emerging business models where standards may not be set or even defined. Virtual workspaces are temporal since theretheir existence is determinate on the existence of the team itself. Once the value or utility of the team is gone the workspace will dissolve.

Collaborative technologies are an integral part of business as we move forward to a more distributed environment. One of the central assumptions is that a collaborative system will be used by the community and generate an active participation within that community. However, this may not be the case, and researchers and designers will want to do everything possible to ensure success in collaborative systems. Grosz (2005) indicated that human-computer collaboration paradigm specifies that the system must act as a partner to its users by supporting them in the increasingly complex environments of modern applications. This indicates that improvement in the usability of an application should improve the utilization of that technology.

USABILITY CRITERIA FOR COLLABORATIVE SYSTEMS

Criteria for evaluating the usability of collaborative systems should follow similar usability issues with traditional web applications and business systems. A common set of criteria needs to be developed which could be used across all collaborative applications. Singh and Wesson (2009) provide some of the common usability criteria including the following items:

- Ease of use
- Usefulness
- Task Support
- Navigation
- Guidance
- Flexibility
- Image Design
- Customization
- Memorability
- Accuracy and Completeness
- Learnability
- Performance and Stability
- Visual Appeal
- System Reliability
- System Responsiveness
- UI Presentation
- Output Presentation

In order to simplify the research, this chapter will condense the list into five basic categories of usability constructs in order to evaluate improvements made on the collaborative applications. These will include the following:

- Visual Appeal of the application and collaborative functionality
- System Performance of the collaborative tool
- Ease of Use which will include the concepts of customization and navigation
- Learnability of the collaborative application
- Task Support which includes workflow, form management, and basic collaborative functionality

The aim of this chapter is to propose a set of characteristics that are specific to collaborative applications. This is necessary to address the inconsistent engagement of most collaborative environments. Many collaborative environments are simply file dumping grounds and fail to take advantage to the collaborative technology as a many to many communication environment. The following sections will look at these five criteria and how they can be applied to collaborative environments. In order to measure usability, we will define a set of heuristics or descriptors to manage the improvements. This will allow us to define specific criteria that can be evaluated in order to show the improved usability. Based on the criteria we can then measure the improvements in the collaborative environment.

Visual Appeal

Visual appeal is a phrase used for application components that impact the presentation of information. Many technical solutions focus on putting as much information on the screen as possible with little regard to how that presentation provides context and meaning. Visual appeal includes components such as page layout, image quality, color palette, font selection, dialog boxes, controls, and form elements. Visual appeal can be reviewed by the following heuristics:

- Visual layout of the information
- Image Quality
- Measuring the accuracy and understanding of the information being presented
- Intuitiveness of the interface
- Consistency of the design

System Performance

System performance is a measurement of the how the system performs in handling the user requests. We can measure the performance by the speed by which processes requests and the number of concurrent users within a specific environment. Research suggests that performance impacts usability with a positive correlation in the areas of efficient access, search success, flexibility, understanding of content, relevant search result, and satisfaction (Janecek & Uddin, 2007). System performance can be evaluated by the following heuristics:

- Transaction Processing Speed
- End User Task Accomplishment
- Expected Results (i.e. search results)
- Learning Times
- End User Satisfaction

Ease of Use

Perceived ease of use is the extent to which a person believes that using a technology will be free of effort. Perceived ease of use is a construct tied to an individual's assessment of the effort involved in the process of using the system (Venkatesh, 2000). Ease of use can be reviewed by the following heuristics:

- Navigation Elements
- End User Task Accomplishment
- Learning Times
- End User Satisfaction
- Ability to locate specific information
- Timeliness of information presented

Learnability

Learnability is in some sense the most fundamental usability attribute of collaborative applications (Nielsen, 2000). The system should be easy to learn so that the user can rapidly start getting value from the application. As Dzida, Herda, and Itzfelt (1978) reported, learnability is especially important for novice users. Learnability can be described as the amount of effort in using a new Web site and to measure how easy a site for new visitors to orient themselves and get a good overview of what the site offers (Jeng, 2005). Ease of use can be reviewed by the following heuristics:

- Time required to learn the application
- Access to online help and community support
- Ability to actively contribute to the conversation is a short period of time
- Consistency of the design
- Complexity of the core tasks

Task Support

The idea of task support is an alignment between the technical world and the business environment. Does the technology support the business environment by ensuring tasks are started, completed, and communicated effectively? Task support deals with how well a product or system enables users to perform their typical tasks to achieve their goals with the product (Anschuetz, L., Keirnan, T. & Rosenbaum, S., 2002). Task support can be reviewed by the following heuristics:

- Consistent terminology is used in the application
- Consistent use of imagery and style based on the organizational style
- Information is real and contextual in nature
- Confirmation of tasks
- Tasks process support and state communication
- Automation of redundant tasks
- Personalization of content and context

CASE DESCRIPTION

This case study reflects on the implementation and integration of a collaborative tool within a large enterprise. The collaborative environments will be designed or implemented in a way to show an increased utilization based on the level of user design principles. This section will review issues and concerns facing large organizations that are looking to implement collaborative solutions.

Technology Concerns

Technology concerns focus on the various technologies used during the implementation and how these technologies will engage the user community. One of the most important technical concerns is scalability of the environment. The studied organization has over 80,000 collaborative environments with several large server farms in order to handle the traffic and data loads required in a collaborative environment. Many design principles are based on the use of images and workflow processes. These types of enhancements will impact the speed of the application and should be taken into consideration. Another technical concern with a collaborative tool is the integration with other technologies such as social media, instant messaging, and traditional office document artifacts. Integration is essential in that forcing the user into various content container applications create confusion and information overload. Organizations should ensure there is a seamless integration to ensure productivity remains high. Another concern from a technology perspective is the level is separation of collaborative environments. For example, Facebook (Global Social Media Applications) provide a single level while other applications create separate environments that create walls of content. IN some cases, these sites or containers of information can be secured or segments from a more global information source.

Technology Components

The environment under study leverages Microsoft's SharePoint 2010. Additionally, the author leveraged Microsoft SharePoint Designer 2010 in order to develop the various collaborative designs. Other technology requirements required knowledge and integration of the following technologies: JQuery, Javascript, CSS, Flash, XML, CAML, and image drawing tools.

Management and Organizational Concerns

From an organizational or managerial perspective, there are several additional concerns that need to be taken into account. First, organizations need to have true HCI professionals available in order to implement many of the recommendations cited in this chapter. Sadly, with the plethora of education and training available on web design, many inexperienced resources see themselves as HCI professionals without the ability to deliver the business benefits of enhancing the end user experience. Another roadblock in applying usability principles to collaborative environments is the propensity to avoid the technology and business change required for collaboration to work effectively. Many organizations have not joined the social media and collaborative technology movement so improvements in usability may not have the business impact required for the investment. The final area to consider is the scalability of the solution itself. Some techniques will scale across a broad collection of environments while other will not. You simply may not have the resources needed to deploy customized solutions to each and every environment.

CURRENT CHALLENGES FACING THE ORGANIZATION

The studied organization is similar to most large scale companies. Organizations are starting to increase the focus on collaborative tools. The idea of a distributed and mobile workforce opens the door for the need of collaborative technology. Collaboration and social media are more critical than ever in today's enterprise, and as collaboration-oriented capabilities continue to advance, new concepts are evolving that challenge the way organizations traditionally operate. Globalization has been a boom for business but the complexity to the business process is more of a challenge. Most of us think of globalization a time zone issue but you also must consider culture and language differences. Organizations are struggling to understand and deploy the right combination of technology to address the issues around globalization. The organization must also understand the gaps in education and training when it comes to collaboration. There seems to be an emerging gap in the knowledge on the best techniques and behaviors required to collaborate effectively. Companies must encourage employees to take the required training and share best practices in order to the entire enterprise to be effective in collaboration.

SOLUTIONS AND RECOMMENDATIONS

The research methodology was designed to provide a basis for usability along with a heuristic evaluation. The goal of the study is to demonstrate that improvements in usability will increase the usage and utility of a collaborative environment. Usage can be defined as the number of times an end user consumes the information which is represented by the number of visits. Utility or utilization is measured by the number of changes in the environment which come in the form of information updates. Updates can be measured by the number of adds, changes, and deletes across all of the content containers.

Control Group Definition

The first step in determining if usability has an impact on the community engagement is to establish a control group of collaborative environments. The studied organization has deployed over 80,000 different collaborative sites across the enterprise. This type of environment creates a diverse set of environments to review from a usage perspective. The company has been using Microsoft's SharePoint for eight years across three different companies which were brought together with an extensive merger. Control sites were selected at random but were required to meet the following criteria:

- The site must have at least 20 members within the community.
- The site must have more than two document libraries.
- The site must have more than five lists.
- The site must contain at least one social media component (i.e. wiki, blog, or forum).
- The site must have a weekly usage metric consistent over a four week period.
- The site must use the standard SharePoint theme.
- The site show demonstrates a less than 5% user growth over a three month period.

Based on the selection criteria, twenty five sites were selected for the study. Each site was reviewed after a period of four weeks to ensure the collaborative environment was being leveraged on a daily basis. It was also important not to choose collaborative sites from a single area of the business with a similar defined user community. The site collection needed to be spread across the entire company in a variety of business areas. From this review, the following information was collected across the entire portfolio of sites:

- Number of user visits
- Number of unique users or membership of the community
- Number of additions, changes or deletes from the environment

Table 1 provides the data collected from the application at the end of the 30 day window. For simplification, the sites have been grouped by business unit and the metrics are averaged across the site collections.

As an example, eight sites were selected from the Information Technology department. On average these sites have 1,606 visits with 231 unique visitors for the month reviewed. Additionally, the sites show an average of 4,946 updates within the environment itself.

Research Design

The research review was broken down into two phases where modifications to the collaborative environment would be made over a period of time. The first phase will focus on enhancing the theme of the site. The theme is a set of colors, fonts, and decorative elements that provide a consistent appearance of a collaborative site. A theme controls the look and feel of the environment and Microsoft's SharePoint comes with several out of the box themes. A theme can alter the visual aspect of the environment by altering the cascading style sheet, page structure, and navigation elements. However, none of the themes are company specific which means that the core look and feel is different versus the company standard. The first phase will implement a new theme which is based on the company standard and adds a degree of usability improvements. A group of twenty sites were updated in order to determine the impact of having a company specific theme versus the standard theme. Themes will only address one of the five criteria from a usability perspective but are easier to implement. Over a period of two week, the sites were evaluated in order to determine the impact of usability improvements. The two week delay is used to ensure the newness of new environment does not drive up the interaction level for a short period of time.

The second phase would not only change the theme but the fundamental structure of the collaboration pages. Many collaborative solutions try to be all things to all users which tend to confuse the user and limit the level of collaboration. Vendor's tend to put as much functionality and complexity as possible on software applications. This results in end user anxiety and poor usage of the system. In order to get the maximum collaborative usage, we must understand how a simplified and context

Table 1. Before metrics for the site collection

Department	Sites	Visits	Users	Updates
IT	8	1,606	231	4,946
Marketing	4	2,101	243	2,864
Finance	2	286	86	1,370
Legal	2	267	44	1,071
Networking	4	650	144	2,594

aware design can improve the usage metrics. This phase will make improvements in all five usability criteria in order to determine the impact to the site collection. Feedback from the first phase was used to enhance the design elements of phase two as needed. In both phases, metrics were collected and compared to the initial control group in order to determine the level of increased utilization. Due to the level of experience, knowledge, and time required, only five of the sites were taken to this level usability in phase two.

Research Results

Figure 1 provides a sample before and after view of the changes made in the usability upgrade for phase 1. The page on the left is the standard out of the box theme while the image on the right is a new theme based on the company style standards.

The modifications to the theme included the following items:

- New standard font and color palette
- Increased size of font
- Included branded logo and tag line
- Removed the clutter and non-functional images
- Additional background images were added
- Several new page structures

Once the theme had been created and deployed into the server environment the application to the specific collaboration envionrments was fairly simply. The system adminstrators were informed of the new theme and making the change had no impact

Figure 1. Example site modifications

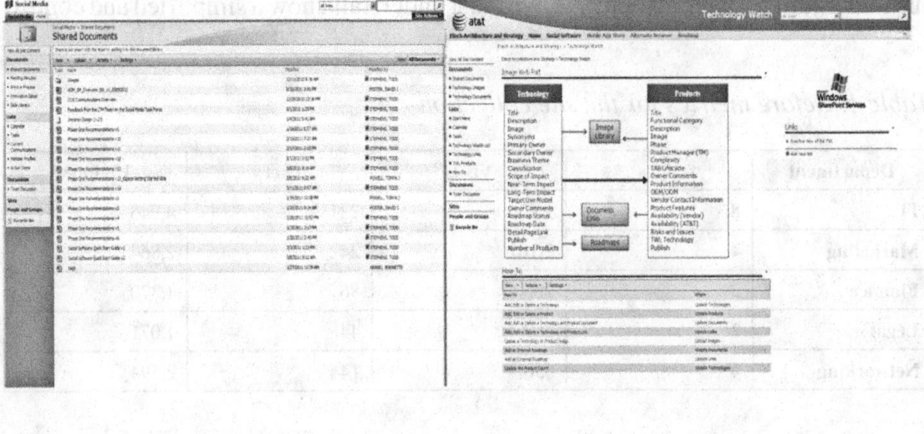

on the environment itself. Members of the community were notifed of the changes via an email along with a list of expectations. After the changes were applied, a four week soaking period was implemented in ensure any initial increase in utilization would be normalized out of the system. Changes to the look and feel tend to increase the activity of the envirnment but this research wanted to look at the impact over a much longer period of time versus any initial jump in activity. Indentical information on users, visits, and activity were collected and then compard to the base level metrics presented in Table 1. Table 2 presents these percentages for comparison.

On average the utilization rate improved by 16.7%. That is to say that across the board our averages improved by 16%. Some environments like the networking group increased as much as 35.9% while the legal enviornment had a reduction of -6%. The reduction of utility on the legal site may have more to do with restructuring than the impact of the improved usability of the environment. An evaluation of the results indicates an improvement in utilization of the environments with slight adjustments to the usability of the environment in the form of a theme.

The second phase took a look at five additional sites with a complete modification to the usabliity of the environment. Each of the five sites were designed by human factors experts with at least 10 years of experience in web design. In addition, the experts consulted with the internal human facors group for recommendations for usability improvements. Figure 2 shows an example of the how the environment was modified with a new site design.

The modifications to the site design included the following items:

- New standard font and color palette
- Increased size of font
- Included branded logo and tag line
- Removed the clutter and non-functional images
- Added background images
- Established a new page structure and layout

Table 2. Phase one results

Phase 1	Sites	Visits	Users	Updates	Utilization
IT	7	16.5%	11.5%	6.2%	11.4%
Marketing	3	19.6%	8.5%	36.2%	21.5%
Finance	1	11.7%	36.7%	13.4%	20.6%
Legal	1	-16.2%	20.0%	-21.7%	-6.0%
Networking	3	58.7%	32.2%	16.8%	35.9%
Averages		18.1%	21.8%	10.2%	16.7%

Figure 2. Complete site redesign

- New navigation and expanded phrases
- Professional images with transparency
- Included hover help on all links, images, and navigation elements
- Customized search function and result sets
- Simplified information flow and more actionable information content
- Added new functionality with personalization
- Added feedback mechanisms such as "Thank You" pages and progress meters
- Additional navigation elements such as cookie trails and location indicators

Site modifications were made over a period of six weeks. Once the application was deployed into production then another six weeks was allowed to pass in order to ensure a level out period was accomplished. Table 3 displays the improvements in utilization that were observed.

On average the utilization of the environment improved by 55% over the standard environment. The best improvement was the Cloud Computing site under IT which showed a dramatic improvement over the standard environment of 136% for site visits. Every environment showed an improvement in visits, unique users, and updates. Figure 3 provides an overall summary of the improvements by each division based on the number of visits. Improvements in the visitation of a site indicate an enhanced utility of the information being provided. With the exception of the theme improvements on the legal environment, every other environment showed in increase in utilization. Table 4 provides the overall statistics for the improvements as well as the total from each of the phases.

In every case, the content collaboration increased indicated that the level of collaborative work increased. While statistically, the level of collaboration and utiliza-

Table 3. Phase two metrics

Business Unit	Sites	Visits	Users	Updates
IT	1	195.2%	17.2%	17.5%
Marketing	1	96.6%	31.0%	11.9%
Finance	1	58.7%	32.2%	34.4%
Legal	1	84.3%	17.1%	16.1%
Networking	1	107.8%	14.2%	16.7%

Figure 3.

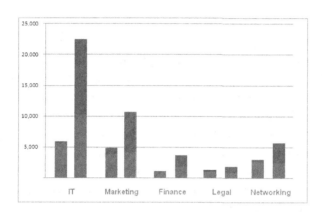

Table 4. Overall improvement metrics

Description	Visits	Users	Updates
Average Total	45.0%	18.5%	16.1%
Phase 1 Average	23.1%	17.3%	13.0%
Phase 2 Average	110.7%	22.0%	25.7%

tion improved, the research wanted to be sure the qualitative information from the user community supported the result. The author interviewed the system administrators of each site in order to collect some qualitative feedback on how the improvements were being received. The response was universally positive in that the design not only welcomed new visitors but engaged the members to contribute more information to the environment. One administrator indicated that the expert design seemed to increase the level of trust the members had with the environment. Another member discussed how much the technology was now being discussed in the team meetings. More importantly, the number of requests for site conversions had dramatically increased as other collaboration customers wanted to have their sites converted to the better design.

One area of concern was expressed by the administrators. They indicated the lack of design expertise could be an issue for a more broad deployment. This concern would not be an issue in phase one in that the modifications had universal applicability while phase required more expertise. In order to deploy the phase two level modifications, a unique set of skills would be required. Designers would need design and usability training, graphic artist ability and collaboration software experience. This skills set would be very unique in any organization.

Discussion

This chapter started with providing a background of collaboration and the evolution of Web 2.0 applications. Additionally, we defined a set criteriaset criteria of usability characteristics from the other researchers which included visual appeal, system performance, ease of use, learnability, and task support. By applying these across the environment we have been able to demonstrate a positive reaction of the end user community to increase the level of collaboration.

Collaboration within individuals and organizations is essential. Several themes of this research case study warrant review and emphasis. First, we wanted to show how improvements in the defined usability would improve the utilization of the collaborative environment. We defined usage by the number of people visiting the site either as a consumer of the information or an active participant within the environment. Our case study made two specific improvements in usability and design. The first was a slight improvement model deployed more broadly across a variety of sites while second was a very specific design model. Both enhancements produced an increase in usage by the community. Our second theme was to not only demonstrate an increase in the usage but also an increase in the content produced by the community. This would indicate an improvement in collaboration and utilization. Again, in both sets of improvement methodologies, we saw an increase in the actual content produced. We can conclude that slight or major improvements in usability will increase the business value of the collaborative environment.

One of the short comings of this research was the number of sites included in phase two. Phase one could easily be distributed to any number of collaborative sites for review but the amount of effort in phase is a limitation. Other researchers could engage a larger group of developers in order to expand this effort in order to see the degree of collaboration improvements that could be observed. Overall it can be concluded that small or extensive improvements in usability will increase the level of interaction and collaborative behavior. By leveraging designs and web developers, organization can improve the level at which the organizations engages in conversation which has been shown to increase the business value.

REFERENCES

Andres, C. (1999). *Great Web Architecture*. Foster City, CA: IDG Books World Wide.

Anschuetz, L., Keirnan, T., & Rosenbaum, S. (2002). Combining usability research with documentation development for improved user support. In Proceedings of the SIGDOC. Toronto, Canada: The Association of Computing Machinery.

Applehans, W., Globe, A., & Laugero, G. (1999). *Managing Knowledge: A Practical web-based approach*. Boston, MA: Addison-Wesley.

Baily, D., & Hinds, P. (2003). Out of sight, out of sync: Understanding conflict in distributed teams. *Organization Science, 14*, 615–632. doi:10.1287/orsc.14.6.615.24872

Becker, S., & Mottay, F. (2001, January). A global perspective on website usability. *IEEE Software, 18*(1), 61–54. doi:10.1109/52.903167

Bock, G., & Qian, Z. (2005). An empirical study on measuring the success of knowledge repository systems. In Proceedings of the 39th Annual Hawaii International Conference on System Sciences. Kona, HI: Institute of Electrical and Electronics Engineers, Inc.

Brennan, S., Fussell, S., Kraut, R., & Siegel, J. (2002). *Understanding effects of proximity on collaboration: Implications for technologies to support remote collaborative work. Distributed work*. Cambridge, MA: MIT Press.

Carr, N. (2003). *Does IT Matter? Information Technology and the Corrosion of Competitive Advantage*. Boston, MA: Harvard Business School Press.

Chellappa, R., & Gupta, A. (2002). Managing computing resources in active intranets. *International Journal of Network Management, 12*(2), 117–128. doi:10.1002/nem.427

Chudoba, K., & Maznevski, M. (2000). Bridging space over time: Global virtual team dynamics and effectiveness. *Organization Science, 11*, 473–492. doi:10.1287/orsc.11.5.473.15200

Davenport, T., & Prusak, L. (1997). *Information ecology: Mastering the information and knowledge environment*. New York: Oxford University Press.

Dingsoyr, T., & Royrvik, E. (2003). An empirical study of an informal knowledge repository in a medium-sized software consulting company. In Proceedings of the International Conference on Software Engineering. Portland, OR: Institute of Electrical and Electronics Engineers, Inc.

Dzida, W., Herda, S., & Itzfelt, W. (1978). User-perceived quality of interactive systems. *IEEE Transactions on Software Engineering, SE-4*(4), 270–276. doi:10.1109/TSE.1978.231511

Grudin, J. (2006). Enterprise knowledge management and emerging technologies. In Proceedings of the 39th Annual Hawaii International Conference on System Sciences. Kona, HI: Institute of Electrical and Electronics Engineers, Inc.

Jeng, J. (2005). Usability assessment of academic digital libraries: Effectiveness, efficiency, satisfaction, and learnability. Libri. *International Journal of Libraries and Information Services, 55*(2/3), 96–121.

Karvonen, K. (2000). The beauty of simplicity. In Proceedings of the ACM Conference on Universal Usability. Arlington, VA: The Association of Computing Machinery.

Krug, S. (2000). *Don't make me think*. Indianapolis, IN: New Riders Publishing.

Lecerof, A., & Paterno, F. (1998). Automatic support for usability evaluation. *IEEE Transactions on Software Engineering, 24*(10), 863–888. doi:10.1109/32.729686

McNay, & Heather, E. (2000). Corporate Intranets: Building communities with data. IEEE Technology & Teamwork, pp. 197-201.

Millard, D., & Ross, M. (2006). Blogs, wikis & rss: Web 2.0: Hypertext by any other name? In Proceedings of the seventeenth conference on Hypertext and hypermedia. Odense, Denmark: The Association of Computing Machinery.

Mohammad Nasir Uddin, M., & Paul Janecek, P. (2007). Faceted classification in web information architecture: A framework for using semantic web tools. *The Electronic Library, 25*(2), 219–233. doi:10.1108/02640470710741340

Nielsen, J. (1998). Introduction to web design. In Proceedings of the SIGCHI on Human Factors in Computing Systems. Los Angeles, CA: Association for Computing Machinery.

Nielsen, J. (2000). *Designing web usability*. Indianapolis, IN: New Riders Publishing.

Nielsen, J., & Tahir, M. (2002). *Homepage Usability: 50 websites deconstructed*. Indianapolis, IN: New Riders Publishing.

O'Reilly, T. (2005). What Is Web 2.0: Design patterns and business models for the next generation of software. Retrieved July 17, 2006 from http://www.oreillynet.com/pub/a/oreilly/tim/news/2005/09/30/what-is-web-20.html.

Pearrow, M. (2000). *Web site usability handbook.* Independence, KY: Charles River Media.

Ruggles, R. (1997). *Knowledge Management Tools.* Boston, MA: Butterworth-Heinemann.

Scanlon, T., Schroeder, W., Snyder, C., & Spool, J. (1998). Websites that work: Designing with your eyes open. In Proceedings of the SIGCHI on Human Factors in Computing Systems. Los Angeles, CA: Association for Computing Machinery.

Sewry, D., & Sunassee, N. (2003). A theoretical framework for knowledge management implementation. In Proceedings of the 2002 annual research conference of the South African institute of computer scientists and information technologists on Enablement through technology. Port Elizabeth, South Africa: The Association of Computing Machinery.

Singh, A., & Wesson, J. (2009). Evaluation criteria for assessing the usability of ERP Systems systems. In Proceedings of the 2009 Annual Conference of the South African Institute of Computer Scientists and Information Technologists. Vaal River, South Africa: The Association of Computing Machinery.

Smith, D., & Valdes, R. (2005). Web 2.0: Get ready for the next old thing. Gartner Research Paper. Stamford, CT.

Veen, J. (2000). *The Art and Science of Web Design.* Indianapolis, IN: New Riders Publishing.

Venkatesh, V. (1985). Determinants of perceived ease of use: Integrating control, intrinsic motivation, and emotion into the technology acceptance model. *Information Systems Research, 11*(4), 342–365. doi:10.1287/isre.11.4.342.11872

Wagner, R., & Sternberg, R. (1985). Practical intelligence in real-world pursuits: The role of tacit knowledge. *Journal of Personality and Social Psychology, 49*(2), 436–458. doi:10.1037/0022-3514.49.2.436

Weiss, A. (2005). The power of collective intelligence. *netWorker, 9*(3), 16–23. doi:10.1145/1086762.1086763

KEY TERMS AND DEFINITIONS

Collaboration: Collaboration is a term used to describe technologies that allow multiple individuals to communicate without requiring a physical presence. Their tools differ from Web 2.0 in that they may or may not have social capabilities.

Collaborative Technologies: The tools for virtual communities include threaded discussions, email, calendaring, surveying, instant messaging, customizable interfaces, document management, and real-time conferencing.

Enterprise 2.0: Enterprise 2.0 describes the integration of Web 2.0 technologies within an organization.

Information Worker: Describes individuals that work with information instead the physical objects of labor. Information workers are individuals who create, manage, share, receive and use information in the course of their daily work, including those who act and react to information.

Usability: Usability is the broad discipline of applying sound scientific observation, measurement, and design principles to the creation and maintenance of web applications in order to bring about the greatest ease of use, ease of learnability, amount of usefulness, and least amount of discomfort for the humans who use the application.

Virtual Workspace: Virtual workspaces are temporal since their existence is determinate on the existence of the team itself. Once the value or utility of the team is gone the workspace will dissolve.

Web 2.0: Web 2.0 is the term used to describe technologies that allow for a many to many conversation in the online environment. That is, many people can create content and many people can consume the information.

Chapter 6
A Practitioner's Approach to Collaborative Usability Testing

Julie Buelow
Ufoundit.ca, Canada

EXECUTIVE SUMMARY

The integration of usability testing into mainstream web development cycles is still in its infancy in many areas of the public sector. Websites are a key means of delivering information and services to residents. However, these websites are often developed and launched within tight timelines without consultation with the public.

To solve the problem, this chapter presents a collaborative approach for successfully launching websites where content experts, design experts, and the public work together for the common purpose of creating a usable website.

The purpose of this case study is to outline a methodology for collaborative usability testing developed in a local government setting where subject matter experts (SMEs), content owners, stakeholders, IT professionals and the public are engaged in the design and development of public sector websites.

DOI: 10.4018/978-1-4666-4046-7.ch006

ORGANIZATION BACKGROUND

In the province of Ontario, Canada, local governments are called municipalities. Municipalities are incorporated areas created by the provincial government of Ontario. Ontario has 444 municipalities. Municipalities are assigned certain powers and responsibilities as set out in The Municipal Act, 2001. The Act denotes which services are mandatory to deliver to citizens and which are not. Non-mandatory services are provided at the discretion of council which is comprised of elected members (Ontario Ministry of Municipal Affairs and Housing, 2011).

Most municipalities comprise several departments that deliver government programs and services ranging from community health and social development to environment and infrastructure projects as guided by council.

SETTING THE STAGE

A typical web project at a municipality is usually part of a campaign to deliver programs and services to the public. A campaign usually originates from a service-facing area such as the Public Health department. Typically a staff member from a program area (Content SME) is tasked with managing the development of a website. The Content SME often works with a project manager from the Communications or IT departments to outline the business requirements and project deliverables to be produced by the web team. Often a communication (marketing) plan is created to announce the initiative and provide a consistent and clear message to the public about the new service. A challenge can arise when members of the public are resistant to the message because they are seeking different information from that which the Content SME and project manager assume they want (Magill, 1998).

Usability testing is one of several activities supporting user-centred design (UCD), a philosophy or approach whereby a product is produced based on the needs and interests of the user. (Norman, 2002, p. 188). The need for usability testing may be identified by the web master through project strategy meetings or by Communication Services professionals assisting SMEs wishing to have a user-centred approach. Usability testing helps to align the user's desire to find information with the program area's need to impart information and deliver services efficiently. Very often the program area's needs and vocabulary differ from the IT department's technical language and security concerns (Zhao J. & Zhao S., 2010) surrounding websites. Usability testing brings together diverse professionals for the common purpose of observing and recording the reactions and feedback of sample users to the websites.

This collaboration and shared experience enables teams to move forward in unison. Usability testing can be used effectively on web projects where increased interaction with the public would be an excellent way to increase users' trust and confidence (Tolbert & Mossberger, 2006).

CASE DESCRIPTION

The case description is presented as follows:

- 1.0 Background
- 2.0 Method
    - ○ 2.1 Initial Client Presentation
        - ▪ 2.1.1 Ten Things to Consider
        - ▪ 2.1.2 Findings
    - ○ 2.2 Homework Assignment
        - ▪ 2.2.1 Key Questions
        - ▪ 2.2.2 Findings
    - ○ 2.3 Test Plan
        - ▪ 2.3.1 Test Plan Elements
        - ▪ 2.3.2 Findings
- 3.0 Observations
    - ○ 3.1 Testing Sessions
        - ▪ 3.1.1 Tester Greeting and Orientation
        - ▪ 3.1.2 Performance Test Items
        - ▪ 3.1.3 Tester Debriefing
        - ▪ 3.1.4 Insights
    - ○ 3.2 Collation of Observations
    - ○ 3.3 Summary of Results
- 4.0 Technology Concerns
- 5.0 Management and Organizational Concerns

1.0 Background

Most government websites are informational in nature. While there is public demand for transactional websites, there are still relatively few of these (Brainard & McNutt, 2010, p. 840). Very often a municipality launches a website as a communication vehicle that works in tandem with call centres, face-to-face reception areas, public information meetings, elected representative communiqués and printed materials. All these initiatives need to be coordinated to deliver the same message in order to avoid confusion.

Regardless of a municipality's organizational structure there are two basic groups of SMEs engaged in building a website: 1) Content SMEs and 2) Technology SMEs. Content SMEs are knowledgeable about the subject matter; they also write and edit content. Technology SMEs including design and User Experience experts are knowledgeable about design, communications and/or technology. They generally, but not necessarily, work in the IT or Communications departments. Each group is very skilled and knowledgeable in their respective areas; however, conflict can arise when the Content SMEs see things one way and the Technology SMEs see things another thereby placing strain on the relationship. Some of the areas of conflict can include such questions as:

- Who knows more about websites?
- Who knows more about content?
- Who knows more about design?

Collaborative usability occurs when these two groups work together with the intended audience to solicit feedback in a meaningful way to make the website more tailored and useful for the intended audience. The inclusion of users adds an element of objectivity and data that helps clarify issues that may be causing of intra group conflict. A good usability test can reveal things that neither the Content nor the Technology SMEs had considered. Figure 1 illustrates the three district groups that come together for collaborative usability.

Many municipalities may not include usability testing in their website development process due to limited resources. Their focus may be on creating and posting content, not the user experience; however, as web teams are introduced to leading usability thinking and best practices, user testing may gain more acceptance. The goal of incorporating usability testing is to collect meaningful input from the ultimate site users. The collaborative usability methodology has the added benefit of engaging and gaining support from the internal stakeholders tasked with developing the site, resulting in increased team collaboration.

In the methodology, an initial client presentation and homework assignment are essential. The initial presentation makes the case for usability testing and seeks buy-in from all participants of the multi-disciplinary team. The homework assignment is an important step requiring Content SME engagement and commitment to complete. The completed homework assignment facilitates the production of a detailed test plan by the usability specialist.

The results of the collaboration can be observed in the testing sessions where Content SMEs, designers and engaged citizens interact to the benefit of the development process. Iterative testing gathers manageable amounts of data which can be incorporated readily into the website development process.

Figure 1. Three distinct groups collaborate for design of a digital product. A good usability test can reveal things that none of the groups would have considered individually.

Collaborative Usability Triangle

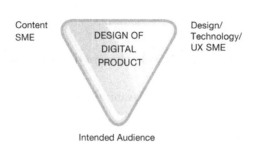

Collaborative Usability involves the coming together of three distinct groups:
Content SMEs, Design, Technology and User Experience (UX) SMEs and the intended audience.

2.0 Method

Usability studies are primarily qualitative in nature, but having a database applies a quantitative approach to capture key data and align project SMEs to a common purpose. A suggested database framework to record studies is as follows:

One *client* could have many *projects*. The client represents the department or division sponsoring the study. A project is the website or digital product to be produced. Projects can be classified in three ways: new, re-design or evaluation. A re-design indicates extensive updates and re-organization. An evaluation indicates that an existing product is deemed to be in need of review, but the extent of updating is not known.

One project could have many *tests*. A test is defined as the actions and methodologies as detailed in the *Project Test Plan* which will be created through the consultation process.

One test may comprise many *sessions*. A session is a specific and appointed time and place where the test is conducted.

One session could have many *observers* and one session could have many *testers*. Observers are the people who are present during the test. Observers can be further categorized as facilitators, time-keepers or note-takers. The facilitator conducts the test. The note-takers take notes throughout the test. The time-keeper times the length of time to complete a task. Testers are the participants who are testing the website or digital project.

2.1 Initial Client Presentation

A presentation explaining usability testing at the outset of a web development project is an excellent way of informing internal partners of its objectives, benefits and next steps. The presentation helps to ensure consistency in the approach to each new project.

2.1.1 Ten Things to Consider

The following ten items are the key elements of the initial presentation:

1. Address the Doubt and Explain Usability Testing
2. Give Examples
3. Consider the Big Picture
4. Acknowledge Frustration
5. Two Basic Questions
6. Review Other Tools
7. Other Sites
8. Cost
9. Roles
10. Show Past Projects

Address the Doubt and Explain Usability Testing

Many people have never heard of usability testing and might not see the value in doing it. What is a usability test anyway? Give an example of a question used on an actual test and then show the starting point and preferred path to the answer. Recognize there's always someone around the table who really doesn't want to go the route of usability testing. Remember, to SMEs who know just about everything on their topic, usability testing appears to be a barrier that will slow down the project. Remind them that they *are* experts, whereas average users are not. You really have to convince SMEs of the return on investment (ROI) of usability testing. Have some facts, figures or graphs ready from past studies of usability cost justification (Bias & Mayhew, 2005).

Give Examples

Give some humorous real life examples of usability errors. For instance, a grown man confessed he thought he was going to be put in jail as a child after seeing the following message when using a word processor: "You have performed an illegal operation." Who knows what the message was really referring to, but it really scared him.

The key point to convey is that a system can be working correctly technically, and be using the "correct" language from the expert's perspective, but still be misinterpreted completely by users. Usability testing provides fresh eyes to the site, helping to identify areas where your intended audience could chuckle at your expense, misunderstand your message or leave your site altogether in frustration.

Consider the Big Picture

Usability testing supports municipality-wide goals beyond the immediate project at hand. A web project is usually one facet of a broader communication campaign that involves coordination of call centres, front-line staff, and printed material messages. It is important to recognize the project's objectives in the context of municipality-wide goals.

Acknowledge Frustration

It's not easy for Content SMEs to take on the development of a website, even when the subject matter of the site is their specialty. Often a Content SME feels overwhelmed about tackling a technical project. Let them know that usability testing will make them feel more confident because they'll have feedback from real citizens upon which to base their decisions.

Two Basic Questions

Two basic questions to ask are:

1. What is the purpose of the site?
2. Who is the intended audience?

Surprisingly often, everyone around the table has a different answer. It's important that a common understanding is reached before a usability test is undertaken.

Review Other Tools

It may be that the project is not ready for usability testing. More discovery work around audience identification may need to be conducted. Talk briefly about other tools, focus groups, surveys, web analytics, and call centre data as ways to discover more about the audience. Usability testing may not be the appropriate tool at this stage. As a first step, the usability specialist may instead develop an online survey or set up a focus group/card-sorting exercise instead of a usability test.

Other Sites

If starting a brand new project, it might look like usability testing is not possible because there is no site to test. However, as Krug (2010, p. 33) suggests, other sites that the SMEs like and wish to use as a model can be tested. Usability testing of other sites has proven invaluable. Very often results from these kinds of tests are a surprise. And a site that may be the first preference of the SMEs may not be the first choice of the testers (the intended audience). It also gives a chance to evaluate features used in other sites as to their usefulness.

Cost

In terms of cost, one usability test with five sessions takes approximately 50 hours of the usability specialist's time using the collaborative usability approach. SMEs can then judge accordingly whether there is room for this in their budget.

Roles

Let SMEs know what is involved and briefly explain their role in the test.

Below is a brief overview of the various roles:

- **Usability Specialist:** Writes test plan; Advises on number of testers, session length, invitations, honoraria, and suitable testers; Facilitates test; Analyzes data; Develops formal recommendations in consultation with SMEs.
- **Content SME:** Provides information for test plan; Finds suitable testers; Provides honorarium to tester; Handles all logistics; Organizes logistics; Observes test and records observations; Collates observations; Presents formal recommendations to senior management for approval to make changes.
- **Secondary Design/Technology/UX SME:** May read test plan; May observe and record during test; May design/write/think differently based on direct observation.
- **Tester:** Never sees test plan; Contacted by Content SME and agrees to participate; Participates in test at designated test site; Provides feedback; May follow up with further thoughts after the session.

Show Past Projects

Provide examples of projects, including before and after images of sites that were usability tested in the past. As well, show some new sites that incorporated usability testing from the start. This can be an effective way of demonstrating to SMEs and other project partners the benefit of usability testing.

2.1.2 Findings of the Initial Client Presentation

The initial presentation takes approximately an hour and uses image-based slides to introduce the notion of usability testing as a tool that will provide a high return on the effort and resources invested.

The presentation establishes an understanding of the purpose of testing and empowers Content SMEs to make decisions about whether to embark on a testing process. Many SMEs may never have considered the importance of having residents participate in the design and development of a website previously.

2.2 Homework Assignment

The homework assignment is the next step after the initial client presentation. It informs SMEs about the next steps and helps them get started. The homework assignment is a list of questions that need to be answered in order to create the test plan.

The homework assignment puts the onus on the Content SMEs to provide user scenarios and really think about a user-centred approach. The time invested produces better scenarios and leads to SME ownership of the testing.

2.2.1 Key Questions

The homework assignment consists of seven questions:

1. Do you have any background information about your project?
2. What is the purpose of your website?
3. How is your website intended to be used?
4. Who is the target audience for your website (and what percentage of the total audience do they comprise)?
5. What are your audience's main concerns regarding the subject matter of your site?
6. What are some issues that you have identified with regards to your site?
7. What are six possible real-life scenarios that would drive your primary audience to your site? Give the scenario and the target page where the information is found on the site.

The rationale for each question follows:

Do you have any background information about your project? For municipalities, websites are usually never a standalone entity without a connection to an existing program or service. Websites are a communication vehicle that support a campaign or provide a service online which can also be performed in person or over the phone. Usually there is other information related to the site that if not specifically asked for, is not provided or considered important by the client.

What is the purpose of your website? It's very important to have clarity on the purpose of the website and that all SMEs agree on that purpose. Some may have a different vision than others. To set up a good usability test, everyone must have the same vision right from the start.

How is your website intended to be used? Sometimes a site's intended use becomes secondary, and unintended uses become important. For instance, a site intended for use by teachers to augment their lessons may in fact be more often used by parents helping their child conduct research.

Who is the target audience for your website (and what percentage of the total audience do they comprise)? This is a very important question, and the percentage is critical. If the split is 80% primary audience to 20% secondary audience, navigation and content should be designed for the 80% primary audience. Asking the percentage is important because it directs SMEs to really think about the proportions of their audience. It can be a real barrier to future discussions if the proportional audience size is not unequivocally agreed to by contributing SMEs. Audience drives scenarios, content direction and navigation.

What are your audience's main concerns regarding the subject matter of your site? Very often the Content SME has personal experience based on informal feedback from clients to answer this question in great detail. The answers to this question can provide an understanding about what should be the top content of the site.

What are some issues that you have identified with regards to your site? Usually an SME has a hunch as to what is wrong or what might go wrong with the website based on client feedback or program delivery issues. As part of collaborative usability, fully understanding and trusting your SMEs gut feelings is critical. Work any concerns into the test.

What are six possible real-life scenarios that would drive your primary audience to your site? Give the scenario and the target page where the information is found on the site (if there is an existing page). This question is the basis for formulating tasks that testers will be asked to do in testing sessions. You may need to re-word the scenarios with neutral language. Sometimes a scenario does not have a target page because the content is new and hasn't been written yet. In that case, you cannot use the scenario until there is content. Always ask for more scenarios than you have time to test.

2.2.2 Findings of the Homework Assignment

The homework assignment is the single most important document in devising the test plan. A well thought-out homework assignment will save hours of work for the usability specialist. Encourage Content SMEs to answer the questions as fully as possible and to supply or give access to any and all supporting documents. Even when first discussing the homework assignment, you may find more information that you needed that the SME didn't think was important.

There's no stated deadline to the homework assignment; it can be completed in a matter of days or take a number of months. The project goes no further until the homework is completed either individually or by a group.

To set up a good usability test you need to see the big picture. You can also look at printed posters and brochures and their relationships to the website. Knowing about existing or planned supporting materials helps set up a test that will truly find valuable insights. If you don't ask for all the available materials, you might miss some important information.

As important as the homework assignment is, a substantial amount of work may still need to be done. If the site already exists, run a content audit of all pages in the site to get an idea of how large the site is. Content SMEs are very often surprised at how many pages their site contains. If no site map is supplied, make a high level site map of the current structure. Look at web statistics to see which pages are the most popular. Do searches for similar content on the site and see what results come up. Do the pages of the site appear at the top of the search results list?

2.3 Test Plan

The initial client presentation and the homework assignment set the stage for a collaborative working relationship.

2.3.1 Test Plan Elements

Every usability test should have a test plan that states exactly what will be done and why (Rubin & Chisnell, 2008, Chapter 5). The test plan allows the Content SME and the usability specialist to review and confirm next steps. It provides the framework for the usability specialist to do the research necessary to fully understand the project. The test plan is drafted by the usability expert based on the information provided by the Content SMEs in the homework assignment.

Test plan elements:

1. Introduction
2. Purpose of the Site
3. Target Audiences
4. Primary Audience Concerns
5. Intended Site Use
6. Issues
7. Home Page Look and Feel

8.   Purpose of Testing
9.   Tester Profile, Acquisition and Sessions
10. Methodology
11. Task List
12. Budget

Introduction

The test plan introduction includes a summary explanation and image. The image could be a screen capture of pages being tested or the identifier of the program for which a website is being created.

   The detail in the introduction signifies the need to put usability testing in the broader context of the entire project. The introduction provides a quick business analysis, the need for the website and the need for the testing itself, to ensure the testing uncovers whether the website meets its stated aims.

Purpose of the Site

This element clarifies the purpose of the website as determined by the Content SMEs on the homework assignment. Everyone on the project should have the same vision of what the purpose of the site is. The purpose may be written down elsewhere in a project charter or another high level document, but it's useful to state site purpose again on the test plan to provide clarity for those who have not seen other documentation.

Target Audiences

Determining target audiences (understanding users) is a basic principle of the user-centred design (UCD) approach (IBM, 2007). Defining the primary and secondary target audiences of a website helps to prioritize tasks to test. Often a campaign, of which the website is only one component, defines the target audience(s) up front. The additional knowledge of the estimated percentage of primary and secondary audience participation is helpful because tasks are audience-specific. If one audience is deemed to have a low percentage of participation, testing (and the website design) can focus on the audience(s) with the greatest anticipated participation.

Primary Audience Concerns

Pareto's Principle - The 80-20 Rule (Lidwell, Holden, & Butler, 2003) can be applied to websites: 80% of your visitors will be interested in only 20% of your site. Acknowledge what visitors are most concerned about and have that front and centre and easy to find. The Content SMEs often have first-hand knowledge of their audiences if they are out in the field working directing with the target groups. In addition, Content SMEs also have access to call centre data, call centre operators and web statistics that can support their first-hand observations. Some municipalities also conduct client satisfaction surveys and focus groups which provide additional information about their audiences.

Intended Site Use

Intended site use identifies the users expected tasks on the site, e.g. whether the site will be used for educational and information gathering purposes, as a feedback mechanism, or as a transactional website. A website could be a combination of these with separate purposes for different audiences. The primary purpose of this section is to understand the audience and how they will use the site.

Issues

An important element of the test plan includes looking at potential challenges or concerns that could impact either the testing or the website development process. Knowledge of issues outside the website, such as important political issues, policy decisions, hot topics in the press, or a requirement to use industry-specific language instead of plain language, provides the test plan reader with greater context. Knowledge of potential issues may also modify the approach a moderator will take during the test including the task selection and questions to explore.

Home Page Look and Feel

The test plan should include a small screenshot of the homepage (and an inside page, if different) or if the site isn't yet live, a small prototype to serve as a marker of the visual appearance of the site at the time of testing. As webpages change in appearance, the screenshot provides a useful record of what the page looked like prior to testing and before subsequent changes occurred. This category can also state the feel or tone that the site is trying to achieve. Most municipalities have brand guidelines and a style guide to which its main sites and intranet have to adhere; in addition, a municipality may also have websites designed with community partners. In this case, the site may only have the municipality's logo and no other identifiers.

Purpose of Testing

This section states the test objectives including any gaps that testing is intended to identify. This section contains specific problem statements that the testing will address or measure.

Tester Profile, Acquisition and Sessions

This section describes the method used to recruit appropriate testers, how many sessions will take place, the number of testers who will participate, and specific testing logistics, if known

Methodology

This section of the test plan defines the components of the usability test and what each is intended to achieve.

- **10.1 Participant Greeting:** This briefly lists who will meet the participant tester (s) and where they will sit.
- **10.2 Orientation:** This describes the scripted introduction, purpose of the session, the need for testers to act as natural as possible, and the role of observers and the facilitator.
- **10.3 Performance Test:** This is the series of tasks that testers will be asked to do while being observed. Prior to completing the tasks, the tester will receive a consent form. Questions will be asked before the performance test to gauge experience and expectations.
- **10.4 Participant Debriefing:** After the performance test observers may ask questions. Brief after and demographics questionnaires will follow.
- **10.5 Test Environment and Equipment Required:** This describes the roles of facilitators and observers and computer or other equipment necessary for the test.
- **10.6 Evaluation Measures:** This describes evaluation measures that will be collected and calculated, such as average time to complete tasks.
- **10.7 Test Report and Presentation:** This describes what happens after the observations are collected.

Task List

Snyder's (2003) detailed task list template provides an associated goal/output, input, assumptions, steps, time for expert, and instructions for the tester for each task. This template is very helpful and gives the reasoning behind each task.

Budget

The importance of delineating a test plan budget will vary by municipality. The collaborative usability method takes approximately 50 hours of the usability specialist's time to do five sessions. Mayhew (2002) states it takes between three and four weeks to complete a test with half the time planning the test, a quarter running the test and a quarter analyzing, interpreting the results. The collaborative approach enlists the content SMEs participation which in turn reduces the number of hours a usability specialist would normally spend.

2.3.1 Test Plan Insights

The writing of the test plan serves a valuable purpose for the usability practitioner. The time invested in writing it provides the context necessary to create really meaningful tasks and set a logical task order. The knowledge acquired when writing the test plan also helps during facilitation by providing the background to probe appropriately.

Another advantage of the test plan is it opens up or allows further discussion about the testing. The test plan describes the testing process in detail to the Content and Technology SMEs. Until this point, many of the ideas were only discussions and PowerPoint slides.

As time goes on and the specifics of testing are forgotten, the plan is a reference of what took place at a certain point in time and why.

3.0 Observations

The following section describes observations of testing sessions conducted at a specific municipality (hereafter "the Municipality") between 2004 and 2011.

3.1 Testing Sessions

Of 41 tests conducted, 32 were usability tests. Of these, three tests were considered "informal" with no consent forms being used and no data collected about the tester. There were many other unrecorded "informal" tests where the purpose of the test was to "test the test." Very often these testers were quickly testing the task list prior to first use to make sure that the tasks were ordered logically and the tasks manageable.

Of 32 usability tests, nine had co-discovery sessions, three had additional card-sorting exercises, three were user acceptance usability tests, six involved paper-prototyping, and all invoked think-aloud protocol.

Of 41 tests conducted, nine were focus groups which are not as structured as usability tests and only require a moderator's guide. Detailed analysis of the focus groups is outside the scope of this study, but it's important to note that usability analyses may indeed highlight the need for other types of studies.

The ideal number of sessions per test is five (Nielsen, 2000). In order to avoid an inordinate time lapse for collating and analyzing data from multiple sessions, the Municipality adopted an iterative approach to testing. Sessions were conducted in groups of two followed by a review. Changes were made as needed which kept project momentum moving forward and led to action.

For the most part, testers were recruited from community contacts of the Content SMEs. The advantage of this is that these testers had a known interest in the subject matter of the sites. Some testers were volunteers who had registered with the Municipality's volunteer program. Testers had a variety of computer and Internet experience and ranged in age from 14 to 81.

Of the 120 sessions only three were located in a tester's private home. The majority (67) of sessions were conducted at the Municipality's offices with the remainder being conducted at various community locations (schools, daycare centres, community centres, etc.).

The key components of the testing session include:

- 3.1.1 Tester greeting and orientation
- 3.1.2 Usability test method
- 3.1.3 Tester debriefing

3.1.1 Tester Greeting and Orientation

The Content SME arranged the testing sessions and greeted the tester.

The facilitator used an introduction/welcome script adapted from Snyder (2003). The facilitator tries to put the tester at ease, explaining that they are in control and that they are helping to test a site and that they themselves are not being tested.

Given the size of the Municipality and the distances that testers travelled to participate, an honorarium was provided. The preferred honorarium was in the form of a gift card and/or promotional item. The Content SME decided whether to present the honorarium at the beginning of the session or at the end. Presenting one at the beginning of the session provides appreciation early for particularly sensitive testers such as teenagers or recent newcomers.

3.1.2 Performance Test Items

The following are the elements of the performance test and

1. Consent Form
2. Before Questions
3. Demographic Questions
4. Session Tasks Timed
5. Five (5) Second test
6. Trust Test

7.   Create Own Scenario
8.   Test Composite Designs
9.   Cue Cards

Consent Form

A consent form was used in 29 of the 32 tests conducted. Only the informal sessions didn't have a consent form. The consent form is handed out during the scripted welcome and explanation session. All testers agreed to sign the consent form which stated they agreed to being observed as long as their comments remained confidential. If the session was to be electronically recorded it was mentioned in the consent form. Only seven sessions were ever recorded electronically.

Before Questions

Questions are asked before the actual tasks begin to gauge the tester's interest in the subject matter of the site and identify any expectations. In early tests, a written questionnaire was presented to the tester; however, experience demonstrated that verbal questions are better as they put the tester more at ease. The specific before questions asked are developed in consultation with the Content SMEs

Demographic Questions

Testers are requested to complete a written demographic questionnaire at the end of the testing session. The questions asked include self-rated computer proficiency, gender, age range and a few project specific questions that were of interest to Content SMEs. Questions related to participants' personal information, address or socio-economic status are not asked. No personal identity information is collected.

Session Tasks Timed

A common practice in usability testing is to time how long it takes a tester to perform set tasks. For highly qualitative studies such as those conducted by the Municipality, timing testers was not critical as project team members were generally present as observers and they could see which tasks created difficulties. Timing testers could be beneficial when reporting findings to team members not in attendance.

Five Second Test

A five-second test asks the tester to look at a page for five seconds and give their initial impressions (Perfetti, 2005). At the Municipality, use of this technique began in October 2006 as an icebreaker before any scenarios were given. The five-second test was so successful as an icebreaker, it has been in use for every test since. The five second question is best worded as "You are going to see a [certain kind] of web page. What are your first impressions?" or "What stood out for you?" On the other hand asking "What do you remember?" seemed more like a test of recall and increased stress levels of the testers.

Trust Test

Following the five second test is a question related to trust. Government organizations want website users to have trust and confidence in their websites (Tolbert & Mossberger, 2006). Questions are worded as follows: "Do you get the impression you will receive reliable information?," "Would you stay on the site?" or "Do you get a feeling that you trust this information?" Feedback on this question is significant. One small change can mean the difference between trust and no trust. For instance, a site about healthy eating with a picture of a hamburger on it, or one with no pictures of food at all does not inspire trust. In keeping with the findings of Beldad, Van der Geest, De Jong, and Michaël, M. (2012) regarding "trust cues, such as a positive organizational reputation," the Municipality's logo on a site inspired trust among those using the site. If a site does not inspire trust, explore why and take action to rectify the situation. The solution may be as simple as changing an image, adding a logo, or displaying the privacy policy more prominently.

Create Own Scenario

Hand-in-hand with the five second and trust questions is a create-your-own-scenario question. "Use the website as if you were at home alone" follows the five second and trust questions because the tester by this point has built their own trust and confidence regarding the testing session. Sometimes the tester covers a scenario you were going to ask later which means that the scenarios created were very realistic.

Another benefit of create-your-own-scenario is that the tester becomes better acquainted with the site which lessens their anxiety about the session. Remember the more relaxed your tester is, the more likely they will be able to act naturally and provide reliable feedback.

Test Composite Designs

In addition to usability questions, six sessions tested composite designs and asked testers to compare and contrast them. This proved very useful, especially since the tester had already tried scenarios and then looked at various designs that would support the scenarios. In every case, the tester liked different elements of each design. Six sessions featured graphic designers as observers. In each case, the designers were grateful for the feedback and the audience's viewpoint and were able to make a new composite design incorporating the tester's suggestions.

Cue Cards

Originally all tasks were printed out on a sheet of paper with the tester reading the questions aloud before beginning each task in turn. This felt awkward even though the intent was to get the tester to talk out loud. A better approach was taken whereby the tasks were written with pencil on cue cards, one cue card per task. The cards could be shuffled like a deck, making it easy to change task order. This finding is similar to Krug (2010, p. 55) who said have "one (task) per sheet for participants."

The cue card method proved superior because since the tester only saw one cue card at a time, the tester was unaware whether all the tasks were competed or not. If one session showed the wording of task was awkward, it was easy to change the wording on the cue card for the next session. Of 32 usability tests, 26 used cue cards.

3.1.3 Tester Debriefing

After the tester has completed the set tasks, observers can ask testers to go back to certain areas of the site and ask them questions about why they made the choices they did. It's a chance to understand why a key area was passed over or missed, and to figure out what is working on the site and what isn't. It is also a chance for observers to really understand their audience and express their appreciation for the valuable feedback they've received.

A written after questionnaire is given to the tester at this time. This document is short and neutrally worded. The purpose is to receive the tester's summary assessment of the site and to discover whether their expectations have been met.

The after questionnaire uses open questions to seek qualitative input where the user's vocabulary may even drive future content changes. To date standard post-test questionnaires such as Brooke's (1996) System Usability Scale (SUS) or the Computer System Usability Questionnaire (CSUQ) (Barnum, 2011) have not been used; however, as usability evaluation begins to be further practiced by the Municipality, the use of a standard post-test questionnaires would allow further comparison between projects. In addition, Papadomichelaki and Mentzas (2012) have devised a scale that could be used called e-GovQual. The scale assesses four dimensions of service quality for government websites and e-products: reliability, efficiency, citizen support, and trust. The four areas have a total of 21 evaluation criteria that could serve as a useful standard of measurement and enable different digital projects to be assessed collectively.

3.1.4 Testing Session Insights

There was little need to change the script modeled from Snyder (2003) over the years as the script very clearly and succinctly explained the purpose and objective of the test and was invariably well-received. Having a prepared script means each tester receives the same explanation.

As Schroeder, Brittan, and Spool's (2005) research suggests, the best testers are people highly engaged in the subject matter of the site, cooperative and articulate. Disinterested testers barely read the content and performed the tasks with very little comment despite being prompted. Testers with low literacy scanned the content and relied heavily on images to help them understand what the site was for. They had difficulty completing tasks and giving feedback.

The Municipality's employees, while willing and available, proved to be unsuitable testers for the Municipality's Internet sites. They knew the Municipality's organizational structure too well (even if it wasn't their own department being tested) and knew intuitively where to look for the information they needed. Using the employees as testers did not reveal the problems that a regular member of the public might encounter.

Usability testing can also be very stressful for the Content and Technology SMEs. Very often it's their work and ideas that are being tested. All observers are given a sheet of instructions in advance of the test requesting that testers are not interrupted while the test is in progress.

In an early project, multiple facilitators were recruited to help with the testing. Different facilitators ran the tests differently despite a detailed facilitator's kit. It was realized that it was best to have the same facilitator for each test session and also have a facilitator who was very familiar with websites and usability testing. From that point forward, the usability specialist facilitated all the sessions in a given test.

Often session details changed after the test plan had been written. Test plans were updated with the final details after-the-fact to capture the actual process followed.

Only seven sessions were ever recorded (with tester's consent), but the recordings proved too time consuming to review. Direct observation by SMEs and discussion afterwards was the approach found to have the most impact.

If going off-site for a session, be prepared in case there's no working Internet connection. Be sure your laptop can function as its own server. Load a back-up working copy of your site that will work using "localhost" in case the Internet connection does not work. Your information technology (IT) department may have to help make a few adjustments to scripts and paths in order that your back-up site works on your laptop.

An LCD projector was helpful for observers; indeed many of the testers would look at the LCD screen instead of the laptop screen because the LCD was larger.

Bring two extra copies of consent forms and questionnaires for the testers, as sometimes testers bring their friends and spouses. If that happens, it is beneficial to run an unexpected "co-discovery" session. Remember, you will get the best feedback based on how comfortable your tester is. If a tester is more comfortable with a friend or spouse present, be flexible. Your scheduled tester will be very grateful.

An adjectives chart from a Microsoft desirability toolkit (Benedek & Miner, 2002) was used in May 2005 to provide words to describe expectations before visiting a site and to describe satisfaction after visiting a site. The adjectives chart provided words describing satisfaction or dissatisfaction with a site. Despite success in some studies (Barnum, 2008, p. 186) this tool proved to be unsuccessful at the Municipality and was discontinued. Our testers were puzzled and surprised at having to pick from so many words.

Tester debriefing is one of the most rewarding aspects of a session. It's a chance for the observers to interact with the tester and ask questions directly.

The purpose of all the collaborative preparation is to design an effective testing session. A good session satisfies all of the SMEs' concerns and your tester will leave feeling valued.

Good test preparation and facilitation are the keys to a great usability test session. Be prepared for extra people, babies, and testers who might need assistance using the computer. At one off-site test session with a faith group, the hosts even offered lunch and prayers. Let people know you want brutal honesty and if you're lucky, you'll get it.

3.2 Collation of Observations/Data

The collection and collation of tester data and observer notes in a timely manner is important to support test analysis and the development of recommendations. Content SMEs often assisted with this activity in the Municipality's usability projects. In fact, as usability testing became more collaborative content SMEs handled the data collection and collation.

A number of forms were developed to facilitate data collection and collation including an observer instruction form to provide guidance to observers during the testing sessions, as well as an observer log form to collect observations in a standardized fashion.

Usability specialists may wish to keep copies of raw data to support future comparative analysis of usability tests.

3.3 Summary of Results

Below are five options for disseminating results following the completion of usability testing sessions:

1. Debriefing Meeting
2. Summary of Observations
3. Report
4. Wireframes
5. Site Map

Debriefing Meeting

Have a meeting as soon as possible with the observers to discuss their observations from the sessions even if the observers have not yet completed and submitted their observations formally. It's a good idea to meet while everything is still fresh in everyone's minds to keep the momentum going. Discuss which observations were expected and especially those that were unexpected.

Have the usability specialist point out which observations had significance. Distinguish between observations that showed usability trends and observations that revealed the tester's personal preferences. Explain the difference.

Summary of Observations

Provide a table summarizing the key observations. Create a row for each significant observation. Insert a screen shot, write a description and list the main issues and recommendations for change. Also provide a priority rating for change. Share your observation table in advance with Content SMEs to get their input. If a report is necessary, include the summary of observations in the report.

Report

As Dumas, Molich, and Jeffries (2004) point out, it's important to stay away from usability jargon when writing reports. Point out things that are working well as well as areas of concern. Use a positive tone and specifically state the usability issue and a specific suggestion for change. The need for specificity led to wireframes and sitemaps as being desirable ways to report recommendations.

Wireframes

From December 2007, ten projects at the Municipality had wireframes as a deliverable. A wireframe is the bridge between observations and recommendations. It provides a tangible visual framework (like a blueprint) for Content SMEs. For example, if the observation revealed that no one saw the "Buy Now" button, a wireframe can provide a suggested solution with a different placement and label for the button. The wireframes can, in turn, be usability tested. Many computer applications generate interactive wireframes allowing the elements to be clickable and act like a website without having to develop code. HTML 5.0 and CSS 3.0 can be used to generate prototypes that take into account the many screen sizes that now exist.

If wireframes are usability tested they allow a tester to focus on the elements on the page and not be distracted or swayed by the colours or images. A wireframe doesn't feel like a finished product to a tester. A tester feels more comfortable commenting negatively about a page that doesn't look finished. Wireframes provide early feedback prior to making look and feel design decisions.

Wireframes ensure that small details that can improve usability are incorporated into the graphic design. Wireframes are also helpful for developers who are building an application. A wireframe can guide them on how to display results pages from a search, as well as how to format and program.

How many wireframes generated depends on the project and the need. For discussion purposes generally a home page and a few key home pages will be sufficient. If testing a site, many more wireframes would need to be generated.

Site Map

The wireframes work in tandem with a proposed site map. Ten projects at the Municipality included site maps as deliverables. The sitemap provides the information architecture of the site and the wireframe provides an idea of what each page will look like. The site map guides the Content SME as to how to organize and write content. It also guides the web designer on how to set up the file structure of the site.

Along with a site map legend include an information box that details the main and secondary audiences (with estimated percentages), to demonstrate that this site map is organized with the audience in mind.

4.0 Technology Concerns

This case study looks at websites only. Websites are straightforward to test as long as there's a computer and a LCD projector (and even the projector isn't absolutely necessary depending on the number of observers). With applications on smart phones and tablets, the testing is more sophisticated. The next step, testing for mobile, requires more specialized equipment and further training.

In addition, there's a need to make websites accessible as well as usable. Under the Accessibility for Ontarians with Disabilities Act, 2005, public and private sector organizations are mandated to make their premises and web properties more accessible. Sub-section 14 (2) stipulates:

Designated public sector organizations and large organizations shall make their Internet websites and web content conform with the World Wide Web Consortium Web Content Accessibility Guidelines (WCAG) 2.0, initially at Level A and increasing to Level AA.

Different browsers display web pages and applications differently. Some test questions involved using an application in one browser and then using it again in another browser.

Another technology concern is the equipment being used by the intended audience. Designers of new sites must take into account the equipment used by the intended audience. In one of the Municipality's studies, it was discovered that PDF files wouldn't open for an entire school board. That was important information since the Technology and Content SMEs were assuming PDF files could be viewed easily and quickly by all users. This issue has now been rectified, but it was an important design consideration at the time. Usability testing revealed the issue early and resulted in content being presented in HTML form and not PDF.

5.0 Management and Organizational Concerns

From a practitioner's viewpoint, a main concern is how to share the valuable information gleaned from usability testing within a municipality. If usability testing reveals a design flaw, it will be rectified for the intended project, but the challenge is to communicate the issue for future projects and potentially other sites. Regular review of projects and findings with key SMEs would be helpful as would the creation of a knowledge base for research and discussion.

Usually usability testing is usually not done routinely. Even where usability testing is occurring, the usability specialist often holds another position such as web designer, user interface specialist or business analyst. Often, the functional testing of websites is an information technology (IT) function that occurs in isolation from subject matter experts (SMEs) and the public.

CURRENT CHALLENGES FACING THE ORGANIZATION

Municipalities are challenged with budget constraints while still mandated to deliver quality services to their residents.

They are also concerned with data security and privacy to a higher degree than many private organizations. They must upgrade aging technology and take into account a variety of new devices that have not existed in the past. Many municipalities are involved with open data initiatives and presenting data to citizens so that it's easy to access. Usability testing can provide citizen input on the best way to organize information on websites for easy access.

With pressure to cut costs and find savings, usability testing may be seen as a discretionary activity and so be excluded from project budgets. In fact the collaborative approach to usability testing offers a high return for a relatively low cost and it generates a genuine appreciation among stakeholders of the importance of feedback from website users.

SUMMARY

This case study offers a methodology that has been highly effective in bridging the gap between user needs and SMEs who are trying to deliver valuable information to the wider world. Members of the public are proud to take part in designing more useful systems and websites. Citizens are pleased to know that governments value their feedback and are creating websites which truly have them in mind.

The working relationship of various SMEs is enhanced as they work together to achieve a solution which is tailored to the needs of the website user. Participating in the testing as observers enables them to see first-hand how users of their sites struggle to find information on the websites they have created. Observing and participating in collaborative usability sessions provides context, focus and purpose for their work.

The unique methodology for collaborative usability testing brings together the various stakeholders to work together to produce user-centred websites. The methodology begins with a presentation to SMEs that explains the value proposition of taking a user-centred approach.

After the presentation the SMEs are given a homework assignment asking them to provide key information such as purpose, audience, and scenarios of use. A detailed test plan is then drawn up where SMEs are completely involved in the testing process. This is a key point: the usability work is not done by a separate user experience group in isolation; instead, the SMEs find the usability test participants from their contacts in the community.

SMEs are the observers and collators of the test data. SMEs see first-hand any changes that need to be made to their sites based on direct observation. Other stakeholders such as graphic designers, web designers, and web developers are also observers. Testing is done iteratively throughout the project, and changes are made rapidly and collectively based on the testing observations. The end result is a report which includes recommendations on how to proceed to develop a site that will meet the needs of the user.

REFERENCES

Barnum, C. M. (2011). *Usability testing essentials: Ready, set--test*. Burlington, MA: Morgan Kaufmann.

Beldad, A., Van der Geest, T., De Jong, M., & Michaël, M. (2012). A cue or two and I'll trust you: Determinants of trust in government organizations in terms of their processing and usage of citizens' personal information disclosed online. *Government Information Quarterly, 29*(1), 41–49. doi:10.1016/j.giq.2011.05.003

Benedek, J., & Miner, T. (2002*). Measuring desirability: New methods for evaluating desirability in a usability lab setting*. Usability Professionals' Association, 2002 Conference Proceedings. Retrieved May 26, 2012 from http://www.microsoft.com/usability/uepostings/desirabilitytoolkit.doc

Bias, R. G., & Mayhew, D. J. (2005). *Cost-justifying usability: An update for an Internet age* (2nd ed.). Amsterdam: Morgan Kaufman.

Brainard, L. A., & McNutt, J. G. (2010). Virtual government-citizen relations: Informational, transactional, or collaborative? *Administration & Society, 42*(7), 836–858. doi:10.1177/0095399710386308

Brooke, J. (1996). SUS: A 'quick and dirty' usability scale. In Jordan, P. W., Thomas, B., Weerdmeester, B. A., & McClelland, A. L. (Eds.), *Usability evaluation in industry*. London: Taylor and Francis.

Dumas, J. S., Molich, R., & Jeffries, R. (2004, July/August). Describing usability problems: Are we sending the right message? *Interactions - All Systems Go: How Wall Street Will Benefit from User-centered Design, 11*(4), 24-29. doi: 10.1145/1005261.1005274

International Business Machines (IBM). (2007). User-centered design. *IBM Design: UCD Process*. Retrieved September 17, 2012, from http://www-01.ibm.com/software/ucd/ucd.html

Krug, S. (2010). *Rocket surgery made easy: The do-it-yourself guide to finding and fixing usability problems*. Berkeley, CA: New Riders.

Lidwell, W., Holden, K., & Butler, J. (2003). *Universal principles of design*. Beverly, MA: Rockport Publishers.

Madill, J. J. (1998). Marketing in government. *Optimum, the Journal of Public Sector Management, 24*(4), 11-18.

Mayhew, D. J. (2002). Usability testing: You get what you pay for. *Deborah J. Mayhew & Associates - Software and Web Usability Engineering Consultants.* Retrieved September 16, 2012, from http://drdeb.vineyard.net/index.php?loc=17

Nielsen, J. (2000). Why you only need to test with 5 users. Retrieved May 26, 2012 from http://www.useit.com/articles/five_second_test/

Norman, D. A. (2002). *The design of everyday things.* New York: Basic Books.

Ontario Ministry of Municipal Affairs and Housing. (2011, July 25). Section 2: An overview of local government. *Local Government.* Retrieved October 12, 2012, from http://www.mah.gov.on.ca/Page8391.aspx

Papadomichelaki, X., & Mentzas, G. (2012). E-GovQual: A multiple-item scale for assessing e-government service quality. *Government Information Quarterly, 29*(1), 98–109. doi:10.1016/j.giq.2011.08.011

Perfetti, C. (2005). 5 second tests: Measuring your site's content pages. Retrieved May 26, 2012 from http://www.uie.com/articles/five_second_test/

Rubin, J., & Chisnell, D. (2008). *Handbook of usability testing: How to plan, design, and conduct effective tests.* Indianapolis, IN: Wiley Publishers.

Schroeder, W., Brittan, D., & Spool, J. M. (2005). *Recruiting without fear: How to find first-rate participants for design studies* (Rep.). User Interface Engineering. Retrieved from http://www.uie.com/reports

Snyder, C. (2003). *Paper prototyping: The fast and easy way to design and refine user interfaces.* San Francisco, CA: Morgan Kaufman Publishers.

Tolbert, C. J., & Mossberger, K. (2006). The effects of e-government on trust and confidence in government. *Public Administration Review, 66*(3), 354–369. doi:10.1111/j.1540-6210.2006.00594.x

Zhao, J. J., Zhao, S. Y., & Zhao, S. Y. (2009). Opportunities and threats: A security assessment of state e-government websites. *Government Information Quarterly.* doi:doi:10.1016/j.giq.2009.07.004

KEY TERMS AND DEFINITIONS

Client: The department or division sponsoring the study.

Observer: The people who are present during the test. Observers can be further categorized as facilitators, time-keepers or observers. The facilitator conducts the test. The observers take notes throughout the test. The time-keeper records the length of time taken to complete a task.

Project: The digital product to be produced. For this study, all the digital products are websites. Projects can be classified in three ways: new site, re-design or site evaluation. A re-design is an existing site that will be extensively updated and re-organized. A site evaluation is used where an existing site that has been deemed in need of review, but where the extent of updating required is not yet known.

Project Test Plan: A document that states in writing exactly what will be done during the usability test, where it will take place, who is involved, what the tasks are, and why the testing is taking place.

Session: A specific and appointed time and place where the test is conducted.

Test: The actions and methodologies as detailed in the Project Test Plan.

Tester: The participants who are testing the digital project.

Usability Testing: An activity to evaluate a system or digital product where testers representing the target audience perform either assigned tasks or create self-assigned tasks while being observed.

Chapter 7
Integrating Semiotics Perception in Usability Testing to Improve Usability Evaluation

Muhammad Nazrul Islam
Åbo Akademi University, Finland

Franck Tétard
Uppsala University, Sweden

EXECUTIVE SUMMARY

User interfaces of computer applications encompass a number of objects such as navigation links, buttons, icons, and thumbnails. In this chapter, these are called interface signs. The content and functions of a computer application are generally directed by interface signs to provide the system's logic to the end users. The interface signs of a usable application need to be intuitive to end users and therefore a necessary part of usability evaluation. Assessing sign intuitiveness can be achieved through a semiotic analysis. This study demonstrates how a semiotic assessment of interface signs' intuitiveness yielded a number of benefits. For instance, (i) it provides an overall idea of interface signs' intuitiveness to the end users to interpret the meaning of interface signs, (ii) it assists in finding usability problems and also in (iii) recommending possible solutions, (iv) provides background for introducing guidelines to design user-intuitive interface signs, (v) helps in constructing heuristic checklist from semiotics perspective to evaluate an application, (vi) no additional resource and extra budget are needed. This study also presents a list of methodological guidelines to obtain the perceived benefits of integrating semiotic perception in usability testing for practitioners.

DOI: 10.4018/978-1-4666-4046-7.ch007

ORGANIZATIONAL BACKGROUND

Assess our designs and test our systems to ensure that they actually behave as we expect and meet the requirements of the user (Dix, Finlay, Abowd, & Beale, 1998)

The user interface (UI) is a crucial as well as complicated component of computer applications. The activities of UI design and development are naturally costly as well as valuable (Janeiro, Barbosa, Springer, & Schill, 2009). Considering only the functional aspect to develop UI is not sufficient to optimize the user experience and usability of a computer application. In several cases, though usability aspects are considered as an additional and optional specification in UI design, but still usability lacks proper association with the functional aspects. However, to optimize the user experience and usability of an application it is rather important to consider usability aspect with each functional aspect to develop UI (Sousa & Furtado, 2005).

Again, from the point of view of users who need to use interactive as well as information intensive web applications, usability is considered as a vital aspect. Usability is also treated as a key quality of an application since high-quality and successful computer applications show a good level of usability. Designers always need to keep usability issues in their mind to design user interfaces of computer applications. In this vein, Greenberg & Buxton (2008) stated that "usability evaluation is one of the major cornerstones of user interface design" (Greenberg & Buxton, 2008). As a result, usability testing is treated as an important part of effective UI design process.

Despite many research efforts in UI design, it still lacks adequate focus on user interface objects like navigation links, buttons, icons, thumbnails, or other symbols, which are called in this chapter interface signs. Interface signs convey the presence of function, navigation, button, image, content, and the like, and are thus treated as the medium of users' interaction and communication with an application. An example of interface signs is presented in Figure 1. This figure presents a weekly calendar view page taken from an online calendar, Ovi calendar by Nokia (http://calendar.ovi.com; copyright © 2010 Nokia). A number of interface signs are marked by rectangles. These signs act as communication artefacts for users to provide information as well as to perform specific tasks with the Ovi calendar. For instance, interface signs '29 Nov – 5 Dec 2010' and 'week' (marked by ellipses) provide information that the current view of calendar body is presented as weekly view. A user needs to click on an interface sign 'month' (marked by an ellipse) to see the calendar body as monthly view.

As a result, interface signs need to be intuitive to the end users in order to maintain user satisfaction, to ensure understanding, or to provide the means to communicate (Bolchini, Chatterji, & Speroni, 2009; Speroni, 2006; Islam, 2008; de Souza,

Figure 1. Interface signs in a user interface retrieved on January 20, 2010 from http://calendar.ovi.com

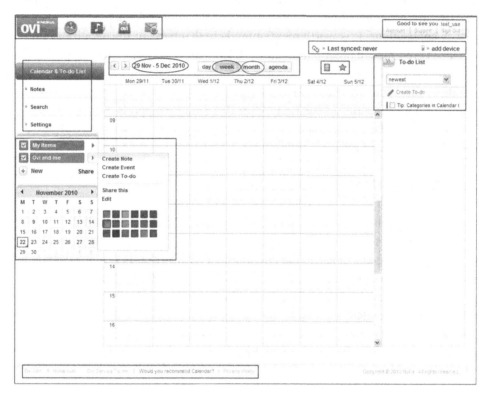

2005a; Islam, Ali, Al-Mamun, & Islam, 2010). In other words, designing user-intuitive interface signs is crucial for improving web usability. Designing intuitive interface sings focuses on sense production and interpretation and thereby involves semiotics, the doctrine of signs, that is, the science of signs (Peirce, 1932-58). A systematic review of semiotics research in UI, reported in Islam (2013), found that the most vital benefits achieved from semiotics research in UI were mainly related to the interface (application) design, users' satisfaction, users' task performance, applications' communicative quality, and uses in usability evaluation. Therefore interface signs are considered as critical elements of user interfaces to improve the application's usability. Considering the interface signs' intuitiveness in usability testing has become essential.

This research focuses on the user-intuitiveness of web interface sign in an attempt to assess the value of integrating the semiotics perspective into usability testing (UT). The research question is then: *What benefits are observed by integrating the semiotics perspective into usability testing?*

The goal of this research is to assess the applicability of integrating semiotics perception in UT and to find possible benefits of integrating semiotics perception in UT. Towards accomplishing this goal, a systematic empirical study was conducted on web applications. It is worth mentioning here that parts of this empirical study have been presented in other publications (Islam, 2011a; 2011b; Islam et al., 2012).

This chapter is structured as follows. Semiotics, interface signs, usability, and usability evaluation are discussed to provide a brief overview of the research background in the following sub-section. After that study method is presented with a brief discussion of the experiments that were conducted. Study results are discussed next. Conclusion and ideas for future work are provided in the final section.

Usability and Usability Evaluation

Usability is a quality feature of interactive systems. An ISO standard defines usability as the effectiveness, efficiency and satisfaction, with which specified users achieve specified goals in particular environments (ISO 9241-11). When designing interactive systems, designers and developers alike strive to build systems that are usable. Usability evaluation is the process during which designers and developers test, verify and validate the results of the design process. A usability evaluation method (UEM) is defined by ISO as any method that can be used to evaluate the usability of a system with respect to criteria such as effectiveness, efficiency and satisfaction of intended users.

Gulati and Dubey (2012) have identified 23 different evaluation methods, categorized as inspection techniques, testing techniques and inquiry techniques. While many usability evaluation methods exist and have been used by practitioners during many years, there is still on-going research to assess the performance of these methods and the need for new methods. For example, in a recent issue of the journal Behaviour & Information Technology (Stewart, 2009), five papers discuss the relevance of conducting usability evaluation within the intended context of use, a component-based usability questionnaire as a new evaluation method, a comparison of the think-aloud protocol with feedback collection, and so on. Assessment of UEMs is still today a relevant issue (Hornbaek, 2010). With this paper, we contribute to the field by proposing a semiotics perception that can enhance the effectiveness of current usability evaluation methods.

Semiotics and Interface Signs

We live in world full of signs. Whatever our eyes take in is pervaded by signs, ranging from traffic signs to the constellation of stars in the night sky; from the silhouette of a mother's image in our dreams to the seven color bands of the rainbow. . . . Conceiving of a world without signs is impossible. (Kim, 1996)

Semiotics is defined as the study of signs and signification. Semiotics is concerned with how human mind generates, communicates and codifies the meaning of a sign. Semioticians are study the what, why and *how*, of Signs (Danesi, 2007). A complete definition of semiotics could be "the study of signs, signification, and signifying systems" (Robert, Robert, & Sandy, 1992).

The notion of "sign" is central in semiotics. A sign is loosely defined as a pattern of data which, when perceived, brings to mind something other than itself (Dillman, 2012). It generally takes the "form of words, images, sounds, odours, flavours, acts or objects and even gestures" (Chandler, 2002). These things are considered as a sign when it provides a meaning to somebody in some respect or capacity. Thus a sign becomes a sign only when we (as designers) invest them with meaning (Chandler, 2002; Morris, 1938).

Ferdinand de Saussure and Charles S. Peirce are considered the fathers of semiotics. Their models are presented here to provide a concise idea about semiotics. In De Saussure's (1965) terms, a semiotic model consists of a *signifier* and a *signified* in the form of a dyad. The *signifier* is the form the sign takes in some material form such as words, shapes, and the like; and the *signified* is the concept in somebody's mind. The traffic light sign for 'stop' (red light on) exemplifies the semiotic model of de Saussure as it consists of a red light facing traffic at an intersection as *signifier*, whereas the driver obtains the concept in the form of the obligation to stop the car as *signified*.

According to Peirce's model (Peirce, 1932-58), semiotics is based on the notion of signs as triadic relations between the following three entities:

- **The representamen:** The form the sign takes to stand to somebody for something in some respect,
- **An interpretant:** Is the sense made of the sign created in the mind of the perceiver, and
- **An object:** Is the actual thing to which the sign refers.

The traffic light sign for 'stop' (red light on) exemplifies the semiotic model of Peirce as it consists of a red light facing traffic at an intersection as the *representamen,* car stopping as the *object*, and the idea obtained by the driver that a red light indicates that vehicles must stop as the *interpretant*.

A user interface of a computer application encompasses a number of signs on the interface between user and computer. Designers design the interface signs as an encoded form to provide the information or services. The end users need to decode these signs to obtain the desired information or services. Thus, users can perform the desired task properly when end user's interpretant matches the referential object of the interface signs with the designer's interpretant, and incorrectly otherwise.

Based on the accuracy level of user interpretation with respect to the designer's intended (assigned) meaning of an interface sign, the users' interpretations of interface signs (Figure 2) are here classified into: (a) *accurate* - user's interpretation completely matches the designer's interpretation and this category reflects semiotics theory, (b) *moderate* – the user interprets more than one distinct object, one of which was the right one about the interface signs and the probability to obtain the right object at the first attempt may be less than the accurate interpretation (for example, if a user proceeds with a sign to obtain a particular object but the sign does not really stand for that), (c) *conflicting* – the user interprets more than one distinct object in his/her mind about the interface signs and the user is confused about choosing the right object that will match the designer's intention, (d) *erroneous* - user's interpretation referred to a completely different object other than the designer's intended meaning, and (e) *incapable* - user was not able to interpret the interface sign at all. This categorization was adopted in this experiment to analyze and synthesize the study data.

SETTING THE STAGE

Three different experiments were conducted sequentially (see Figure 3). The experiments' primary purpose was to reveal usability problems and to find solutions to those problems.

The experiments were designed as follows:

- In experiment 1 (exp1), a usability test was conducted on a web application, the Ovi Calendar by Nokia (http://calender.ovi.com), during early 2010 at the usability testing laboratory of Åbo Akademi University, Finland. This experiment was conducted with four participants from different educational institutions in Finland.
- In experiment 2 (exp2), two user tests, Interface Sign Intuitive Test (ISIT) – see test description below - and a conventional think-aloud usability test, were conducted sequentially on a web application, the Ovi Calendar by Nokia (http://calender.ovi.com), during late 2010 at usability testing laboratory of Åbo Akademi University, Finland. This experiment was conducted with seven participants from different educational institutions in Finland.

- In experiment 3 (exp3), three user tests, Interface Sign Intuitive Test (ISIT1), a conventional think-aloud usability test, and a second Interface Sign Intuitive Test (ISIT2), were conducted sequentially on an e-health application. This application is designed as a support tool for daily use in homecare in Finland. This experiment was conducted with four health care professional as test subjects in Finland during late 2011.

Finally, systematically collected data from these experiments were synthesized, examined and compared to observe the value of integrating semiotics perception in usability testing as well as to provide reflection on the methodological approach for practical implications.

Two types of user tests (Usability Test – UT and Interface Sign Intuitive Test – ISIT) were designed to be used in the above experiments as separate or integrated.

1. *Usability Test (UT)* was performed following a think-aloud method (Hertzman & Jacobsen, 2003; Nielsen, 1993) to observe how users perform the given tasks and to find the usability problems. The discount usability testing approach was followed in this test. The approach involves testing only a small number of participants to yield reliable results, thus limiting costs and time. Research shows that carefully designed usability testing with five participants might reveal 80% of the usability problems (Nielsen, 1994). Even though discount usability evaluation is not guaranteed to find a large portion of the usability

Figure 2. Possible interpretations of a web interface sign 'faculties'

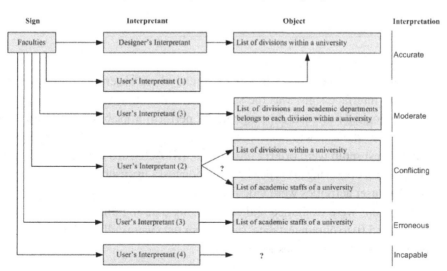

Figure 3. Structure of our experiments' methods

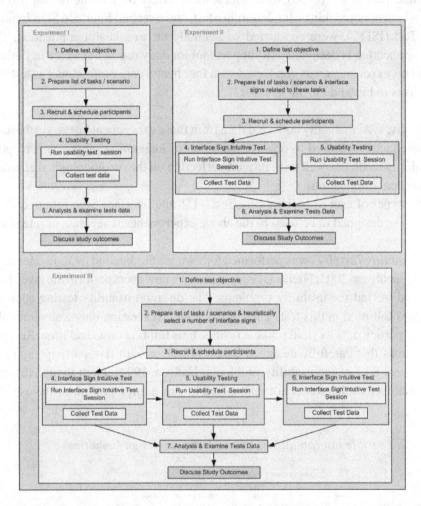

problems (Faulkner, 2003); in this research, where observing users interacting with interface signs was the scope of evaluation, it was sufficient to use 4-7 participants in each experiment. To perform a usability test with each participant, the following activities were followed: (i) The given application and the test setup were briefly introduced. (ii) Activities during test sessions consisted of observing users performing their tasks in a usability test laboratory. (iii) Test user activities were video-recorded. (iv) The video recordings of the test sessions were examined and coded using data-logging software (Noldus Observer 5.0) to obtain test data. (v) Further data were collected from pre-test, post-ask and post-test questionnaires.

2. Interface Sign Intuitive Test (ISIT) was conducted to understand users' interpretations of interface signs and their interpretation accuracy. This user intuitive test was conducted mainly through user interviewing. The main reasons for choosing interviewing were (Teoh, 2012): interviews need few facilities, are easy to organize, enjoyable, as well as a good way to obtain in-depth information. User interviews were conducted one by one following the think-aloud method (Lewis, 1982). At the beginning of the test, the interviewer gave a very short introduction to the participant regarding the purposes of the interview and the web applications being tested. In ISIT, a number of signs were presented to the test subjects; test subjects were asked to tell for every sign: (i) what they thought the sign meant or what action would happen from it, (ii) why they thought as they thought, and (iii) how confident they were about their interpretation. Finally, we classified their interpretations with respect to the designer's intended meaning as *accurate*, *moderate*, *conflicting*, *erroneous*, and *incapable* (an example of this classification is presented in Figure 2). During the test session, the interviewer was careful of two main things: (i) to prompt the user to keep up the flow of comments and (ii) to provide help when necessary. The interviewer was always alert while prompting and helping, to avoid distorting the results. For example, if someone missed any important interface element, then a word from the interviewer helped them to focus their attention right on it. The interview sessions were video-recorded. Later the video recordings of the interview sessions were examined to obtain data of users' interpretations of interface signs.

CASE DESCRIPTION

The first experiment (exp1) was treated as a control group in this empirical study and was left alone. The data in the two other experiments (exp2 and exp3) were compared in an attempt to observe the benefits that were obtained by integrating semiotics perception in usability testing. In this section, firstly we summarized the observed benefit in Table 1 and then each benefit is discussed elaborately. To discuss a benefit we firstly stated the benefit and its importance in usability evaluation. After that, we present an example from the study experiments to provide (i) a concise idea of stated benefit, and (ii) the procedural (methodological) way of obtaining this benefit.

B1: Provided an overall idea of interface signs' intuitiveness to the end users.

An accurate interpretation of interface sign leads users to access the desired information or to perform a specific task properly (e.g., with satisfaction, effectively, without making an error, and the like). Few basic properties of interface signs are:

1.   Different users may interpret an interface sign in a different way and refer to the several objects rather than to a single object (Islam, 2012a; 2012b).
2.   Multiple signs may refer to the same object rather than multiple objects, i.e., there is no one-to-one link between the sign and its object (Frege, 1879).
3.   Signs in a web user interface are recommended to be designed in a one-to-one fashion. In other words, a sign needs to be consistent to represent particular information or function (as an object) throughout the entire website to obtain better user experiences (Islam, 2008).

These properties make it clear that designers need to choose the most appropriate sign so that end users may easily interpret its meaning to perform their tasks properly. Therefore, observing the intuitiveness of interface signs to the end users is important to evaluate an application's usability. In this vein, we can assume that if we compare two identical applications which are identical in all other design aspects (e.g., navigation, information architecture, etc.) except the interface signs, then the application having more intuitive interface signs will show better usability than the another one. Our study observed that the exp-2 and exp-3, where semiotics perception is integrated by conducting a user test (ISIT), provides an overall idea of interface signs' intuitiveness to the end users.

Table 1. List of benefits obtained from the experiments

	Benefits	Exp1	Exp2	Exp3
B1	Provided an overall idea of interface signs' intuitiveness to the end users	-	X	X
B2	Conveyed understandability (improving the users' interpretation accuracy) of interface signs	-	-	X
B3	Indicated how learnable the applications are by the real users	-	-	X
B4	Helped to find usability problems and recommend possible solutions	-	X	X
B5	Gave background for introducing guidelines to design user-intuitive interface signs	-	X	X
B6	Helped in constructing checklists from semiotics perspective for heuristic evaluation	-	X	X
B7	Received customer's contentment	-	*	X
B8	No additional resources or extra budget is needed	-	X	X

*: The usability report of exp2 was not sent to the customer/developer, thus we could not observe the possibility of getting this benefit from exp2.

Let us discuss a simple example from exp2 to show how integrating semiotics perception in UT obtained this benefit (B1). Users' interpretations data collected from ISIT were classified into accurate, moderate, conflicting, erroneous, and incapable. This classification bases on the accuracy level of user interpretation with respect to the designer's interpretation of an interface sign. Examples of users' interpretations for five interface signs of Ovi calendar and its accuracy classification is showed in Figure 4. This accuracy classification showed how their interpretation varied comparing to the original (designer's) meaning. Data of users' interpretations of interface signs are then summarized in a tabular format. A complete synthesized view of data related to users' interpretation accuracy is presented in Table 2. A number of observations related to the interface signs intuitiveness to the end users came out from this synthesized data. Examples of these include:

- On average, about one third of total signs (30.22%) of Ovi calendars were inaccurately interpreted by the test participants.
- Users were unable to interpret the meaning of interface signs (*Incapable* interpretations) for a very limited number of signs (M=3.86 & SD=2.41).
- Almost a similar outcome was observed for the *Erroneous* interpretations of interface signs (M=3.57 & SD =2.51).
- For users' inaccurate interpretations of interface signs, the maximum number of interpretations belonged to the *Moderate* (M=13.57 & SD = 2.99) and *Erroneous* (M=10.43 & SD= 3.87).
- Maximum number of accurate interpretations (75.96%) was observed for the participant P3, whereas P2 showed maximum inaccuracy (37.50%) in interpreting the interface signs.

Thus the integration of semiotics perception in UT provides an overall idea of users' interpretations of the intended/referential meaning of interface signs.

B2: Conveyed understandability (improving the users' interpretations accuracy) of interface signs.
B3: Indicated how learnable the applications are by the real users.

A user interface encompasses a number of interface signs that act as communication artifacts for human to interact with the application. For end users, a proper interpretation of interface sign is the prerequisite for understanding the logic of the application, for learning to use the application, and for having a satisfactory use experience, among others (Salgado et at., 2009; de Souza et al., 2006; de Souza & Cypher, 2008). Moreover, learnability is defined as the capability of application's

Figure 4. An example of user's interpretations of an interface sign and its categorizations

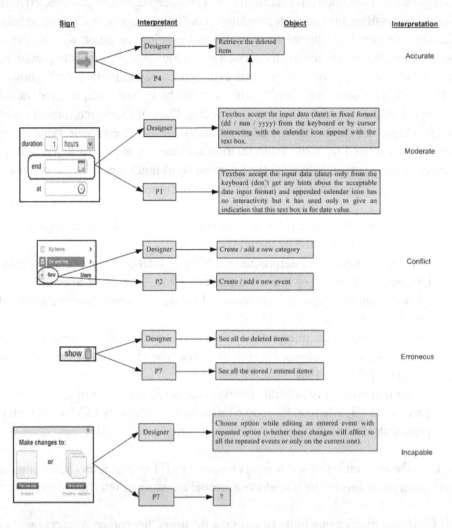

user interface to enable end users to learn it quickly and effectively measured by learning time (Usability first, 2012). Since learning depends on the capability of UI and interface signs are considered as communication artifacts of UI, this implies that accurate interpretation or proper understanding of interface signs provides an indication of system's learnability. Our study showed that the integration of semiotics perception in UT conveys understandability (improving the accuracy of user interpretation) of interface signs. As a consequence it also provides an indication of applications' learnability by the real users. In other words, it showed the ease as well as the efficiency to learn the communication artifact (interface sign).

Table 2. Participants' interpretations of interface signs

Participant	Accurate	Inaccurate				Accuracy (%)	Inaccuracy (%)
		Moderate	Conflict	Erroneous	Incapable		
P1	67	18	3	12	4	64.42	35.58
P2	65	13	8	16	2	62.50	37.50
P3	79	16	0	8	1	75.96	24.04
P4	73	14	5	4	8	70.19	29.81
P5	71	14	3	11	5	68.27	31.73
P6	77	11	2	9	5	74.04	25.96
P7	76	9	4	13	2	73.08	26.92
Mean	72.57	13.57	3.57	10.43	3.86	69.78	30.22
SD	5.22	2.99	2.51	3.87	2.41	-	-

Figure 5. Learning effect: interpretations accuracy level changed within the users' inaccurate interpretations (left figure) and increased interpretations' accuracy (right figure)

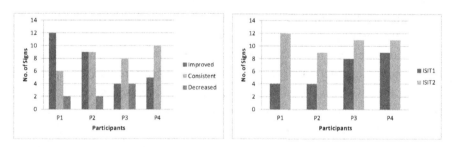

Let us discuss a simple example from exp3 to show how integrating semiotics perception in UT obtained benefit B2 and B3. The improvement of user interpretation accuracy data were obtain by observing the differences between (i) the users' interpretations accuracy observed in ISIT1 (ISIT conducted before the UT), and (ii) the users' interpretations accuracy observed in ISIT2 (ISIT conducted after the UT). Experiment data were synthesized to observe this improvement through the following ways (see Figure 5).

- Interpretations accuracy level changed within the users' inaccurate interpretations - these changes were grouped into three ways: (i) improved, that is, the interpretation accuracy changed from *Conflicting* to *Moderate*, *Incapable* to *Conflicting/Moderate*, *Erroneous* to *Conflicting/Moderate;* (ii) consistent, that is, the *Conflicting* and *Moderate* interpretations remain consistent in both ISIT1 and ISIT2, and accuracy changed from *Erroneous* to *Incapable* and *Incapable* to *Erroneous;* and (iii) decreased (e.g., interpretations accuracy changed from *Moderate* to *Conflicting/Incapable/Erroneous, Conflicting* to *Incapable/Erroneous*).

- Interpretations' accuracy changed - Users' interpretation accuracy changed in ISIT2, that is, the differences of users' *accurate* interpretations observed in ISIT1 and ISIT2.

The exp3 showed that users' inaccurate interpretations averagely improved by 42% in average, remained consistent by 47%, and decreased by 11%. Users' accurate interpretations increased for each participant and the accurate interpretations were 26% in ISIT1 and 47% in ISIT2.

B4: Helped to find usability problems and recommend possible solutions.

Finding usability problems is one of the central goals of every usability evaluation method. In some cases it may happen that evaluators may fail to identify the main reasons for a particular usability problem in UT. As a consequence, their recommendation does not focus on the definite point that creates the problem. Thus all clues pointing to the issue at hand as well as recommending the solution to the problem are very important for the evaluators. To perform a specific task, the user needs to interact with the interface signs. Therefore user interpretations' accuracy of these signs is considered as a hub to observe user behavior to identify usability problems and recommend solutions. Integrating semiotics perception in UT provides a clear idea of users' interpretations accuracy to grasp the meaning of interface signs. Therefore, exp2 and exp3, where users were observed based on the accuracy of interpretation, showed the possibility of getting support to find usability problems and recommend possible solutions to these problems.

Let us discuss a simple example from exp2 to show how integrating semiotics perception in UT obtained benefit B4. Data obtained from both tests (ISIT and UT) in exp2 were analyzed and synthesized to observe the following three issues:

1. Users' understanding (accuracy level) in interpreting the intended meaning of interface signs,
2. Users' behaviors to perform a specific task with respect to his understanding (accuracy level) of the task-related interface signs, and
3. Usability problems raised by users' inaccurate interpretations.

To observe these, the following steps were followed for each participant:

1. Firstly, re-viewed the data of user's interpretation of task-related interface signs.
2. Then, observed user's behavior to interact with a task-related sign, while his understanding for that sign was not accurate.
3. After that, observed how user's behavior (observed in step b) leads to usability problems.

Thus semiotics perception integration with UT helps to find the usability problems and also to recommend possible solutions to these problems. Let us show an example from exp2. The date input text boxes on event entry page (see Figure 6) accepts data (date) in two ways: (i) by keyboard, and (ii) also by cursor via interacting with the calendar icon appended besides the text boxes. A participant thought that the text boxes accept input data (date) only by keyboard. He also thought that the appended calendar icon has no interactivity but it was used only to give an indication that this text box is for date value. Therefore, he entered the date value into the text boxes in two different formats. In Figure 6, the square marked shows his date input, above two rectangles show the incorrect date format and below one show the correct one. As a result of saving the incorrect input, it obviously led to an input error and this input error generated a system error and failed to perform this task at the first attempt. Then, these failures and errors led him to ask for help twice, and spend time at confused and wrong navigation state for 32 seconds. These eventually directed him to make the navigational errors and also to increase interact variation (51.85%). As a consequence, these comparatively increased his task completion time (8:26, whereas minimum time was 2:57) and finally these also affected his subjective rating (rate to 3; where satisfaction score was give as 1: *very satisfied* to 5: *not at all*). The user's behavior observed here showed two things:

- An inaccurate interpretation of a task-related interface sign is significantly aligned with a usability problem and as a consequence it affects on the application's overall usability. Figure 7 depicts how a test participant encounters problems to perform a task because of inaccurate interpretation of interface sign. Here, two nodes linked with one side arrow means arrow sided node affected by other side node. For example, inaccurate sign interpretation affected input error, and this input error eventually affected interaction variation and this eventually affected task completion time, and so on.
- A few important considerations of sign representation from semiotics point of view. These are: (i) do not provide any hints about acceptable date format; and (ii) text boxes accept data in both ways (keyboard and icon). Therefore, when user uses the calendar icon then by default date is entered into the text

Figure 6. Snapshot of Ovi calendar retrieved on November, 2010 from http://calendar. ovi.com (above one) and examples of possible re-designs (below two)

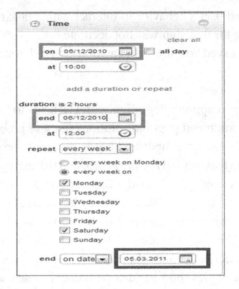

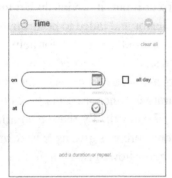 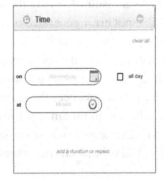

boxes as acceptable format and when user uses keyboard then he chose the date format arbitrarily (possibly the format he/she is more familiar with).

There could several solutions to this problem by redesigning these signs semiotically. Among these, one solution could be to append an indicative sign to provide an idea of acceptable input date and time format for text boxes (see the two lower snapshots in Figure 7). This presentation could make sense to the user and lead them to enter the accurate date and time by keyboard. As a consequence, this re-design obviously reduced input error, system error as well as increased the overall task completion performance.

B5: Gave background for introducing guidelines to design user-intuitive interface signs.

B6: Helped in constructing checklists from semiotics perspective for heuristic evaluation.

The ultimate purpose of a computer application is to improve user performance (Mayhew, 1992). Numerous user interface guidelines as well as principles have been identified to enhance application's usability standard so that human performance can be improved (Ford & Gelderblom, 2003). Most of these guidelines and principles focus on designing system interface, mostly covering navigational issues, contents, information architectures, and the like, which are encapsulated into the fundamental usability design approach of User Centered Design (UCD). Unfortunately a very limited number of guidelines are available that focus user-intuitive interface sign design. Thus producing semiotics considerations as design guidelines seems a good contribution to enhance application's usability. The design guidelines can also be used as heuristics checklists that might be used as an additional toolkit to evaluate an application heuristically. Our study observed that the exp2 and exp3, where

Figure 7. User's inaccurate interpretations lead to usability problems and affect overall web usability

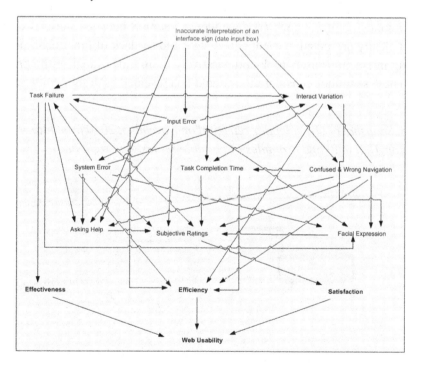

semiotics perception was integrated by user tests (ISIT), introduced guidelines as well as produced heuristic checklist to design and evaluate interface signs.

Let us discuss a simple example from exp2 to show how integrating semiotics perception in UT obtained benefit B5 and B6. Systematically collected data from both tests were analyzed and examined from semiotics perspective to observe the same things and followed the same steps as stated above (in benefit B3). However, after finding the usability problem based on users' inaccurate interpretations of task-related signs, we enumerated important considerations of designing the interface signs to reduce usability problems from semiotics point of view. These considerations might be treated as design guidelines to design user-intuitive interface signs and also be used as a heuristic checklist. Heuristics checklist produced from these guidelines could be used in heuristics evaluation to check whether it adheres to the semiotics design principle or not. Let us show an example from exp2. At event entry page of Ovi Calendar (see Figure 8, left one), the check box appended with "all day" sign (marked by rectangle) is always shown as selected by default. The input text box appended beside a linguistic sign "at" and an iconic sign of time (marked by rectangle) showed consistently enable to take input data. Since the system selected the "all day" option by default, this time entry input box was not accepting any input data. Users tried for comparatively long time by clicking on the text box and also the time icon. These increased their interaction variation. They were despaired. These eventually led them to complete the task with worse performance. The users' behavior observed here show two important considerations of sign representation from semiotics point of view: (i) dependency relation between these two signs were not clearly presented in event entry page; and (ii) lack of functional message for wrong interactions users took comparatively more time to realize the problem he did. These semiotics considerations could be presented as design guidelines as:

Figure 8. Snapshot of Ovi calendar retrieved on November, 2010 from http://calendar.ovi.com (left one) and examples of possible re-designs (right one)

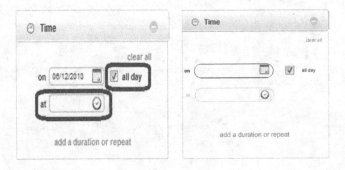

1. Present clearly the dependency relation (if present) among interface signs.
2. Provide understandable message for wrong interaction with an interface sign.

These semiotics considerations could also be presented as checklist for heuristic evaluation as:

1. Are all the dependency relations among interface signs of the application present clearly?
2. Does the application provide understandable message for a wrong interaction with an interface sign?

Among a set of semiotic ways to solve this problem one solution could be to present the input time entry box, and its appended signs as disabled. An example is presented in Figure 8 (on the right). This presentation could make sense to the user to understand the reasons of disabling this (time entry) sign. This would eventually increase task completion performance. Again for a wrong interaction with the time input box and time icon while "all day" are selected, providing a proper message like *"please clear the 'all day' check box"* could be another useful solution to realize the problem user did.

B7: Received customer's contentment.

Getting feedback for every work is important, because it really can improve work. Positive feedback obtained from the customer/developer is expected to motivate practitioners to their work, to support the method employed in UT, and also to show the customer satisfaction with their evaluation results. Exp3, where semiotics perception was integrated in UT, received customer's contentment for the testing method and evaluation report.

Let us discuss a simple example from exp3 to show how integrating semiotics perception in UT obtained benefit B7. The usability testing report of exp3 was received by the project customer of the application with content. One representative of the project customer was part of the testing team and saw how semiotics was applied in the usability test. We asked the project customer for feedback on the importance of using semiotics evaluation as part of the usability test; for instance, the project customer stated that "… mielestäni ikonien testaaminen oli hieno lisä tähän käytettävyyden arviointiin…." ("… I think sign testing was a great addition to the usability evaluation…."). From a practitioner's point of view, this demonstrated that sign testing was an applicable method in the given context.

B8: No additional resources or extra budget is needed.

It is a great challenge for the usability practitioners and customers to conduct an integrated usability testing without asking for any additional budget or resources. Some people may think that performing a user test for usability evaluation is very complex and costly and this test is applicable only for a very limited web design project with a vast budget and a plentiful time schedule (Nielsen, 2000). In our study, both exp2 and exp3 showed that integrating semiotics perception in UT does not imply additional resources and extra budget; whereas this integration method produced a number of benefits that contribute to the usability evaluation.

Let us discuss few experimental issues from exp2 and exp3 to show how integrating semiotics perception in UT obtained benefit B8. In our exp2 and exp3, we conducted the sign test(s) and a usability test sequentially in each session with a short break for each participant. In exp2, the ISIT test last for 18-22 minutes per test session where a total 114 interface signs were presented. Again in exp3, the ISIT tests last for 5-8 minutes per test session where a total 24 interface signs were presented. Thus, our study findings showed that the only resource that this integrated approach demands is testing time. Other resources like laboratory equipment, number of test participants, and data analysis software (observer 5.0) remained identical in all three experiments.

SOLUTIONS AND RECOMMENDATIONS

In this empirical study, we conducted three experiments to observe the value and the applicability of integrating semiotics perception in usability testing. This study showed that (i) it is possible to obtain a number of benefits that contribute to the usability evaluation, and (ii) we could construct some methodological guidelines for practitioners to obtain these benefits. In a nutshell, integrating a semiotics perception into usability testing:

- Provides an overall idea of interface signs' intuitiveness to the end users to interpret the meaning of interface signs properly (*B1*),
- Conveys the understandability (improving the users' interpretations accuracy) of interface signs (*B2*),
- Indicates how learnable the applications are by the real users (*B3*),
- Helps to find usability problems and recommend possible solutions (*B4*),
- Gives background for introducing guidelines to design user-intuitive interface signs (*B5*),
- Helps in constructing checklists from a semiotics perspective for heuristic evaluation (*B6*),

- Receives customer's contentment (*B7*), and
- Requires no additional resources or extra funds (*B8*).

Again, the examples discussed provide methodological guidelines for the usability practitioners to design an UT experiment integrating semiotics perception and obtain the perceived benefits. It was also observed that few benefits (i.e. *B2* and *B3*) were not obtained from both the exp2 and exp3 because the experiments were designed differently. Practitioners need to design the experiment based on their test objectives. For instance, if evaluators want to obtain benefits *B2* and *B3* then an experiment design similar to exp2 will not produce the results for them. In that case practitioners may plan and conduct (i) an experiment like exp3 or (ii) an iterative experiment of exp2 and then compare the users' interpretations accuracy data to the previous ISIT's data to observe the improvement of users' interpretation accuracy (*B2*) and getting an indication of applications learnability from semiotics perspective (*B3*).

Moreover, this experiment also showed few directions for conducting future research. For instance: (i) a semiotic-based conceptual framework for interface design and evaluation is essential to improve the usability evaluation, thus an extensive empirical study might be designed and employed to propose this framework; (ii) this study provides to usability practitioners a methodological approach that can be used and applied in other domains; (iii) assessing the significance of considering cultural issues in semiotics research to design and evaluate web interface; and (iv) conducting a similar study on mobile web/apps might be another appealing area of further research, and the like.

REFERENCES

Bolchini, D., Chatterji, R., & Speroni, M. (2009). Developing heuristics for the semiotics inspection of websites. In *Proc. of the 27th ACM international conference on Design of Communication (SIGDOC 2009)* (pp. 67-71). Indiana, USA: ACM Press. Retrieved from http://doi.acm.org/10.1145/1621995.1622009

Chandler, D. (2002). *Semiotics: The basics*. London, UK: Routledge. doi:10.4324/9780203166277

Danesi, M. (2007). *The quest for meaning: A guide to semiotic theory and practice*. Toronto: University of Toronto Press.

De Saussure, F. (1965). *Course in general linguistics* (Baskin, W., Trans.). New York, NY: McGraw-Hill.

de Souza, C. S., & Cypher, A. (2008). Semiotic engineering in practice: Redesigning the CoScripter interface. In *Proceedings of the working conference on Advanced Visual Interfaces (AVI 2008)* (pp. 165-172). Napoli, Italy: ACM Press. Retrieved from http://doi.acm.org/10.1145/1385569.1385597

de Souza, C. S., Leitão, C. F., Prates, R. O., & da Silva, E. J. (2006). The semiotic inspection method. In *Proc. of VII Brazilian symposium on Human Factors in Computing Systems (IHC 2006),* (pp. 148-157). Natal, RN, Brazil: ACM Press. Retrieved from http://doi.acm.org/10.1145/1298023.1298044

de Souze, C. S. (2005). *The semiotic engineering of human-computer interaction.* Cambridge, MA: The MIT Press.

Dillman, R. W. (2012). Tutorial: Signs and language. Retrieved May, 2012 from http://www.rdillman.com/HFCL/TUTOR/Semiotics/sem1.html

Dix, A., Finlay, J., Abowd, G., & Beale, R. (1998). *Human-computer interaction* (2nd ed.). Hertfordshire, UK: Prentice Hall.

Faulkner, L. (2003). Beyond the five-user assumption: Benefits of increased sample sizes in usability testing. *Behavior Research Methods, Instruments, & Computers*, *35*(3), 379–383. doi:10.3758/BF03195514

Ford, G., & Gelderblom, H. (2003). The effects of culture on performance achieved through the use of human computer interaction. In *Proceedings of the 2003 annual research conference of the South African institute of computer scientists and information technologists on Enablement through technology* (SAICSIT 2003) (pp. 218-230). Republic of South Africa.

Greenberg, S., & Buxton, B. (2008). Usability evaluation considered harmful (some of the time). In *ACM Conference on Human Factors in Computing Systems (CHI 2008)* (pp. 111-120). Florence, Italy: ACM Press.

Gulati, A., & Dubey, S. (2012). Critical analysis on usability evaluation techniques. *International Journal of Engineering Science and Technology*, *4*(3), 990–997.

Hertzum, M., & Jacobsen, N. E. (2003). The evaluator effect: A chilling fact about usability evaluation methods. *International Journal of Human-Computer Interaction*, *15*(1), 183–204. doi:10.1207/S15327590IJHC1501_14

Hornbæk, K. (2010). Dogmas in the assessment of usability of evaluation methods. *Behaviour & Information Technology*, *29*(1), 97–111. doi:10.1080/01449290801939400

Islam, M.N. (2008). Semiotics of the web interface: Analysis and guidelines. *Journal of Computer Science and Technology (JCS&T)*, *8*(3), 166-167.

Islam, M. N. (2011a). A semiotics perspective to web usability: An empirical case study. In *Proc. of IADIS International Conference on Interface and Human Computer Interaction (IHCI 2011)* (pp. 19-28). Rome, Italy: IADIS.

Islam, M. N. (2011b). Beyond users' inaccurate interpretations of web interface signs: A semiotic perception. In *Proc. of the IFIP 13th International Conference on Informatics and Semiotics in Organizations (ICISO 2011)* (pp. 31-40). Leeuwarden, The Netherlands: Fryske Akademy.

Islam, M. N. (2012a). Semiotics perception towards designing users' intuitive web user interface: A Study on web sign redesign. In Hakkikur, (Eds.), *Knowledge and technologies in innovative information systems* (pp. 139–155). Berlin, Germany: Springer Verlag. doi:10.1007/978-3-642-33244-9_10

Islam, M. N. (2012b). Towards designing users' intuitive web interface. In *Proc. of the 6th International Conference on Complex, Intelligent, and Software Intensive Systems (CISIS-2012)* (pp.513-518). Palermo, Italy: IEEE CS.

Islam, M. N. (2013). *A systematic literature review of semiotics perception in user interfaces. Accepted to be published in Journal of Systems and Information Technology (JSIT), 15(1)*. UK: Emerald Publishers.

Islam, M. N., Ali, M., Al-Mamun, A., & Islam, M. (2010). Semiotics explorations on designing the information intensive web interfaces. *International Arab Journal of Information Technology*, 7(1), 45–54.

Islam, M. N., Tetard, F., Reijonen, P., & Tarkkanen, K. (2012). Integrating semiotics perception in usability testing: A light-weighted experiment on an e-health application. In *Proc. of IADIS International Conference on Interface and Human Computer Interaction (IHCI 2012)* (pp. 141-148). Lisbon, Portugal: IADIS.

ISO 9241 -11. (1998). Guidance on usability standards. Retrieved September, 2012 from http://www.iso.org/iso/iso_catalogue/Catalogue _tc/catalogue_detail. htm?csnumber=16883

Janeiro, J., Barbosa, S. D., Springer, T., & Schill, A. (2009). Enhancing user interface design patterns with design rationale structures. In *Proceedings of the 27th ACM international conference on Design of communication (SIGDOC 2009)* (pp. 9-16). Indiana, USA: ACM Press.

Kim, K. L. (1996). *Caged in our own signs: A book about semiotics*. Berkeley, CA: Greenwood.

Lewis, C. (1982). *Using the thinking-aloud method in cognitive interface design. IBM Research Report RC 9265*. NY: Yorktown Heights.

Mayhew, D. (1992). *Principles and guidelines in software user interface design.* NJ: Prentice Hall.

Morris, C. (1938). Foundations of the theory of signs. R. Carnap et al. (Eds.), *International Encyclopedia of Unified Science*, 2:1. Chicago: The University of Chicago Press.

Nielsen, J. (1993). *Usability engineering*. London, UK: Academic Press.

Nielsen, J. (1994). Guerrilla HCI: Using discount usability engineering to penetrate the intimidation barrier. In Bias, R. G., & Mayhew, D. S. (Eds.), *Cost-justifying usability* (pp. 245–272). Boston, MA: Academic Press.

Nielsen, J. (2000). Why you only need to test with 5 users. *Alert box*. Retrieved May, 2012 from http://www.useit.com/alertbox/20000319.html

Peirce, C. S. (1932-52). *Collected writings (8 Vols.)*. Charles Hartshorne, Paul Weiss & Arthur Burks (Eds.). Harvard University Press.

Robert, S., Robert, B., & Sandy, F. L. (1992). *New vocabularies in film semiotics: Structuralism, post-structuralism and beyond*. London: Routledge, Taylor & Francis.

Salgado, L. C. d-C, de Souza, C.S., & Leitão, C. F. (2009). *A semiotic inspection of ICDL*. Monografias em Ciência da Computação, No. 31/09. ISSN: 0103-9741.

Sousa, K., & Furtado, E. (2005). From usability tasks to usable user interfaces. In *Proceedings of the 4th international workshop on Task models and diagrams (TAMODIA 2005)* (pp.103 – 110).Gdansk, Poland: ACM Press.

Speroni, M. (2006).*Mastering the semiotics of information-intensive web interfaces*. (Unpublished doctoral dissertation). Faculty of Communication Sciences, University of Lugano, Switzerland.

Stewart, T. (2009). Usability evaluation. *Behaviour & Information Technology, 28*(2), 99–100. doi:10.1080/01449290902786510

Teoh, C. (2012).User interviews – a basic introduction. Retrieved May 3, 2012, from http://www.webcredible.co.uk/user-friendly-resources/web-usability/user-interviews.shtml

Usability first. (2012). Website. Retrieved March, 2012 from http://www.usability-first.com/glossary/learnability/

KEY TERMS AND DEFINITIONS

Interface Sign: User interfaces of computer applications encompass a number of navigational links, command buttons, images, symbols, logos, etc. These have a referential/intended meaning that refers to another object. Therefore these user interface elements are defined as interface signs. For instance, the interface sign 'Admission' in a university web user interface stands for providing admission information for prospective students.

Semiotics: The central concept of semiotics is the concept of 'sign.' Therefore, semiotics is mainly concerned with sign, signification, and signifying systems. In other words, semiotics is defined as the study of signs and its process of signification.

Sign: Anything like a sound, a word, an image, etc. can be defined as a sign if it refers to some object rather than itself. For instance, the word 'EXIT' on a door inside a hall room provides an indication to use that door to leave the hall room. In this case, we may treat the word 'EXIT' as a sign.

Think-Aloud Method: The think-aloud method is a method used to encourage users to voice their thoughts while performing some actions. This method is often used in conjunction with usability evaluation methods as a means to gather insights in how users think about a product and the actions they perform with this product.

Usability: Usability, as defined by the ISO 9241 standard, is defined as the effectiveness, efficiency and satisfaction, with which specified users achieve specified goals in particular environments.

Usability Evaluation Method: A usability evaluation method is any method that can be used to evaluate the usability of a system with respect to criteria such as effectiveness, efficiency and satisfaction of intended users.

User-Intuitive Interface Sign: User-intuitive interface sign refers to an interface sign which is very easy as well as intuitive to the end users to interpret/understand the intended/referential meaning properly.

Section 2
Usability of Mobile Applications

Chapter 8
Developing the Intel® Pair & Share Experience

Joshua Boelter
Intel Corporation, USA

Cynthia Kaschub
Intel Corporation, USA

EXECUTIVE SUMMARY

Intel developed the Intel® Pair & Share application with dual purposes. The first purpose was to deliver a high quality user experience that allows users to share photos seamlessly from their smartphone or tablet to a PC. The second purpose was to serve as a real world application we could use to develop and document a set of best known methods for cross-device user experiences. In this chapter, the interdisciplinary approach taken is outlined to develop a cross-platform consumer software product that allows users to share pictures from iOS* and Android* devices to their Windows* PC. An initial question was posed, "What can we do to maintain PC relevance given the widespread use of smartphones?" This question eventually evolved into a much larger question, "What can we do to improve user experiences and interactions across all of users' devices?" In this rapidly changing landscape, the authors have seen the disruptive influence of smartphones and tablets on the consumer experience. Each platform has different user interface conventions and interactions that impact the user expectations. In turn, the authors have embraced the notion of cross-device, cross-platform connected user experiences and strive to create best–in-class applications that take advantage of the benefits of each platform.

*Other names and brands may be claimed as the property of others.

DOI: 10.4018/978-1-4666-4046-7.ch008

ORGANIZATION BACKGROUND

Intel has a long history of being a semiconductor manufacturing company, which to be successful has followed a few philosophies that have permeated our approach toward product development; Moore's Law (Moore, 1965) states that the processing power will double every two years and Copy Exactly! These mantras have served Intel extremely well when the emphasis and focus was solely on hardware manufacturing, which is largely hidden from the end user. In recent years, Intel has begun the journey toward the user with their products. Specifically, we have started to place emphasis on software and solutions that inherently bring Intel closer to the consumers and their user experience. The company's unprecedented focus on user experience will continue to benefit our consumers for years to come.

SETTING THE STAGE

Intel is amidst a transition from a PC computing company into a computing company that includes a significant effort on both software and solutions for consumers. The Intel® Pair & Share application was developed in a software group that is located within the PC Client Group. This is an interdisciplinary team that includes Software Architecture, Developers focused on prototypes, Human Factors Engineers, Interaction Designers, and Visual Designers. The key role of a software architect is to partner with key stakeholders to refine product architectures and identify future product opportunities. A prototype developer focuses on evaluating the software architecture and design, usage-driven path finding and evaluating technical constraints to promote the design and development of sound solutions via empirical analysis. A Human Factors Engineer uses what they know about human capabilities to design products, processes, and systems to improve ease of use, system performance, and user satisfaction. In contrast, an Interaction Designer focuses on creating product workflows that communicate its function to the user so they can complete their intended tasks. A Visual Designer is someone who develops visual materials to create an experience using elements of visual expression and style. These roles form a core team that works together to develop the user experience of a product incorporating technical constraints, stakeholder requirements, and end user needs into a product with a quality user experience. We have structured our product design and development around interdisciplinary teams that work together to iteratively develop products from a user perspective.

We define a cross-device experience as one in that a single user or multiple users are using the same (or compatible) application simultaneously on two or more connected devices in which the experience is more than the 'sum of the parts'. Examples include: sending a file directly from my phone to my PC; playing a multi-person game on our phones; using your phone as a remote control.

CASE DESCRIPTION

We wanted to create interactions that take place on both a smartphone and a PC, and together create a great user experience. This chapter will review how we include the users' needs into experience design through iterative concept and product testing throughout the development process (Nielsen, 1993). The targeted devices included phones, tablets and PCs with different operating systems, form factors and user interface guidelines. As we worked through various concept usages, we determined there were common interactions that needed to be completed repeatedly by users, regardless of the application they were using. The key questions we were faced with included:

- What sort of cross-device experiences do users desire?
- Is there more to cross-device experiences than just syncing?
- How do people find and connect to another device in the context of a single-user experience?
- How do people find and connect to another device in the context of a multi-user experience?
- What are users' mental models for how they would achieve their desired goal? For example, did users know that they needed the application on both devices to deliver the experience?
- Did users understand how to acquire applications on each device since each platform has a different method for acquiring applications?
- Did users know that this experience was delivered by an application as opposed to resident functionality (application) on the platform? For example, texting is a resident application on a smartphone whereas other applications must be downloaded from an application store.

The initial interaction of finding and connecting devices was a barrier for unlocking the experience we wanted to deliver to the user. We will discuss how we both directly and indirectly developed and tested these foundational elements of the experience flow in the context of the Intel Pair & Share application in addition to the development of the Intel Pair & Share application.

Figure 1. Product development phases

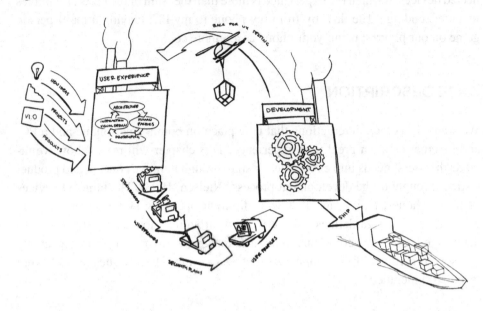

This chapter presents these steps in a linear fashion as discrete project phases, however, that is far from reality. Agile practices are adopted throughout and phases overlap, repeat and iterate as necessary on both a macro and micro level. While you will generally apply these techniques sequentially, you can think of these 'phases' as tools in your toolbox to apply to the problem at hand (see Figure 1).

Research Methods

Research methods fall along a continuum with qualitative methods at one end, and quantitative at the other. The choice of which method to use is dependent on a variety of factors such as research goals, product development timeline, cost, and team structure. The continuum of methods and terms will be introduced first, followed by a detailed review of how to choose methods, review of how we used focus groups, and steps to complete focus groups and the impact they had on our product direction.

Qualitative methods tend to be generative in nature and include gathering subjective feedback on specific concepts or subset of, from a relatively small number of people. Subjective feedback is data that is specific to an individual and is impacted by factors that are not consistently experienced across people (e.g., emotion and types of previous experience). Obtaining subjective feedback from a sample of users enables the product team to better understand some of the issues or concerns that people may have around a given concept. Examples of qualitative methods are focus groups (Kreuger & Casey, 2009), paper prototyping (Snyder, 2003), and in-home observations (Mateus et al., 1996). In contrast to qualitative research methods, quantitative methods tend to be evaluative in nature and include gathering objective data from a relatively large number of people so statistical inferences can be made. Objective feedback is data that can easily be compared across users in that it is observable performance behaviors that can be translated into summary statistics. Gathering objective data enables the product team to use inferential statistics to make informed product decisions. Examples of quantitative methods are experience sampling methodology, world-wide surveys, and in-field beta testing.

While this methodological continuum may seem daunting, there are a few simple guiding questions that can help. The factors that help narrow your methodological choices are all fairly interdependent but still important to think about before you make the decision. Start by asking the following questions:

- What is the product development timeline?
- What is your research goal?
- What is your research budget to achieve your goals?
- What skill sets do I have on my team to help me achieve my research goals?

Focus Groups

When we began, we did not have a specific product in mind. Instead, we were simply exploring the following question, "What can we do to maintain PC relevance given the widespread use of smartphones?" We recognized that the prevalence of smartphones and their respective applications had met a number of user needs. We also recognized that most users had relatively simple PC usages. Combined, these points led to two general industry perspectives. One perspective stated that faster smartphones would eventually lead to users no longer needing a PC. The other perspective stated that each platform had its respective advantages and disadvantages and therefore both devices users would continue to be needed but, that their usages would likely change. Consistent with the later thinking, we were interested in talking with users to better understand how they perceived their smartphone and PC within the context of their own life. To do this, the qualitative methodology of a focus group was chosen because it served as a needs assessment (Kreuger & Casey, 2009) around the PC-Smartphone interactions.

A focus group is when a small sample of 6-10 people are brought into a central location and, with the help of a facilitator, provide their thoughts and opinions on specific topics. People are chosen for participation based on criteria that are developed by the team that is interested in the outcomes. Criteria are created and then converted into a series of questions that are used by a participant recruiting firm to choose people to participate in your focus group that possess the criteria you deemed important. The series of questions that are developed combine to create a participant screener. Screeners typically include some general questions about age, sex, socioeconomic status (income, education and occupation), and perspectives on their own level of technology adoption. In addition to the general questions that are obtained to contextualize the user relative to their responses to the specific criteria questions. The specific criteria questions typically have discrete responses choices (e.g., A, B, C, or D) with each response serving as either a positive indicator that the user may possess the criteria for participation or a negative indicator for participation. For example, if one of the strict criteria for the research is that the user must own a PC and own a touch-enabled smartphone then this would be determined by a user's response to two questions. The first question would be, "I own a PC." A positive response of "Yes" would mean that the recruiter would ask the user the next question of, "I own a touch-enabled smartphone." Another positive response of "Yes" would mean the user would then provide the name brand and model of their smartphone as verification to insure the user understood the question. This example demonstrates a participant that would be included in, and invited to participate in the focus group, assuming their smartphone brand and model was verified as being touch-enable and the user met the other distribution requirements outlined by the team. In contrast, a user that answered "Yes" to the first question and "No" to the second question would have been terminated from the screening questions and not invited to participate in the focus group. This type of contingent progression questioning continues until the desired number of participants is recruited to attend the group. Typically recruiting for a focus group begins 2-3 weeks before the actual groups take place.

The number and location of focus groups is important to think about when planning. Completing four to eight focus groups in total across a few different geographical locations is recommended to insure that you are not getting a geographically-biased perspective on the topical area of interest. The specific geographical areas should be chosen based on where you anticipate you will be applying the information you obtain. For example, for our team, we knew that we would be creating a product that would ship within the US initially and if it resonated, we would entertain the idea of shipping it to other countries. Because of this decision early on, we decided to limit our focus group locations to the US but to distribute the sampling within this country to different states (e.g., Portland, Oregon and Dallas, Texas).

Preparing for successful focus groups is time-intensive. A successful focus group is one where the attendee feels like their contribution is effortless, low-pressure, and engaging from start to finish. Each focus group is usually 1.5-2 hours in duration. This may sound like a significant amount of time to obtain information from users, but it is actually relatively short when you realize that none of the participants know why they were chosen to participate and therefore have no idea what they will be talking about. Participants are also talking about this unknown topic with a group of strangers they just met. When you consider these facts, a significant portion of the group time is spent insuring participants feel comfortable speaking within the group on all of the topics that are brought up and that they are engaged in all activities. You can leave the details of making the group comfortable to the facilitator that you hire. The actual subject content is what your team is responsible for.

For the Intel® Pair & Share focus groups we had three key research goals: a) Obtain current PC and Smartphone usages and pain-points from users, b) Obtain user perception of usage concepts and gain novel ones from users, c) Explore user expectations for product positioning of these usages based on perceived value. The section below will discuss how we achieved the research goals.

To obtain the current usage behavior of smartphones and PCs, we needed to know where participants were using each device, for what tasks, with what type of data, why they chose to use one device over another, and whether there were things they wish they could do better. Participants were asked to complete a worksheet where they indicated their usage patterns after which each individual shared theirs with the rest of the group. To obtain user perception of usage concepts, participants were then presented with a visual of each concept followed by discussion. The three key concepts introduced were smartphone as a controller for your PC, smartphone as an extended display and easy sharing between both of your devices. Each usage concept discussion was broken into a few sections: whether they thought it was interesting, useful for them, concerns or reservations about the usage concept, what else they would want it to do. After the discussion for each usage concept slowed, users were asked to make individual ratings such as: "How likely would you be to use your smartphone and/or PC in this way?" After all three usage concepts discussions were completed we asked participants whether they thought having this capability would impact their decision-making for future personal computer purchases and how might they expect to acquire this capability. This allowed us to explore how users would expect this product to be positioned in the market.

Given the range of research goals and focus group content you can understand how it is a challenge to obtain all of this data in a way that insures the focus group participants stay engaged. It is a good idea to have team members from various disciplines observe the sessions to gain insights from various domains and insights that may otherwise be missed. Various individuals took away a broad range of insights, product features and ideas just from listening to the participant interactions during the focus groups. Focus groups are typically conducted at a facility that has a two-way mirror with one side designed for the focus group participants and the other side for the observers. Additionally, each group is typically videotaped for post-session processing.

From the focus groups, we acquired a deeper understanding of how people use their PCs and smartphones. More importantly, we discovered how they perceived each of the devices within their life. Some users perceived their PC as their primary device with the smartphone simply filling the gap until they returned to the PC. As one user stated, *I use my iPhone when I am not around my laptop because the screen is too small to use otherwise.* Other participants perceived their smartphone as their primary device. As one user stated, *I rarely go to my PC because it is so much easier to use my phone. I'm never out of touch and now it has come to a point that I only turn on my computer once a day to download long email or do something in Photoshop.* Current perception of the devices is only one piece of the puzzle for us, pain-points revealed where we were able to provide direct value to consumers. Another user lamented, *I wish I didn't need wires/cords to sync my phone to my PC.*

User perceptions on the specific usage concepts were also interesting. When users were introduced to the usage concept of smartphone as a controller for your PC they immediately understood the benefit, leveraging the inherent advantages of multiple devices for a better experience. One user said, *I would play games on my PC if it has this because the screen is bigger and my kids would like it!* When users were introduced to the smartphone as an extended display they were able to see that the value of monitoring time consuming PC activities on their phone so they could do other things and return to the PC when they need to, as one user put it, *I am constantly needing to RUN from my computer to the front door, phone, bathroom, kitchen, laundry room, and being able to monitor my computer needs would be immensely helpful.* When users were introduced to the easy share between both devices they were able to contextualize how it would make their life easier. As one user stated, *Pictures would be great for this type of share zone. I am responsible for my daughter's year book. We could meet at a coffee shop and exchange pictures in real-time.*

The main benefit of focus groups is that while you are trying to get specific information on the usage concepts introduced, you also uncover users concerns about the ideas. For example, *I hate playing games with the stupid keyboard, I would love this – I would be concerned about the security aspects of this…so I would want to know that it was secure…phone can get lost easily.* This comment about security demonstrated that users were aware of the inherent risk in making wireless connections between devices and that they would expect some way to verify the two devices to enable the experience. This is a concern we spent a considerable amount of time addressing later in the development phase. In addition to the focus group users concerns, we were able to get a relative appeal ranking for the usage concepts presented to the users. The most appealing usage concept to the focus groups was the easy share concept, with most users expressing they wanted this experience for photo sharing.

As a team, we intuitively knew that at best, the relationship between the PC and smartphone was clunky and disjointed. We also knew that users had certain types of data that they work with and share more than others. The most popular data item was photos. During the focus groups, the Easy Share concept was fairly ambiguous and simply showed that you could share content across devices seamlessly. This concept resonated with participants and prompted a series of statements expressing how difficult and annoying it is that their smartphone enables them to take photos but not to easily share them with someone in real-time other than by looking at your small smartphone screen. While users were aware that they could send them to others via email or text, they acknowledged that this was a time consuming task and they desired sharing to be easier. There were countless examples of participants stating they wished to share photos with others in an easier way. The data from the focus group provided directional qualitative data to our team that led us to start exploring a way to provide secure pairing between smartphones and PCs for an easy sharing experience for the photos that people love to share with each other.

Product Vision

Based on the focus group findings and internal interest, we started with a proposed usage of 'photo flipping' that evolved into Pair & Share. The core idea was to make it quick and easy for one person or a small group of people to share photos from their phone to their PC to create a collaborative viewing experience with their photos. The physical metaphor we mimicked and the vision for the product was as follows:

Imagine you are sitting around a table with a few friends, and each friend has a shoebox of photos. You each select photos from your shoebox and drop them on the table between you to share. As the photos are dropped on the table, you have a shared experience and a conversation around the photos you are sharing. When you are done, each person takes their photos back home with them in their own shoebox.

Our desire was to translate this idea to a digital experience with a collaboration that is free-form and guided by the participants. Each person's shoebox is their handheld device (phone/tablet) and the common table is a PC or TV. Since you are within physical proximity of your friends, you can talk about each photo in turn and you can see the location where your photos are being shared.

Whiteboarding

The first step is translating this vision into a product begins with 'whiteboarding.' Sketching on whiteboards provides our team with a high-bandwidth, low-cost method to quickly iterate through ideas as we transition from the vision to designing a product. We collectively refer to this activity as 'whiteboarding,' but you may know it by other names. During this process it is important to sketch and talk through ideas in an open and non-threatening environment where any idea is welcome, but not necessarily worth pursuing (see Figure 2). We like to follow a method that encourages the team to clarify, compliment and challenge each other. It is important that ideas are challenged in a constructive manner to build on ideas, and it is equally important that ideas are actually challenged to make them better (Lehrer, 2012). A particular idea may not make it into the product, but the shared conversations and insights will prompt new ideas and create a common language. This process can take a considerable amount of time from tens of hours to hundreds of hours depending on the size and complexity of the product. We spent 100+ hours on Pair & Share over the course of a few months cycling through this activity. We have also found it quite valuable to use large uninterrupted blocks of time of approximately half a day at a time to really work through ideas in addition to considerable time spent thinking individually. Most importantly, remember that this stage of product development is a lot of fun.

Although you could use flip charts or colored pencils and paper, a white board allows you to focus on the flows and not get distracted by the artwork at this stage. We have also found that whiteboards tend to level the playing field when differing levels of artistic skill is involved. A big white board, a little bit of hand waving and gesturing goes a long ways to explaining and working out ideas. A key consideration for this is to involve just enough of the right people to form a cross-disciplinary team. This team will form a nucleus of knowledge and expertise that provides continuity through delivery and future versions. A large team may deadlock in discussions and too small of a team may lack enough breadth of expertise and experience. During this phase of the project the team typically consisted of two or three people representing Interaction Design, Human Factors Engineering and Software Architecture. It is also important that stakeholders are periodically consulted or informed on the current direction and progress.

Throughout this process, it is important to continuously reflect on the user needs and the personas you are developing for. Our vision for the Pair & Share application required us to translate the physical world into the digital world. Insights from the focus groups and previous projects led us to design the product to comprehend the spectrum of users from those that had a disorganized set of photos on their smartphone to carefully arranged albums of photos. The need to address very large albums of

Figure 2. Example sketches

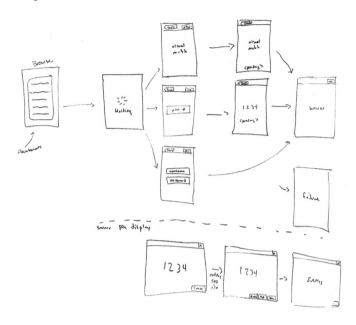

hundreds to thousands of photos quickly became a difficult technical challenge the developers began addressing very early through prototypes. Our interactions with users new to smartphones led us to develop interactions that were easily discoverable and minimized and simplified features where possible. Developing a common understanding of the user needs and expectations guided the design, and allowed the definition of the feature requirements. We strive to deliver an intuitive design that allows the users natural behavior to teach them how it functioned with minimal instruction. Reflecting on our user personas and acting out the interactions allowed us to identify needs such as: how to know what others have shared; how to know who shared it; and how to go back and look at a picture.

Transforming the Pair & Share vision into an experience started with a series of discussions to explore potential interactions and work flows that would meet the goals. In parallel with the whiteboard sessions, from the initial concepts generated, various technical feasibility research efforts and prototypes were executed to determine whether there were any technical limitations that would constrain the space for the user experience. For example, iOS* and Android* both presented different methods of accessing albums and photos on the devices that required further investigation. The outcome of these white-boarding sessions provided a first pass at the interaction design, information flows and technical needs to feed into a low-fidelity prototype we could put before users and identify areas that required technical feasibility assessment.

When considering an experience, we generally start with some entry point – and there may be more than one depending on the application. The starting point for the Pair & Share began by mapping the core sharing idea to the digital realm. This included selecting albums, sharing images and incorporating a multi-user experience with the second screen. When we consider each screen presented to a user during an interaction, whether it be a phone, tablet or laptop, we break the interaction into a few distinct components. Each screen, or state, in the interaction provides the user with a few simple components (a) data they can consume, (b) data they can input, and (c) the ability to take action(s) that transition to another screen or manipulate the current screen. The cross disciplinary perspective enables us to reduce the amount of re-explaining of ideas by having all parties involved immersed in the context and richness of information flowing. This allows us to develop a few concepts with actionable and testable hypothesis, including both usability and technical. It is important to capture the sessions in some fashion. We typically capture the whiteboard sketches on phones and email the images to ourselves. The 'really good' ideas also tended to be re-sketched in a project notebook to provide a progressive record of the changes and ideas as we progressed.

As we iterated through the design ideas, it became apparent that the initial connectivity and pairing aspect of the application presented a variety of challenges for both technical and usability domains. We did not want to subject users to random people connecting and displaying pictures on their devices, that led us down a path to develop an initial pairing interaction. This was a doubly difficult challenge, because the first thing you encounter when launching the Pair & Share application is the discovery and pairing interactions. The pairing interaction acts as a barrier to get to the core experience of sharing pictures. It became very challenging throughout the development of the application to properly communicate the notion of connecting to another device without confusing users with the language of connecting to wireless networks that they were more typically familiar with. A careful balance of usability and security was necessary to provide a solution that met the security requirements, yet did so without a difficult interaction. Through a number of design attempts and detailed discussions, we chose an interaction that first requires the user to choose the device they want to connect to, and then authorize the connection by entering a PIN# displayed on the remote screen. This interaction still remains one of the pain points in the application. Securely and wirelessly connecting applications across two devices is a difficult problem to make easy given the constraints of devices today.

It is important that the team is able to not only begin developing the desired user experience, but also considers the scope of the greater project. Each person brings their experience, opinions and expertise to bear on the problem at hand, and the individual specialties are also heavily relied on. We imagined the interactions as our target users would experience them as we sketched through various mock-up interfaces and flows. The Interaction Designer provides a guiding hand to the workflows and user experience. The Human Factors Engineer provides insights into potential pain points and identifies areas of concern and risk to be addressed in usability testing. The Software Architect identifies potential areas that require research for technical feasibility or desired performance characteristics. Of course, contributions are not restricted to an individual's official role. Throughout this early effort we are also beginning to gain an appreciation for the size and scope of the project. This serves as input to product planning, staffing and budgeting activities.

There are a variety of outputs from this phase. As mentioned previously, the primary goals are to develop the interaction design including the data flows and user workflows. These form the basis for the future steps as you begin to test the ideas with end users. During the whiteboarding sessions, you also begin to develop an appreciation for the scope of the work. This includes the amount and types of usability testing necessary (prioritizing usability testing of actions we have never done before versus things that are trivial), the quantity of artwork necessary (visual design, motion design, etc), and the localization and internationalization needs. Finally, you will also begin to appreciate the scope of the technical domain and identify areas for technical feasibility, items to license or build, and the necessary skill sets to execute the development of the product.

The greatest amount of whiteboarding effort in this phase occurred early on during the program, but it is also a tool that is applied to address usability feedback or, in some cases, to revisit large chunks of an experience that needs to be reconsidered. This part of product development also tends to be a lot of fun and exercises the creative side of the whole team.

Low Fidelity User Experience Testing

The outcome of the white-boarding sessions provided the necessary information to begin developing paper prototypes of the workflows to test out various hypotheses with real end users. At this point during the process we began developing a paper prototype to address the high-priority (i.e. what we believe are high usability risk features) interactions from the previous efforts. Examples of high priority user experience areas include: a new or unfamiliar mental model for the user, a feature with a high cost of failure (unrecoverable), and unfamiliar or non-traditional interactions. The paper prototype for the Pair & Share application initially focused on two areas. The first area developed was the core notion of sharing pictures. The second area was the necessary flows to connect your device to the second screen. In our case this was discovering and pairing your smartphone and/or tablet to your PC over the user's wireless network.

The creation of paper prototypes also serves a secondary purpose in addition to usability testing (Snyder, 2003). The activity provided a low cost method to really dig into the next level of details of the flows and interactions developed previously. In this case, we eventually developed a feature rich set of 'screens' for both the smartphone and the PC that exercised the majority of the 'happy path' flows. For example, we did not create a screen that would indicate that a user failed to transfer a photo (representing network errors or device errors), but we did create all of the screens to allow a user to experience the complete product without overtly artificial constraints. We chose to only do happy paths because the model of interaction was novel and we knew that we would need significant time to work those details out in terms of workflows. Additionally, we were not sure of all the potential error paths yet as development had not identified them all. Paper prototyping is also not an optimal method for testing items that are very reliant on a user seeing the dynamic interactions real-time and the cause and effect of their actions. While we typically choose not to develop the screens for errors or failures, developing the paper prototype does serve to identify these for consideration and later implementation. These screens were constructed from a life-size paper mockups and color pencil with fake data and layouts representative of a real application including the buttons of the smartphone. Depending on the complexity of a screen, small overlays were also created that could be combined together to augment and modify the screens as a user 'used' the paper prototype application.

The initial paper prototype for Pair & Share was on the order of 50 or 60 paper screens and overlays that allowed a user to experience a broad range of flows and interactions. The phone prototype was constructed primarily of complete individual screens since the user was expected to touch and interact with it, or even hold it. A screen composed of a bunch of parts doesn't hold up well to user interactions. Many of the screens were very similar with small tweaks to information as the screen would 'update'. As the user interacted with the prototype, the facilitator would swap the screen or hand the user a new screen to replace the previous one. Another benefit of using paper prototypes is the ability to easily augment the experience between test subjects if desired. New screens and overlays can be easily created to quickly test new ideas or fix 'bugs' like misspellings or other oversights with an eraser and scissors. Throughout development and use of the prototype it is very important to develop a method of organizing the screens and flows. The usability test facilitator also needs to be intimately familiar with the flows in order to provide a smooth experience for the test subjects. Consider laminating your prototype if it is going to be used by a large number of test subjects or is subject to smearing from handling.

In testing the paper prototypes, we told users that a new capability enables them to share photos seamlessly to their PC from their smartphone. We then asked them to show us how they would do this. Users indicate their actions by interacting with paper representations of a mockup of the application on a smartphone and computer. Users very quickly became accustomed to the interactions with paper, to the point where they recognized *that didn't do anything* when attempts to double-tap a non-interactive part didn't result in the facilitator providing them a new screen. Within the context of Intel Pair & Share, we indirectly obtained insights into how a user would look for and find the application, how they would connect to another device/PC. We were also able to get direct feedback on the interactions users would expect if they were to share photo(s) to their PC. Some of their expectations were already features that we had planned to implement in the product; others were novel and impacted out feature list. This feedback then enabled further refinement of the concept.

This method of testing is very interactive and the user is actively encouraged to talk aloud as they interact with the product. In our case the user was working with the facilitator to show the effect of action on the server to give the user a true understanding of the interactions between the two devices. After the initial pass of the test was complete, we also provided the users the opportunity to show us how they would design an interaction or add how features they wanted would work. They were given a combination of pencil and paper or allowed to rearrange and assemble the experience through the components we had already provided.

During this process, we identified the initial discovery and pairing process as a high risk part of the product and user experience. However, we did not want to explicitly test pairing on as a standalone feature, but instead we tested it in the context of the Pair & Share. A user was presented with a phone mockup with an icon representing the application. When the application was 'touched' we swapped in a mockup showing the initial screen of the application as it was performing discovery. Discovery is the process where the application is searching for the PC on the network in order to allow the user to initiate a connection to the PC. Given the discovery screen is dynamic, we would first provide the user with a screen showing no PCs discovered, and then momentarily replace it with a screen showing one PC discovered. The user would then select the PC to connect to, sometimes hesitantly. The user would then be presented by a new screen on the PC showing the application with pin # to enter and a pin entry dialog on the phone. Once completed, the experience would then proceed to the core picture sharing experience. We were pleasantly surprised that the users showed a high comprehension for what occurred and the reasoning for the pairing interaction. However, we also noted the need to test for edge conditions and failure cases that were difficult to simulate with a paper prototype (see Figures 3 and 4).

We followed up the paper prototype with a real, but low fidelity implementation. The implementation was developed by the product team based on the paper prototype flows and interactions. Feedback from the usability testing was also integrated into the application. With the revised workflows we wanted to determine if the corrections we made were sufficient, and we began adding functionality that could not be tested with paper prototypes. We continued to incrementally build out the application over the course of weeks until it reached the point where it contained the complete functionality envisioned, albeit with minimal effort spent on the visual presentation. However, we were still able to prioritize features and test them with the real application at intermediate milestones as the development occurred. For this application, it was deemed sufficient to present an 'in-process' application to users and not concern ourselves with the quality of the artwork incorporated into the application.

We tested multiple iterations of interaction models in early testing of the prototype. This included orientation, selection method (e.g., touch, double-tap, drag), sort order, the indication that a picture was in transit, and more. As the prototypes were implemented we would be forced to work through another level of interaction details in order to provide complete workflows. This testing occurred in 2010–2011. One of the more interesting observations made in early testing tended to segment users that were familiar with touch devices (e.g. an iPhone) from those that were not. There was a very distinct difference in the ability of a user that was not familiar with touch devices (iPhone, Android) and those that were.

Moving from testing the paper prototype to the low fidelity implementation allowed us to gain insights into the user expectations and frustrations. For example, users familiar with the iOS* or Android* environments began to express opinions

Figure 3. Example paper prototypes

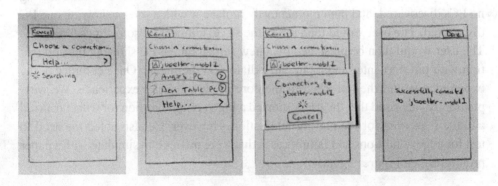

Figure 4. Example paper prototypes

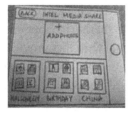  

 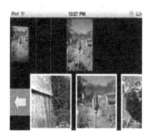 

about particular interactions inherent to the platform such as the placement of back buttons, or using swipes or a long press for certain actions. They also expressed some surprise that we didn't support both landscape and portrait modes for the application, a decision driven by the minimal screen space on a smartphone. An initial version of the application contained a relatively complicated model for pairing that allowed the user to make choices to allow a connection permanently, allow a connection or to deny or cancel a connection. The user feedback ultimately provided the necessary motivation to greatly simplify the pairing interactions while continuing to meet the security requirements. The ability to have a cross-disciplinary team discussion of the security requirements, interaction design and usability results enabled us to quickly adapt the implementation. Early implementations of the application also used a drag-and-drop method to share photos, however we quickly learned that this method of sharing was quite difficult to discover as compared to a tap or double-tap. Finally, testing also uncovered a number of defects in the implementation that were addressed by the developers.

High Fidelity User Experience Testing

After several rounds of low fidelity prototyping, we were able to define a workflow that seemed to meet users' expectations for the pairing and photo sharing interactions. This workflow was then refined in partnership with an external firm that provides interaction and visual design work. Our choice to engage an outside design house was based on internal priorities and available resources. They also provided us with a fresh perspective on the interactions and were able to further refine the experience based on the input we had received up to that point. With the application implemented and working, usability feedback was obtained from users within the full context of use in a way that was impossible to do within the context of paper-prototyping. The primary difference between high-fidelity user experience testing and paper prototype testing is the completeness of the interactions and the amount of the experience, such as errors, that you can test. For example, in low-fidelity user experience testing we were able to hash out which flows are likely to work and should be implemented. With high-fidelity testing we were able to get feedback on the artwork and critical pieces that impact the experience like discovering and downloading an application from the online stores, detection and verification of identity on both devices, ease of use for sharing to the PC, the ability to understand the temporary nature of the sharing, and the ability to understand who is currently sharing in the context of a multiple person sharing context.

In this high fidelity user experience testing, we were not only interested in the sharing workflows that we had tested in earlier low-fidelity testing, but we were also interested in what we call the out-of-box-experience (OOBE). OOBE is always an interesting area to test as it can never be exactly true to the actual experience that a user has with a product because we are testing in a usability lab with unreleased products. Having said that, when doing a high fidelity user experience test it is important to insure that you create an ecologically valid test plan. Ecological validity is an experimental term for external validity - that is, it is important that your testing environment and methodology closely map to the environment in which a user would actually be using a given product. This is important in that you want to have confidence that the data you achieve from a given round of testing can be used to make modifications on the product that reflect the reality of how consumers would be using it.

For our team, this meant that we did not train users on how to use the product prior to using it, nor did we tell them the mental model that they would need to actually use the product successfully. That is, to use Intel Pair & Share, a user would need to first download the application on both the smartphone and the PC then complete the security pairing successfully and only then could they actually begin sharing their photos from their smartphone to the PC. To mimic the way a user would encounter the application in real life, we simply provided users with a smartphone and a PC and told them, "You just got a brand new computer, and your friend told you about an app that allows you to share media from your mobile device to your computer wirelessly and you want to try it out. You know the app is called Intel Pair & Share. What would you do now?" With this minimal amount of information, we were able to see how a user would work toward this goal. While the task scenario is ecologically valid, we do ask users to use "speak aloud protocol" so we can note where users were confused so we could improve it in the final product (see Figure 5).

The simple task scenario that users started their session with enabled us to learn which device they initiated the experience on and gain insight into the users' expectations on what they were required to install on the devices. Once they realized that you do indeed need the application on both devices, we were able to see whether the workflows we had created could successfully guide them to download the application on the other device. Then, once users went to the application store, we were able to observe what search strings they tried to use to find the application. This was informative to the marketing team so they could insure that the search strings all resulted in the Intel Pair & Share application. Once they tried entered their search string, we provided them with fake marketing collateral by saying,

Figure 5. Final product UI

"Imagine that when you went to the application store, this is what you saw." This simple action enabled us to see whether users read the content, looked at the photos, ratings, and what their general thoughts were. Following their "download" users then proceeded to start the application so they could try out the photo sharing. In this portion of the workflow, users were faced with a potentially new phenomenon of device pairing. This is when the user had to find the computer that they would like to share their photos to and complete a connection that required the entry of a six-digit code. After a successful pairing, users were then able to start sharing their photos to the larger PC screen. Later in the session, participants were asked to switch devices and begin sharing photos with a tablet now. From this, we were able to see whether users thought that the sessions were only capable of being one-to-one or whether they assumed that they were able to have multiple users share photos to the same PC. Following this discussion, users were asked to end their connection with the PC. From this, users were able to express their understanding of the temporal nature of the photos they have shared. Hopefully, what you will notice from the structure and flow of the session is that it is critical to have users experience the interactions that you have developed in a way that allows them to reveal to you their understanding of the application functionality across platforms. It is only when users reveal to you what their understanding is of the functionality can you see where the product needs to be improved. Of course, no all users successfully navigated this sequence of steps and actions were taken to improve flows as necessary.

From this round of testing we had the pleasure of seeing our users smile and laugh with delight when they shared their first photo to the PC screen. This is the type of interaction you hope for after months of design, implementation, evaluation and redesign. We were also able to fine tune the experience by expanding the marketing collateral to include a frequently asked questions section that was eventually launched on the application stores. Additionally, the testing uncovered functional bugs, usability issues, and a list of additional functionality that users wished the application had. A functional bug is when the application was designed to behave in a particular way but fails to perform that way due to coding error. An example of a functional bug that was uncovered in testing is when the user was trying to share a photo from a smartphone or tablet and accidentally hit the whitespace between the photos instead of having that singular photo appear to be blue highlighted, the entire row appears blue highlighted. A usability issue is an element of the application design or interaction that is consistently confusing and/or surprising to users that should be fixed to improve the user experience. An example of a usability issue found in this testing was that users wanted a way to access frequently asked questions to help them troubleshoot when they can't find the PC they wanted to connect to. The list of additional functionality is a list of items that users said they would want the application to have as a core feature or functionality. An example of this would be to have remote photo sharing sessions with family and friends within Intel Pair & Share.

The overall user experience of the product is largely dependent on the full experience that a user has with a product that includes the way that they download the application, complete the initial connection and the first time they share photos from their smartphone to a computer. Accomplishing this is not a simple, brief task, rather, as you have seen throughout this case study, it requires the collaboration of multiple disciplines to design, develop, evaluate, and redesign when necessary. This requires thinking about who the user is, learning from them, determining what they are missing from their current computing experiences, and determining what type of experience would enable them to have a richer experience. Along the way, it is important to continually check-in with the user to see whether you have strayed from that vision and whether you have been designing an experience that is easy for them to understand and to achieve their goals with relative ease. A successful user experience allows users of the Pair & Share application to share photos without letting technology get in their way.

Shipping Product

The Intel Pair & Share application was delivered to the market in Fall 2011 and was the first of what is expected to be many cross-device applications developed by Intel and others. This project allowed us to indirectly explore difficult concepts encountered in cross-device experiences in the context of a real application. The fast-paced interdisciplinary team allowed us to quickly iterate from concept to product with very little rework that was not a direct result of observations and user feedback.

CURRENT CHALLENGES FACING THE ORGANIZATION

Intel has a long history of being a manufacturing company that is driven to copy exactly, which is only possible through the rigorous use of quantitative data to make decisions. The reliance on quantitative data to make decisions has permeated our group's culture. Traditionally, we prefer to rely on hard data to make decisions versus qualitative data. This works well within the technical domains when managing project scope and features but data driven decisions from user studies, which are inherently qualitative in nature, creates challenges. As this case study has demonstrated, many of the decisions required to create a quality user experience are fed by qualitative data. Today the organization continues to develop a variety of consumer software products and the methods and practices described throughout this paper continue to be refined and applied. As our organization continues to expand software and solutions, we will need to find scalable methods to integrate both qualitative and quantitative data into the hands of key decision makers.

SOLUTIONS AND RECOMMENDATIONS

We recommend two key findings from our experience on this project and others as we continue to refine our product development methodologies. The first recommendation is to construct interdisciplinary teams that represent the technical, interaction and usability domains. The second recommendation is to incorporate qualitative data into decision making processes in addition to traditional quantitative data.

One of the key challenges faced when developing the user experience of a product is communication. Without communication across disciplines, the experience of a product will suffer. Teams that are not integrated or working closely together will struggle to work effectively together. The shared knowledge that is developed by jointly progressing through the product development phases from concept to final product provides a solid basis for clear communication between team members. The various disciplines that are represented on an interdisciplinary team allow the members to express their individual skills, and at the same time take advantage of the unique experiences and viewpoints of the other members. These same unique viewpoints also allow the team to identify risk areas such as technical, usability and scope. Finally, we have found that interdisciplinary teams will accomplish amazing feats.

In our environment, qualitative data can be difficult to act on. Decision making must be structured so that it can accept both quantitative and qualitative input. One way to achieve this is to translate qualitative data into actionable recommendations that the team, management and stakeholders can digest. We have found it important to build trust by presenting the underlying methodology and observations in addition to any resulting recommendations. We have also found it enlightening to invite team members to observe participants during tests. These methods have been helpful in gaining consensus and alignment to act on feedback. The organization is now more comfortable relying on qualitative results as input to product design decisions. In the absence of team buy-in, efforts that generate qualitative data will have a scattered influence on the end product experience. It is also important that a plan is put in place that provides ample resources and time, not only to execute usability tests, but also to incorporate the feedback and findings into the product.

The practices described throughout have allowed us to create a user experience that did not exist before, and set new standards as we develop new products.

Traditional approaches we have used in the past involved long lag times between various disciplines, and unbalanced requirements between interaction design and technical feasibility. As with most products, we are challenged in various degrees by schedules, feature creep, differing opinions of stakeholders, technical constraints and requisite skill sets. It is critical that you are able to reach a mutually acceptable outcome through both qualitative and quantitative data. We believe that a quality user experience is developed with an interdisciplinary team that blends the user needs and technical constraints into a fast moving iterative process.

REFERENCES

Kreuger, R. A., & Casey, M. A. (2009). *Focus groups: A practical guide for applied research* (5th ed.). Thousand Oaks, CA: Sage Publishers.

Lehrer, J. (2012). Groupthink: The brainstorming myth. *New Yorker.* Retrieved from http://www.newyorker.com/reporting/2012/01/30/120130fa_fact_lehrer?currentPage=all

Mateus, M., Salvador, T., Scholz, J., & Sorensen, D. (1996). *Proceedings from CHI: Engineering Ethnography in the Home.* New York: ACM Press.

Moore, G. (1965). Cramming more components onto integrated circuits. *Electronics, 38*(8).

Nielson, J. (1993). *Usability engineering.* San Diego, CA: Academic Press, Inc.

Rudd, J., Stern, K., & Iseness, S. (1996). Low versus high fidelity debate. *Interaction, 3*(1), 76–85. doi:10.1145/223500.223514

Snyder, C. (2003). *Paper prototyping: The fast and easy way to design and refine user interfaces.* Boston, MA: Morgan Kaufmann Publishers.

ADDITIONAL READING

Android User Interface Guidelines. (2013). Website. Retrieved from http://developer.android.com/guide/practices/ui_guidelines/index.html

Buxton, B. (2007). *Sketching user experiences: Getting the design right and the right design.* San Francisco, CA: Morgan Kaufmann.

Cooper, A., Reimann, R., & Cronin, D. (2007). *About Face 3* (3rd ed.). Indianapolis, Indiana: Wiley.

iOS Human Interface Guidelines. (2013). Website. Retrieved from http://developer. apple.com/library/ios/#documentation/UserExperience/Conceptual/MobileHIG/ Introduction/Introduction.html

Windows User Experience Interaction Guidelines for Windows 7 and Windows Vista. (2013). Website. Retrieved from http://www.microsoft.com/en-us/download/ details.aspx?id=2695

KEY TERMS AND DEFINITIONS

Focus Group: A carefully planned series of discussions designed to obtain perceptions on a defined area of interest in a permissive, nonthreatening environment (Kreuger & Casey, 2009).

Human Factors Engineer: Uses what is known about human capabilities to design products, processes, and systems to improve ease of use, system performance, and user satisfaction.

Interaction Design: How a device/product communicates its function to the user so they can complete their intended tasks.

Low Fidelity Prototypes: Generally limited function, limited interaction prototyping efforts. They are constructed to depict concepts, design alternatives, and screen layouts, rather than to model the user interaction with a system (Rudd et al., 1996).

Software Architecture: Partner with key stakeholders to define product architectures and identify future product opportunities.

Visual Design: The field of developing visual materials to create an experience using elements of visual expression and style.

Whiteboarding: Sketching on whiteboards during early discussions provides our team with a high-bandwidth, low-cost method to quickly iterate through ideas as we transition from the vision to designing a product.

Chapter 9
A Usability Study of Mobile Text Based Social Applications:
Towards a Reliable Strategy for Design Evaluation

Ricardo Mendoza-González
Instituto Tecnológico de Aguascalientes, Mexico

Francisco Álvarez Rodríguez
Universidad Autónoma de Aguascalientes, Mexico

Jaime Muñoz Arteaga
Universidad Autónoma de Aguascalientes, Mexico

EXECUTIVE SUMMARY

The authors present a usability study where three of the most popular mobile Social Applications (mobile Facebook, mobile Twitter, and mobile Windows Live) were analyzed. The evaluation focused on four text-based tasks: Text-lines visualized at one time (Number of Turns), contacts visualization, conversation tracing, and text entry. The evaluation was performed using an adapted version of the System Usability Scale (SUS), which was answered by ninety participants (each mobile Social Application was analyzed by thirty participants). The authors firmly believe that the results of the study could lead to create a reliable strategy for design evaluation which could be structured into a set of heuristics.

DOI: 10.4018/978-1-4666-4046-7.ch009

ORGANIZATION BACKGROUND

Nowadays the *Instituto Tecnológico de Aguascalientes* is part of the *Sistema Nacional de Educación Superior Tecnológica* (SNEST) which coordinates over 261 Institutes of Technology throughout the country (Mexico). This national network provides support to almost 500,000 students, both undergraduates and postgraduates.

The *Instituto Tecnológico de Aguascalientes* will hold its 45th anniversary in September in 2012; this institute has its educative process certified by ISO 9001: 2008 and all their programs accredited and recognized by Secretariat of Public Education (SEP, Mexico) as a good quality Institute in the country.

This Institute is also certified by the Gender Equity Model (GEM: 2003) and runs a business incubator model recently authorized by the secretariat of economy in Mexico. The *Instituto Tecnológico de Aguascalientes* offer the following degrees: Chemical Engineering, Mechanical Engineering, Electrical Engineering, ICT Engineering, Bachelor in Informatics, Electronic Engineering, Management Engineering, Industrial Engineering, Bachelor in Business Administration, and this year release the Materials Engineering program. Additionally offer the online degrees on Engineering in Computational Systems. A PhD on Engineering programs was released this year as well, this program is currently in evaluation by *Consejo Nacional de Ciencia y Tecnología* (CONACYT) to be incorporated into the *Programa Nacional de Posgrados de Calidad* (PNPC) which belong the most prestigious graduate programs in Mexico. There are above of 4,400 students currently registered in the different degrees offered.

Meanwhile, the *Universidad Autónoma de Aguascalientes* was created at 1973, having their origins at the *Instituto Autónomo de Ciencias y Tecnología de Aguascalientes* established on 1867 in the Aguascalientes City.

In 1968 it began offering two degrees, Public Accountant and Business Administration. Currently it offers many programs, including middle and high school education, 40 undergraduate careers, two post-basic, eleven specialties, seven master's and two PhD programs.

The *Universidad Autónoma de Aguascalientes* is distinguished from other institutions for its departmental structure, separate from traditional systems but according to the needs of our time. Thus, education is taught through academic centers, allowing you to organize the sciences related to different groups of professors who teach interchangeably in different courses and careers.

As a decentralized institution of the state with legal personality to acquire and administer property, it aims to impart the secondary and higher education in the state, to perform scientific and humanistic research, and extend the benefits of culture to the various sectors of the population.

Teaching and research are planned and developed with special attention to the training of professionals and researchers in scientific disciplines related to technological, scientific, cultural and economic development, according to the national and international requirements.

The education in this Institution is focused on developing of the personality and abilities of the students, fostering in them patriotism and humanity, and awareness of social responsibility. The *Universidad Autónoma de Aguascalientes* examines all the currents of human thought, historical events and social doctrines, with rigorous objectivity that corresponds to their purposes.

Currently the *Universidad Autónoma de Aguascalientes* offer sixty one degrees, six of them are directly related to Computer Sciences: ICT Engineering, Bachelor in Informatics, Electronic Engineering, Engineering in Intelligent Computing, Bioinformatics, and Engineering in Computational Systems.

It is important to mention that we are members of public Mexican Universities and we performed this study for academic research purpose only, nevertheless our findings could be applied to benefit the industry.

SETTING THE STAGE

This research project involves researchers and students of Instituto Tecnológico de Aguascalientes and Universidad Autónoma de Aguascalientes. Both institutions have over thirty years of experience on IT. The professors who participated as researchers in this study hold a PhD in Computer Science and are specialists on Human-Computer Interactions and Software Engineering. Our survey application team was comprised by twenty five students in social service at the *Instituto Tecnológico de Aguascalientes*.

CASE DESCRIPTION

Technology Concerns

The use of mobile devices to access information is very popular today. People have mobile phones, smartphones and PDAs which they take with them almost everywhere. Mobile devices have become a pervasive part of our everyday lives. Similarly, a number of novel approaches are available oriented to provide users with the possibility of accessing and sharing social information particularly using textual messages e.g. social networks as Facebook (see www.facebook.com), microblogging as Twitter (see www.twitter.com), chat-rooms, e-mail, among others.

Considering this, it is easy to understand that the join between social applications and mobile devices was a natural consequence. According to Pabllo et al. (2009), the use of mobile computing can seriously contribute to enhance the relationships between users (in a: public, personal, or professional context).

Nevertheless, other works (e.g. Harding et al., 2009) pose that interacting with mobile applications and services remains difficult for users because of the impact of mobility on both device capabilities and the cognitive resources of users. According to Kuen Seong Su & Siew Yen Yee (2007) current text-based mobile applications as chats hinder navigation with long archives in a limited screen display. Moreover, it is time consuming and cumbersome to track messages that are sent by specific virtual-community members. A very similar assumption is addressed by Schuster-itsch et al. (2007) and Vronay et al., (1999), they states that despite popularity the user interfaces of most of text-based mobile applications, as chats, are very limited consisting merely of a list of participants, a type message text-area, and the text-file history of messages, in fact no many design improvements has been from the initial.

It is common to find in literature insights as above, which emphasize the need of having more focus on the interface between users and the mobile applications for several areas and fields. But in these efforts to support mobile applications another obstacle appear "*the small physical size of the devices*" being the principal concerns the limited size of screens and keyboards, which negatively impact on the correct information presentation. Kuen Seong Su & Siew Yen Yee (2007) particularly found that in text-based social applications the screen size could seriously limited the number of displayable text lines at one time seriously hamper the tracing of a conversation and subsequently the usability of the application. This prevalent prob-lem in text-based applications was previously analyzed by (Vronay et al. 1999) in stationary applications, they called *Turns* to each of these text lines, and highlighted the importance of the number of *Turns* which must be presented at one time (5 to 7 lines) in order to maintain a conversation clear and engaged. Additionally, the screen size of the mobile devices impedes a large number of logged-users in a so-cial application as well as the correct visualizations of contacts. Jung et al. (2008) focused their research in improving the contacts design in order to provide users novel benefits by becoming more personal and enriched with social information, beyond the simple communication enabler.

According to literature presented by Cui, et al. (2010), Nguyen & Oh(2010), and Jung & Blom, (2008), another important aspect is related to the limited pro-cessing capacity of the mobile hardware which straiten the computational tasks of the applications. Similar consideration should be given to avoid high consumption of limited storage and memory (e.g. The storage of the history consume a lot of memory). Additionally, the nature of wireless connectivity can delay or hinder the interaction among users.

Technology Components

Software

For this study we considered the mobile versions of three very popular text-based social applications: Facebook (http://m.facebook.com/for social network category, Twitter (https://mobile.twitter.com/signup) for microblogging category, and Windows Live (mobile.live.com/) for e-mail category. We briefly describe these applications in the following list:

- **Facebook mobile:** We used the mobile version of the website of Facebook, nevertheless Facebook offer an alternative suitable for over 2500 cellphones and other mobile devices, for Android and Apple devices (http://www.facebook.com/mobile/). These mobile versions are downloadable without any charges from the Facebook site.
- **Twitter mobile:** In the same way, for this study we used the mobile version of the Twitter's website, additionally the new version of this microblogging application is free available and is suitable as a native application for iPhone and for Android. This mobile application allows people who access Twitter mobile from feature phones, low-bandwidth networks or older browsers to enjoy the entire services of the application.
- **Windows Live mobile:** We used the mobile version of the website of Hotmail, but an application for Windows Live Mobile is available also. This app is a set of personalized Windows Live specifically created for mobile devices. Is offered through three channels: As a client (for windows mobile and other compatible mobile devises such as Nokia phones), Web based (for mobile WAP or GPRS with Web browsers), and SMS based services.

Hardware

Undoubtedly another important technology consideration is the huge diversity, features, and capabilities of the mobile devices. In order to trim this concern we focused this study on cellphones and smartphones that participants had. We found that the most popular models between the participants were (see also subsection "*Study Protocol*"):

- **LG GM 360:** Cellphone with WiFi, screen size 3 inches (240 X 400 pp), touch screen, Twitter, SMS network Facebook, see also http://www.lg.com/global/products/mobile-phones/index.jsp.
- **Samsung S5560 Tocco:** Cellphone with Internet browser (WAP 2.0), WiFi, screen size 3 inches (240 X 400 pp), touch screen, connectivity facilities. Detailed information is presented in www.samsung.com/us/mobile/.
- **LG P500 Optimus One:** Smartphone with Android system, WiFi, screen size 3.2 inches (320 X 480 pp), touch screen, supports Java applications, XHTML applications, 3G connection. see also http://www.lg.com/global/products/mobile-phones/index.jsp.
- **Nokia C3 - 00:** Cellphone with Internet browser of Nokia (WAP 2.0) and Opera MINI, facilities for web applications, WLAN IEEE 802.11 b/g, screen size 2.36 inches (240 X 320 pp). Detailed information is presented in http://www.nokia.com/mx-es/productos/celulares/c3-00/(inSpanish).
- **iPhone 4:** Smartphone, with Apple iOS, multi touch screen, screen size 3.5 inches (960 x 640 pp), WiFi. See also: www.apple.com/iphone/iphone-4/specs.html.

Usability Evaluation

Related to the usability evaluation, we selected the System Usability Scale (SUS) 10 items questionnaire as the principal base. According to Jeff Sauro, founding principal of Measuring Usability LLC (see http://www.measuringusability.com/), SUS was released by John Brooke in 1986. It was originally created as a "quick and dirty" scale for administering after usability tests on systems like VT100 Terminal ("Green-Screen") applications. SUS is technology independent and has since been tested on hardware, consumer software, websites, cell-phones, IVRs and even the yellow-page phone books. It has become an industry standard and has been referenced in over 600 publications. A revitalized version of SUS is following presented strictly based on Brooke (1996):

1. I think that I would like to use this system frequently.
2. I found the system unnecessarily complex.
3. I thought the system was easy to use.
4. I think that I would need the support of a technical person to be able to use this system.
5. I found the various functions in this system were well integrated.
6. I thought there was too much inconsistency in this system.
7. I would imagine that most people would learn to use this system very quickly.
8. I found the system very cumbersome to use.

9.   I felt very confident using this system.

10.   I needed to learn a lot of things before I could get going with this system.

For this particular study we adapted the original SUS replacing "System" with "Social Application" and slightly directing some questions to specific requirements without altering the substance of their original purposes. Our suggested SUS version is presented below:

Q1: I think that I would like to use this Social Application frequently.

Q2: I found the Social Application unnecessarily complex.

Q3: I thought that visualization and selection of contacts through this Social Application was easy.

Q4: I think that I would need the support of a technical person to be able to use this Social Application.

Q5: I found the functions for contacts visualization and read/write messages in this Social Application were well integrated.

Q6: I thought there was too much inconsistency in this Social Application.

Q7: I would imagine that most people would learn to use this Social Application very quickly.

Q8: I found this Social Application very cumbersome to use, especially when I write/read messages.

Q9: I felt very confident using this Social Application.

Q10: I needed to learn a lot of things before I could get going with this Social Application.

Each item is a statement (positive items 1, 3, 5, and 7; or negative items 2, 4, 6, and 8) and a rating on the following seven-point scale:

- Strongly Disagree (SD)
- Disagree (D)
- Moderately Disagree (MD)
- Neither Agree Nor Disagree (NAND)
- Moderately Agree (MA)
- Agree (A)
- Strongly Agree (SA)

We decided to use a seven point-scale bearing in mind the findings of Findstad (2010). The author noted that the 5-point items were more prone to contribute to inaccurate measures through subtle but repeated data loss, especially when utilized in an electronic, non-moderated format. Seven-point Likert items have been shown to be more accurate, easier to use, and a better reflection of a respondent's true evaluation. In light of all these advantages, even when compared to higher-order items, 7-point items appear to be the best solution for questionnaires such as those used in usability evaluations. These assumptions are consistent with those reported by (Brooke, 1996). We follow the scoring SUS process described in (Brooke, 1996) which textually says

SUS yields a single number representing a composite measure of the overall usability of the system being studied. Note that scores for individual items are not meaningful on their own.

To calculate the SUS score, first sum the score contributions from each item. Each item's score contribution will range from 0 to 4. For items 1,3,5,7, and 9 the score contribution is the scale position minus 1. For items 2,4,6,8 and 10, the contribution is 5 minus the scale position.

Multiply the sum of the scores by 2.5 to obtain the overall value of SU.

SUS scores have a range of 0 to 100 (Brooke, pp. 193).

Note: In order to use a 7-point Likert scale we adapted the scoring SUS as follows: Each item's score contribution will range from 0 to 6. For odd items the score contribution is the scale position minus one. For pair items, the contribution is seven minus the scale position. Then we multiply the sum of the scores by 60/100 (1.67 approximately, to have a range of 0 to 100 SUS scores).

Tullis & Stetson (2004) performed a comparison study in order to analyze the effectiveness of SUS against other usability questionnaires such as: QUIS (Maryland University), CSUQ (IBM), Words (Microsoft). The authors concluded that SUS is one of the simplest questionnaires (only 10 rating scales), yielded among the most reliable results across several sample sizes. Additionally, all the items/statements of SUS address different aspects of the user's reaction to the website as a whole. Just a few participants are needed to get reasonably reliable results.

General Context and Purposes of the Study

How can interaction with real-world entities help people? Currently this is one of the most interesting questions in HCI (Human-Computer Interaction). In this way, the HCI community is creating and adapting methodologies, tools, and infrastructure for specific challenges and opportunities, such as social mobile technologies evaluation (Nakhimovsky et al., 2009).

In the field of usability evaluation, experts as Schusteritsch et al. (2007), points that for most mobile usability studies enabling natural interaction with the device can be more challenging than in a desktop-based environment because mobile devices come in a diverse range of shapes and run a variety of operating systems. In this way, it is necessary to focus on the user interface interaction.

Considering these aspects and in order to contribute to previous research works on usable mobile technologies, we conducted a wide usability study for text-based social applications (see subsection *"Technology Components"*), which is focused on the user interface interaction.

Our work is oriented to provide a starting point to developers and testers with some guidance in designing adequate interfaces for mobile text-based social applications, but certainly our findings could be applied to other scenarios in different areas of HCI and mobile usability through slight adaptations.

As mentioned before in subsection *"Technology Components"* we use a SUS questionnaire version to find:

1. The common usage and usability issues in mobile social text-based applications when users perform tasks related to reading, writing, and visualizing text.
2. The usability flaws related to contacts visualization in mobile text-based social applications.
3. The general perception of the users on the text-based social applications usability.

Also, in this study, we aimed to answer the following questions with regard to the efficacy of the mobile social applications considered (Mobile Facebook, Mobile Twitter, and Mobile Windows Live) when text-based operations were performed:

- What are users' perceptions, challenges, concerns, and perceived benefits when using these mobile social applications during the reading, writing, and visualizing textual conversations?
- What specific usability factors influence users' adoption intentions?
- What changes in the interface of the text-based mobile social applications could improve users' experience and adoption incentives?

At a first glance the three social applications considered (Mobile Facebook, Mobile Twitter, and Mobile Windows Live) have very different features and functionality, which do not allow a fair comparison. Nevertheless, some of the essential text-based tasks are commonly performed for users of these applications. This research work is focused on the usability evaluation of four of these common tasks:

- Text-lines visualized at one time (Number of Turns)
- Contacts visualization
- Conversation tracing
- Text entry

We think that the usability analysis of these tasks could lead to a set of general design guidelines oriented to enhance the user interactive experiences with text-based social applications regardless of the specific applications purposes: Social networking, microblogging, chat, or e-mail.

Study Protocol

At the beginning of this study it was established as a goal to survey ninety people, thirty for each application. In this fact, we recruited ninety participants of which thirty two were female, and fifty eight were male. All the participants were members (students and personnel) of both the *Instituto Tecnológico de Aguascalientes* and the *Universidad Autónoma de Aguascalientes*, being students the vast majority of the participants (77 undergraduate participants). We invite to these people directly during "tours" in libraries, cafeterias, laboratories, and cubicles of both institutions.

Ages of participants were varied, forty one participants were between 20 and 25 years old, thirty six between 26 and 31, and thirteen were older than 31 years old. The seventy seven undergraduate participants were students of a diverse range of specialties not directly related to Computer Sciences. Seven participants were professors of majors such as: Management Engineering, Industrial Engineering, and Chemical Engineering. And six participants were members of the administrative staff at both Institutions. All the participants were native Spanish speakers but all of them had a considerable level of English proficiency.

For this study we tray to recruit novel or non-experts users of mobile social applications in order to capture a realistic perception of the usability of these software. This concern was not a problem because only one participant had a couple of previous experiences with Facebook mobile. It is noteworthy that eighty three participants were regulars of Facebook and/or Twitter use not on the mobile but on the desktop.

The majority of the participants used their own phone to perform the requested tasks (eighty three participants); in others, the survey application team provided them with one of two smartphones: An iPhone 4, or a BlackBerry Curve 8300. These latter cases were minimal (only seven participants requested a smartphone).

The models of cellphones and smartphones used by the participants during this study are presented in Table 1. We considered the two models of our smartphones, thus the total sample of mobile devises models was seven.

After a brief introduction to the purposes of the study, participants were asked to perform the following tasks:

1. To include a researcher in their contact lists in order to start a brief conversation with him.
2. To write one of the following message (in English): Message a) "Hello, I'm participating in a research performed by Instituto Tecnológico de Aguascalientes and Universidad Autónoma de Aguascalientes in order to determine the usability of mobile text-based social apps, so I wrote this message from a mobile device. What do you think? ", for Windows live and Facebook, or Message b) "Hi, I'm participating in a research to determine the usability of mobile text-based social apps, so I wrote this message from a mobile device", for Twitter. We use two messages considering that messages posted in microblogging systems consist of 140 characters including white spaces (see "Microblogging" in additional section "Key Terms and Definitions").
3. To send this message to the added contact.
4. To read the response message.

Note: It is very important to mention that the participants agree to include us in their contact lists. All the contacts and e-mail addresses were treated as confidential and were deleted after each contribution.

Then the participants were asked to completing the version of the SUS questionnaire presented in subsection *"Technology Components"* summarizing their perceptions and experiences through the seven-point Likert scale provided for each question. In some few cases we received additional contextual feedback of the participants,

Table 1. Frequency of cellphones and smartphones used by the participants during this study

Model of Cell or Smartphones	Frequency
LG GM 360	14
Nokia C3 - 00	14
iPhone 4 (Including our own)	14
LG P500 Optimus One	13
Samsung S5560 Tocco	12
Various cellphones' models	16
Various smartphones' models (Including our own Blackberry Curve 8300)	7

which contributed to better understand the problems encountered, as well as their potential concerns, perceived benefits, and desired features in the usability of text-based social applications.

Survey Application Schedule

At the beginning this study appear to be "too complex" to coordinate, nevertheless we had a very important help from the twenty five students in social service at the *Instituto Tecnológico de Aguascalientes.*

Tying to keep low the workload, we organize the research staff in five teams of four people, and one more of five, additionally we structured the following simple schedule for survey applications, see Table 2.

As shown in Table 2, we evaluated an application biweekly, first two weeks Facebook mobile was analyzed, then the following two weeks we analyzed Twitter, finally, we consider weeks five and six to evaluated Windows Live.

The "*Team*" column presents the consecutive team numbers (1 to 6). Last column shows the weekly expected number of respondents (participants), fifteen in this case. The research staff had to survey three people daily on working week.

Collected Data

We first analyze the perception of participants in general, and then we individually discuss the feedback for the three applications considered (Facebook, Twitter, and Windows Live). The survey asked about how frequently people would like to use a particular mobile social application. Twenty people responded that they are strongly agreed with this statement. Another twenty participants were in agreement with this idea. Thirteen selected the option "Moderately Agree". Fourteen were strongly dis-

Table 2. Survey application activities schedule

Activity	Week #	Team #	Expected Respondents #
Application of the SUS for mobile Facebook	1	1	15
	2	2	15
Application of the SUS for mobile Twitter	3	3	15
	4	4	15
Application of the SUS for mobile Windows Live	5	5	15
	6	6	15
Totals	*6*	*6*	*90*

agreeing, and nine were disagreeing with this statement like other eight people who were moderately disagree, meanwhile, six people responded to the neutral option.

Twenty participants found the Social Application unnecessarily complex. Nevertheless thirteen people responded selecting the very opposite "Strongly Disagree". In the same way twenty one participants thought that visualization and selection of contacts through the Social Application was easy, but sixteen do not shared this idea choosing "Strongly Disagree", eleven were in disagree, and ten were moderately disagree. Thirteen think that they do not would need the support of a technical person to be able to use the Social Application, another thirteen shared this perception, and fourteen more did so moderately, but thirty five people altogether think the opposite; fifteen more remained neutral.

Sixteen respondents strongly considered that the functions for contacts visualization and read/write messages in the Social Application like well integrated. Eighteen were agreeing and seven more were moderately agreeing with this perception. Twelve could not decide, while eleven were strongly disagreed, fourteen disagreed and twelve more moderately disagree.

Thirteen people could not to decide on level of inconsistency in the Social Application. Seven selected the option "Strongly Agree", thirteen selected "Agree" and other thirteen "Moderately Agree". However, twenty people found strongly consistent the Social Application used followed by eight respondents which selected the option "Disagree", and fifteen selected "Moderately Agree".

Just six people strongly think that most people would learn to use the Social Application promptly, eleven agree with this assumption as well as twenty people which were moderately agreed. Nevertheless, nine do not perceive this, selecting the option "Strongly Disagree", twelve disagree, and sixteen were moderately disagree. Sixteen respondents were neutral.

Sixteen participants found the Social Application very cumbersome to use during reading or writing messages. Six people think in the same way by selecting "Disagree", followed by eight which selected "Moderately Disagree". Twelve participants were neutral.

Just ten participants felt strongly confident using the Social Application. In contrast, fourteen respondents were strongly disagreeing with this perception. Most participants selected one of the options at the negative pole of this statement (forty participants).

Finally, forty five people altogether accepted the idea that they needed to learn a lot of things before I could get going with this Social Application. The number of opposite perceptions of this statement was close, eight participants selected the option "Strongly Disagree", nineteen "Disagree", and twelve "Moderately Disagree". Just six people could not decide.

Table 3 shows the general perception of the participants on the usability of the three mobile Social Applications considered: Mobile Facebook, Mobile Twitter, and Mobile Windows Live.

The column titles of Table 3 are based on the following: Strongly Disagree (SD). Disagree (D). Moderately Disagree (MD). Neither Agree Nor Disagree (NAND). Moderately Agree (MA). Agree (A). Strongly Agree (SA).

In addition we analyzed each mobile social application separately. Our survey reveals that fifteen respondents think that they would like to use this Social Application frequently. Meanwhile twelve participants thought different, and just three participants were indifferent. Seventeen people perceived this application as easy enough, but thirteen respondents found it unnecessarily complex. In the same way, fourteen participants perceived that, visualization and selection of contacts through this Social Application were easy, eleven were disagree with this statement and five were not either agree or disagree.

Table 3. General frequency of responses for each question

Questionnaire Items	SD	D	MD	NAND	MA	A	SA
Q1. I think that I would like to use this Social Application frequently.	14	9	8	6	13	20	20
Q2. I found the Social Application unnecessarily complex.	13	10	10	12	12	13	20
Q3. I thought that visualization and selection of contacts through this Social Application was easy.	16	11	10	11	14	7	21
Q4. I think that I would need the support of a technical person to be able to use this Social Application.	13	13	14	15	12	13	10
Q5. I found the functions for contacts visualization and read/write messages in this Social Application were well integrated.	11	14	12	12	7	18	16
Q6. I thought there was too much inconsistency in this Social Application.	20	8	15	13	13	13	7
Q7. I would imagine that most people would learn to use this Social Application very quickly.	9	12	16	16	20	11	6
Q8. I found this Social Application very cumbersome to use, especially when I write/read messages.	16	6	8	12	20	16	12
Q9. I felt very confident using this Social Application.	14	12	14	16	19	5	10
Q10. I needed to learn a lot of things before I could get going with this Social Application.	8	19	12	6	15	15	15

Twelve people thought that they would need the support of a technical person to be able to use mobile Facebook, but fifteen disagree with this idea.

Fifteen people found the functions for contacts visualization and read/write messages in this Social Application were well integrated. Nevertheless, eleven do not think that, and five can not make a decision.

Thirteen respondents think that this Social Application is very consistent. Nevertheless thirteen people think different and five selected the neutral option.

Fourteen participants would imagine that most people would learn to use this Social Application very quickly. Ten disagree with this idea and six could not decide.

Nineteen people found mobile Facebook very cumbersome to use, especially when they write/read messages. Eight people were not agreeing and three were neutral.

Fourteen people felt very confident using this Social Application. Twelve participants did not share that opinion. Four were not agree or disagree. Thirteen people think that they needed to learn a lot of things before they could get going with mobile Facebook, fourteen had a different view and three people were neutral. Table 4 shows the perception of the participants on mobile Facebook.

The column titles of Table 4 are based on the following: Strongly Disagree (SD). Disagree (D). Moderately Disagree (MD). Neither Agree Nor Disagree (NAND). Moderately Agree (MA). Agree (A). Strongly Agree (SA).

Now we present the participants' feedback on mobile Twitter. The majority of the participants (twenty one) thought that they would like to use this mobile Twitter frequently, and just six people perceived this Social Application as unnecessarily complex. Fifteen participants think that visualization and selection of contacts through mobile Twitter, and eleven people had a different view. When participants were asked if they would need the support of a technical person to be able to use this Social Application, twelve people answered in a positive way, but fourteen think different.

Fifteen participants found the functions for contacts visualization and read/write messages in mobile Twitter were not well integrated, and eleven people think that this assumption is incorrect. Similarly sixteen people think that Twitter is very consistent. Thirteen people would imagine that most people would learn to use this Social Application very quickly. But thirteen participants do not think so. Fourteen people found mobile Twitter as very cumbersome to use, especially when they write/read messages. Fifteen respondents did not felt very confident using this Social Application. And fifteen participants think that they knew enough to get going with mobile Twitter. See Table 5.

The column titles of Table 5 are based on the following: Strongly Disagree (SD). Disagree (D). Moderately Disagree (MD). Neither Agree Nor Disagree (NAND). Moderately Agree (MA). Agree (A). Strongly Agree (SA).

Table 4. Frequency of responses for each question when mobile Facebook was used

Questionnaire Items	SD	D	MD	NAND	MA	A	SA
Q1. I think that I would like to use this Social Application frequently.	5	4	3	3	5	5	5
Q2. I found the Social Application unnecessarily complex.	7	4	6	0	3	3	7
Q3. I thought that visualization and selection of contacts through this Social Application was easy.	4	4	6	5	4	2	5
Q4. I think that I would need the support of a technical person to be able to use this Social Application.	3	5	7	3	2	5	5
Q5. I found the functions for contacts visualization and read/write messages in this Social Application were well integrated.	5	4	2	4	5	6	4
Q6. I thought there was too much inconsistency in this Social Application.	5	2	6	5	6	5	0
Q7. I would imagine that most people would learn to use this Social Application very quickly.	4	4	2	6	12	1	1
Q8. I found this Social Application very cumbersome to use, especially when I write/read messages.	3	1	4	3	10	6	3
Q9. I felt very confident using this Social Application.	0	4	8	4	9	2	3
Q10. I needed to learn a lot of things before I could get going with this Social Application.	3	7	4	3	3	6	4

With respect to mobile Windows Live we could observe that seventeen people think that they would like to use this Social Application frequently, despite the fact that sixteen participants found the Social Application unnecessarily complex. In the same way sixteen respondents think that visualization and selection of contacts through mobile Windows Live was easy. We observed a draw on the statement "*I think that I would need the support of a technical person to be able to use this Social Application.*" where eleven participants agree with this idea and other eleven disagreed, and eight people neither agreed or disagreed.

Fifteen participants found the functions for contacts visualization and read/write messages in this Social Application were well integrated. Another draw was detected when fourteen participants perceived too much inconsistency in mobile Windows Live, and other fourteen think the opposite.

Seventeen respondents would imagine that most people would learn to use this Social Application very quickly, Nevertheless fifteen people think that this Social Application very cumbersome to use, especially when I write/read messages.

Table 5. Frequency of responses for each question when mobile Twitter was used

Questionnaire Items	SD	D	MD	NAND	MA	A	SA
Q1. I think that I would like to use this Social Application frequently.	5	2	0	2	2	8	11
Q2. I found the Social Application unnecessarily complex.	2	3	1	8	6	4	6
Q3. I thought that visualization and selection of contacts through this Social Application was easy.	7	2	2	4	6	3	6
Q4. I think that I would need the support of a technical person to be able to use this Social Application.	7	4	3	4	6	4	2
Q5. I found the functions for contacts visualization and read/write messages in this Social Application were well integrated.	2	8	5	4	2	5	4
Q6. I thought there was too much inconsistency in this Social Application.	9	5	2	6	3	2	3
Q7. I would imagine that most people would learn to use this Social Application very quickly.	2	3	5	7	3	6	4
Q8. I found this Social Application very cumbersome to use, especially when I write/ read messages.	6	4	1	5	4	6	4
Q9. I felt very confident using this Social Application.	6	8	1	6	5	2	2
Q10. I needed to learn a lot of things before I could get going with this Social Application.	5	7	3	1	4	3	7

Thirteen people did not felt very confident using this Social Application, and six selected the neutral option for this particular perception. And fifteen participants think that they needed to learn a lot of things before I could get going with mobile Windows Live. See Table 6.

The column titles of Table 6 are based on the following: Strongly Disagree (SD). Disagree (D). Moderately Disagree (MD). Neither Agree Nor Disagree (NAND). Moderately Agree (MA). Agree (A). Strongly Agree (SA).

CURRENT CHALLENGES FACING THE ORGANIZATION

One of the main challenges was the variety of mobile devices used by users, which affected the correct visualization of the interfaces on certain equipment; in fact the speed of interface-display was different in many mobile devices of the participants. It was evident that interfaces allowed better visualization and handling in smart

Table 6. Frequency of responses for each question when mobile Windows Live was used

Questionnaire Items	SD	D	MD	NAND	MA	A	SA
Q1. I think that I would like to use this Social Application frequently.	4	3	5	1	6	7	4
Q2. I found the Social Application unnecessarily complex.	4	3	3	4	3	6	7
Q3. I thought that visualization and selection of contacts through this Social Application was easy.	5	5	2	2	4	2	10
Q4. I think that I would need the support of a technical person to be able to use this Social Application.	2	9	0	8	4	4	3
Q5. I found the functions for contacts visualization and read/write messages in this Social Application were well integrated.	4	2	5	4	0	7	8
Q6. I thought there was too much inconsistency in this Social Application.	6	1	7	2	4	6	4
Q7. I would imagine that most people would learn to use this Social Application very quickly.	3	5	9	3	5	4	1
Q8. I found this Social Application very cumbersome to use, especially when I write/read messages.	7	1	3	4	6	4	5
Q9. I felt very confident using this Social Application.	8	0	5	6	5	1	5
Q10. I needed to learn a lot of things before I could get going with this Social Application.	0	5	5	2	8	6	4

phones. These aspects could surely influence the perception of people about the interfaces' usability.

Another important aspect to consider was the lack of more formal statistical evaluations which were not carried out due to time and specific purposes on this stage of the research. Obviously, these analyses and other traditional (but important) usability testing were established as part of subsequent steps in this research.

The third major challenge is to justify the reliability of the (under construction) new measurement strategy. However it is difficult to venture into the affirmation of this statement at this stage of the research. A second stage of the research will involve the comparison of a preliminary version of the proposed strategy with other already available and check their performance by statistical tests complemented by in-depth discussion regarding the reliability of these methods.

While this study focuses on the three (perhaps) most popular social applications, exist a wide number of this kind of software which could be most usable than the considered applications. Also we just evaluate a single use of the applications. According to Sun et al. (2011), expanded (more applications) and longer term studies (daily usage of the applications) are recommended to obtain better and clear perspectives on usability. Additionally, we just analyzed four specific tasks related to visualization of contacts and write/read text messages, because were considered as sufficiently general to be carried in the three kinds of applications alike. In addition, our empirical study results highlight other limitations related to the participants, which were primarily young adults and none under twenty years old. Currently, several teens and even elders could access to social applications and must be considered into the study in order to provide a complete perspective on social applications usability.

SOLUTIONS AND RECOMMENDATIONS

Study Findings and Discussion

Our study result shows that, on average, almost 59% percent of the participants whose age ranged from 20 to 31 (the vast majority) think that they would like to use mobile Social Applications frequently, although they found these mobile tools unnecessarily complex (almost 50%), even at level of require the support of a technical person to be able to use this Social Application (39%); another 53% perceived the applications as very cumbersome to use, especially when they write/read messages.

These results demonstrates that (at least at a certain level) possibilities (and even some virtues) of mobile versions of Facebook, Twitter, and Windows Live, outweigh his faults. The majority of the participants (47%) thought that visualization and selection of contacts through this Social Application was easy enough. Additionally almost 46% of the participants found the functions for contacts visualization and read/write messages in these applications were well integrated. This perception contributed to almost 48% of the respondents noticed the consistency of these applications. These virtues certainly could influence to increase the confidence of people using the considered mobile Social Applications (44%).

An interesting result was observed in the answers given to statement "*I needed to learn a lot of things before I could get going with this Social Application,*" 50% responds affirmatively. Bearing in mind some additional comments of the participants was possible to establish that this behavior occur due to the view of possibilities and new advantages, and lack of technological knowledge (even including some features of their own mobile devices). We could say that this study awoke the curiosity of the participants and encouraged them to "*want*" to learn more about these technologies usage. Therefore, we could to perceive this as a positive thinking.

Nevertheless the positive perceptions on the usability of these applications are very close to the negatives. In fact approximately thirty eight people perceive the applications in a negative way, and twelve participants could not decide. Only 44% of the respondents perceived these applications on a positive way. This is consistent with the results of the SUS analysis performed for each mobile Social Application following the scoring process described in subsection *"Technology Components"*. Table 7 shows the individual SUS scores obtained.

According to Jeff Sauro (http://www.measuringusability.com/) sixty eight represents the average SUS score (based on the evaluation of five hundred studies performed). A SUS score above a sixty eight would be considered above average and anything below sixty eight is below average. In this way the three results (and the overall) were under the suggested average.

Concluding Remarks and Future Work

We detected several opportunities to improve the interaction and usability of the mobile Social Applications. The perceived drawbacks are closely related to the user interface design. A redesign of the entire interface complemented with a simplest interaction model could lead to mitigate the perception of complexity. In the same way the incorporation of visual elements as icons, and pictures, could to improve the visualization and identification of contacts. Other important aspect is related to contacts representation, combining multidimensional and one-dimensional avatars to represent the presence of the users/members in the community will allow enriching the user experience by integrating behavioral expressiveness (such as happiness, interest, motivation, anger, among others) into avatars and emoticons.

Additionally interface elements as tabbed-pane could to contribute to makes easier the access to a specific contact. Another important concern was the number of turns (number of text-lines visualized at a time), we suggest to design the user interface in order to displaying at least seven lines of text at a time. The number

Table 7. Results (on average) of the individual SUS evaluation

Mobile Social Application	SUS score
Mobile Twitter	49
Mobile Facebook	47
Mobile Windows Live	46
Overall Average	47

of *turns* is directly related to an adequate implementation and configuration of the Up-Down Scroll., avoiding at any cost the incorporation of lateral scrollbar.

Effective strategies to mitigate these issues are frequently presented in guidelines and best-practices fashion, these alternatives could benefit directly to developers and programmers.

On other hand, some researches such as (Paavilainen, 2010; Mendoza et al. 2011) reflects that results of usability studies could represent a reliable source for these alternatives including also heuristic for usability evaluation. In fact, heuristic evaluation is the most popular of the usability inspection methods. Heuristic evaluation is done as a systematic inspection of a user interface design for usability. The goal of heuristic evaluation is to find the usability problems in the design so that they can be attended to as part of an iterative design process (Nielsen, 2005). In this vein, the findings of this research could represent a convenient starting point to structure a preliminary set of heuristics oriented to evaluate usability in user interfaces for mobile text based social applications. A proposed strategy to analyze the reliability of the evaluation method consists in generate a prototype based on the recommendations derived from this study. Then, evaluate the usability of the prototype by other usability questionnaire (e.g. CSUQ, Lewis [1995], albeit would be necessary an in-depth revision of the reliability of the available methods). The results could be corroborated by statistical analyzes of variance and significance tests.

This research reveals additional potential avenues for future work. One of them consist in complement the data collection by including additional classical usability measurements such as time for task completion, error rates, among others; which provide a wide outlook on the usability of the mobile text based social applications. In this way, it will be necessary also consider a wider range of mobile devices including tablets and tablet-smart phones (e.g. The Samsung Galaxy Tab 2, see http://www.samsung.com/in/consumer/mobile-phone/mobile-phone/tablet-smartphone). Another aspect to consider is the analysis of emerging technologies such as video chat services and their communication tools which have become increasingly popular (e.g. Tian et al, 2012).

REFERENCES

Brace, I. (2008). *Questionnaire design: How to plan, structure, and write survey material for effective market research* (2nd ed.). London, England: Kogan Page Publishers.

Brooke, J. (1996). SUS: A "quick and dirty" usability scale. In Jordan, P. W., Thomas, B., Weerdmeester, B. A., & McClelland, A. L. (Eds.), *Usability evaluation in industry*. London, England: Taylor and Francis.

Cui, Y., Honkala, M., Pihkala, K., Kinnunen, K., & Grassel, G. (2010). Linked Internet UI: A mobile user interface optimized for social networking. In *MobileHCI 2010* (pp. 45–54). Lisbon, Portugal: ACM Press. doi:10.1145/1851600.1851611

Dansky, H. K., Thompson, D., & Sanner, T. (2006). A framework for evaluating ehealth research. *Evaluation and Program Planning, 29*(4), 397–404. doi:10.1016/j.evalprogplan.2006.08.009

Finstad, K. (2010). Response interpolation and scale sensitivity: Evidence against 5-point scales. *Journal of Usability Studies, 5*(3), 104–110.

Harding, M., Storz, O., Nigel, D., & Friday, A. (2009). Planning ahead: Techniques for simplifying mobile service use. In *HotMobile 2009*. Santa Cruz, CA, USA: ACM Press. doi:10.1145/1514411.1514422

Hewett, T. T., Baecker, R., Card, S., Carey, T., Gasen, J., Mantei, M., et al. (1996). *ACM SIGCHI Curricula for human-computer interaction*. Retrieved October 13, 2009, from http://www.acm.org/sigchi/cdg/cdg2.html

ISO International Organization for Standardization. (1998). International ISO standard 9241-11, ergonomic requirements for office work with visual display terminals (VDTs) - Part 11: Guidance on usability (1st ed.). Switzerland.

Jung, Y., Anttila, A., & Blom, J. (2008). Designing for the evolution of mobile contacts application. In *MobileHCI 2008* (pp. 449–452). Amsterdam, the Netherlands: ACM Press. doi:10.1145/1409240.1409311

Kuen Seong Su, D., & Siew Yen Yee, V. (2007). Designing usable interface for navigating mobile chat messages. In *OZCHI '07* (pp. 291–294). Adelaide, Australia: ACM Press. doi:10.1145/1324892.1324953

Lewis, R. J. (1995). IBM computer usability satisfaction questionnaires: Psychometric evaluation and instructions for use. *International Journal of Human-Computer Interaction, 1*(7), 57–78. doi:10.1080/10447319509526110

Mendoza-González, R., Vargas Martin, M., & Rodríguez Martínez, L. (2011). *Identifying the Essential Design Requirements for Usable E-Health Communities in Mobile Devices, E-Health Communities and Online Self-Help Groups-Applications and Usage* (Smedberg, Å., & Global, I. G. I., Eds.).

Nakhimovsky, Y., Eckle, D., & Riegelsberger, J. (2009). Mobile user experience research: Challenges, methods & tools. In *Workshop on Human-Computer Interaction and Security Systems, ACM CHI 2009* (pp. 4795-4798). Boston, Massachusetts, USA: ACM Press.

Nguyen, V. T., & Oh, H. A. (2010). Users' needs for social tagging and sharing on mobile contacts. In *MobileHCI 2010* (pp. 387–388). Lisbon, Portugal: ACM Press.

Nielsen, J. (1993). *Usability engineering*. San Francisco, CA: Morgan Kaufmann.

Nielsen, J. (2005). Heuristic evaluation. Technical Report. UseIt, ISSN 1548-5552, 2005. Retrieved February 1, 2012 from http://www.useit.com/papers/heuristic/

Paavilainen, J. (2010). Critical review on video game evaluation heuristics: Social games perspective. In *ACM Future Play 2010* (pp. 56–65). Vancouver, BC, Canada: ACM Press. doi:10.1145/1920778.1920787

Pabllo, C., Soto, R., & Campos, J. (2008). Mobile medication administration system: Application and architecture. In *EATIS'08*. Aracaju, Sergipe, Brazil: ACM Press. doi:10.1145/1621087.1621128

Schusteritsch, R., Wei, C. Y., & LaRosa, M. (2007). Towards the perfect infrastructure for usability testing on mobile devices. *In Proceedings of CHI 2007* (pp. 1839-1844). San Jose, CA, USA. ACM Press.

Sun, S.-T., Pospisil, E., Muslukhov, I., Dindar, N., Hawkey, K., & Beznosov, K. (2011, July). *What makes users refuse web single sign-on? An empirical investigation of OpenID* (pp. 1–20). Pittsburgh, PA, USA: SOUPS. doi:10.1145/2078827.2078833

Thompson, D., Canada, A., Bhatt, R., Davis, J., Plesko, L., & Baranowski, T. (2006). eHealth recruitment challenges. *Evaluation and Program Planning, 29*(4), 433–440. doi:10.1016/j.evalprogplan.2006.08.004

Tian, L., Ahn, J., Cheng, H., Xing, X., Liang, L., Han, R., et al. (2012). Demo – MVChat: Flasher detection for mobile video chat. In *MobiSys 2012* (p 457). Low Wood Bay, Lake District, UK.

Tullis, T. S., & Stetson, J. (2004). *A comparison of questionnaires for assessing website usability*. Paper presented at the Usability Professionals Association Conference. Minneapolis, Minnesota.

Universidad de Granada. Spain. (2013). *Mobile devices*. Retrieved May 23, 2012 from http://leo.ugr.es/J2ME/INTRO/intro_4.htm

von Niman, B., Rodríguez-Ascaso, A., Brown, S., & Sund, T. (2007). User experience design guidelines for telecare (e-health) services. *Interaction, 14*(5), 36–40. doi:10.1145/1288515.1288537

Vronay, D., Smith, M., & Drucker, S. (1999). Alternative interfaces for chat. *UIST'99 CHI Letters, 1*(1), 19-26.

KEY TERMS AND DEFINITIONS

Human Computer Interaction: According to (Hewett et al., 1996), from a computer science perspective, human-computer interaction (HCI) deal with the interaction between one or more humans and one or more computers using the user interface of a program.

Likert Scale: According to Brace (2008), is frequently known as "agree-disagree scale" and the scale was named after its inventor, psychologist Rensis Likert. "The technique presents respondents with a series of attitude dimensions, for each of which they are asked whether, and how strongly, they agree or disagree, using one of a number of positions on a five-point scale." Also it is common to find seven to eleven point-scales. Likert scale is the most widely used approach to scaling responses in survey research, such that the term is often used interchangeably with rating scale, or more accurately the Likert-type scale, even though the two are not synonymous (see also http://en.wikipedia.org/wiki/Likert_scale).

Microblogging: esTwitter (http://estwitter.com/microblogging/) Defines microblogging as a new form of Internet communication that wins followers every day being Twitter (https://twitter.com/) the most popular microblogging system today. The messages posted in are very simple; most microblogging systems allow a maximum of 140 characters per message. In those 140 characters a person can tell to others from what he/she is doing, interact with others through replies and private messages, post things, promote themselves, make friends and networking, find a job, among other conversation topics. Microblogging could be perceived as a kind of mixture of chat, forums, blog and the "*state*" that people put in the Messenger.

Mobile Devices: Aka information device, handheld device, handheld computer, consumer electronic, embedded device, or small device. Represent pocket-sized computing gadgets which are small enough to be carried and used during transportation, even wirelessly.

Text-Based Social Applications: For this research we define *Text-based Social Applications* as those software tools which facilitates the interactive communication between people, on the web or network, through sending/receiving text messages.

These tools include: Text-chat, e-mail, microblogging, instant-messaging, social networks, blogs, among others.

Usability: The standard ISO 9241-11(ISO, 1998, pp. 1-2) defines usability like "Extent to which a product can be used by specified users to achieve specified goals with effectiveness, efficiency and satisfaction in a specified context of use."

Usability Test: According to Jakob Nielsen (1993), "User testing with real users is the most fundamental usability method and is in some sense irreplaceable, since it provides direct information about how people use computers and what their exact problems are with the concrete interface being tested."

Section 3
Usability of Critical Systems

Chapter 10
Pilot Implementation Driven by Effects Specifications and Formative Usability Evaluation

Anders Barlach
Roskilde University, Denmark

Morten Hertzum
Roskilde University, Denmark

Jesper Simonsen
Roskilde University, Denmark

EXECUTIVE SUMMARY

This chapter reports on the usability-engineering work performed throughout the pilot implementation of an Electronic Healthcare Record (EHR). The case describes and analyzes the use of pilot implementations to formatively evaluate whether the usability of the EHR meets the effects specified for its use.

The project was initiated during the autumn of 2010 and concluded in the spring of 2012. The project configured and implemented an EHR at a Maternity ward at one hospital located in a European region and then transferred this system to another ward at another hospital in the same region.

DOI: 10.4018/978-1-4666-4046-7.ch010

The project was conducted using effects-driven IT development: a process comprised of workshops with specification of the usage effects by management and end-users followed by an agile development process progressing through mock-ups, prototypes and finally the pilot system. Effects were iteratively refined and evaluated to achieve alignment with the intended design, and quantitatively measured to document the desired effects.

The pilot implementation is analyzed, and the lessons learned are discussed in relation to usability engineering in general.

ORGANIZATION BACKGROUND

This section introduces the chapter and describes the experiences of the IT vendor CSC Scandihealth in working with pilot implementation on the basis of effects-driven IT development and the EHR client, a large hospital complex located in a European region, the Hospital for short.

A pilot implementation is defined as: "a field test of a properly engineered, yet unfinished system, in its intended environment, using real data and aiming – through real-use experience – to explore the value of the system, improve or assess its design, and reduce implementation risk." (Hertzum, Bansler, Havn, & Simonsen, 2012). Pilot implementations are field trials and in that sense constitute a continuation of prototype evaluations into the field. In this chapter, we describe a case where the preparations were carried out before a pilot implementation included using workshops with mock-ups as well as several versions of prototypes. The pilot implementation was supported by so-called 'effects-driven IT development' (Hertzum & Simonsen, 2011) by which the desired effects of using the system were specified, used as specifications for the mock-ups and prototypes, and finally measured as part of a formative usability evaluation based on the system used during actual work as part of the pilot implementation. In the following, we outline the strategies of both the vendor and client and the circumstances making the pilot implementation and effects-driven IT development relevant. We set the stage and describe the effects specified to produce the input to the succeeding usability evaluation. Then, we describe the case and the pilot implementation including planning and design, technical configuration, organizational adaption, use of the system, and the learning that took place. We conclude the chapter by discussing challenges, solutions, and recommendations.

Organizational Facts and Strategy: CSC Scandihealth

CSC Scandihealth is a company within the Computer Sciences Corporation and is part of its global healthcare Vertical, which specializes in delivering IT to public and private healthcare providers. CSC Scandihealth (in the following referred to as CSC, for short) employs 375 healthcare IT specialists in Denmark with an annual turnover of USD78 million.

The CSC's mission is to "deliver a *solution* to the client," rather than "delivering a *product* to the client." This marks a decisive shift in attitude towards the vendor-client relationship in CSC. To achieve this goal, the company and its employees must engage in various processes that must be aligned with the clinical work the solutions are to support. The increase in intimacy with the client's core business and the need of establishing technology consistent with individual healthcare providers is stated by CSC's CEO Freddy Lykke:

The vision we have is that the healthcare community is increasingly integrated into the various sections of society, coming closer and closer together, and our mission is that we [CSC] can help to make the linkage of the Healthcare community (Barlach & Simonsen, 2011).

Freddy Lykke elaborates how this vision can be implemented through a bottom-up approach:

The bottom-up approach is basically another way of saying that it is the clinicians themselves that are to define how their work processes are to be supported, rather than we [CSC] come with a system where we have defined how we think the work-flow should be at the various hospitals and their wards. We present a system that allows the clinicians to dynamically describe how the system should work in their specific situations (Barlach & Simonsen, 2011).

Organizational Facts and Strategy: The Hospital

Denmark is divided into five regions, each responsible for providing publicly funded hospital services to approximately 1 million citizens. Rehabilitation and prevention is delegated to the municipalities within the regions and to General Practitioners, who are self-employed and funded directly by the national government. The Hospital is situated in one of the five regions and comprises:

- 1,753 beds plus an additional 50 beds in the patient hotel.
- Approx. 8,700 employees.
- An annual budget of nearly USD1279 million.

The overall goals of the Hospital are to deliver a consistent service of high quality while remaining an effective organization within the financial limits of the region (Region North Jutland Consolidated, 2011). The Hospital management has defined five strategic focus areas for IT in the region:

1. Stable and reliable operation of the solutions supporting the end-users.
2. Effective utilization of IT in the region.
3. Coherence in services and decisions across the organization.
4. Innovation as a factor in creating growth and an attractive workplace.
5. Ensuring ownership and clear responsibility in management and planning.

The first two focus areas calls for the use of effect as the actual use of the systems becomes a success parameter for any IT implementation and therefore must be subject to an evaluation. The complexity of healthcare work and the uncertainties in requirements defined in advance of a project start, means that the Hospital needs a process enabling learning during IT projects. Experimentation becomes a mean to acquire knowledge on how to achieve desired effects. The tool is formative evaluation of effects specifications that set the success criteria of the design in use (pilot implementation).

The Overall Software Development Context

We look at the different life-cycle models present in relation to the case to illustrate how pilot implementation interacts with both models from an industry perspective. The development of the technical framework in a slow forward moving Waterfall life-cycle dictates how the prototyping process can evolve and adds to the complexity of mounting a pilot implementation. On the other hand the framework development has the potential to gain valuable knowledge from the prototyping and later pilot implementation.

By comparing Prototyping (Nielsen, 1993) (Jansson, Handest, Nielsen, Saebye, & Parnas, 2002) and "traditional" Water-fall (Royce, 1987) project life-cycle models in this client setting we aim to illustrate how the project benefit from the pilot implementation and help identify challenges.

The Waterfall model is characterized by an assumption that the lifecycle of software development is a sequential process beginning with specification and ending with test and delivery. Requirements can be identified in advance before programming is carried out and testing is intended to confirm the fit between the specified requirements and the actual needs of the end-users once implemented (Royce, 1987). A pilot implementation in this setting would not make much sense; since the majority of resources available to the project have already been spend on implementing the knowledge (requirements) available, and changes would not scheduled before the system goes into production.

Prototyping differs from this approach by using experiments (prototypes) to learn as requirements are specified and understood in a simulated context of use before putting large amounts of resources into implementing the requirements (Floyd, 1984; Nielsen, 1993; Stapleton, 1998). Pilot implementation takes this approach a step further by evaluating the use in a restricted but real work environment (Hertzum et al., 2012).

How come the Water-fall approach is applied in the first place? The reason could be collaboration between client and supplier is regulated by commercial contracts regulating the transfer of responsibility during the system development lifecycle. This transfer requires strict boundaries between requirements before the development and delivery of a system in accordance with predefined specs, and the Waterfall approach is deemed particularly suited for this type of process by the CSC and Hospital organizations. In the client case with the CSC, it is a public institution (The Hospital) with a standard contract that governs the overall implementation project. These contracts are regulated by government agencies and contracts are only beginning to allow for specifications to be discovered during the development lifecycle, but still with the lion's share of the risk carried by the vendor.

Another reason for choosing the Waterfall approach can be found in the complexity of the systems being developed. The complexity of making Reliable, Adaptable systems that can be Maintained and Perform in the environment for which it is intended requires much effort and time to be successful and advocates against the use of prototypes as the primary model for the project, in short these high level requirements are called RAMP (Davis, Bersoff, & Comer, 1988).

To illustrate the differences between the two life-cycle models we adopt the metrics suggested by Davis et al. (Davis et al., 1988). The metrics suggested are; *shortfalls* as how far are the developed system from fulfilling the actual requirements while applying the two different models (Davis et al., 1988). Another metric could be *lateness* since the process of learning is characteristic for most project models they all generate new requirements and has different degrees of latency from discovery to implementation (Davis et al., 1988). *Adaptability* to new requirements or longevity of the system as seen in how long before it needs to be replaced could be candidates for these metrics too. Finally, *inappropriateness* as the ability or lack of same, to meet new requirements without delay during the remaining lifecycle, e.g. ideally a new requirement can be met with an existing functionality (Davis et al., 1988).

In the CSC-Hospital case, both life-cycle models are present for several reasons. The primary reason for the Waterfall model to be implemented is a consequence of the contract dictating changes of lifecycle phases where money and responsibility are exchanged between the client (The Hospital) and the vendor (CSC). This means specifications are made before development or programming begins and requires careful negotiations to be changed once the contract is signed. The other significant reason for the Waterfall model to be present can be seen as a consequence of the complexity of an EHR. The RAMP requirements in a mission critical system like an EHR, is demand for a stable and performing platform while being adaptable to a large organization as found in the case. These requirements are not specified by end-users directly but are found in the service level agreements of a typical client-vendor contract such as the one governing the project in the case.

The project needs both models; the handling of RAMP requirements by the Waterfall model and the agility of Prototyping while learning and adapting to end-user requirements. The solution is to implement a two layered design by building the system in a technological framework with configured elements.

The framework is developed in a strict Waterfall organized project environment, and covered by the main client-vendor contract. This means *shortfalls*, both originating from the contract specifications and changes discovered during the project, are approximately one year underway. This latency would be responsible for a high degree of lateness since the process of design, programming and test before being released means learning is slow to be incorporated. If this was the only way development was undertaken, the project would be too slow to learn. The appendix of the contract allows for more agile configuration processes to negotiate the risks of *lateness* and *shortfall* as confirmation of requirements implemented in the system fit the actual need experienced by the end-users, would not be possible before the final system implementation was completed.

By splitting the system and project process into two, the project is making up for this latency in meeting requirements, and the ever changing organization of work carried out by the client end-users. With the introduction of prototyping and pilot implementation in the configuration process, the project is attempting to adapt and close the gap between specified and actual requirements. This configuration is organized with effects driven method and adoption of elements from different sources of process improvement, which have been integrated and adapted internally to local conditions. It involves elements of agile development methods such as the Dynamic Systems Development Method (DSDM) (Stapleton, 1998) and Scrum (Schwaber & Beedle, 2002).

The purpose of designing with prototypes is to negotiate uncertainties in the specification and challenge the participant's visions, expectations, and hypotheses through concrete IT experience (Bødker, Simonsen, & Kensing, 2009; Simonsen, Hertzum, & Barlach, 2011). The purposes of effects in this prototyping and pilot implementation setting are dual; Effects are used in specifying requirements during the configuration process resulting in the prototypes. Effects are also used to evaluate how the end-users experienced the actual requirements as the system is first used in a laboratory setting before it is put to use in a pilot implementation.

The EHR is built in a configurable standard system or technical framework; CSC Clinical Suite (CCS) as the Hospital's overall electronic healthcare record (EHR). CCS is implemented in overlapping stages as the Hospital gradually adopts the new technology.

The main EHR project has been underway for 4 years and has entered a phase where the technological framework is in place, and the need for adapting the configurable elements to the end-users' work requirements are the main focus. The pilot implementation presents the Hospital organization and CSC with an opportunity to learn about the new challenges facing them onwards in the implementations process. It further allows them to experiment with ways of achieving the goals set out by the Hospital management in the strategy; effective use of IT and a stable platform across the organization. Further the Hospital aims to establish the necessary competences to configure and organizationally implement IT systems within of the organization. In other words, Hospital staff must learn to undertake agile processes while experimenting with design to support clinical work.

To meet the strategy's call for organizational learning and effective utilization of IT, the project studied in this case choose to apply a pilot implementation in the process.

Pilot Implementation

It is well known to use various prototype versions of an IT system during the development process as it allows the designer to learn how end-users respond to the design (Floyd, 1984; Nielsen, 1993) and make a formative evaluation with input on how to improve the design. In order to determine the fit between the use experienced by the end-users and the design proposed, a common approach is to use mock-ups and prototypes (Floyd, 1984) during design and development to move still closer to real-use conditions. A pilot implementation is the last step before a system enters the lifecycle stage where it is finalized for operational service and, contrary to prototyping; it involves using the system in the field for real work. We are looking into the challenges of this transition from prototype to pilot-system. The elements of pilot implementation are planning and design, technical configuration, organizational adaptation, use, and learning (Hertzum et al., 2012):

Planning and design, the project defines how it will acquire data to evaluate the design, logistic issues like where the pilot should take place, how long it will last and how participation among the involved organizations and end-users will be coordinated.

Technical configuration, this element considers the technical tasks required to perform the transition from prototype into the pilot-system. To some extent it resembles the final phases of the development process, but since the pilot is operating in an end-user context not yet covered by the main implementation project, the pilot implementation must handle the finalization to a specific instance of real-use. Considerable re-use of this work can be expected when concluding the development project, but it is often postponed until the final design has been implemented to save development costs.

Organizational adaptation is concerned with how the organization is prepared for the use of the system. Tasks like training of end-users, coordination with adjacent units which are supporting the work performed at the pilot organization or the adoption of new or different work practices due to the system being taken into use.

Use, the system must support work in a realistic end-user environment. During use, the pilot participants can observe and experience how the design fits end-users' requirements and make measurements to support the formative evaluation.

Learning is the process of acquiring new knowledge regarding how the design was interpreted by the intended end-users, what was supportive towards the goals of the development project and which anticipated effects failed to emerge in the pilot context (Hertzum et al., 2012).

EDIT

The project needed a method that would allow for learning through formative evaluation and the need for pilot implementation to negotiate implementation risks while adhering to the strategy of both CSC and the Hospital. The choice was made to apply the effects-driven IT development (EDIT) method (Simonsen et al., 2011). The development project was organized as a Rapid Application Development (Hainey, 2007) process involving methods like short iterations – typically 2 weeks – and prototyping following CSC's effects driven IT-development. The Hospital provided the project management and the configuration of the electronic Partogram-Record while CSC was to provide process support, design suggestions and ensure documentation and evaluation of the project.

The EDIT process is a series of workshops driven by effects as the specification and usability evaluation tool with participation of different usability actors or stakeholder representatives (Figure 2). The usability actors in the project are:

- **Hospital organization managers:** Senior management representing local management across the Hospital organization, responsible for budget and strategy implementation at the political level.
- **Hospital organization project staff:** Responsible for the project deliveries, planning and configuring the actual system, employed by the Hospital organization.
- **End-users:** Clinical staff having first-hand experience with work performed in relation to the use of the system during the pilot.

The process is initiated with two parallel workshops involving management and end-users. They are held separately since experience shows the two groups have different priorities and needs regarding the process, and outcome. In both workshops design requirements are specified using effects rather than functional descriptions of the future system. Effects relate to the actual work the system is intended to support by taking into account variables like, who are the end-users, and what is the expected outcome of the task supported. An example of an effect specified in the project could sound like this:

The Midwife on call must be able to gather the general picture of the relevant tasks performed and interventions planned regarding an individual patient in her care.

This effect can evaluated as it is performed at the end of a watch/shift or while handing over the care responsibility of an individual patient. The midwife must experience sufficiency in the knowledge presented and not feel the need for looking elsewhere for missing information. The measurement of the effect lies in asking for the experience of the midwife in the context of use. E.g. *"Do you miss any information after having used the system to gain an overview of the patient?"*

Considering the technical configuration and the organizational adaptations (see Figure 1) the project learns as it moves forward in iterations with new versions of the mock-up or prototype each time. Progress is documented by the fit of the Effects specification with the prototype as it is evaluated in the workshops, which aim to move still further away from simulating work and towards conducting actual work (Use).

The formative evaluation allows the project to learn and progress toward more complete representation of a system with each iteration. Using mock-ups and prototypes as tools during the EDIT process can be seen as a progression towards the pilot system, which is capable of supporting real work (Figure 3).

To understand how mock-ups and prototypes differ from each other and the pilot system we adopt an ANSI/SPARC (Tsichritzis & Klug, 1978) inspired perspective on what an information system consists of on a general level. In short, the model has three layers: an external layer represented by the graphical user interface (GUI), the conceptual layer containing functions and providing the necessary means to access data in the internal layer and transfers them to the external layer. The in-

Figure 1. A model of pilot implementation showing the four elements: planning and design; technical configuration; organizational adaption and use contributing to learning (Hertzum, et al., 2012)

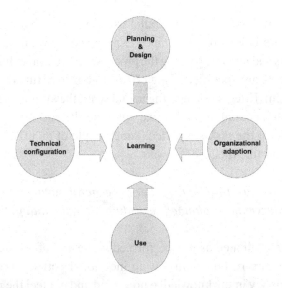

Figure 2. EDIT process, starting out with effects specification workshops, followed by iterations of workshops with mock-ups/prototypes before culminating with a pilot implementation

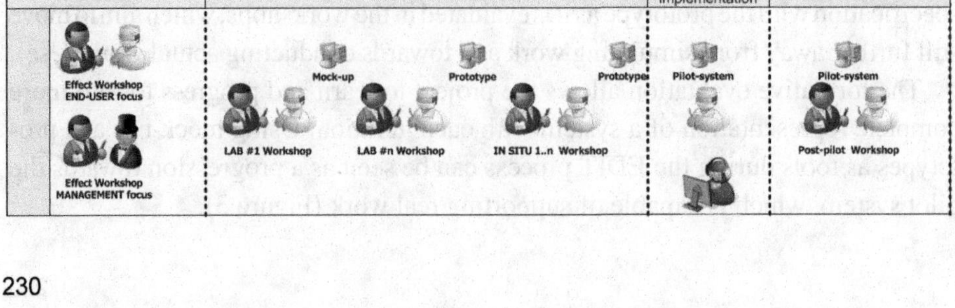

Pilot Implementation Driven by Effects Specifications

Figure 3. During the EDIT workshops, the role of the effects design diminishes in relation to the role of mock-ups and prototypes when performing the formative evaluation to determine progression towards enabling real use

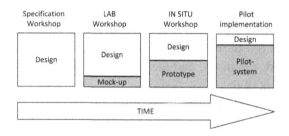

Figure 4. Differences among mock-up, horizontal prototype, vertical prototype and the pilot-system from an ANSI/SPARC three layer perspective

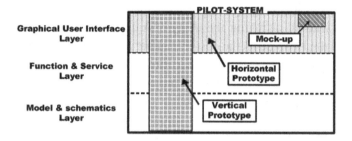

ternal layer contains the data model and is an extension of the database allowing for persistence of data (Figure 4).

If we look at the different representations of the pilot-system design during the EDIT process, they start out as mock-ups. This is a simple way to experiment with design ideas, and represent only a very small part of the GUI with no function or model representation in comparison to the envisioned pilot system.

Evolving through the EDIT workshops (Figure 3) the prototypes can be horizontal or vertical (Nielsen, 1993) depending on the nature of formative evaluation the EDIT process requires.

The pilot system is the goal of the process, encompassing all the envisioned use performed by the intended usability actors and fulfilling the requirements set for the project. It is important to realize that each step made in the process requires effort as with each new prototype and finally the pilot system covering all three layers both vertically and horizontally must the realized.

SETTING THE STAGE

The prototypes and pilot system are developed in CCS, which is a highly configurable framework tool based on the Oracle Healthcare Transaction Base (HTB). It is a multi-tiered platform and can be configured by various mark-up technologies XML, XSL etc. to define the elements of the EHR; overviews, clinical notes, results, standard plans, work situations, and the structure of the patients' medical record within the framework of the CCS.

In accordance with the strategy of the Hospital and considerations within the team of Hospital IT configurators the project defined the scope for knowledge of the pilot implementation as;

- Can the CCS support work in a clinical context? If not CSC and the Hospital have a serious problem delivering a working EHR?
- Can the end-users in another location adapt to a solution implemented in one location without changing the design? Again this is a major concern with CSC and the Hospital as the cost of making a new design for each unit would challenge the entire project. Further extension of project activities would tie up CSC resources in a development project longer than anticipated jeopardizing other deliveries.
- Can the Hospital learn to develop solutions in CCS using pilot implementation? It is the intension of the Hospital to become independent of CSC when it comes to configuration and implementation of CCS. Being able to rely on internal resources provides the necessary agility to achieve an ambitious implementation plan. Alternatively the Hospital is forced to spend time and money buying these services from external partners on a consulting basis.
- Can effects (EDIT) provide the project with a tool for formative evaluation? The Hospital's strategy states that they want to be able to evaluate the use of IT and work focused towards effects from the use of the CCS.

Effects in EDIT

Effect specifications are descriptions of the effects that the usability actors or end-users would like to obtain when they start using the envisioned IT system. CSC uses a generic template for effects specifications. This template has five parts: *Effect* (the effect to be obtained in a specified situation), *agent* (the end-user of the system in this situation), *practice* (a description of the clinical activity and intervention involved in the situation), *outcome* (the result of the activity), and *evaluation* (a description of how to assess the extent to which the effect has been achieved). The template represents an anticipated effect generated by the end-user in a specific work situation and when performing a given activity using the system.

The effects to be obtained from using the system can be assessed from multiple perspectives and at multiple levels of abstraction. Therefore, the effects are specified in a five-level hierarchy, as described in Figure 5. They range from abstract to concrete, being more and more technical. The hierarchy organizes effects to describe them as means to achieve other more abstract ends. This means–ends hierarchy is inspired by cognitive work analysis (Rasmussen, Pejtersen, & Goodstein, 1994; Vicente, 1999) and the participatory design method, MUST (Bødker et al., 2009).

The properties represented in the effects means–ends hierarchy are purposes and reasons at the top (high level of abstraction), general processes in the middle, and more specific information processes and the physical configuration of the IT system at the bottom.

Each level is described in the following section, inspired by work by Rasmussen and Vicente (Rasmussen et al., 1994; Vicente, 1999):

1.   **Purpose:** This is the highest level of abstraction and represents the goals and purposes in relation to the organizational environment and the goal pursued

Figure 5. Effects specification in five levels, ranging from abstract to physical effects. The stakeholder groups are located at the different levels in the hierarchy.

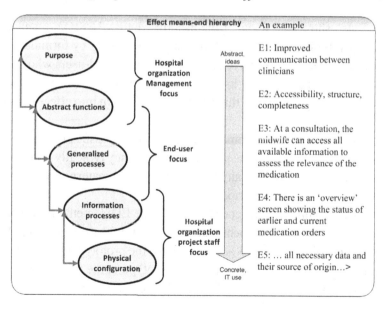

through the lower levels. It is typically identified as policies, service goals etc. regarding quality and efficiency at the enterprise level of the client organization.

2. **Abstract functions:** This level addresses the prioritization and allocation of resources to the various generalized processes and activities on the *Generalized processes* level below. The level describes the client's response, or strategy, to the environmental demands from level one and often relates to efficiency or the quality of service.

3. **Generalized processes:** This level represents business processes in terms of recurrent input–output processes and overall activities which are general and well-known in the work domain. It is not a detailed specification of an activity but might be compared to the "black box" metaphor because subprocesses or sub-activities are not specified at this level.

4. **Information processes:** This level represents information-processing tasks that define the generalized processes, including the human activities, as well as the use of equipment. Typically, these tasks precede or succeed a clinical intervention. Example: One of the tasks during the preparations for a consultation involves looking at the overview listing past consultations to determine whether there are any topics or events of relevance to the upcoming consultation. At this level, it is possible to map activities to the forms and views in the prototype.

5. **Physical configuration:** This is the lowest level of abstraction and consists of tools or objects which are the sources of information for a given tasks. At this level, detailed descriptions of user interfaces are given as screen mock-ups or interactive prototypes.

Figure 5 also shows the focus of the usability actors. Hospital management is involved in specifying effects at levels one and two, usually by formulating strategies. These overall effects are the reference point for the end-users who specify the effects they want to obtain in their use or clinical practice. The Hospital project staff then interprets the effects at level three and translates them into effect requirements at levels four and five.

The effects specified were primarily concerned with issues regarding viewing information at critical stages of the patient pathway. They typically described handover of responsibility from the outpatient clinic to the maternity ward or among staff during the shifting work periods of the day.

The process was initiated in accordance with the EDIT method (Figure 2). The workshops progressed from the specification of effects with the involved stakeholder from the Hospital (Figure 5). CCS accommodated the prototypes during workshops and after an IN-SITU workshop, testing the prototype in the ward intended for the pilot implementation, it was concluded that the design was ready for pilot imple-

Figure 6. EDIT pre-pilot: the workshop process of design and development of the midwife record, up until the preparations for the pilot implementation, at site 1 (University Hospital Maternity ward). EDIT pilot implementation: the timeline from pilot implementation and transition to full scale implementation at site 1 and 2.

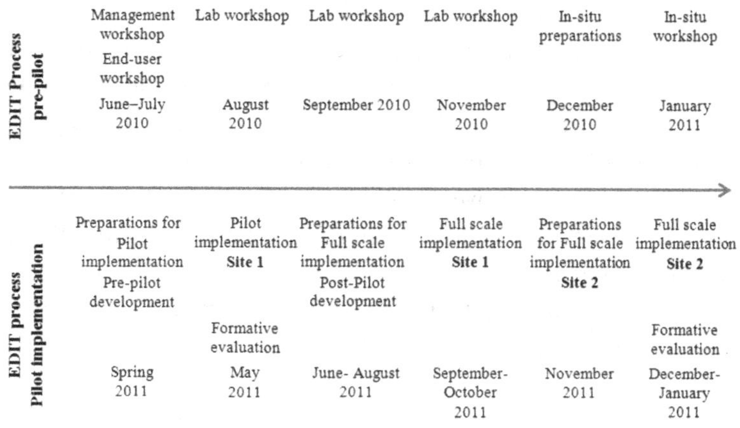

	Management workshop / End-user workshop	Lab workshop	Lab workshop	Lab workshop	In-situ preparations	In-situ workshop
EDIT Process pre-pilot	June–July 2010	August 2010	September 2010	November 2010	December 2010	January 2011

	Preparations for Pilot implementation / Pre-pilot development	Pilot implementation Site 1 / Formative evaluation	Preparations for Full scale implementation / Post-Pilot development	Full scale implementation Site 1	Preparations for Full scale implementation Site 2	Full scale implementation Site 2 / Formative evaluation
EDIT process Pilot Implementation	Spring 2011	May 2011	June- August 2011	September-October 2011	November 2011	December-January 2011

mentation, Figure 6 EDIT pre-pilot phase. Preparations began immediately after and are described in the case, Figure 6.

The lessons learned, regarding CSC's use of effects in the specification and development work with the client, are listed below:

Effects are easier for clinicians to understand, formulate, and prioritize than functionality specifications (Barlach & Simonsen, 2011).

One of the major concerns during requirement specification is the representation of end-users' actual needs in various work situations. In traditional specifications at the CSC, there is a tendency for documentation to be biased toward the configuration staff in terms of being dominated by technical vocabulary and system functionalities rather than exploring solutions to work problems in a language familiar to the end-user or clinical staff.

By specifying the system in terms of effects, the intension was to reduce the distance between what end-user expressed as requirements and what their actual needs were while working. This meant the effects could be challenged in a qualitative investigation during the workshops by asking the participants whether they could recognize the effects and whether they considered them relevant. During the pilot implementation, the effects were evaluated in a quantitative fashion using questionnaires as the usability-actors used the system at work.

Effects are stable, tempting, yet ambiguous for the IT developers (Barlach & Simonsen, 2011).

Effect specifications do not change after the early EDIT workshops (see Figure 2), and in CSC's projects they have proven to be very stable.

Effects create a tempting innovative "free space" for the configuration technicians. The technical domain is allowed to more or less freely translate the requirements related to specified effects without the constraints of traditional technical specifications of IT requirements. This "free space" (and dealing with the lack of technical requirements) can, however, prove problematic and require more experimentation with prototypes. The ambiguity inherent in the effects as they are subject to interpretation by the technical staff is a serious issue to be taken into consideration by any project that applies the effects method and relies on the collective knowledge of the configurators responsible for implementing the pilot system *(Barlach & Simonsen, 2011).*

The inherent ambiguity lies in the effects' requirement notation capability, and, as reported by earlier work on goal methods; effects can also be disruptive as communication and pose a risk by not providing any detailed technical specifications (Jureta, Faulkner, & Schobbens, 2008; Stacey & Eckert, 2003). In this project and previous projects end-users tend to tolerate these imperfections and value the negotiation benefits stemming from the speed or lack of lateness of using workshops with prototypes (see Figure 1).

Effect measurement at implementation requires technically robust framework systems of a reasonable quality (Barlach & Simonsen, 2011).

The systems for which effects are to be measured and evaluated must be technically both robust as defined by the RAMP requirements (Davis et al., 1988) and flexible so that *shortfalls* (Davis et al., 1988) identified can be corrected within a relative short time-frame in the configured elements – otherwise it will interrupt the implementation process and put the pilot implementation at risk of being terminated prematurely. The quality of the solution must be sufficient for effects to be realizable. This entails that framework changes must not emerge as necessary when the clinicians' start using the pilot system because framework implementation is performed according to a Waterfall process and would seriously slow the overall project and contract completion. However, it is possible to ensure the prompt inclusion of immediate and emerging requirements in the technological framework, but it requires careful planning of available resources from vendor and the acceptance of re-prioritizing other deliveries from the client.

CASE DESCRIPTION

In May 2011, a pilot implementation was planned at the first site (Figure 6), including both the maternity ward at a University hospital and 4 affiliated pregnancy outpatient clinics (Site 1).

After the pilot implementation, the design was evaluated, and while preparations for full-scale production were made on the technical element, the organizational adaptation was undertaken among the remaining end-users at Site 1. This included end-user training and dissemination of the documentation model among the clinical staff.

After implementing the system at Site 1, the Hospital turned its attention to the next site (Site 2). Site 2 is a smaller hospital with a maternity ward and one affiliated pregnancy outpatient clinics (Figure 6). The preparations undertaken at Site 2 were not technical configurations, but primarily organizational adaptation as the documentation model devised by the end-users at Site 1 had to be adopted by the clinical end-users at Site 2. Site 2 went into full-scale production on the system in December. The evaluation performed during the pilot implementation (Site 1) and the full-scale implementation (Site 1 and Site 2) provided input to the management both at hospital level but also at the corporate level with reference to the Hospital management and product strategy and the considerations outlined in the section *Setting the Stage*.

PLANNING AND DESIGN

There are several considerations involved in planning a successful pilot implementation. It requires effort of the entire organization either coming into direct contact with the pilot system or dealing with the consequences of work related to other aspects of using the system. The project team planning the pilot must consider both the resources readily available for the project to draw upon and the planning of contingencies of unforeseen events. The project manager and participants in general must consider the triple constraints allocated (time, resources and content) at every step in the pilot implementation, starting at the planning of the pilot. Some of the key considerations are discussed in the following:

Duration, how long can the organization handle the risk of the pilot implementation and allow staff to involve themselves in the system design? From the project point of view, too short a period of real-use will not allow for sufficient learning, while too long a period will tie up project resources in a redundant process and delay the completion of the project. The required length is dictated by the measurement and evaluation considerations, but there is a negotiation with the line-management involved since it is their budget and responsibility to ensure that "business" prevails without endangering the safety of the patients. As part of this negotiation the project promised hotline support on-site and a direct line to the management on the ward/outpatient clinic, in case events presented themselves warranting a fall-back maneuver. Experience from earlier pilot implementations with the CSC suggests that one week is a minimum duration to achieve a level of stable use allowing for an evaluation. Two weeks are preferred, but it requires a steady hand from management and in this case the project was the first-mover, and there was no previous experience within the organization to rely on.

Measurements, if there are to be a formative evaluation it is necessary to gather data with regard to user experience while using the system. How long must the users experience the system to be able to evaluate it with a satisfactory degree of confidence? This depends, among other things, on whether the project intends to apply qualitative, quantitative or statistical methods of evaluation. A spin-off from the pilot implementation can emerge if the evaluation is adopted by the line management, considerable goodwill can be expected as good design resulting in "business as usual" or improved quality or efficiency is in the direct interest of these usability actors and management.

From the project´s usability point-of-view, speed and agility is of the essence since a credible formative evaluation means input to either design changes or adding confidence in the existing design supports the end-users' work and brings the project closer to completion. Measurement instruments like the TLX or TAM are described in more detail in (Hart & Staveland, 1988; Venkatesh, Morris, Davis, & Davis, 2003) or how they can be utilized in Hertzum et al. (Simonsen et al., 2011). During the pilot implementation, different methods of measurement were utilized; questionnaires handed to individual usability-actors providing responses about their experience of using the EHR. Another approach was the observations made by on-site support staff from the Hospital and CSC. The measurements and observations were collected in a spreadsheet and evaluated by project staff during and after the pilot implementation.

Practical issues regarding the duty rosters: To understand the challenges involving clinical staff, it is necessary to understand the terms which they work under, and the complexity of planning depending on which parts of the organization that is involved in the pilot implementation.

There are typically 3 types of clinical work organizations interacting in conjunction over time: bed ward, outpatient clinic and day-hospital ward.

- The bed ward or just 'ward' is a traditional location with patients admitted for treatment and care around the clock; it is active 24 hours a day and can be found in highly specialized or general versions depending on the size of hospital and affiliation to the university. Emergency rooms, operation departments etc. are considered bed wards although they do not have patients staying overnight, but they are staffed and perform they function 24 hours a day.

- The Day-hospital ward is similar to the bed ward; however, it is not staffed at night, and consequently cannot house patients during the night. The only impact this has on the work or use of the Pilot-system is the nature of treatment and care which is limited to daytime and can be left to the patients to monitor at home.
- The outpatient clinic has a different workflow and often a supporting role in relation to the bed ward. Patient flow and tasks are well-defined and can be performed with short interactions between the staff. Typically tasks are follow-up on treatment and care initiated by the ward, but the patients do not need a continued monitoring by doctors and nurses to recover.

When planning the involvement of one or more of the above mentioned types of wards, it is easier to handle day-time operation since staffing are present in greater numbers. However, complexity and workload is higher during daytime and there are more staff and adjacent organizations to coordinate with, train and support. From a project perspective, planning must start ahead of the development process for two weighty reasons. First, keeping the momentum of the development process and still allowing for feedback from the formative evaluation means that planning cannot begin until the solution has reached the required degree of completion mentioned in the technical configuration section. Second, the planning must take into consideration that the Hospital must continue to operate at normal capacity. A pilot implementation is not undertaken without effort being invested by the Hospital. Rosters are made ahead and regulated by rules that cannot be manipulated by the project. E.g. a duty roster must be available 8 weeks before it is scheduled to be carried out. The pilot implementation described in this case thus began planning as early as in February for the pilot implementation to take place in May.

Patient-safety: Another issue regarding the successful pilot implementation is related to the fact that clinical work is sometimes a matter of life and death. It was agreed, although the design had proved itself at the IN-SITU workshop in January (Figure 6), that unanticipated events leading to breakdown in communication or reports would have to result in a fall-back procedure where the organization returned to the paper record. This provided one of the requirements for preparation for the pilot; in case of fall-back, the end-users must be able to print a hard copy of the record. This was an issue for the technical configuration of the pilot implementation as print was not implemented on the framework version available for production. Further a work procedure was agreed upon between the project management and line-management.

The projects had staff on location during the entire pilot implementation, and there was always a "duty-officer" on-call in case of events described by the fall-back procedure. Each morning and afternoon the project management made a status and could evaluate whether fall-back was required. The pilot progressed however without any incidents leading to a fall-back to the paper record.

Post pilot: What happens after the pilot? It is necessary for both the project and management in general to consider what is going to happen after the pilot, regarding the system and the work involved in Use. Does the project need more design itera-tions (post-pilot, Figure 2) or is the pilot-system ready for full scale implementation (Figure 6)? While the project may only consider implications regarding the pilot-system there are consequences when moving into the clinical domain. In clinical work, the record is a legal document regulated by law by the healthcare provider. It describes all clinical interventions performed. This means the project cannot scrap data created during the pilot and will have to consider either making a hardcopy or continue documenting in the system. The last option means the project has to be ready to keep up the momentum of the implementation, and continue to train and involve staff in the remaining organization.

In this case, the Hospital decided that if full scale implementation was postponed they would make hard copies the records made during the pilot implementation to avoid historic information being inaccessible. In case of a successful pilot, they made plans for a rapid escalation and involvement of end-users and usability-actors resulting in the remaining staff being trained and the organization upgraded to full scale within 4-6 weeks after completing the pilot implementation.

TECHNOLOGICAL CONFIGURATION

One of the major concerns while using an agile process in the pilot implementation was how technically robust the framework was. To keep momentum and eventually measure effects, errors identified initially must be corrected immediately – other-wise an interrupted implementation will result in the expensively built end-user motivation being lost and the effects-driven process being terminated prematurely. In addition, reasonable changes in the framework design must be handled within the transition process (Figure 7) without workshops in order to prevent interrupting the process. It is possible to ensure the robustness of a technological framework and to establish a prompt inclusion of immediate and emerging requirements, but it requires careful planning of available resources from CSC. It was anticipated that some minor changes were required to the framework.

Figure 7. An example on the evolution of the different layers of the system during the process. The final transition required by the system from prototype to pilot-system, presents several challenges to be negotiated by the project organization.

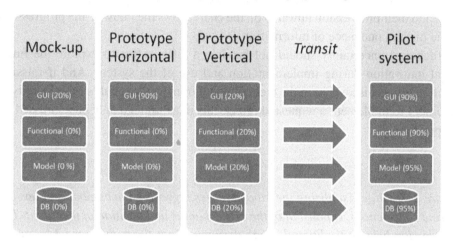

To illustrate some of the challenges in preparing the prototype for the pilot we have adopted the ANSI/SPARC inspired model described in Figure 4 to illustrate the evolution at different system levels from the mock-up, prototypes towards the pilot system (Figure 7).

The different degrees of completion are illustrated by exemplary percentages. In the Case several prototypes were made and compiling those made up the pilot system. The transition from prototype to pilot system is not trivial and involved much effort as each layer must be considered during the transition:

Considering the GUI Layer

The formative evaluation performed during the workshops resulted in the improvement of the solution presented to the usability-actors; see the examples of the satellites in Figure 8 (version 2). The first version could convey the status of the birth to the midwives, but interpretation was slow and cumbersome. E.g. the dark line in Figure 8 (version 1) shows the distance traveled by the infant in the birth channel, but it could not convey how the infant was rotated. This information had to be accessed in another satellite using a clock-dial analogy to convey the message of how the infant is rotated. E.g. 12-6 being in the middle of the birth channel facing upwards. The change in design was the result of a formative evaluation of the effects stating it should be easy and quick for the end-users to determine the progression of the birth of an individual pregnant on record. The new design shown in Figure 8 (version 2) has a satellite illustration using the position and rotation of the infant's head as well as the distance traveled to convey the same message as in Satellite version 1. The icons are stylized representations of the top of the infant's head, and by looking at them and their progression upwards on the chart shows the midwife the progression of the birth in one piece of information.

Technical uncertainty should not become a disincentive to explore the functional innovation during implementation and use of the system. And if missing functionality is discovered in the technological framework and this functionality is necessary to implement a requested effect, this must immediately be addressed be the project.

Figure 8. Satellite visualizing the labor process regarding the number and level of uterine contractions, expansion of the birth channel and position of the infant. The first version being a traditional graph drawing where the midwife must hover the mouse cursor over each entry to get a detailed reading. The second version incorporating a small illustration of the top of the infant's head allowing the midwife a direct reading of position and rotation.

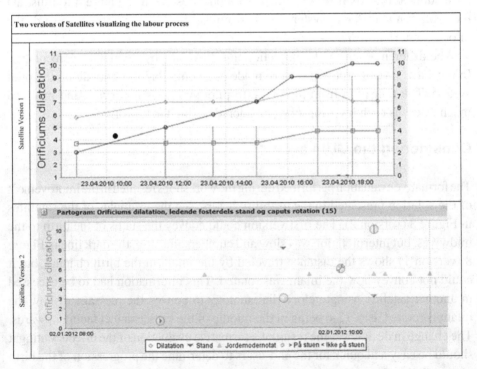

Considering the Functional Layer

The technical framework CCS is highly configurable, but in order to provide this degree of freedom much effort must be invested in implementing the functional layer in CCS.

CCS framework evolves continuously and does not contain all anticipated functionalities. Identified functionalities are described in the road map for the development of the framework in the near future, say 1-2 years. When a workshop discovers a new requirement or raises a need for a specific service the project is left with three choices: (1) Make do with what is available, (2) try and make a workaround or (3) ask the development organization within the CSC to implement the requirements ahead of schedule. During prototyping, the end-users can be asked to envisage the missing functions or a lack of coherence in the prototype.

In order to make the apparently small change of allowing icons in satellites, development on the framework was required. This means the project has to take into consideration the unforeseen task of specifying and testing new functionality before it can implement the solution. To illustrate the extent of a change of the type we see in Figure 8, a change in GUI may also require functional changes. Fortunately, no change was needed in the model layer. Consequently, a request for a functional-layer change was issued to the development team in CSC. Making this new functionality was not identified by the framework development project, and the pilot implementation was the sole owner of the request. Depending on the effort required to implement such requests, pilot projects risk not getting the solution they need. In this case, there was a lot of political interest as both Hospital and CSC management had an interest in the pilot implementation, and this made it possible to accelerate development within the pilot implementation time-frame.

Environment versioning is an issue as prototypes usually only mimics the real system. The system consisting of a technical framework and configuration elements means the configuration elements rely on functionality and background data such as terminology and classifications provide and managed by the framework. Moving the prototype from an environment where inaccurate terminology can be accepted towards a production grade environment means different rules for updates and another speed at which tasks can be completed. This increase of effort required for production grade configuration and background data, usually stems from activities such as quality assurance; design reviews and test or having to consider all three layers of the for coherence (Figure 7).

While the pilot-project only included a small area of the hospital organization, and while the rest of wards depend on the existing record for their work, changes in terminology design may have a consequence on a larger scale than just the project scope. For example introduction of Problem classifications required the project to select and map relevant official diagnosis classifications with the terminology recorded in order to support the reporting requirements dictated by national law.

Another major task in the preparations for pilot implementation, and pre-pilot development is not confined to programming, but also relies on the organization being able to implement new framework functionality required to support the con-figurations made during design workshops. An example was the usability regarding the reading of notes which needed substantial improvement and the project had to choose if it would go for a hard-coded "display print" to support this need better or wait for the framework to implement the correct solution. As indicated in Figure 7, the pilot-system has to come close to 100% in all layers in order to support real use as defined by the pilot implementation (Figure 1). In this case, the project chooses to invest time and effort to configure a workaround, rather than wait for the frame-work to present an easy solution. Special overviews were made for the sole purpose of serving as print templates; they provided readability improvements otherwise scheduled for later releases of the CCS framework.

Considering the Model Layer

The final layer of the system is the model layer and database. Moving from pro-totype to the pilot-system environment means the solution must co-exist with the rest of the IT portfolio. An example was the terminology implemented with the pilot system; the EHR is a distributed system, which means that it communicates with many other systems. For example, the records made by the midwives contain reports of clinical procedures; these procedures end up in national databases and are used in calculating performance and funding of the Hospital. In the case, CSC and the Hospital had to invest the time and effort in finding the correct terminol-ogy and load it into the CCS for the pilot system to operate on equal terms with the remaining systems in the Hospital portfolio.

ORGANIZATIONAL ADAPTATION

The task of ensuring the correct terminology led the project to a revision of work procedures and new praxis of registration and reporting. It was discovered that a considerable amount of redundant registration was carried out because communica-tion between local and national databases could not be mapped.

A spin-off was the discussion initiated among the staff regarding the documenta-tion model that had been adopted by the small group of midwives directly involved in the project. It concerned a large overview with a graphical representation of the progression of the birth. The illustration in Figure 8 is the electronic version of it. This model was developed by midwives for midwives but had not been fully assimilated into the organization. The design was made from the principles outlined in this model and end-users were required to adhere to it in order to benefit from the effects of use. The hospital management was concerned that it could spark unrest when the group of staff that had not been directly involved was going to use the system or later when Site 2 was to implement the EHR. This was one of the scope goals for knowledge set out in the beginning of the pilot implementation by the Hospital and CSC.

Another aspect of adaptation was the physical facilities surrounding the midwives. They were located often in small rooms with the woman giving birth, the father, sometimes a doctor and often bulky equipment (monitors etc.). This meant ergonomics and issues of network access had to be raised and addressed by management and local IT support. Another related issue was the training of the staff, as the final version of the pilot system was not ready until the week before the pilot implementation. Staff had to be trained in the actual version to understand the documentation model in order to have sufficient skill with the pilot system without having to call hotline too often. Training was carried out by two members of the project staff in classroom sessions of 1½ hours, and the staffs were issued a short-list to carry with them as a first resort when in doubt.

Post-pilot consideration mentioned in planning should include choosing a part of the organization which is well defined and preferably can be contained in case of fall-back or escalating the implementation. In this case, the midwives were chosen because they had a well-defined area of responsibility with regards to patients (pregnant women), and relations to other units at the Hospital. Escalation was relatively easy to plan and execute since there are only one main group of staff (midwives) and the doctors were a small and specialized group. In contrast, most other wards are staffed with nurses, doctors and various therapists.

In this case, the planning had included two scenarios: fall-back to the paper record or escalation of the EHR to the rest of the staff. The later scenario was the outcome of the pilot implementation and two months later when site 1 was at full scale the implementation team moved to site 2.

USE

The goal of the pilot implementation was to allow the staff to perform "business-as-usual" with the exception of records being made entirely in the EHR. The midwives at the hospital performed the usual amount of births during the pilot without extra staff and without needing to apply the fall-back procedure for reverting to paper.

During the pilot implementation, hospital management insisted on support staff being readily available. The project had called upon project participants and staff from the remaining implementation organization to perform the role of an on-site hotline service. A hotline roster had been prepared to ensure a person with clinical knowledge and technical skills was available at any time during the pilot. In addition, a person with the role of managing a potential fall-back and being able to stop everything had to be designated and to be on call.

It was the responsibility of the Hospital to ensure that the staff used the EHR as planned. They were not allowed to keep a paper record for private use. Further they had to use the system as it was described by the design. E.g. if they wanted to learn the status of the birth they had to open the EHR and read it there before seeking additional information elsewhere. On a larger scale, the staff at the outpatient clinics had to record their work in the EHR since their colleagues relied on the information when reading about the pregnant women when they arrived at the maternity ward. If the staff failed to support the pilot implementation in this way it would have been impossible to measure the effects of sharing information among maternity and outpatient clinic.

LEARNING

Three groups of end-users have the possibility to learn from the pilot implementation experience. They each have their own perspectives and areas of responsibilities spanning from across the organization to practical issues and tasks.

The three groups are;

- **Hospital management:** Senior management representing local management across the Hospital organization, responsible for budget and strategy implementation at the political level.
- Hospital IT configurators responsible for the project deliverables, planning and configuring the actual system.
- **End-users:** Midwives from the entire organization and clinical staff working with patients on an everyday basis.

The knowledge they can expect to acquire is defined in the scope for the pilot implementation including support of a clinical context, if change is necessary when implementing at a new location, whether the Hospital organization achieve independence of the CSC configurators and finally how can EDIT support the overall process?

Hospital Management

The EHR platform as a Hospital organization spanning project is a complicated undertaking. It involves the entire organization and the primary concern of the senior management was to see whether the CCS platform could support clinical work without compromising patient safety and could it do so within the budgets and staffing of the business unit (Maternity). Secondly there was a concern that local differences in work organization and practices would require adaptations that were costly in both time and effort each time a new location implemented the system. The pilot implementation answered these concerns by example; although staff was kept on call in the event that record keeping proved more time consuming, the amount of staff involved at the maternity ward and the outpatient clinics was not increased, neither was the intake of pregnant women admitted or referred for consultation reduced. The business units operated at normal capacity during the pilot implementation. Patient safety was not compromised as the project management did not use the fall-back procedure but recommended the continued implementation after the pilot first at Site 1, and later at Site 2.

When implementation was conducted at Site 2, the Hospital management was assured that the concerns for huge costs due to local demands for configuration were unfounded. Again the evidence for these claims is that production was not interrupted, and patient safety was not compromised, and no problems were reported regarding the adaptation of the documentation model supported by the design.

In contrast to previous learning experiences, the strategy involves that effects evaluation must be undertaken to ensure "Effective utilization of IT in the region" and the effects specifications used during design and development was used to measure the effects of use by the end-users. This documented not only the individual user experience but also the aggregated experience of a group of users with regard to how they rate the effectiveness of the IT implemented during the pilot.

Hospital IT configuration unit is charged with the responsibility of implementing the CCS EHR and business strategy in practice.

From their point-of-view, the greatest learning experience from the pilot implementation is that of putting a system into production as they have been concerned with the prospect of upgrading 6000+ users from paper to IT in an extremely short period of time. Their implementation strategy relies on the scalability of design and the ability to start using the system in rapid successions throughout the Hospital.

The Hospital IT configuration unit had the opportunity to try real implementation with all the safety features available. They experienced confidence because they knew exactly what the pilot system could do and not do as they had themselves configured it from the beginning with the end-users.

By using effects, they had the opportunity to receive formative feedback from the end-users in a structured way and keep the design effort focused on the priorities agreed upon from the beginning of the project.

Secondly, they could experience learning as the vendor-customer responsibilities shifted due to the Hospital business strategy demanding more *"Coherence in services ...,"* *"Innovations as a factor in creating growth and an attractive workplace,"* *"Ensuring ownership...."* This was in part made possible due to the nature of the CCS and through the initial organization of work in the project team. The Hospital IT configuration unit was responsible for the project process as well as for the configuration of a design that met the effects specification. This was a new role for the business unit as it usually had a consulting role, and left the project management and development to CSC. In a way, the Hospital IT configuration unit was being an apprentice as a vendor, learning to reflect on all levels of the system (Figure 5) to end up with a usable pilot system.

A final concern was that professional differences among the midwives could result in resentment towards the system since it had been designed at the university clinic (Site 1) and transferred unchanged to another group of midwifes without direct representation from this group during design and development (Site 2). The risk of the end-users having a strong sense of professional integrity combined with a feeling of being left without influence in matters of professional values was a potential show-stopper. This would be the case if the local midwives at Site 2 could not accept the documentation model devised by the University group at Site 1. During the introduction and training, the midwives referred to this concern in various terms, by saying; "It is better to have this kind of structure rather than the old mess where it was up to everyone to decide what was relevant to document" or "I can see my profession in this and that is what is pertinent to my work" (Interviews with midwives during preparations for Full scale implementation Site 2, Figure 6). Further evaluation of use at Site 2 showed no significant difference in the effectiveness or quality of service due to the new record keeping practice.

End-Users

When we look at the end-user group, there are 2 significant learning opportunities: a technology related and a work related.

The most important aspect of work, when dealing with clinical staff, is the patient–professional relation. It is not the technology that motivates and drives the staff while delivering service. At best the technology involved in performing clinical work assumes a discrete presence, and in some cases, it is an endured necessity. In either case end-users had the opportunity to become familiar with the standardized documentation model, but also doing it in a new technology. In a way, they made two steps at once, learning and working with the Partogram could have been introduced on paper before they implemented the CCS. However, as the Hospital IT configuration unit in charge of the planning and design experienced the absence of negative effects from using the CCS, they decided to make the implementation at Site 2 without trying on paper first.

The end-users saw that business (clinical work) could be performed as they were used to, and they did not experience issues threatening patient safety or causing a reduction in the quality of service. It was not without extra effort involved, as staffs were required to attend training before they could use the CCS effectively and in accordance with the design.

The effort experienced, besides training, was that they had to seek out a PC when they needed information or wanted to document their work. For example, at the maternity ward there is a national quality indicator stating that a midwife must be present continuously during the active phase of delivery. In the event that the midwife has to leave for more than 15 minutes, she would not adhere with this indicator, so she must quickly and continuously be able to document her presence. In the paper record, this was easily done by marking absence on a timeline, but in the CCS, they had to make a record of leaving by entering the time manually as they left the room and again when they returned. It was not possible to make an exception from this requirement to document quality and since there was no easy way of supporting this work practice, the end-users experienced extra effort involved in using the CCS during work.

Another learning experience was observed during discussions on how to adopt the standardized documentation model. This was undertaken during training or ordinary staff meetings, and it was emphasized that the midwife could carry out the same work they used to, and they had been represented during design by highly qualified senior midwives. The effects evaluation supported the experience by acting as a facilitator between individual opinions by offering a shared statement of the end-users experiences. E.g. if one midwife would say "I feel insecure relying on the CCS for information," the effects stated that the majority did not share this experience. This made the discussion focused on what the end-user was missing rather than starting a discussion on shortcomings of the technology.

CURRENT CHALLENGES FACING THE ORGANIZATION

It seems two potential and major challenges related to technical configuration and organizational adaptation were absent in the case: the need for local design and development of the CCS to support staff at Site 2, and there was no un-willingness with the midwives at Site 2 to accept a solution made by the midwives at Site 1. This does not mean that pilot implementation is the solution to all challenges among CSC and the Hospital. During the pilot implementation, CSC and the Hospital experienced that the role of apprentice and mentor was more complex than anticipated. The CCS has been envisioned as a standard tool, a framework in which technical staff with a relatively basic understanding of technology can develop the system required by the end-users.

The agile process adopted (Figure 2) by the project made it necessary to work intensely between workshops. These bursts of peak activity with high workload challenged the Hospital. The Hospital IT configuration unit, although skilled in organizing projects, was not staffed and organized to cope with both the continuous support of other projects and the allocation of large tasks with critical deadlines. In addition, they had to learn technical skills as they went along as the CCS came in new versions at regular intervals, making new functionality available or setting the conditions for design differently. For example, readability is essential when clinical staff scans records for clues about the problems experienced by the patients.

The amount of work involved in design and planning was underestimated, and CSC was asked to assume responsibility for the configuration tasks required to develop the pilot system. It was not difficult to discover what to develop. The challenge was production coordination related to configuration of the pilot system. The Hospital IT configuration unit had to learn how to coordinate configuration tasks as a vendor rather than as a customer. Being responsible for planning meant estimating work tasks in order to monitor if the plan is on schedule and making progress. In order to make accurate estimates, experience with the task anticipated is needed and keeping the project on track requires the discipline of follow-up on progress and prioritizing when necessary to reach deadlines. This also put the CSC's strategy for client intimacy into perspective.

Another new experience was setting up the facilities of quality assurance. Being responsible for developing and managing meant that the Hospital IT configuration unit had to assume responsibility for prioritizing the implementation of changes discovered during workshops, but also internal testing and correction of errors discovered during internal work processes. Normally CSC would perform a system and delivery test before handing over the system for acceptance, usually only involving clinical staff as technical issues should be solved by the time the system reaches the end-user representatives. Again the pool of available and skilled staff was underestimated, and management of resources versus completion of tasks was a new experience for the Hospital IT configuration unit staff.

After the pilot implementation, the Hospital IT configuration unit was upgraded with staff skilled in both project management and configuration.

SOLUTIONS AND RECOMMENDATIONS

The difference between pilot implementation and prototyping can be seen in challenges raised by the different aspects motivated by the desire to evaluate the fit between simulated and real-use.

Technical configuration aspects raise the issues defined by the transition from prototype to pilot system. The project assumes responsibility for either substituting missing functionality in the technical framework or qualifying the system. This must be to a completion level where work can be performed sufficiently close to the intended use in the pilot-system without compromising patient-safety.

Use implies that usability-actors cannot be limited to specific work situations, e.g. using the CCS for one type of tasks and paper for another. The pilot implementation must support the work specified by the end-users and the project management can benefit from contemplating a reduction in complexity when selecting the business unit they want to target for learning. This means pilot implementation requires a relatively mature technical framework and a skilled project team to plan and monitor the elements of both organizational adaptation and technical configuration.

The Hospital wanted to learn how to make pilot implementation and chose the midwives for the pilot implementation because they form a homogeneous group of skilled professionals. Their work is defined by one particular group of patients (pregnant women), and they have been working with this clinical domain for a very long time. In addition, they only interact directly with doctors on well-defined tasks. For example, the midwife attends the patients independently from the beginning in the outpatient clinic to delivery at the maternity ward. If complications introduce a need for treatments that are outside the midwife's competences, she contacts the doctor on call. This means that the pregnant woman can carry her child and give birth without seeing other hospital professionals than the midwife. She does however, see her General Practitioner (GP), but he or she only shares information with the midwives on a need-to-know basis. This information is typically entered in a small dedicated record; the "Pregnancy record" (Hertzum et al., 2012); the midwives and GPs do not share information or coordinate work directly, although both groups use the EHR in their individual work. This may be the reason why a similar project aimed at sharing information among these two independent professions (i.e., midwives and GPs) turned out unsatisfactorily in the case described by (Hertzum et al., 2012). This project involved a heterogeneous group of professionals with a pilot implementation as a way of investigating the collaboration and coordination between the groups.

Another recommendation for pilot implementations is the ability to assess and negotiate risks for first-movers, both when spanning different geographic locations in large organizations and when dealing with mission critical systems. All three groups of end-users had concerns regarding these issues and benefited from the approach utilizing pilot implementation during the process.

REFERENCES

Barlach, A., & Simonsen, J. (2011). Innovation in partnership sourcing from a vendor's perspective. In Hertzum, M., & Jørgensen, C. (Eds.), *Balancing sourcing and innovation in information systems development* (pp. 193–212). Trondheim, NO: Tapir Academic Publishers.

Bødker, K., Simonsen, J., & Kensing, F. (2009). *Participatory IT design: Designing for business and workplace realities*. Cambridge, MA: MIT.

Davis, A. M., Bersoff, E. H., & Comer, E. R. (1988). A strategy for comparing alternative software-development life-cycle models. *IEEE Transactions on Software Engineering, 14*(10), 1453–1461. doi:10.1109/32.6190

Floyd, C. (1984). A systematic look at prototyping. In R. Budde, K. Kuhlenkamp, L. Mathiassen, & L. Zullighoven (Eds.), *Approaches to prototyping: Proceedings on the working conference on prototyping* (pp. 1-18). Heidelberg: Springer Verlag.

Hainey, T. (2007). Information systems development methodologies, techniques & tools (4th ed.). *International Journal of Information Management, 27*(1), 58-59. doi: doi:10.1016/j.ijinfomgt.2006.09.002

Hart, S. G., & Staveland, L. E. (1988). Development of NASA-TLX (Task Load Index) - Results of empirical and theoretical research. In Hancock, P. A., & Meshkati, N. (Eds.), *Human mental workload*. Elsevier Science Publisher B.V. doi:10.1016/S0166-4115(08)62386-9

Hertzum, M., Bansler, J. P., Havn, E. C., & Simonsen, J. (2012). Pilot implementation: Learning from field tests in IS development. *Communications of the Association for Information Systems, 30*(1), 313–328.

Jansson, L., Handest, P., Nielsen, J., Saebye, D., & Parnas, J. (2002). Exploring boundaries of schizophrenia: A comparison of ICD-10 with other diagnostic systems in first-admitted patients. *World Psychiatry; Official Journal of the World Psychiatric Association (WPA), 1*(2), 109–114.

Jureta, I. J., Faulkner, S., & Schobbens, P. Y. (2008). Clear justification of modeling decisions for goal-oriented requirements engineering. *Requirements Engineering, 13*(2), 87–115. doi:10.1007/s00766-007-0056-y

Nielsen, J. (1993). *Usability engineering.* Boston: Academic Press.

Rasmussen, J., Pejtersen, A.-L. M., & Goodstein, L. P. (1994). *Cognitive systems engineering.* Wiley.

Region, N. J. C. (2011). IT strategy 2014. [Aalborg Oest.]. *Niels Bohrs Vej, 30,* 9220.

Royce, W. W. (1987). *Managing the development of large software systems: Concepts and techniques.* Paper presented at the Proceedings of the 9th international conference on Software Engineering. Monterey, California, United States.

Schwaber, K., & Beedle, M. (2002). *Agile software development with scrum.* Upper Saddle River, NJ: Prentice Hall.

Simonsen, J., Hertzum, M., & Barlach, A. (2011). Experiences with effects specifications. In Hertzum, M., & Jørgensen, C. (Eds.), *Balancing sourcing and innovation in information systems development* (pp. 145–163). Trondheim, NO: Tapir Academic Publishers.

Stacey, M., & Eckert, C. (2003). Against ambiguity. [CSCW]. *Computer Supported Cooperative Work, 12*(2), 153–183. doi:10.1023/A:1023924110279

Stapleton, J. (1998). *DSDM* (Repr. ed.). Harlow: Addison-Wesley.

Tsichritzis, D., & Klug, A. (1978). ANSI-X3-SPARC DBMS framework - report of study-group on database management-systems. *Information Systems, 3*(3), 173–191. doi:10.1016/0306-4379(78)90001-7

Venkatesh, V., Morris, M. G., Davis, G. B., & Davis, F. D. (2003). User acceptance of information technology: Toward a unified view. *Management Information Systems Quarterly, 27*(3), 425–478.

Vicente, K. J. (1999). *Cognitive work analysis: Towards safe, productive, and healthy computer-based work.* Lawrence Erlbaum Associates, Inc.

KEY TERMS AND DEFINITIONS

Effect: The anticipated clinical outcome of work performed by an agent typically being a person (doctors, nurses, etc.) in rare instances the agent can be a technology (drugs, etc.).

Electronic Healthcare Record (EHR): A tool for planning and documenting clinical work, facilitating collaboration among clinical staff towards common patient related health goals.

Learning: The process of acquiring or modifying information into knowledge. In this case knowledge is applied to the design and implementation of an EHR.

Patient-Safety: The considerations involved in preventing adverse effects from clinical interventions either directly or indirectly involving the patient. E.g. abstaining from performing specific actions because they pose a risk of harming the patient to an extent that cannot be justified by the anticipated benevolent effects from the action.

Pilot Implementation: Pilot implementation is an Information Systems Development (ISD) technique that aims to feed experiences from real use back into development by having users try out a system on a restricted scale before the design of the system is finalized. Pilot implementation is a field test during which a pilot system is used in its intended environment with real data. Pilot implementations are conducted to learn about how a system may support its users in their work and, thereby, to create information and insight about how to improve the system, adapt the organization, and capture the benefits of introducing the system in the organization. By providing feedback from target-environment use of the system to the on-going development activities, pilot implementation supplements prototyping, which in most definitions is restricted to the development phase (Hertzum et al., 2012).

Prototyping: The use of prototypes to facilitate learning during the software development process. The prototypes are the main artifact to illustrate the interpretation of user requirements and feedback from stakeholders.

Technical Framework: A set of electronic building blocks in which prototypes and applications can be configured by combining relevant features and functionalities offered by the framework to a specific customer.

Chapter 11
Design and Development of a Digital Error Reporting System for a Rural Nursing Home

Barbara Millet
Texas Tech University, USA

EXECUTIVE SUMMARY

Error reporting systems are traditionally facilitated through completion of paper forms. These forms are largely flawed in design and usability. Use of digital reporting forms may be advantageous in reducing data entry errors, minimizing documentation time, and collecting consistent data items. This case study is a site-specific exploration of error reporting systems for a rural nursing home. A comparative evaluation was conducted of the nursing home's existing narrative, paper form against a newly developed, digital interface. Empirical results showed no overall difference in performance between the interfaces. Expected performance gains may have been offset by the novelty of the digital interface and user familiarity with the existing paper forms. There were, however, differences in user preference, with the digital interface significantly preferred. Furthermore, data entry of accident and near miss information into computer systems was projected to streamline data collection and analysis.

DOI: 10.4018/978-1-4666-4046-7.ch011

ORGANIZATION BACKGROUND

The study site is a nursing home facility located in West Texas. The facility is a 120-bed geriatric nursing care facility that employs over 120 employees (with 82 employees in the Nursing department). The center provides round the clock support and three levels of care: traditional long term care, specialized care for patients diagnosed with dementia and related conditions, and skilled care for short term patients needing therapy. This study was focused specifically on the safety perceptions and reporting practices of the Nursing department of the selected facility.

SETTING THE STAGE

Safety and error prevention is a major concern in the workplace. Safety experts generally categorize error events that have actually occurred as accidents, while near misses are referred to as unplanned events that did not result in damage, illness, or injury, but have the potential to do so. Accident and near miss information collected directly from workers are critical to occupational health and safety. Furthermore, error reporting is essential for facilities to shift from a reactive to a proactive approach to safety. The Occupational Safety and Health Administration (OSHA) mandates the collection, investigation, and reporting of all accidents for regulated industries. The collection of near miss information is also required for most regulated industries (Yandziak, Lima, Verboonen, Gomes, & Guerlain, 2006). However, underreporting of accidents and near misses is a major problem across industries (Clarke, 1998).

Traditional accident and near miss reporting is generally facilitated through manual efforts such as completion of paper forms and verbal reports to management. These traditional methods are limited in the type of data that are collected and are generally thought to be too time consuming (Wagner, Capezuti, & Ouslander, 2006; Evans, Berry, Smith, Esterman, Selim, O'Shaghnessy, & Dewit, 2006; Wagner, Capezuti, Taylor, Sattin, & Ouslander, 2005), may not yield sufficient and accurate data (Wagner et al., 2005), and limits the opportunities to conduct quantitative analyses for quality improvement (as cited in Wagner et al., 2006). Johnson (2003) describes that there are also practical problems in the submission of printed reporting forms. The forms are not easily obtained, the staff must be motivated to find one, fill it in, and then submit it to the appropriate manager.

Johnson further explains that many organizations have responded to these problems by introducing digital systems (2003). Use of computerized systems is advantageous in reducing errors in data entry, minimizing documentation time, collecting consistent data items (Wagner et al., 2005), and increasing overall reporting (as cited in Wagner et al., 2006). Furthermore, data entry of accident and near miss information into computer systems by workers streamlines data collection and provides data for tailoring preventative measures and programs in the workplace. This implies that digital error reporting systems generally provide a more effective safety strategy than its paper-based counterparts. However, these efforts are largely flawed in system design and usability (Johnson, 2003). There is agreement in the literature that accident and near miss reporting should be easier to use, non-punitive, readily accessible and better designed to encourage voluntary reporting (Johnson, 2003; Ulep & Moran, 2005).

To successfully deploy an accident and near miss reporting system, the system itself must be designed for its users. A well-designed, digital interface can improve reporting performance by assisting users in information management and other cognitive demands in real-time. However, no digital error reporting systems have been developed that are designed specifically to meet the needs of the broad spectrum of nursing home employees.

CASE DESCRIPTION

The purpose of this case study is to identify issues related to interface design for a web-based, data entry system administered to a diverse group of workers. Specifically, the design of an error reporting interface that is usable (measured as a function of efficiency, effectiveness, and user satisfaction). This research is a site specific exploration of error reporting systems for nursing homes. All phases of work relied on the User Centered Design (UCD) process. The UCD process ensures that design and development efforts result in usable products by focusing on usability goals, product functions, user characteristics, and contexts of use (Rubin & Chisnell, 2008). The project was completed in three phases of work: 1) data collection, 2) prototype design, and 3) prototype implementation and evaluation.

The data collection phase included secondary analysis and design research. Secondary analysis is essentially the analysis of previously compiled data. The results of the secondary analysis led to the identification of the types of error events that had been reported. Design research, on the other hand, is primarily a front-end analysis leading to concept exploration and ideation. Design research efforts generally lead to a better understanding of those who will be using a product and the context in which it will be used. Design research techniques were used in this study specifically to get a better sense of the nature of the work and to assess factors affecting reporting system use. Design research data were collected via interviews and focus groups and relied on participation across user segments (e.g. managers and employees). Techniques such as focus groups and interviews focus on what people say and think. These methods provide insight into the "true user profile, user needs, and user preferences" (Wilson, 2010, p. 46). Specifically, one-on-one user interviews pose questions to an individual. Interviews are ideal for understanding what an individual thinks about a topic, without being influenced by others. Focus groups, on the other hand, are small groups of informed people who are gathered to address product research questions. Focus groups are helpful for gathering multiple points of view in a short period of time (Courage & Baxter, 2005).

The prototype design phase also relied on the design research data and was supplemented by a review of the literature to identify design parameters to be incorporated in the interface prototype. Once design concepts were materialized, the focus shifted to evaluating usability. Usability evaluations assess the degree to which users can effectively operate a product, the product efficiency, and user satisfaction with the product. There are three main types of usability evaluation techniques. These are usability inspection, inquiry methods, and usability testing. At the prototype refinement stage, inspection techniques were used to identify usability problems early in the development process. Inspections are diagnostic techniques whereby usability specialists decide whether product design elements follow established usability standards and guidelines. There are three key inspection methods: best practices and guidelines reviews, heuristic reviews, and expert reviews (Millet & Patterson, 2012). In this study, the inspection method of best practices and guidelines review were employed. Best practices and guidelines reviews are expert evaluations of a product to assess conformance against a comprehensive list of usability guidelines and best practices.

The last phase of work was concluded with the evaluation of system attributes for the existing and the newly developed reporting systems. The evaluation relied on comparative usability testing. The main objective in conducting a usability test is "to discover whether the product elicits the necessary human performance to meet the requirements established for it" (Millet & Patterson, 2012). Comparative usability tests allow comparison of two or more developed products against one another. Comparative usability tests are appropriate in this situation given their ability to reveal which design is more efficient, effective and satisfying to use. The primary deliverable from this phase of work was then a collection of performance data (time on task, errors, and task completion rates), preference data (ranks and ratings) for each design (new digital interface vs. existing paper form), and a comparison of the results.

The sub-sections below represent efforts completed for the data collection and prototype design phases, and describe test methods and study findings for the comparative evaluation. All work completed in this project was approved in advanced by the study site. All data collected was held confidential. Prior to data collection, a proposal was submitted to and approved by the Texas Tech University Institutional Review Board.

Secondary Analysis

We conducted a systematic review of the nursing home's existing accident and near miss reporting activities to identify the rate and types of events that have been reported. This effort represents a descriptive study of reported events using the facility's "First Aid" logs, completed OSHA 300 & 301 forms, safety meeting minutes, and worker compensation reports between August 2009 and November 2010. The facility provided the reports for review and therefore determined the time range for the error reports. Any duplicated event documentation was removed. As a consequence, we reviewed 129 reports. Of these reports, 76% were accident related events and the remaining represented near misses documented in the safety meeting minutes.

Given the lack of information captured by the reporting forms, it was not possible to identify who completed the report (in terms of job type). As the reports were provided de-identified, we could not request that the facility provide job type as a function of employee name. Therefore, we could not explore event rates and event types by job function.

Of the 98 accidents reported, 57% of employee injuries were caused by patient handling and violence. The next major contributor to employee injury was slips, trips and falls (15%). Consequently, 29% of the near misses reported were related to facility issues. The facility issues reported detailed uneven flooring surfaces (possibly contributing to slips and trips) and poor or overdue inspections. Another main contributor of near misses reported (29%) is due to equipment related events (mostly for overdue inspections and broken equipment). Examples of the types of accident and near miss events are listed in Tables 1 and Table 2, respectively. The data collected, overall, was insufficient for further analysis.

Interviews and Focus Group

One-on-one interviews and focus group meetings were held at the study site in order to gain an understanding of 1.) the work domain and different worker roles, 2.) error data collection process and systems, 3.) types of error data that are currently collected, and 4.) to explore the quality of the error data currently collected and user opinions of implemented systems. The overall goal was to identify issues related to interface design for error data entry systems administered to a diverse group of workers. To satisfy this objective we employed interviews and focus groups as the research technique. Interviews and focus groups are appropriate in this situation given their ability to reveal motivations, experiences, attitudes, and perceptions of the target audience towards a product, process, idea, or technology. This phase of work relied on participation across user segments (e.g. managers and employees), but was focused exclusively on the Nursing department.

Table 1. Types of accident reported

Reported Accidents (n=98)	% Reported
Handling Resident	33%
Resident Violence	24%
Slip/Trip/ Falls	15%
Chemical/Bio- Hazard	7%
Equipment	6%
Physical hazard	5%
Needle stick or sharp object	4%
Job Hazard	3%
Other	3%

Table 2. Types of near misses reported

Reported Near Misses (n=31)	% Reported
Facility	29%
Equipment	29%
Chemical Hazard	12%
Slip/Trip/ Falls	10%
Fire Hazard	10%
Other	10%

Fourteen employees from the nursing department, all females, were recruited to participate in this phase of work. Of the participants there were 6 nurse aides (certified nurse aide (CNA) or certified medical aide (CMA)), 5 nurses (licensed vocational nurses (LVNs)), 1 assistant director of nursing (ADON), 1 director of nursing (DON), and 1 executive director. Eight of 14 participants had less than 3 years of work experience in their current job.

Nine topics were discussed within each of these types of sessions (interviews or focus groups). The topics explored in the sessions are presented in Table 3. Review of participant responses followed the sessions. This analysis uncovered critical information for what employees feel and think about the existing reporting process.

All participants correctly defined an accident, but only 43% correctly defined a near miss. Ten of 14 participants expressed that error events (accidents and near misses) they would experience are more likely to occur in patient rooms and common areas. Very little distinction was made, across participants, when asked to

Table 3. Interview and focus group discussion topics

Category	Topics
Introduction	Name
Introduction	Job Type
Introduction	Years at Job
Accidents & Near Misses	Define an accident
Accidents & Near Misses	Define a near miss
Accidents & Near Misses	Accident types, frequencies, and locations
Accidents & Near Misses	Near Miss types, frequencies, and locations
Reporting Process & System	Types of events reported
Reporting Process & System	Reporting process (e.g. procedures, systems, forms)
Reporting Process & System	System frequency of use
Reporting Process & System	System likes and dislikes
Reporting Process & System	Ideal system

describe the types of accidents and near misses that occur at the facility. Twelve of 14 participants agreed that the top error types were as follows: 1. slips, trips, and falls, 2. needle pricks, 3. medical waste, and 4. back strain from handling residents. However, no consensus was reached on which error event was the most likely. One participant indicated that near misses are most often a consequence of defective equipment and employees failing to follow standard operating procedures.

Participants claim that all accidents are reported at this facility. It is believed that the existing worker's compensation policies influence accident reporting. The facility does not use the Texas sponsored worker's compensation plan, but instead has a facility funded program. Accident reporting is mostly motivated by the facility's worker compensation policies in that all accidents must be reported prior to the end of the shift in which the event occurred in order to receive any compensation if indeed it is needed.

To report an accident the employee (or ADON) must first enter information about the event in a first aid log. The first aid log has the following data elements: event date and time, employee name, manager name, injury description. These data elements are presented in a table where data specific to one event are recorded across one row. If the injury requires medical attention, or if the employee requests time off, then a worker compensation form must be completed by the ADON. The worker compensation form has the following data fields: employee name, home address, home phone, birth date, social security number, gender, hire date, marital status, location, job type, incident location, work phone, manager's name, manager's phone, date and time of incident, date and time for reporting the incident, who the incident was reported to, names of witnesses, description of activities preceding the incident, description of the incident, description of body parts affected and the type of injury, description of where the incident /injury occurred, past treatment for similar injuries, and whether or not treatment is being requested on form completion. Additionally, the OSHA 300/301 forms are then submitted, as needed, by the Human Resources Supervisor.

The nursing employees do not generally report near misses. Management reports near misses they detect via safety meeting minutes. In the monthly safety meeting, management representatives across facility departments (Nursing, Therapy, Environmental Services, Housekeeping, Maintenance, Activities, Marketing, Admissions, Human Resources, Social Services, and Dinning services) discuss and document error likely events and set forth action plans to remediate these problems. However, as only management reports near miss events many opportunities for proactive safety improvements are missed.

Most participants expressed strong, negative opinions toward the existing system. Six of 14 participants indicated that there were too many forms to complete in order to report an event and that the forms were not readily available. Overall, participants were negative about the system with the only positive statement being that they are happy that there is an existing process for reporting at all. The results from this phase of work were used to inform the design of the new, digital reporting interface.

Guidelines and Best Practices for the Development of Reporting Systems

Based on published research, system development has been separated into the following five phases: (1) research and goal identification, (2) instrument development, (3) determination of feedback mechanisms, (4) prototype development and analysis, and (5) training and implementation (as identified in Smiley & Millet, 2011). Research findings indicate that during the research and goal identification phase, the existing system at the facility should be reviewed, the needs of the facility and users in question should be identified, and system goals for functionality and usability should be set. Instrument development involves defining an accident and near miss, developing a standard taxonomy, identifying necessary data elements, and deciding on field types, system modalities, and confidentiality policies. Determination of feedback mechanisms includes identifying mechanisms to provide feedback to the individual reporter, to the facility employees as a group, and to the system. In the prototype development and analysis phase, a prototype is developed and analyzed using heuristics and other evaluation methods, a pilot system is implemented, and changes are made prior to the final phase. The final phase comprises training and implementation in which training goals are set, training materials are developed, and the system and training are implemented.

Digital Form Design

In designing an error reporting system that captures both accidents and near miss information, the first step is to define what is and is not classified as an accident or a near miss. Therefore, the new digital reporting system provided clear and simple definitions of the types of error events. These definitions allowed reporters to select the appropriate incident type that occurred.

The next step involved identifying the necessary data elements. Data elements selected allowed collection of objective, factual, and relevant data that can be used to break down accidents and near misses by different demographics and types. The form content was customized to fit the individual facility. Specifically, the facility has different possible event locations, reporter positions, contributing factors, and shifts. The form included reporter demographics, the location of the accident or near miss, the type of accident or near miss, a description of the event, and the potential causes of occurrence. The error event type was divided into categories. The categories included: 1) Strain, Slip, Trip, or Fall, 2) Needle stick or sharp object, 3) Equipment/Technology, 4) Chemical hazards, 5) Physical hazard and 6) Other. The causes of occurrence were divided into the following categories: 1) Communication, 2) Environment, 3) Equipment, 4) Fatigue, 5) Patient/Family issues, 6) Patient's cognitive status or activity at time of the event, 7) Rules, policies, or procedures, 8) Scheduling or workload, 9) Training or experience, and 10) Other. Presentation of the data fields followed design best practices and guidelines (as specified in Smiley & Millet, 2011). Furthermore, the digital system was offered in both English and Spanish, as many nursing home employees were native Spanish speakers.

Digital Reporting System Evaluation

The goal was to develop a usable, digital error reporting system specific to the nursing home domain. Preliminary efforts included heuristic evaluation of existing reporting systems in the following industries: Health Care, Petroleum, Nuclear, and Chemical. We applied best practices and guidelines described in the preceding section to the development of the digital reporting system. We relied on information collected via interviews and focus groups to get a better sense of the nature of the work, to identify job hazards, and to assess barriers to reporting system use. The results from these efforts were used to inform the system user interface design and the data elements collected.

Next, wireframes of the application were constructed to serve as the specification for the development of low fidelity prototypes of the reporting system. Initial system designs (low fidelity) were generated in Adobe InDesign. We then conducted heuristic reviews to further refine the usability of the system. Next, a prototype of the digital reporting interface, used in the evaluation phase of the work, was developed. The prototype was developed as an html application that is accessible through a web browser. As designed, any data collected were stored in a local database to facilitate on-site testing flexibility and to support participant privacy. The final prototype was tested and debugged prior to the usability test.

We conducted a comparative usability test, evaluating system attributes of the existing, paper form and the newly developed digital error reporting system. The primary deliverable from this evaluation was the collection of performance and preference data for each design (new interface vs. existing paper form) and a comparison of the results.

The facility agreed to allow employees to complete the usability test during their normal working hours. The usability test was conducted one participant at a time, using a designated room, which is located in an isolated area to ensure privacy and eliminate distractions. To schedule the usability test sessions, the facility administration worked with our team to create a timetable, which was conducive to the various workflow agendas existing in the work areas from which the participants were gathered.

Twelve nursing employees, all right-handed, with normal or corrected-to-normal vision, participated in the usability test. There was 1 Male and 11 Female participants. All participants had worked at the facility less than 5 years, with 7 of these participants having worked at the facility less than 1 year. Seven participants were recruited from day shifts (6 AM- 2 PM or 8 AM- 5 PM) and 5 were from night shifts (2 PM-10 PM or 5 PM – 9 PM). Seven participants had a vocational certificate or less, while only 5 participants had "some college" or more. There was an equal mix of job types (nursing assistants and licensed vocational nurses) and computer experience groups (non-expert and expert). Modifying the criteria of Staggers (1994), an "expert" was someone who scored more than 160 points on the Staggers Nursing Computer Skills Questionnaire (a 30 item instrument with a maximum score of 240 points, instrument was modified for the purposes of this test). All participants had experience only with the existing, narrative paper form.

Each participant submitted one error report with each reporting system. The experiment was a mixed design with one within-subject factor, reporting system (New: Digital interface and Existing: Paper form) and two between-group factors: job type (nursing assistants and licensed vocational nurses) and computer skill (non-expert and expert). The user test was conducted as a repeated measures design (each participants was tested under both conditions). The experimental design used a diagram-balanced Greco-Latin rectangle (Lewis, 1993) to simultaneously counterbalance the presentation of user interface, the error scenario, and the pairing of the user interface and scenario.

The overall results for mean completion time (or time on task) were: Digital (New) M= 443.3 seconds (SD= 192.2) and Paper (Existing) M= 364.8 seconds (SD= 93.1). To determine whether system or other factors were associated with completion time, mixed effects ANOVA was conducted. The results indicated that the mean completion time was not associated with system, $F (1, 8) = 2.787$, p= 0.134, with computer skill, $F (1, 8) = 0.414$, p= 0.538, or with job type, $F (1, 8) = 0.216$, p= 0.654. The interface developed was new to the participants so it is promising that at first use it is not requiring greater completion time than their existing (and already well learned) paper form. Furthermore, significantly more questions (improving the quality of the data collected) are asked in the digital system than that of the existing narrative paper form and yet there was no statistically significant increase on time on task.

All reports regardless of the reporting system used were submitted successfully (completion rate of 100%). However, there were unexpected responses regarding how the error events were categorized in the digital system. The digital system required that the participant select the category that was representative of the scenario provided. All 12 participants initially selected "physical hazard" to categorize the error event for one of the scenarios presented. However, we had categorized this event as a "strain" due to "handling a resident." This implies that the digital interface design would benefit from use of card sorting, a technique used for organizing elements of an information system, in order to categorize the event types and root cause attributes in a way that makes better sense to the end users.

The rating for each layout was the composite score of the System Usability Scale (SUS: Brooke, 1996) questionnaire, given after participants finished submitting a report with each system. SUS scores have a range of 0 to 100, where higher scores indicate greater perception of system usability. Specifically, SUS scores above 68 are considered "above average" and below 68 "below average" (Sauro, 2011). The overall mean SUS scores were: Digital (New) M= 76.04 (SD= 13.25) and Paper (Existing) M= 57.92 (SD= 17.67). A mixed effects ANOVA was conducted to assess whether system, computer skill, job type, or other factors were associated with SUS ratings. Results indicated a system by job type effect was significant $F (1, 10) = 10.382$, p= .009, with nurses rating, on average, the digital system more favourably than nursing assistants. Furthermore, the digital system received the most first-place votes (11/12).

CURRENT CHALLENGES FACING THE ORGANIZATION

As evident from the usability evaluation, design modifications are needed to optimize the digital reporting system given that some system terminology did not match user expectations. Therefore, the developed system needs minor modifications before facility implementation. Furthermore, based on the design research conducted early in the program, some of the nursing staff were unfamiliar with reporting error events and had low levels of computer skills. Consequently, staff training is needed prior to system implementation.

SOLUTIONS AND RECOMMENDATIONS

Encompassed by the user centered design model is the notion of iterative design. This enables designers and developers to incorporate user feedback, allowing them to incrementally refine the design until the product reaches an acceptable usability level. As detailed previously, not all participants readily understood some of the terminology presented in the digital interface. Different usability methods should be applied throughout the development process to ensure that the stated requirements are being met. As an immediate next step, we recommend use of card sorting in order to categorize the event types and root cause attributes in a way that makes better sense to the end users. This effort should be followed by design modifications and subsequent user testing to ensure product usability.

Furthermore, it is highly recommended that some type of training, whether individual or group, be completed prior to system implementation. If the individuals who will be using the system do not understand the processes, nomenclature, or structure of the system there will be a high tendency not to report. After this initial training has been completed and the reporting system has been implemented, it is important to continue improving the system and to periodically repeat the training process.

ACKNOWLEDGEMENT

Funding supported by Grant No. T42CCT610417 from the National Institute for Occupational and Environmental Health (NIOSH)/Centers for Disease Control and Prevention (CDC) to the Southwest Center for Occupational and Environmental Health (SWCOEH), a NIOSH Education and Research Center.

REFERENCES

Brooke, J. (1996). SUS: A quick and dirty usability scale. In Jordan, P., Thomas, B., Werdmaster, B., & McClelland, I. (Eds.), *Usability evaluation in industry* (pp. 1189–1194). London, UK: Taylor and Francis.

Clarke, S. (1998). Organizational factors affecting the incident reporting of train drivers. *Work and Stress, 12*(1), 6–16. doi:10.1080/02678379808256845

Courage, C., & Baxter, K. (2005). *Understanding your users: A practical guide to user requirements methods, tools, and techniques*. San Francisco, CA: Morgan Kaufmann.

France, D. J., Cartwright, J., Jones, V., Thompson, V., & Whitlock, J. A. (2004). Improving pediatric chemotherapy safety through voluntary incident reporting: Lessons from the field. *Journal of Pediatric Oncology Nursing, 21*(4), 200–206. doi:10.1177/1043454204265907

Johnson, C. W. (2003). How will we get the data and what will we do with it then? Issues in the reporting of adverse healthcare events. *Quality & Safety in Health Care, 12*(2), 64–67. doi:10.1136/qhc.12.suppl_2.ii64

Martin, S. K., Etchegaray, J. M., Simmons, D., Belt, W. T., & Clark, K. (2005). Development and implementation of the University of Texas close call reporting system. *Advances in Patient Safety, 2*, 149–160.

Millet, B., & Patterson, P. (2012). User centered design. In *Design and designing*. Oxford, UK: Berg Publishers.

Oktem, U. G. (2002). Near-miss: A tool for integrated safety, health, environmental and security management. (Unpublished manuscript). The Wharton School, University of Pennsylvania, Risk Management and Decision Processes Center.

Phimister, J. R., Oktem, U. G., Kleindorfer, P. R., & Kunreuther, H. (2000). Near-miss system analysis: Phase I. (Unpublished manuscript). The Wharton School, University of Pennsylvania Risk Management and Decision Processes Center.

Rosenthal, J., & Booth, M. (2005). Maximizing the use of state adverse event data to improve patient safety. Retrieved from http://www.premierinc.org/quality/tools-services/safety/safety-share/03-06-downloads/01-patient-safety-gnl61.pdf

Rubin, J., & Chisnell, D. (2008). *Handbook of usability testing: How to plan, design, and conduct effective tests* (2nd ed.). New York, NY: Wiley.

Sauro, J. (2011, February 2). Measuring usability with the system usability scale (SUS). In *Measuring usability*. Retrieved September 29, 2012, from http://www.measuringusability.com/sus.php.

Smiley, L., & Millet, B. (2011). Near miss reporting systems: Best practices and development guidelines. In *Proceedings of the International Society for Occupational Ergonomics and Safety*. Baltimore, MD.

Staggers, N. (1994). The staggers nursing computer experience questionnaire. Clinical method. *Applied Nursing Research*, 7(2), 97–106. doi:10.1016/0897-1897(94)90040-X

Ulep, S. K., & Moran, S. L. (2005). Ten considerations for easing the transition to a web-based patient safety reporting system. In K. Henriksen, J.B. Battles, E.S., & D.I. Lewin (Eds.), *Advances in patient safety: From research to implementation*. Rockville, MD: Agency for Healthcare Research and Quality.

Wagner, L. M., Capezuti, E., & Ouslander, J. G. (2006). Reporting near-miss events in nursing homes. *Nursing Outlook*, 54, 85–93. doi:10.1016/j.outlook.2006.01.003

Wagner, L. M., Capezuti, E., Taylor, J. A., Sattin, R. W., & Ouslander, J. G. (2005). Impact of a falls menu-driven incident-reporting system on documentation and quality improvement in nursing homes. *The Gerontologist*, 45(6), 835–842. doi:10.1093/geront/45.6.835

Wilson, C. (Ed.). (2010). *User experience re-mastered: Your guide to getting the right design*. Burlington, MA: Morgan Kaufmann.

Wu, A. W., Pronovost, P., & Morlock, L. (2002). ICU incident reporting systems. *Journal of Critical Care*, 17(2), 86–94. doi:10.1053/jcrc.2002.35100

Yandziak, J. J., De Lima, O., Verboonen, M., Gomes, J. O., & Guerlain, S. (2006). Critical review and redesign of a petroleum industry accident/incident reporting system. In Michael DeVore (Ed.), *Proceedings of the 2006 IEEE Systems and Information Engineering Design Symposium* (pp. 222-227).

KEY TERMS AND DEFINITIONS

1-on-1 Interviews: Posing product research questions to one individual (e.g. product user) to find out what they think, feel, and expect.

Accidents: Error events that have actually occurred and result in damage, illness, or injury.

Card Sorting: A technique used to understand how people organize information. It is conducted by presenting participants with written or pictorial cards conveying product characteristics and then asking them to sort the cards in a meaningful way.

Focus Group: Posing product research questions to a small set of people (e.g. product users).

Near Misses: Unplanned events that do not result in damage, illness, or injury, but have the potential to do so.

Usability Test: A technique used to evaluate a product by testing with representative users completing tests tasks.

Chapter 12
The Usability Evaluation of a Touch Screen in the Flight Deck

Stefano Bonelli
Deep Blue Srl, Italy

Linda Napoletano
Deep Blue Srl, Italy

EXECUTIVE SUMMARY

This chapter presents and discusses an Expert Usability Evaluation for a flight deck touch screen prototype, carried out in one European co-funded project called ALICIA (www.alicia-project.eu). Through the presentation of this evaluation activity and its impact on the rest of design process, this chapter will address some methodological issues on usability in complex domains: 1) The specific context in which the technology is introduced has to be well known by the designers as it provides crucial constraints to be taken into account; 2) Evaluating complex safety critical systems entails the use of a holistic multidisciplinary approach and an iterative design process that involve, in different phases, several type of experts (engineers, human factors, usability experts, end users and stakeholders); and 3) The level of maturity of the technology and the evaluation objectives contribute to the definition of the evaluation methods to be used.

DOI: 10.4018/978-1-4666-4046-7.ch012

ORGANIZATION BACKGROUND

Nowadays, a range of technologies and interfaces design approaches exist which together have the potential to address the management of the flight deck's complexity, whilst maintaining crew situation awareness, reducing workload and simultaneously addressing the issue of through life cost. Example technologies include Direct Voice Input/Output, Auditory Displays and 3D Audio, Graphical User Interfaces with task tailored controls, Improved Display Technologies (Large Area Displays, Head Up/Head Mounted Displays, 3D Displays), Touch screen controls, Multi modal input/output devices. ALICIA is one EU co-founded project started in 2009 and lasting for 4 years, aiming at extending aircraft operations in degraded visibility conditions by developing a new aircraft flight deck architecture facilitating the introduction of new technologies and applications. One of the research challenging concepts of the project is the introduction of touch screens as a means to provide and better manage the information needed to operate efficiently and safely in all weather conditions.

SETTING THE STAGE

In the following paragraphs the importance of the context and the appropriate complexity is highlighted.

The Flight Deck Complexity

The flight deck (also known as cockpit) is the area where a pilot controls the aircraft. This area is located in front of the plane or helicopter and, from it, the aircraft is controlled when moving on the ground and when flying in the air. The cockpit of an aircraft contains flight instruments (providing information such as height, speed and attitude) and controls (which enable the pilot to fly the aircraft).

Early commercial aircraft crew stations featured systems with dedicated control and monitoring facilities. This means that every function (e.g. radio, altimeter) had a dedicated instrument in the cockpit. All these controls were analogic ones as, prior to the 1970s, computer based technology was not mature enough and no sufficiently light and powerful circuits were available. The increasing complexity of transport aircraft and the growing air traffic congestion around airports turned this approach became unsustainable because there was insufficient space to accommodate all the dedicated controls and displays (the evolution in the distribution of the space is illustrated by the Concorde crew station in Figure 1). A commercial aircraft in the mid-1970s had more than one hundred instruments and controls, and the primary flight instruments were already full of indicators, crossbars, and symbols, and the growing number of cockpit elements impacted cockpit space and pilot attention. This design also imposed a high system management and control workload on the crew resulting in the need for three crewmembers on the flight deck of large aircraft.

The advent of digital systems changed this approach. By the end of the 1990s, Liquid crystal display (LCD) panels were increasingly introduced by aircraft manufacturers because of their efficiency, reliability and legibility. This is the so called "glass cockpit," featuring electronic (digital) instrument displays, typically large LCD screens, as opposed to the traditional style of analogue dials and gauges. Where a traditional cockpit relies on numerous mechanical gauges to display information, a glass cockpit uses several displays driven by flight management systems that can be adjusted to display flight information as needed. This simplifies aircraft operation and navigation and allows pilots to focus only on the most pertinent information.

This approach has allowed the industry to accommodate new requirements and operating procedures and removed the need for the third crew member. The A380 cockpit (depicted in Figure 1) represents the current state-of-the-art using this level of technology.

Bringing the Touch Screen into the Flight Deck

Many projects[1] within the aeronautical domain are working to find a better way to present information to pilots and a better way to interact with the system. Touch screens seem to be the suitable way to continue the process of simplification of the cockpit presented in the previous paragraph (Norman, 2011).

Technologies such as touch screens are largely used, with success, in many other domains, from the customer electronic sector, to the automotive and industrial plans ones. The use of touch screens has became quite common in everyone life. So why not introduce them in the aeronautic sector? They would allow greater

Figure 1. Concorde cockpit (1970) and A380 crew station (2005)

use of graphical-based interfaces that facilitate gesture interaction techniques in a complex environment like the aircraft cockpit. Several advantages and opportunities can be envisaged:

- Graphical representations of aircraft systems can provide more intuitive visual representations,
- No more physical or space constraints, as all the information and input keys can be accessed through the same interface,
- Direct manipulation as interaction mode to select an object/element of the interface,
- Touch screens interfaces can be personalised and present only the information and inputs necessary for the specific flight phase, thus reducing "visual noise" and positively impact on workload by clearing crew's peripheral attention,
- Touch screens interfaces can merge all the different kinds of information at stake (texts, icons, videos, maps, etc) and ease direct interaction with digital maps and other applications for air traffic avoidance.

However, despite its opportunities, the introduction of a new technology in the flight deck needs to be fully assessed in order to design solutions adequate to the complexity of the crew's activities. In fact, some advantages deriving from the use of touch screens in one domain can be lost when the same technology is introduced in a totally different activity. Three aspects can vary (also dramatically) when moving form a domain to another:

1. The steering design principles can be very different.
2. The weight and balance of several aspects, such as usability, safety and errors management can greatly change.
3. The number of stakeholders can be very different, and so the quantity and heterogeneity of requirements to implement.

The Environmental Constraints

When designing a tablet or a phone interface, there are consolidated rules that can be followed. Literature (Parhi, Karlson, & Bederson, 2006; Saffer, 2008) provides several studies about the design of buttons for touch screens. For example, regarding button size, ISO and ANSI (ISO 13406-1, 1999) standards recommend making them .75″ (3/4″) square, as it is considered to be most effective at maximizing both user performance and satisfaction.

This knowledge, however, cannot be directly applied to the cockpit because many factors differentiate the use of touch screens on a cockpit compared with other uses. The more obvious one is the presence of vibrations, that reduce the precision of users in touching the right part of the screen (see Figure 2B). Also the possible gestures to interact with the instrument is deeply determined by its use in vibrating situations (see Figure 2A). Even if touch screen units have already started founding their way into aerospace applications, there is still a lack of published qualitative assessments on the performance of this technology when integrated within existing avionics components. This means that a dedicate investigation has to be performed, in order to understand if there is a right size of buttons in this specific context, if it can be personalised by the pilot, if there can be a personalisation depending on the different phases of the flight the pilot is engaged in, or also depending on the difficulty of the specific manoeuvre.

The Importance of Safety

Making an error when interacting with your pc at work can lead to the loss of data (meaning money). Making an error in a cockpit can lead to incidents or even accidents. This means that safety issues have a huge importance in the design in the avionic domain that must develop reliable technologies and error free interfaces. These aspects are normally less considered in other domains, so the design of touch screens interfaces for cockpits requires additional considerations and new investigations on the realistic scenarios of application that should carefully consider that degraded conditions of usage should maintain the same level of safety and reliability (Chiuhsiang, Chi, Chin, & Hung, 2010).

This implies, for example, that the failure of the system should be considered in the design solution generated and anticipated by backup solutions (see Figure 2C);

Figure 2. Design constraints for touch screen in the cockpit (as studied in ALICIA)

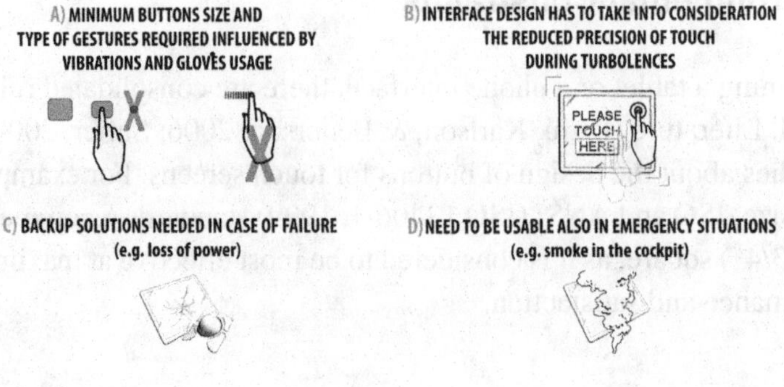

A) MINIMUM BUTTONS SIZE AND TYPE OF GESTURES REQUIRED INFLUENCED BY VIBRATIONS AND GLOVES USAGE

B) INTERFACE DESIGN HAS TO TAKE INTO CONSIDERATION THE REDUCED PRECISION OF TOUCH DURING TURBOLENCES

C) BACKUP SOLUTIONS NEEDED IN CASE OF FAILURE (e.g. loss of power)

D) NEED TO BE USABLE ALSO IN EMERGENCY SITUATIONS (e.g. smoke in the cockpit) and emergency situation, such as smoke in the cockpit, should be considered when designing the introduction of a touch based device in the flight deck (see Figure 2D).

Harmonise Stakeholders' Needs

As preliminary work on the project, a definition of the stakeholders' chain of the civil Aeronautic sector was done. It is immediately clear that several factors influence the design process with their specific objectives. Each of them unfolds a complexity articulated in several requirements that the designer has to collect, analyse and measure in the future scenarios he/she envisages:

- *Pilots* ask for usable instruments, capable of dealing with the complexity of the tasks of flying an aircraft, and with the specific issues that the airborne environment presents (vibrations, possible system failures, lens flares effect on screens surface and so on).
- *Designers* have to master the intrinsic complexity of human cognition, the physical constrains of the human body, the unexpected critical interactions between humans and the system, and the specific tasks making off the flying activity.
- *Aviation Industry* (avionics and aircraft) requires to take into consideration the limitations in space and weight of a cockpit. As many technologies have not reached an adequate maturity level or are produced only in few quantities, there is the challenge of finding quite off the shelf hardware and software, trying to reduce development costs. In addition, industry is looking for technical solutions that lower the costs related to certification.
- *Airlines*, that are Industry's clients, lose a lot of money every year because of delays, very often caused by bad weather; they ask for solutions that permit aircraft to fly safely even in degraded visual conditions. Moreover, they want systems that are not only usable and reliable, but also require as little maintenance as possible. Moreover, new aircrafts (having updated instruments or philosophy of use) usually require some new training for pilots; these costs are on the shoulders of airlines.
- The aircraft is not a close system; it has to integrate with the *Air Traffic Control*. And it is not just a technological problem: pilots and controllers have a well-defined division of work and also responsibilities. Any technology that, for example, provides new information to the pilots, can modify this division of labour.

This means that, when designing in complex socio-technical systems, even if focusing on specific aspects such as usability, a certain knowledge of the requirements coming from the different actors involved has to be taken into consideration. The design process should include specific activities in which the requirements are collected from the different stakeholders through the use of the appropriate means, and then evaluated and validated.

CASE DESCRIPTION

In the previous paragraphs it was explained why consolidated and commonly used technologies such as touch screens needs to be thoroughly assessed before their introduction in a safety critical domain, and how the expected improvements should not compromise the level of safety of the whole system. Now the way technologies can be assessed in complex domains, such as the aeronautic one, is introduced.

The Design Process in the Air Transport System

When designing for the Aeronautic there are several aspects of complexity to tackle with, and they do not only relate to usability. They are entailed by the intrinsic complexity of the different "systems" that have to interact with each other, so that the challenge for the designer is not only to design a cockpit that efficiently supports all the tasks related to the activity of flying an aircraft, but to take into consideration and harmonize aspects such as production costs, interaction with the ATM (Air Traffic Management) system, specific requests from airlines, and so on. Alternative versions of future scenarios have to be considered, especially during the initial phases of development, trying to prioritize and balance all the requirements elicited by the different stakeholders. One of the aims of the designer is to explore these different versions and select those that are more promising for the later phases of the design process. This is particularly true in Research&Development (R&D). In fact, projects are used as a mechanism for investigating specific aspects of the scenarios during specific lifecycle phases. While developing innovative scenarios, the designer shall also refine them and provide evidence that they are adequate for evolving towards an operational status. Moreover, these concepts have to be accounted of being able to deliver the planned enhancements, and thus encounter the stakeholders' objectives stated. This evidence shall demonstrate that the new scenarios developed can work safely in a real life environment while providing the benefits they are developed for. The evidence is essential to support the decision making process regarding the adoption, or the further improvements and refinements, or the rejection of the concepts under study.

The Design Process in ALICIA

A highly iterative design process is what in ALICIA allows the constant (re)defini-tion of the design opportunities and constraints, while early evaluations guarantee that the issues from different stakeholders are taken into account.

The process adopted in ALICIA is holistic and iterative. In fact, ALICIA's ob-jective is to integrate different technologies using a comprehensive and integrated approach to ensure that the design and implementation of a technical, human, and/ or procedural system can deliver the desired performance improvements. In such iterative process the design outcomes are the result of a series of feedback loops in which requirements and designed solutions are iteratively refined based on the feedback of formative evaluation activities. Iterative design and evaluation together attempt to mitigate the discomforts that technological innovation could bring to working practices by custom tailoring the systems interfaces to the users in all of the design phases of a system, in such a way that they are able to steer the design process.

In such a holistic process the design choices are the result of a trade-off be-tween the requirements coming from different dimensions. In generating a concept and selecting between different options, designers have to envisage which are all the effects that every choice would have at all the dimensions for all the relevant stakeholders. Often the designer's role is not easy: for example, a solution that can improve usability for pilots can have some undesired effects:

- The solution can provoke an uncontrolled increase in the costs of production to the industry.
- The solution could require the use of a technology that is too heavily increas-ing fuel consumption and so costs for the airlines.
- The solution could burden Air Traffic Controllers work.

The design process applied to explore the potential of touch screens for the cockpit of the future couldn't be only driven by final users' requirements (the pilots). The presence of market logics, interactions with cooperating systems (such as ATC), requirements coming from the certification and regulation authorities, entail the need to apply a systemic approach to manage the complexity and face the new challenges of the domain, guaranteeing the safety of the whole system.

In the presentation of this case, a small part of this design and evaluation process will be presented. As illustrated in Figure 3, the Usability Evaluations in ALICIA, followed a study on haptic feedback in the aircraft flight deck environment, and a *user* test carried out to determine the "right" buttons' size.

The first study (Bolton, 2012), over a complete set of experiments, has demon-strated that the haptic feedback could provide some performance benefits and that the technology was well received by users. In the second study, the test aimed at identifying and assessing all the issues related to the interaction with the touch screen in a vibration environment (Vibration trial). The test was based on the observations of pilots performing simple tasks (such as entering an alphanumeric string of characters) using the touch screen in a cockpit simulator that simulated the vibrations. Post-test questionnaires and system logs (providing task execution time and error rates) were also used to gather feedback. A set of requirements for the design of the single elements of the touch screens (buttons) has been generated.

The results of these tests were considered for the next step of design process: the design of an *Interface Philosophy* to be used as a common reference and guide for the design and the implementation of different applications for both helicopter and airplane cockpits. The Interface Philosophy is a list of guidelines that describe the characteristics of the user interface and user experience for the ALICIA cockpit. It contains several guidelines, ranging from Location of Key Functions to Graphical Object Behaviours, to Colour Palette, Error Policy, Touch Gestures, Feedback Policy and so on.

Figure 3. A view of the evaluation and design activities performed before and after the usability expert evaluation presented in this case (as developed in ALICIA)

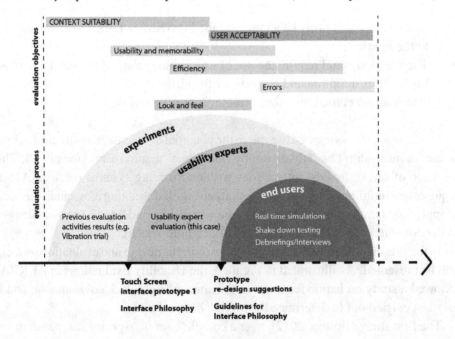

This Interface Philosophy was used as a reference for the implementation of a *digital prototype*, presenting the interface look&feel and its behaviour (buttons status, icons animations, etc.) as well as some navigation examples. Figure 3 shows the evaluation activities presented in this case study within the overall ALICIA evaluation process.

At this stage of the project, the concept was mostly based on construction requirements, constrains related to the use on different aircraft and the standards implemented in already existing products. The Human Factors point of view was still lacking. Therefore, a usability evaluation was planned for the digital prototype developed.

Selection of the Evaluation Method

The cockpit is a complex socio-technical system in which several tools have to be used synchronously, different procedures are applied, and as consequence the resources of pilots are absorbed by several concurrent tasks. The airline (and test) pilots provide great and indispensable feedback when testing technologies in a real operational context in the latest phases of a design process (see Figure 3). Thus, involving pilots in a simulation can provide crucial information about the whole activity and the impact of new designs on attention, workload, fatigue and stress.

However, the usability evaluation here presented, was based on a prototype consisting in a non-interactive slide show presenting an interface that allowed the management of several applications and avionics, including radios, flight management system, lights controls, fuel, etc. At this early stage of the design process the evaluation needed was purely related to the interface usability and coherency, trying to anticipate and reduce error prone configurations.

For this reason, a discount technique was chosen that would allow to unfold issues related to effectiveness and efficiency and could be used to guide the next steps of the iterative design process. The *Heuristic Evaluation* (Nielsen & Molich, 1990) is a Human Factor method aimed at understanding whether each element of a user interface follows a list of established usability heuristics.

In a heuristic evaluation the usability expert checks features of an interface or product against a checklist that details a pre-defined set of criteria/heuristics. Several heuristics are available, such as the ones proposed by Jacob Nielsen (1994). This is a quick and easy method to employ, offering an immediately useful output. Once the set of heuristics has been established the analyst worked through it to determine:

1. Which aspects of the system/device match the criteria identified in the checklist
2. In which areas there are gaps

The adherence to the heuristic ensures that about 75% of usability problems of an interface are identified (Nielsen & Landauer, 1993). A heuristic evaluation carried out successfully in the early phases of a design, allows focusing the next evaluations with the end users on operational aspects (functionalities, procedures, impact on workload, attention, task sharing and other human factors) as the majority of the usability flows was already addressed.

Usability Expert Evaluation for Touch Screen

The evaluation performed was made up of six steps:

- **Step 1:** Definition of the evaluation objectives
- **Step 2:** Analysis of the context
- **Step 3:** Adapt the evaluation method to context
- **Step 4:** Analysis of the prototype
- **Step 5:** From heuristics to design
- **Step 6:** From design to philosophy

Step 1: Definition of the Evaluation Objectives

The usability evaluation conducted on the touch screen prototype was aimed at:

1. Providing analysis of the design issues and suggesting possible solutions on the interface of the prototype.
2. Integrate/correct the Interface Philosophy to guarantee its usability and reduce error prone interactions.

Based on the extensive literature on usability in complex domains (Cardosi & Murphy, 1995; Peryer, Noyes, Pleydell-Pearce, & Lieven, 2010; Nielsen, 1993; Stanton, 2004; Bannon, 1992; Harris, 2011) and taking into considerations the specific objectives of the ALICIA project, the "usability for touch screens in the cockpit" was defined as composed of four elements:

1. Human Machine Interaction relates to the perceptual and physical aspects of the interface (display formatting, graphics, feedback, etc.).
2. Workload is determined by the contents and display representation, the appropriateness of the information and the functions for supporting the cognitive tasks of the pilot.
3. Learnability relates to the intuitiveness of the solutions, the easy- to-learn and easy-to-adapt solutions.

4. Awareness relates to the full and real-time picture of the activities during all phases of flights.

Step 2: Impact Analysis

With respect to each of these elements, a first evaluation of the *impact of the introduction of touch screens in the cockpit* was performed. This study allowed identifying in the first place risks and opportunities for the introduction of the touch screen. This evaluation entails a thorough knowledge of the domain and the operational context, together with a Human Factors expertise. The information needed to perform this study was collected by a literature review and dedicated interviews with operational experts and pilots.

A brief summary of the results of this preliminary study is presented in Figure 4. It presents some of the impact (pros and cons) of the introduction of touch screens in a flight deck on the four components identified in the first step. In the upper left part of the Figure, the expected positive and negative consequences on *usability* are presented. In general, touch screens are expected to have a positive impact on the human machine interaction. In fact, they permit a direct manipulation of information (that is generally considered more intuitive than a menu-based interaction); there are no physical constrains to the shapes and sizes of the different elements of the interface (within the size of the screen, all formats can be used: buttons, tables, synoptic representations, synthetic vision, etc); there are several robust and already knew interactions modalities that can be applied (e.g. the "pinch movement" to zoom in and out); there is the possibility to access more information through the same interface: as you don't need a dedicated instrument for each function, you can use instead different pages in the same screen. On the other hand, there are some aspects that have to be considered, in order to assure a good level of interaction with touch screens in the cockpits. Some lights conditions make the screen unreadable; vibrations can make it difficult to touch the intended part of the screen; there is no physical feedback (e.g. when you press a button there is a graphic feedback but not a haptic one, this means that the only feedback to the action requires active visual attention to be perceived).

In the upper right part of Figure 4 it is presented how the introduction of touch screen is expected to influence the easiness in learning how to use the cockpit system. This is a very important aspect in the aeronautic domain as it impacts on pilots' training needs, and so on costs. Touch screens are expected to improve *learnability* as they permit to implement more intuitive interfaces, thanks to direct interaction with objects, no physical constraints to the design (text, figures and also videos can be accommodated in the screen space, etc.), contextual help functions and so on. The use of touch screens also enables the implementation of similar interfaces in

Figure 4. Aspects to consider when evaluating the introduction of touch screens in cockpits. For each element pros (upper semicircle) and cons (bottom semicircle) are provided.

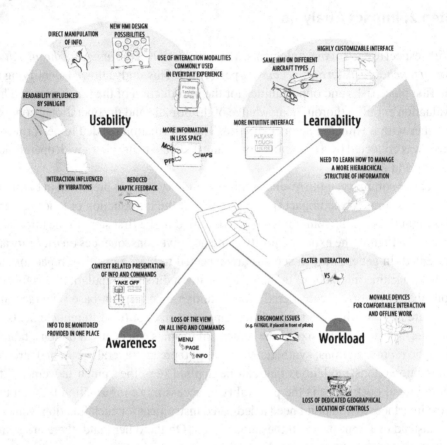

different models of aircraft and also on different types of aircraft (i.e. airplanes and helicopters), reducing, for example, the training needs for a pilot moving from a model of aircraft to another. The interface would also be highly customizable, enabling pilots to adjust some aspects (e.g. the positions of information within a screen or among different screens) to their specific needs or to a specific phase of flight. The drawback is the need to interact with information that is no more always visible (like in the old fashion cockpit with an instrument for each function, always present on the cockpit) but structured in menus and pages, leading the need for pilots to remember in which page is the information/command he/she wants to use.

The *situation awareness* of pilots is expected to be improved by touch screens, as they permit to present just the information needed in the current phase of flight (reducing the number of information that pilots have to monitor at the same time) and they permit to have all the information needed in one specific place of the cockpit, reducing pilots need to look for the desired information among different instruments spread on a large space (the whole cockpit). On the other hand, this positive aspects imply the risk that some potentially important information are not presented to pilots; the crowded old cockpit had the pros of presenting all the information at the same time, implying difficulty in monitor them and find the needed one, but also implying the possibility for pilots to have an holistic view on all flight data and information.

Workload should be lowered thanks to the faster interaction permitted by touch screens if compared with the current interaction means used in cockpits (e.g. the trackball); they also enable the possibility to share cockpit information with portable devices (e.g. dedicated tablets) permitting a faster and comfortable interaction (pilots don't need to extend their arms on the cockpit instruments) and enabling them to work together on the same screen, improving team work and lowering the possibility of misunderstanding. Nevertheless touch screens imply some issues, especially related to ergonomics and so physical workload: for example in today's cockpits pilots use the frames of the several instruments, as well as other physical holds, to support their hands while interacting with instruments. This lowers their fatigue (especially during turbulences), an aspect that plays an important role, especially in long distance flights. With touch screens the possibility to rest arms holding hands and fingers on instruments surface is lower, as touching the screen would probably activate some command. In addition, the use of direct interaction implies pilots to extend their arms and reach the screens. Armrests, as well as alternative interaction means, should be considered to lower pilots' fatigue. A possible aspect that could increase mental workload is the loss of dedicated geographical locations of information: pilots today knows where in the cockpit they can find a particular information, while with touch screens at least some of them will be hide within menus and pages that are not visible; pilots would so need to remember not a position in the space but a position within a abstract structure (the interface menus), that is a more demanding cognitive task.

In addition to the list of advantages and disadvantages, two other important considerations have to be highlighted:

1. Some cons are specific for this context: for example the highly vibrating environment that interfere with the interaction (while we use our tablets or phones mainly in static environments); or the ergonomic issues: pilots have to interact with instruments for prolonged times, so they have to be comfortable (think about intercontinental flights).

2. Some cons have a completely different importance than in other domains: for example the reduced haptic feedback is a common drawback that we experience every day with our touch screen based devices, it is, however, considered

tolerable for the task we use them for; in the cockpit, the feeling of touching buttons or levels is more important, because pilots often need to interact with instruments while watching outside the aircraft; there are also emergency situations in which pilots cannot see the instruments (e.g. smoke in the cockpit), but they can still use them because they can understand which command they are touching by its specific shape.

Step 3: Adapting the Evaluation Method to the Context

The third step of the evaluation process was based on Heuristic Evaluation technique carried out by a usability expert on the low-fi prototype developed. The list of heuristics used for the evaluation of the prototype was created ad-hoc tailoring and adapting to the specific context existing heuristics in which the technology was expected to be used by users (i.e. a touch screen in a rotorcraft) and depending on prototype's characteristics and functionalities (e.g. level of possible interaction allowed, limitations, functionalities available, etc). The final list was built on different references for usability heuristics: Molich e Nielsen (1990), Ravden and Johnson (1989), Cardosi and Murphy (1995), Peryer et al. (2010).

A selection of the heuristics used in the case presented is reported in the Table 1.

Step 4: Analysis of the Prototype

Once objectives and heuristics for the usability evaluation were decided, the analysis was performed. The analyst inspected the prototype against each point on the checklist. The output of this phase of evaluation was a list of issues and possible solutions, recorded in Table 2.

The issues identified and the level of severity assigned to each of them, was deeply influenced by the operational context. For example, the violation of user expectations coming from standards, training and previous aircraft experience in this context has been rated as a high severity issue (see Table 3) as it can lead to errors and increase workload, while the same could be considered a minor issue in another context, such as the consumer electronics.

Once generated, this list has been used:

- To prepare a summary of the main issues found
- To select some issues for which to present redesign solutions
- To generate more general guidelines to be integrated into the Interface Philosophy (starting from the most violated heuristics and the related possible solutions)

Table 1. Selection of heuristics used during expert evaluation

HF Issues	Keywords	Referred Heuristics
Usability To evaluate the ease-of-use of the new concept	Accessibility	• Controls can be operated in all operational conditions • Controls and displays are visible
	Visibility	• Needed information is promptly available • Needed information is visible • The information provided is relevant and really needed • The system clearly indicates data-entry mode and location • The system clearly indicates current position within menu structure
	Understanding	• The information provided to user is easy to interpret correctly • Data are directly usable by the user • Data are directly usable by the user
	Interaction	• The actions that a user can perform on a device are obvious • Menus are effectively designed • The interaction with the system is effective
	Errors	• The system supports the user in preventing the execution of unwanted actions • Errors can be minimised/recovered • Errors messages are provided when needed
Situation Awareness To evaluate if the system supports the flight user in correctly understanding the situation, in anticipating future events and in taking the appropriate actions	Understanding	• The information provided to the user supports him in building the correct picture of the situation
	Planning	• The information provided to the user supports him in anticipating how the situation could possibly evolve
	Acting	• The information provided to the user supports him in taking the correct actions
	Emphasis	• Important information that requires flight user awareness, is properly evidenced • Warning and alerts do not produce negative effects on user activity
	Consistency	• The system (colours, symbols, wording, etc.) is designed to match user expectations (coming from standards, common life experience, training, previous a/c experience, manufacturer philosophy, internal system logic, etc.)
	Feedback	• The system keeps users informed about what is going
Safety To evaluate if the system supports the flight user in the discovery of safety critical events		• The system supports the flight user in dealing with critical events
		• The system does not induce to safety critical events (i.e. does not induce hazards)

Two examples of the analysis performed are proposed below. As the prototype is protected by copyright, the images presented are sketches that represent the main elements of the interface, but they do not directly reproduce the prototype developed. They reproduce only the contents of the pages, without the navigation and radio

Table 2. Example of template for heuristic analysis results

Violated Heuristic	Issue	Severity	Possible solution
The reference or the description of the specific heuristic that has been violated	*Description of the problem: how the heuristic has been violated and consequences of this violation*	*Description of the severity of the issue; a rate (low, medium, high) is associated to each issue. Impact on usability, workload, awareness and safety is highlighted*	*How the interface can be modified in order to solve/mitigate the problem*

menus (placed on the top and on the right of the pages). Moreover, some aspects have been simplified to make easier to understand the analysis performed even with no aeronautic prior knowledge.

Example A: The Lights Page

Figure 5A represents one of the pages of the interface, as implemented in the prototype. This page presents controls related to the external lights (the lights outside of the aircraft) and internal lights (the flight deck and the cockpit's instruments brightness). Pilots can act on these controls to turn on or off some lights (e.g. the fasten seat belts light) or to tune lights luminosity (e.g. the general cockpit light luminosity). The rounded buttons are *"Toggles"* (e.g. the "Position" button). A toggle selection is a means of selecting one or other option from a choice of two. On touch release, the button toggles to the other selection and the two toggle options retain their relative position on the button. The current selection is shown in a white background and the alternate (not selected) option is shown in a smaller font. The rectangular buttons are *"Dimmers"* (e.g. "Overhead"). Acting on the + or - it increases or decreases the value of the related parameter. The number next to button's name indicates the current value (that is also graphically indicated by the triangle). The "Main dimmer" toggle does not act on any lights. It selects on which ambient (cockpit or cabin) the dimmer below will act.

Based on the template in Table 2, an analysis based on the usability heuristics has been carried out. Three main issues emerged and they are described in Table 3.

Example B: Checklists Page

Pilots have to follow different checklists in different phases of the flight. A checklist is a tool for error management and performance improvement. It consists in a list of actions (e.g. activate a device, set a parameter) that pilots have to perform in a

Table 3. Heuristic analysis results for the lights page

Violated heuristic reference	Issue encountered	Severity	Possible solution
The information provided to user is easy to interpret correctly	The function related to several buttons are not obvious, and it is difficult to anticipate the consequence of each command; for example, the dimmer "Cockpit" acts on the intensity of the lights. It acts on the cockpit light if the "Main dimmer" button is set to "Cockpit," on the cabin lights if the "Main dimmer" button is set to "Cabin." This behaviour is not easily predictable by users	Medium: impact on errors, workload, situation awareness, efficiency, effectiveness of the interaction and time needed for training	Use separated dimmers for cockpit and cabin lights
The information provided is relevant and really needed	Pilots do not need to act on external and internal lights at the same moment. There is no procedure that requires this and no added operational value in having the commands of the external and internal lights in the same page	Medium: impact on errors, workload, efficiency	Remove the external lights commands
The system (colours, symbols, wording, etc.) is designed to match user expectations (coming from standards, common life experience, training, previous a/c experience, manufacturer philosophy, internal system logic, etc.)	Buttons acting on complete different and separated functions (as the dimmers acting on lights and the ones acting on instruments luminosity) are positioned close to each other; this doesn't help in understanding the difference in the consequences of the commands and can induce to errors	High: impact on errors, workload, situation awareness, efficiency, effectiveness of the interaction and time needed for training	Group the buttons with similar functions

specific order in specific moments of the flight (e.g. before starting the engines, or during emergencies); it guarantees the effectiveness when performing routinely tasks that could be subject to lapses.

Figure 6 refers to the page of the prototype used to present the list of available checklists. Pilots can navigate through them scrolling up and down using the "List" up and down buttons; once the needed one is selected, they can activate it in two modalities: "Auto check" or "Manual check." Once one of these two buttons is pressed, the list of actions related to the selected checklist is shown. The "Page" buttons are used navigate through the different pages (in this case the Normal checklists occupy four pages).

Figure 5. The lights page as implemented in the prototype under analysis (up) and the redesign proposal (down)

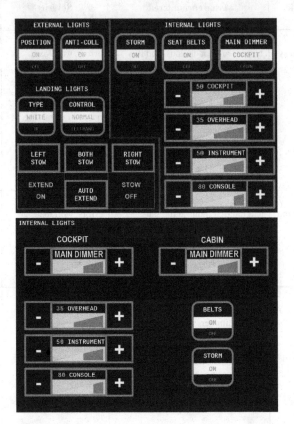

Two main issues have been identified; they are described in Table 4.

Step 5: From Heuristics to Design

Following the possible solutions listed in the previous step, some redesign suggestions solving the issues encountered have been realised. This would help designers in understanding the problems and solutions reported in the expert evaluation results.

Example A: The Lights Page

Figure 5 presents the redesign proposal for the lights page; this proposal tries to solve the problems found during the Heuristic Analysis.

The following modifications have been made respect to the original prototype:

- The external lights related buttons are removed.
- The "main dimmer" selector is removed, and dedicated dimmers for both cabin and cockpit have been added.
- Buttons are grouped in a logical way, divided into cabin and cockpit. This meets pilots' expectations and matches with the real world, in which cockpit and cabin are separated. Moreover pilots acts on cockpit's and cabin's light in different moments.
- The cockpit buttons are grouped, divided into main dimmer (1 button) and panel related dimmers (3 buttons) and ordered following logic of "importance" (illumination of the all cockpit above the illumination of the panels). The three buttons related to panel brightness are ordered following a spatial relationship: the Overhead button is the first (up in the page) because overhead panel is above pilot (up from pilot's perspective), then instrument button is under overhead (as instrument panel is under the overhead one from pilot's perspective), then at the bottom the interseat button (as interseat console is the lowest console from pilot's point of view).

In this example of redesign the interface uses a logical spatial correlation (up/front, down/back), universally accepted and used, that helps pilots to better remember the buttons that they have to use (minimizing workload) and reducing errors.

Example B: Checklists Page

In Figure 6 a redesign proposal for the checklist page is presented.

The original page has been modified as the following:

- The "Manual Check" and "Auto Check" buttons produce an action related to the currently selected item (i.e. they will visualize the selected checklist). For this reason the buttons acting on the selected item are moved on the right, next to the checklists list (and so to the element they act on).
- Page buttons and scroll buttons, all navigation elements, are grouped in the same area, on the right.
- They are ordered following the logic: the buttons in the centre move the selection (small movement), the buttons far from the centre move page (bigger movement).
- Page number is moved next to the other elements related to navigation (List and Page buttons).

Figure 6. The Checklists page as implemented in the prototype under analysis (up) and the redesign proposal (down)

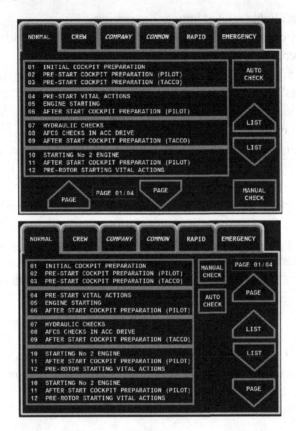

Step 6: From Design to Philosophy

At the end of the evaluation activity, the most violated heuristics were transformed in "positive" sentences to be adapted to the specific context and included in the Interface Philosophy. Table 5 reports some of the guidelines generated starting from the heuristics and solutions related to the previous two examples.

As you will see, they all refer to one of the biggest issue found at the end of the analysis, the *lack of a rationale* for the positioning of the elements in the space of the screen.

With these and similar guidelines, it has been filled one important gap that was present in the Interface Philosophy. A rationale behind elements' order, elements' position in the page and the relative position to each other helps pilots to understand

Table 4. Heuristic analysis results for the checklists page

Violated heuristic	Issue encountered	Severity	Possible solution
The system (colours, symbols, wording, etc.) is designed to match user expectations (coming from standards, common life experience, training, previous a/c experience, manufacturer philosophy, internal system logic, etc.)	Buttons should be placed in the page following a specific logic. In particular, commands with similar functions should be placed close together. In this case the navigation buttons are scattered within the page	Medium: impact on workload, efficiency	The navigation buttons should be grouped in one specific area. This would help pilots remembering where the navigation buttons are and in better identifying these buttons among others
The system clearly indicates current position within menu structure	The current location within the contents is indicated by the page number, that is placed in the middle of the page	Light: Impact on awareness, workload	The current page buttons should be placed in the area related to navigation buttons

their functions and the relationship between them. The logic chosen can be based on operational needs (e.g. elements can be ordered following the order the associated functions/commands are used within a procedure), usability heuristic (e.g. a button acting on a list should be placed near the list), coherence with the real word (e.g. the button related to front lights can be placed up in the page, creating a easy to understand and remember association up (in the screen) = front (in the helicopter), or coherence with standards. To group and place elements using a rationale that can be shared by pilots would also positively affect efficiency, training time and errors.

An important aspect that does not emerge from the few examples provided is that the Expert Analysis is not just focused on the single pages, but it considers the all interaction experience. The second major issue found in the prototype was in fact the *lack of coherence* in the positioning of the elements in the space of the screen. The analysis found in fact that navigating the different pages of the prototype the same kind of information (e.g. list of items) or commands (e.g. the buttons for navigating a list) were often presented in different formats and in different positions. To solve this it was suggested the implementation of a set of standard layouts to be used for pages presenting the same kind of information or commands. This would affect: efficiency, effectiveness of the interaction and time needed for training. The coherence in the interface layout helps pilots finding the wanted information and commands; it eases the training phase and reduces errors and indecisions. It also is also a first step towards the certification and standardisation process. See Figure 7 for a possible layout for these pages.

Table 5. Guidelines related to positioning of the elements in the space of the screen

Topic	Guideline	Example
Logic in the positioning of the elements within the page	Keep commands related to different aspects of an avionic/procedure in different places within the page	Buttons related to lights in the cockpit on the left, buttons related to lights in the cabin on the right
Some logic in the order of the elements within the page	If there is any spatial, logical, or procedural order in the activated action or related avionics, always reflect it placing the related commands in a coherent way	Buttons activating lights placed on the front of the helicopter should be up in the page, above the buttons activating lights placed in the back of the helicopter, that should be down in the page/below the other ones
Relevance of the contents provided	Keep commands and information related to different avionics/places/procedures separated using different pages, in order to have a view on related information and elements as simpler and consistent as possible	If internal and external lights are not usually managed at the same time, they could have two dedicated pages
Navigation	The information related to navigation should always be placed in the same place in the page; in other words, some place in the pages should be devoted to present the position of the current page within menu structure. When navigations elements cannot be placed here, they should be placed next to navigation buttons	The "current page/total numbers of page" text should always be provided above the page (up/down) buttons

To incorporate that in the Interface Philosophy several guidelines have been generated. Table 6 provides a simple example.

Figure 8 presents a proposal of a standard layout for pages containing lists of objects, such as checklists. The list of objects (e.g. waypoints) is displayed in the upper left rectangle area, the commands acting on the list (e.g. add a waypoint) are in the lower left rectangle area, the command acting on the object currently selected (e.g. edit a waypoint) are placed in the middle rectangle area, the buttons related to navigation (e.g. change page) are in the right rectangle area.

CURRENT CHALLENGING FACING THE ORGANISATION

Nowadays pilots and controllers communicate between them via radio; a concept under study within the ALICIA project includes the use of textual messages instead of radio as primary communication means between pilots and controllers. An excerpt of a page dedicated to communication with the ground controllers is presented as

Figure 7. An example of possible layout for pages providing lists of times to navigate and interact with

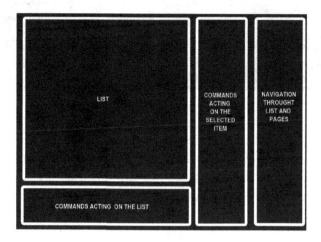

Table 6. Guidelines related to the coherence among pages

Topic	Guideline	Example
Coherence	Once a logic is used for placing elements in the screen, this should be used in all pages that present the same elements; in other words, pages having a similar purpose (e.g. select and/or act on items of a list) should have the same layout, and buttons with the same action (e.g. scroll up, delete/remove, edit) should maintain the same position/size	Different layouts can be developed according to page purpose. For example, pages containing lists of objects (e.g. waypoints) could have all the same layout, like the one provided below

example. The focus is just on a function in this page that was simplified to make it easier to understand the underlying issues and solutions.

In the upper rectangle, textual messages coming from controllers are displayed. They are requests for pilots to perform some actions, such as changing altitude, speed or route. The procedure that has to be followed when a message is received is: the pilot reads and understands the message, he presses the "Read" button in order to make the controller aware that the message has been received; the controller waits for an answer to the request; pilot checks if the flight conditions permit to execute the requested manoeuvre; if yes, he presses the "Wilco" (that means I Will Comply) button, if not, he presses the unable button; once one of the two buttons is pressed, the air traffic controller is acknowledged of pilot answer.

Figure 8. An excerpt of the communication page (left) and a redesign proposal (right)

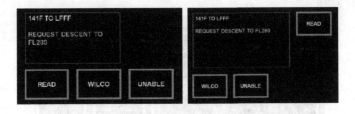

For this example, no heuristic violation has been found. However, the redesign suggestion is an example of a design that violates a heuristic on purpose, to adapt the interface to a specific context and somehow scarifying usability in favour of safety.

The original design is not particularly wrong. The buttons are placed near to the elements they refer to and they are in an order corresponding to the set of actions that has to be performed (confirm that you read, communicate your decision). Some space could be added between the "Read" button and the other two to make visually clear that they refer to two conceptually different kind of action. But in this case a major problem has been found.

Pilots need to interact with this communication function while performing other tasks (navigate the aircraft, perform checklists, etc.). Sometimes this communication can be received in very busy moments of the flight. As the answer to controllers requests is generally "yes," it is highly probable that pilots will develop an automatic reaction to this messages, like pressing the two buttons in rapid sequence, without really performing the two separated cognitive tasks that are associated to the two buttons (understand, decide). As the screen will be most probably situated in the console between seats, it is probable that pilots will use the thumb to give stability to the hand (placing it on the frame of the screen) and the index and middle fingers to press the two buttons almost simultaneously.

This would have no consequences in the majority of the cases, but situations can be envisaged that can lead to safety problems. For example, it is possible that a very busy pilot sends the wilco message to a request, and only later realises that he cannot comply (e.g. he misunderstood the message or he/she realizes later that weather conditions do not allow the manoeuvre). In this case the pilot has to advise the controller via radio (increasing workload to both pilot and controller); this operation needs time, in the meanwhile the controller is taking decisions with the belief that the aircraft will act in a certain way (like changing route), maybe requesting manoeuvres to another aircraft in a way that will create a conflict (like authorizing it on the same route of the other).

In this case, as safety is a fundamental requisite in this particular context, the choice is to break a consolidated rule in order to help pilots performing the right action before pressing the buttons, and make more difficult for them to develop automated movements. The design suggestion is to move the "Read" button on the right, as far as possible from the other two buttons. This layout increases the perception of the different meanings of the buttons; moreover in this configuration is no more possible for pilots to press in rapid sequence the "Read" and "Wilco" buttons, as they are farer than medium extension between index and middle fingers.

SOLUTIONS AND RECOMMENDATIONS

Presenting this case the reader was introduced to some aspects that characterise the design approach in complex safety critical socio-technical systems, such as the aeronautic domain. From the design of a touch screen based device as an example, some first understanding of the different levels of complexity that influence the choice of evaluation methods and design solutions were presented. They range from the peculiar characteristics of this context (the environmental constrains, the importance of safety, etc.) to the heterogeneity of stakeholders' requirements (needs coming from: pilots, related industries and other actors such as controllers), to the complex design process into which the designer work has to be integrated (choice of a prototype type and method that meet evaluation objectives of the specific phase of design). An example of preparation and execution of a specific evaluation method was offered, together with its results and how they can be used to feed of a subsequent design cycle.

REFERENCES

Bannon, L. (1992). From human factors to human actors: The role of psychology and human-computer interaction studies in system design. In *Design at work: Co-operative design of computer systems*. Hillsdale, NJ: L. Erlbaum Associates Inc.

Bolton, L. (2012). Enhancement of aircraft touchscreen HMI through use of haptic feedback. To appear in *the Proceedings of the HCI Aero 2012 conference*. Brussels.

Cardosi, K. M., & Murphy, E.D. (1995). *Human factors checklist for the design and evaluation of air traffic control systems*. DOT/FAA/RD-95/3.1. Research funded by the Federal Aviation Administration's Office of the Chief Scientific and Technical Advisor for Human Factors (AAR-100).

Chiuhsiang, J. L., Chi, N. L., Chin, J. C., & Hung, J. C. (2010). The performance of computer input devices in a vibration environment. *Ergonomics*, *53*(4), 478–490. doi:10.1080/00140130903528186

Harris, D. (2011). *Human performance on the flight deck*. Farnham, England: Ashgate.

ISO 13406-1:1999 (2007). Ergonomic requirements for work with visual displays based on flat panels. ISO.

Nielsen, J. (1993). *Usability engineering*. San Diego, CA: Academic Press Inc.

Nielsen, J., & Landauer, T. K. (1993). A mathematical model of the finding of usability problems. In *Proceedings ACM/IFIP INTERCHI'93 Conference* (pp. 206-213). Amsterdam, The Netherlands.

Nielsen, J., & Mack, R. L. (1994). *Usability inspection methods*. New York: John Wiley & Sons.

Nielsen, J., & Molich, R. (1990). *Heuristic evaluation of user interface*. In *Proceedings of CHI 90* (pp. 249-256). New York, NY: ACM.

Norman, D. A. (2011). *Living with Complexity*. Cambridge, MA: MIT Press.

Parhi, P., Karlson, A. K., & Bederson, B. B. (2006). Target size study for one-handed thumb use on small touchscreen devices. In *Proceedings of the 8th conference on Human-computer interaction with mobile devices and services*. New York, NY, USA.

Peryer, G., Noyes, J., Pleydell-Pearce, C. W., & Lieven, N. (2010). Auditory alert characteristics: A survey of pilot views. *The International Journal of Aviation Psychology*, *15*(3), 233–250. doi:10.1207/s15327108ijap1503_2

Ravden, S., & Jonhson, G. (1989). *Evaluating usability of human-computer interfaces*. Chichester, UK: Ellis Horwood Limited.

Saffer, D. (2008). *Designing gestural interfaces*. Sebastopol, CA: O'Reilly Media.

Stanton, N. (Ed.). (2004). *The handbook of human factors and ergonomics methods*. Boca Raton, FL: CRC Press. doi:10.1201/9780203489925

KEY TERMS AND DEFINITIONS

Air Traffic Control (ATC): It is a service provided by ground-based controllers who direct aircraft when taxing on the ground and through controlled airspace.

Cockpit: A cockpit or flight deck is the area, usually near the front of an aircraft, from which a pilot controls the aircraft. From the cockpit an aircraft is controlled when taxing on the ground and flying in the air.

Human Factors: Is the scientific discipline concerned with the understanding of interactions among humans and other elements of a system, and the profession that applies theory, principles, data and methods to design in order to optimize human well-being and overall system performance.

Prototype: A prototype is an early sample or model built to test a concept or process or to act as a thing to be replicated or learned from.

Usability: The extent to which a product can be used by specified users to achieve specified goals with effectiveness, efficiency, and satisfaction in a specified context of use.

Usability Heuristics: General principles for design. They are called "heuristics" because they are more in the nature of rules of thumb than specific usability guidelines.

Validation: Is the process by which the fitness-for-purpose of a new system or operational concept being developed is established. In practice, validation can be defined as the process of answering a question like 'Are we building the right system?'. The answer is then provided to stakeholders to support their decision-making activity. Therefore the validation process is structured in order to satisfy the information needs of relevant stakeholders about performances of systems/concepts.

ENDNOTES

[1.]   Among others we mention: VIEW (Enhanced & synthetic representation), HILAS (Innovative flight deck technologies), FLYSAFE (Airborne Integrated Systems for Safety Improvement, Flight Hazard Protection and All Weather Operations), OPTIMAL, PEGASE (Approach management & guidance), ODICIS (Innovative displays).

Section 4
Usability of Virtual Environments, Simulations, and Video Games

Chapter 13
BCI-Based User-Centered Design for Emotionally-Driven User Experience

Valeria Carofiglio
Università degli Studi, Bari, Italy

Fabio Abbattista
Università degli Studi, Bari, Italy

EXECUTIVE SUMMARY

In order to develop a complex interactive system, user-centered evaluation (UCE) is an essential component. The new interaction paradigms encourage exploring new variables for accounting the users' experience in terms of their needs and preferences. This is especially important for Adaptable Virtual Environments (AVE). In this context, to obtain a more engaging overall user's experience, a good designer should perform proper formative and summative usability tests based on the user's emotional level, which become a UCE activity. Our methodology tries to overcome the weaknesses of traditional methods by employing a Brain Computer Interface (BCI) to collect additional information on user's needs and preferences. A set of preliminary usability experiments has been conducted for (i) determining if the outcome of a BCI is suitable to drive the designer in organizing the user-system dialog within AVE and (ii) evaluating the user-system dialog, in terms of dynamic increase of the emotionally-driven interaction's customization.

DOI: 10.4018/978-1-4666-4046-7.ch013

ORGANIZATION BACKGROUND

The University of Bari (http://www.uniba.it), created on 1924, is the second largest university of South Italy. The university includes 1058 professors, 1060 non-teaching employees, and 58000 students.

The Dipartimento di Informatica (http://www.di.uniba.it) is composed of 10 full professors, 14 associate professors, 20 assistant professors, and 10 postdocs. Currently the department provides three undergraduate courses (500 students per year), a Master science course (150 students per year), and a postgraduate course in computer science (10 PhD students per year). The Dipartimento di Informatica performs research in several fields of Information and Communication Technology, such as intelligent systems, software engineering, human-computer interaction, and others.

Within this department, the Collaborative Development Group (Collab) is a research group which addresses those challenges that must be overcome in collaborative environments to accomplish a common task, even if users are distributed by time or distance.

The general domain of expertise and innovation of Collab is the development of tools for virtual teams with a special focus in the domain of distributed software development. Research at Collab address topics such as collaboration in software development, collaborative knowledge sharing, object-oriented technology, interactive virtual environments and emotion in computer-mediated communication. More detailed information about the research group and current projects, together with publication lists can be found at http://cdg.di.uniba.it/.

SETTING THE STAGE

In the global race for more intuitive interfaces that must allow non-expert users to operate increasingly complex technology, we explored Virtual Environments, paying attention to the role of emotions in the design and use of such interfaces. The area to which our past work belonged most directly was Multimodal Interfaces. Our work specifically addressed the objective of this area to develop natural and adaptive multimodal interfaces and its focus on interaction between and among humans and the virtual and physical environment, with particular emphasis on recognizing and responding to emotive user reaction.

The employment of 3D Virtual Environments (VEs) is continuously growing in several different applicative domains. VEs show great potentialities in fields such as Virtual Heritage, Serious Gaming and Visual Analytics. The flexibility of a VE allows domain experts to communicate specific views and interpretations of the reality in a way accessible to final users by a proper choice of contents, representation and rendering. Interaction with 3D VEs is inherently multi-modal, spatial input devices (such as trackers, 3D pointing devices, gesture and vocal devices) and multisensory output technologies (head mounted displays, spatial audio and haptic devices) allow interaction to be carried out with advanced input/output devices involving different sensorial channels (sight, hear, touch, etc.) in an integrated way. Each device addresses a particular sense and exhibits a different interface: Bowman (Bowmann et al., 2005) offers a broad review of multimodal interaction while Salisbury (Salisbury et al., 2004) represents a good introduction to haptic. Interaction with VEs needs 3D user interfaces to be organized in metaphors based on user tasks (navigation, selection and manipulation) (Bowmann et al., 2001). Currently one of the most important issues in designing multimodal interaction for 3D VEs is to develop engineered methods to design multimodal interaction with VEs.

On the other side, the development of emotion-oriented systems related to more objectives: (i) To develop interfaces that were natural and intuitive (that should appear "believable" and easy to use and accepted by the human side of the interaction loop) and that were either capable of pro-active emotion-oriented behaviour or of adapting to the user environment (in particular emotion-related aspects) through continued interaction; (ii) To respond intelligently and in a way that were emotionally appropriate; (iii) To achieve robust dialog capability.

Our work spanned: Critical analysis of existing models and system, identification of needs regarding research, applications, good practice and usability; basic cross-disciplinary research; and specific joint activities.

While the project described in this case is different from previous activity, it is built upon several researches carried out by the authors in past years, in different organizations. More recent works of Valeria Carofiglio were in the key areas of information technology and the science of emotion.

The general aims were the *development* and *the evaluation of believable systems that register, model and/or influence human emotional and emotion-related states* (emotion-oriented systems). Fabio Abbattista is mainly involved in the research concerning artificial intelligence and videogame, with a focus on the development of believable characters.

State of the Art

Since the early 1970, a lot of work has gone in BCI research, and due to the improvements in hardware performance, the last four decades have witnessed an exponential growth of BCI-based applications (Wolpaw et al., 2002; Dornhege et al., 2007; Allison et al., 2007). BCI has proven effective in several contexts: In Millan et al. (2004) the authors proposed a BCI system for driving a mobile robot. They introduced the novel idea of controlling robots by mapping asynchronously high-level mental commands into a finite state automaton. This automaton is a key feature for the efficient control of the mobile robot. In (Millan et al., 2009) a BCI system for driving a wheelchair is proposed. In this paper, three subjects participated in two experiments where they steered the wheelchair spontaneously, without any external cue. To do so the users learnt to voluntarily modulate EEG by executing three mental tasks that are associated to different steering commands. The results show that the three subjects could achieve a significant level of mental control, even if far from optimal, to drive the intelligent wheelchair. In Birbaumer et al. (1999) slow cortical potentials (SCPs) of the electroencephalogram were employed to drive an electronic spelling device. Similar spelling devices were described in Obermaier et al. (2003) and Williamson et al. (2009), in which the EEG were modulated by mental hand and leg motor imagery. An Internet browser by BCI was presented in Mugler et al. (2008). Here, World Wide Web access was made possible through real-time classification of the P300 event related potential. Standard page navigation tools, hyperlink selection and page scrolling were available through user selection of symbols presented on a separate screen. In Leeb et al. (2007), a 3-channels BCI was employed to enable subjects to freely navigate through a virtual apartment with a goal-oriented task, a high mental workload and a variable decision period for the subject. Here subjects can be trained in a synchronous paradigm within three sessions to navigate. Navigation commands were carried out from the analysis of the subject stable motor imagery over a minimum time of two seconds. In the videogame domain, most of the research effort concerns using the BCI as a new game controller (Krepki et al., 2007; Nijholt et al., 2008). Several authors propose the so called motor-control based BCI as an alternative to classical game controller (mouse, keyboard, etc.). However, the BCIs are currently too much slow as compared to a keyboard. A new interaction schema is needed in order to fully exploit the BCI.

In Plass-Oude Bos et al. (2010), authors propose a deep overview of neurofeedback-based games, in which the user ability to control the brain signal is the goal of the game. These games cannot' be experienced using other control modalities and they offer a new game experience.

A third kind of BCI game is the evoked response based (Plass-Oude Bos et al., 2010). In this case user' actions depend on stimuli from the game system.

Very often, the speed of the games is reduced to allow the use of BCI, for example transforming the game in a turn based one.

Future research should focus on how to use BCI to improve the game experience. A main research goal aims at using neurophysiological signals, and consequently BCI, to dynamically acquire a more accurate affective user profile with respect to the classical sensory devices such as camera and microphone. Actually, the BCI are used in labs and in controlled domain because their efficacy is largely influenced from noise in the neurophysiological signals due, for example, to user movements.

CASE DESCRIPTION

Technology Concerns

By viewing serious games as one of the most representative examples of Emotional Adaptive Virtual Environment (EAVE), but also as elicitors of complex user emotion synthesis, we explore Brain Computer Interface (BCI) for assessing the emotional user experience, as a variable to support a user centered evaluation (UCE) design. We start from the idea that traditional methods such as self-report or interviews, are not ideal within EAVE because they rely either on sampling approaches or the users' perception of the environment. Also methods for capturing the interaction experience in an unconscious and continuous approach (e.g. log experience) may be troublesome, as they do not collect subjective feedback from (potential) users. Once our EAVE has been developed we planned several formative and summative usability tests. These tests were useful to evaluate the emotional state of the users, as detected from the BCI in the course of their interactions with the 3D environment. Moreover, they gave us a way to investigate on:

1. How emotional user experience within EAVE may be evaluated: This is linked to the possibility of implementing a BCI that is able to efficiently recognize emotions from the EEG signals. Scientific research in this area is very active.
2. How the outcome of this evaluation can be used to enhance emotional user experience. The expected result is a dynamic increase of the interaction's customization and therefore an improvement of the user's engagement, focusing on the chance of better reaching the intended emotional effects on each individual user. This result strongly relies on the reproducibility of the aforementioned correspondences between the emotions and the EEG signals. The research in this area aims at validating such correspondences.

The field of Brain Computer Interface (van Gerven et al., 2009) has recently witnessed an explosion of systems for studying human *emotion by the acquisition and processing of physiological signals* (Kim et al., 2004). A BCI is a direct communication pathway between the brain and an external device. Several researchers (Choppin, 2000; Murugappan et al., 2007) have shown that it is possible to extract emotional cues from electroencephalography (EEG) measurements, which become a way to investigate the emotional activity of a subject beyond his conscious and controllable behaviors, such as speaking and facial expressions. Moreover, EEG signals can be measured at any moment. However, the use of EEG signals to this aim still needs a lot of improvement. In the medical field, the automatic recognition of emotions from physiological clues could be used to objectively assess the emotional state of people (by therapists and/or psychologists, by physician to evaluate the results of clinical tests whose results are affected by the emotional state of the patient, by the people as a bio-feedback to learn the control of their internal state, etc.). Another application is to enable people suffering from severe muscle diseases to express emotions.

For those patients, the creation of brain-computer interfaces would greatly improve the communication of the internal emotional state. In the field of human-machine interaction this technique could be applied in many different situations such as software adaptation, educational games or tutoring systems. Moreover, a brain computer interface could add emotional information to computer mediated human-human conversation (e.g. instant messaging, online games, chat rooms and social networks).

Psychologists worked at decoding emotions for decades, by focusing on two main questions: (i) How can emotions be classified? and (ii) Which is their functioning?, i.e. how are they triggered? How do they affect behavior? Which is the role played by cognition? Two points of view prevailed: the first one assumes that a limited set of basic emotions exists, while the second one consider emotions as a continuous function of one or more dimensions: see, e.g., the Russell's "Circumplex Model" of affect (Russell, 2003). Theories following the "discrete trend" agree on the idea that a limited set of basic emotions exists, although consensus about the nature and the number of these basic emotions has not been reached. Ekman defines a basic emotion as having specific feelings, universal signals and corresponding physiological changes (Ekman, 1999); emotions may be triggered by either an automatic (very quick) or extended (slow, deliberate and conscious) appraisal mechanism. Plutchik defines discrete emotions as corresponding to specific adaptive processes: reproduction, safety, (Plutchik, 1980). In Izard's "Differential Emotion Theory," distinct discrete emotions are triggered by neural activation, which induces a specific experience and influences behavior and cognition (Izard, 1993). Lazarus describes nine negative (anger, anxiety, guilt, shame, sadness, envy, jealousy, disgust) and six positive (joy, pride, love, relief, hope, compassion) emotions, with their appraisal patterns: positive emotions are triggered if the situation is congruent with one of the individual's goals; otherwise, negative emotions are triggered (Lazarus, 1991). Some physiological theories assume that stimuli produce a physiological activation that creates emotions, with no cognitive intervention (James, 1984). Evolutionary theories assume that emotions were inherited during evolution and are automatically triggered with no cognitive intervention (Ekman, 1999). On the contrary, cognitive theories assume that cognition is essential in the triggering of emotion. Among the cognitive theories of emotions, "appraisal theories" assume that emotions are triggered by the evaluation of a stimulus, using different criteria. To Arnold, "appraisal" is the process for determining the significance of a situation for an individual, i.e. if a given situation is good or bad for him or herself (Arnold, 1960). Appraisal triggers an emotion that induces an "action tendency" of attraction or repulsion, with a corresponding physiological change (to favor the individual's adaptation to the environment). Ortony, Clore, and Collins focus their theory on the cognitive elicitors of emotions. They postulate that emotions represent balanced reactions to perceptions of the world. Thus, one can be pleased or not about the consequences of an event; one can endorse or reject the actions of an agent or can like or dislike aspects of an object (Ortony et al., 1988). Lazarus assumes that the human emotional process is made up of two separated processes: appraisal (which characterizes the person relationship with their environment), and coping (which suggests strategies for altering or maintaining this relationship). Cognition informs both these processes; it informs appraisal by building mental representations of how events relate to internal dispositions such as beliefs and goals, and informs coping by suggesting and exploring strategies for altering or maintaining the person envi-ronment relationship (Lazarus, 1991)

In the new research on automatic human affect recognition the development of more comprehensive data sets of training and testing materials for eliciting emo-tions is a central issue (Zeng et al., 2007). Here researchers focus on studying the correlations between the different modalities (audio and visual) and between various behavioural cues (e.g., facial, head, body gestures and speech).

Given the complexity of emotions, there is no universal method to measure them. Methods for measuring human emotions may be categorized into subjective and objective ones. Questionnaires, adjective checklists or picture tools could be used as self-report instruments. Self-Assessment Manikin (SAM) (Bradley & Lang, 1994) and the Affect grid (Russell et al., 1998) are examples of this method. Objec-tive methods use physiological cues derived from the theories of emotions which define universal pattern of autonomic and central nervous system responses related to the experience of emotions. Some systems for recognizing emotions are based upon theories such as the theory of Ekman. This theory suggests that there is a link between facial expressions and an affective state (Ekman, 1999; Fasel & Luettin, 2007). Research has been done to enable the automatic recognition of emotion also from speech (Carofiglio et al., 2009; Bickmore & Giorgino, 2006). Other modalities used for measuring or automatically detect emotions include blood pressure, heart rate, and respiration. This paper exploits emotion assessment via EEG.

A BCI records human activity in form of electrical potentials (EPs), through multiple electrodes that are placed on the scalp. Depending on the brain activity, distinctive known patterns in the EEG appear. In general, EEG rhythms are classified in five basic types: Alpha, beta, gamma, delta and theta. Variation in the frequency bands shows the humans' functional and emotional changes. These rhythms are used to investigate different brain's states.

An important distinction, in the psychology literature, is made between two dimensions of emotion: The valence (ranging from negative to positive) and the arousal (ranging from calm to excited) (Russell, 2003). Cognitive researchers have investigated how changes along these two dimensions modulate the EEG signals and have determined that the position of an emotion in this two dimensional planes can be derived from EEG data (Chanel et al., 2005; Heller et al., 1997).

To infer emotions from EEG signals, according to the literature, alpha band is the most distinctive range of frequencies by which we can make use of. In Coan et al. (2002) positive emotions are associated with relatively greater left frontal brain activity whereas negative emotions are associated with relatively greater right frontal brain activity. In Kostyunina and Kulikov (1996) emotions such as joy, aggression and intention results in an increase in the alpha power whereas, emotions such as sorrow and anxiety results in a decrease in the alpha power. Musha et al. (1997) showed that valence of emotion is associated with asymmetries in the frontal lobe, whereas arousal is associated with generalized activation of both the right and the left frontal lobes. Also, EEG signals acquired from the right hemisphere can be a good predictor of negative emotions such as sadness, anger and fear whereas, EEG signals acquired from the right hemisphere can be a good indicator of positive emotions such as joy. To account for user emotional state during BCI operation, most of the literature suggests an exhaustive training of the BCI classification algorithm under various emotional states: In the general approach, the user is exposed to an opportune affective stimulation. The type of mental activity elicited is recorded and then processed to obtain features that could be grouped into features vectors. Such features vectors are then used to train the BCI classification algorithm, which can then recognize the relevant brain activity (see Figure 1(a)).

If a passive BCI is employed, as in our case (Figure 1(b)), active user involvement is not required. The interpretation of his mental state could be a source of control to the automatic system adaptation (from the application interface to the

Figure 1. (a) Conceptual model of an emotional BCI, (b) conceptual model of the employed emotional BCI

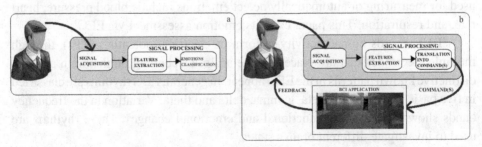

virtual environment), for example in order to motivate and involve the user by the application feedback. In Figure 1(b), the module for emotion classification is included into the translation to command one.

Technology Components

The electrical activity of the human brain is recorded through the Emotiv™ Epoc (http://www.emotiv.com). Emotiv™ Epoc have developed a non-invasive, dry, biosensor headset to read the electrical activity in the brain to determine different cognitive and emotional states. It is a high-resolution, low-cost, easy to use neuroheadset developed for games. Based on the International 10-20 locations, it captures neural activity using 14 dry electrodes (AF3, F7, F3, FC5, T7, P7, O1, O2, P8, T8, FC6, F4, F8, AF4) plus CMS/DRL references, P3/P4 locations (see Figure 2).

The headset samples all channels at 128 Hz, each sample being a 14 bit value corresponding to the voltage of a single electrode. Moreover, it provides a research SDK that enables to display real-time the Emotiv™ Epoc headset data stream, including EEG, contact quality, FFT, gyro, wireless packet acquisition/loss display, marker events, headset battery level. Directly based on the user's brain activity, Emotiv™ Epoc reads different emotion-related measures. Among the other, the Instantaneous Excitement (IE) and the Long term Excitement (LTE). The first is experienced as an awareness or feeling of physiological arousal with a positive value (see Figure 3). In the figure the diagram represents the valence-arousal bidimensional space, according to the circumplex model of emotion. The upper hemisphere (in red) represents the positive arousal (ranging from neutral to excited) for all the valence's value (ranging from negative to positive values).

In general, the greater the increase in physiological arousal the greater the output score for the detection. The Instantaneous Excitement detection is tuned to provide

Figure 2. The Emotiv™ Epoc headset electrodes placement

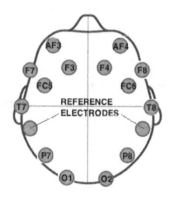

Figure 3. Instantaneous excitement vs. the circumplex model of emotions

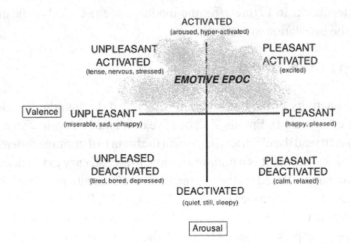

output scores that more accurately reflect short-term changes in excitement over time periods as short as several seconds; the Long Term Excitement is experienced and defined in the same way as IE, but the detection is designed and tuned to be more accurate when measuring changes in excitement over longer time periods, typically measured in minutes. Both these measures are time-independent: At each arousal variation the IE and LTE are detected.

Experimental Concerns

The experimental environment was chosen among the applications requiring detection of and management of user's emotions to provide an appropriate user experience or even to avoid psychological harm. As main example of this kind of application, we consider a *Nazi extermination camp*. We chose this domain as representative example of elicitors of complex human emotions. Moreover, sooner the only way to preserve the remembrance of that terrible historical period will entrusted on indirect documentation in the form of videos, images and texts reporting interviews to last witnesses. A way to maintaining alive the dramatic meaning of that experience could be to reconstruct a 3D virtual environment of one of those camps, such as Auschwitz. In our view, this could represent a valid alternative to the standard channels (e.g. movies) as these exhibit a real poor ability to deliver contents which are tailored to the emotional attitude of an individual.

In our VE a digital character representing a prisoner guides users through different parts of the camp. During the navigation, the VE activates links to videos, photos documenting the Jewish and Gipsy's lifestyle in the 1940-1945 period, or plays songs that some prisoners composed during their permanence, in an interactive way. By means of the BCI we aim at capturing the user' reaction to presented contents in order to allow the virtual prisoner to dynamically adapt the visit to the user profile, choosing to avoid some media judged too upsetting for the users sensibility or visiting only some zones of the entire virtual camp, in order to maintain the current user's emotional state or to induce a desired one. In this way users could be guided along well defined emotional and informative paths.

Our virtual environment has been interfaced with the Emotiv^{TM} Epoc headset (see Figure 4).

The headset detects the EEG signal of the user and pre-processes them, by means of some C# script:

1.   A script manages the connection between the headset and the virtual environment.
2.   Another script receives and saves user's affective values, i.e. long-term excitement and instantaneous excitement.
3.   A third script detects user's head movements to adjust the camera perspective.

In the first experiment, each session lasted about 13 minutes. The environment includes 8 different scenes; among these, six scenes contain historical multimedia documentation; the remaining two include only the 3D reconstruction of the camp. At the end of the interaction each user answered a self-assessment questionnaire (see Figure 5). In choosing the scenario we avoided scenes that could objectively induce psychological harm and, we discard people who reported a strong knowledge of the domain to avoid the lack of reaction to the selected scenes. The subjects were preventively informed about the details of the experiment, and only those who have

Figure 4. Functional model of the employed BCI

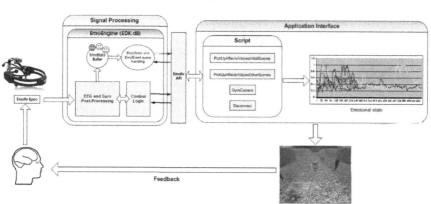

deliberately declared their intention to participate in the experiment were taken into account.

The final sample was composed of eight different subjects (50% males and 50% females), 25% ranged between 18 and 25 years old; 12,5% ranged between 26 and 35 years old and 62% aged more than 46 years old. All of the subjects, but one, were experienced PC users. Among them, 38% were undergraduate students. The goals of this first experiment were to evaluate some factors that could have impact on the emotional experience of users interacting with our 3D environment:

1. How much the 3D environment is inherently emotive. For each user, we measured the global emotional response due to the whole interaction process, by:
    a. **A subjective evaluation:** Analysis of the user answers to the questionnaire;
    b. **An objective evaluation:** Analysis of the recorded user EEG signal;
    c. Comparing the two previous analyses to evaluate their consistency;
2. How much each scene contributes to the inherent emotional level of the 3D environment, by analyzing the EEG signals of each user for each scene and by measuring the average IE and LTE;
3. How much the multimedia content of each scene contributes to the emotional response with respect to the scenes not enriched with multimedia contents.

Concerning the first research question, we compare the values of excitement (both instantaneous and long term) detected by the headset with the emotion felt by the users (as declared in the questionnaire) to verify if the proposed environment was actually capable to induce an emotional response in the users.

Table 1 reports the results concerning the emotional response of the 8 users. Experimental data show that most of the users claimed they felt different levels of sadness, while the others felt both anger and fear (see Table 1).

Figure 5. The procedure of the experiment

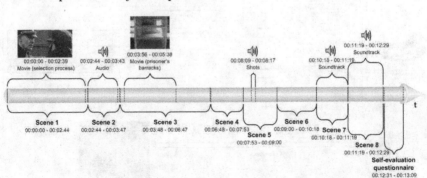

The values are moderately low but the coherency between both IE and LTE values indicates that a user emotional response actually occurred.

Next, we analyzed the contribution of each scene to the emotional response. From Figures 6a and 6b, it could be noted that the scene with higher average IE value is the scene 6, a scene lacking multimedia content; this *anomaly* can be due to an external source of distraction. However, the scene 7 has the higher average LTE value, and this means that users were very involved during all (or most of) the scene 7.

Finally, we evaluated the effectiveness of the multimedia contents to the elicitation of the emotional response of the users. Table 2 shows, for each user, the number of scene(s) with, respectively, IE and LTE greater than the two scenes with no multimedia contents, that is scenes 4 and 6. The EEG signals detected indicate that 62.5% of the users consider the six scenes with multimedia contents more emotionally engaging than the other two scenes (see Table 2a); moreover, for 85% of the users the emotional engagement of the six scenes with multimedia contents has a longer duration (see Table 2b).

The exploitation of experimental results may serve as a guide for the designer of the multimedia application. In this case, results concerning the first issue allow the designer to evaluate the emotional engagement of the whole application. If a more detailed analysis is needed according to the designer view, the investigation concerning the last two issues is useful to evaluate each single content and, consequently, to identify scenes to be discarded and/or scenes to be included.

The second experiment aims at enhance the user experience by dynamically adapting the interaction to the user emotional state. The environment is the same as in the first experiment, it includes the same 8 scenes and, among these, six scenes contain historical multimedia documentation; however, each of this six "enriched"

Table 1. Average IE and LTE values detected by the BCI wrt. users' declared emotions

	Average IE values	Average LTE values	User emotional response (as declared)
User 1	0.343	0.338	Sadness (4)
User 2	0.543	0.535	Sadness (4)
User 3	0.411	0.402	Sadness (3)
User 4	0.368	0.360	Sadness (6)
User 5	0.467	0.458	Anger (5)
User 6	0.369	0.375	Sadness (4)
User 7	0.463	0.458	Fear (5)
User 8	0.447	0.438	Sadness (5)

Figure 6. (a) Minimum and maximum average IE values for each scene, (b) minimum and maximum average LTE values for each scene

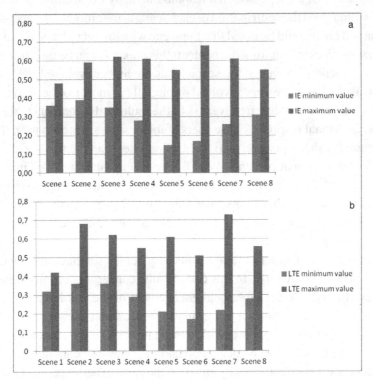

scenes contains three different multimedia contents, with increasing level of violence. The remaining two include only the 3D reconstruction of the camp.

In the course of the interaction, the system proposes more violent content first, and if the user should feel uncomfortable, the system switches to a less violent content. This process is repeated until the less violent content is proposed. If the user should still feel unpleasant the system quits the current scene and starts to show the next scene. If the user does not feel uncomfortable with the multimedia content, the interaction goes on to the end of the scene. The duration of these sessions is unpredictable because it is based on the user's emotional state and his/her sensitivity to the multimedia content proposed by the system.

Moreover, we are interested in the validation of the rules used to recognize the emotional states of the users. In fact, in Mandryk and Atkins (2007) a set of fuzzy rules are reported to detect the emotion of players of computer games. Due to the entertaining nature of computer games, in their work, the authors are mainly interested in the detection of excitement, fun and challenge with respect to boredom

Table 2. Number of scenes with multimedia content with greater IE value (a) and greater LTE value (b) wrt the two scenes without multimedia content (a zero in the cell indicates that the scene corresponding to the column has an higher IE/LTE value.

(a)	Scene 4	Scene 6
User 1	0	5
User 2	0	0
User 3	3	3
User 4	6	2
User 5	4	2
User 6	0	0
User 7	4	6
User 8	4	0
(b)	Scene 4	Scene 6
User 1	0	6
User 2	4	5
User 3	3	2
User 4	5	3
User 5	1	1
User 6	3	3
User 7	4	5
User 8	2	0

and frustration. Concerning our 3D environment, the goal is to detect and identify unpleasant emotional state, characterized by combinations of valence and arousal.

The hypothesis under this work is that a more natural and credible interaction is plausible by using an interface that is based on extra-rational aspects (e.g. physiological aspects of emotions).

We proposed a test case in the context of virtual environments, with the intent to evaluate users emotional attitude level as central in the human computer interaction design.

The results seem to be encouraging, but they strongly depend on the device and proprietary algorithms that the device provides. According to a typical machine learning approach, the task of prediction works on a very high amount of features which can be extracted by the brain signals. Even if these techniques are said to be excellent in terms of predictive accuracy from a purely methodological point of view, their use in real-time interactive multimedia applications may cause problems in terms of user experience. As the most of existing EEG-based emotion recognition systems do operate offline, accurate comparisons with these systems are not profitable at this stage. To compare this work with the literature, further topics of investigation should be considered, some of which are listed and described in the following section.

CURRENT CHALLENGES FACING THE ORGANIZATION

Our current challenges can be categorized as follows:

Challenge 1: The evaluation of how self-induced emotions could be utilized in a BCI paradigm (real-time data processing), according to UCD.

The real-time acquisition of information about the emotional state of the user provided by the system is being used to adapt the characteristics of the interaction. In order to achieve this goal, the virtual environment proposed in this case is being enriched with more multimedia content. The system will be able to choose the proper content according to the sensibility of the current user, in order to avoid him unpleasant feelings due for example to violence of multimedia contents. This, in fact, could drive the user to quit the 3D environment threatening the goal of our system. This challenge represents a main usability factor that needs of formative tests to be evaluated.

Challenge 2: The replacement of Emotiv™ Epoc proprietary processing algorithms: This in order to recognize further aspects of the users' emotional experience, according to the emotional correlates. Two issues are under investigation.

1. If a BCI is employed for recognizing emotions, the brain signals are recorded by devices in the form of a helmet which has different electrodes and references to the system 10-20. Actually, there are many commercial devices able to measure brain activity, but the most of them includes software that does not allow adopting their potentials to different research interests. The main goal of this work is to replicate part of the BCI cycle, by means of an open source software (named BCI2000). In the following the phases of the cycle that are being accounted: Brain Activity Recording; Pre-Processing; Feature-Extraction and Evaluation. We use the Emotiv™ Epoc helmet, to record the brain activity.

2. The most of existing emotion recognition systems does operate offline. The task of prediction makes use of methods of classification. According to a typi-

cal machine learning approach, the task of prediction works on a very high amount of features which can be extracted by the brain signals. Even if these techniques are said to be excellent in terms of predictive accuracy from a purely methodological point of view, their use in real-time multimedia interactive applications may cause problems in terms of user experience. To be able to actually use them, the number of features and their power of discrimination should be balanced.

Challenge 3: *The generalization of our BCI-based adaptation approach to different kinds of applications.*

We investigate a novel approach to detecting emotions in a computer role-playing game using a BCI (Brain-Computer Interface), with the aim to provide game developers with (i) crucial information with respect to difficulty adjustment, suitability of content according to a player profile, (ii) the ability to procedurally generate game content.

These challenges have in common the need (i) to quickly (at real-time) collect information on the emotional mental state of the users beyond their conscious and controllable behaviors, and (ii) to employ collected information to build applications able to react to the users' activity in a credible way. Even if BCIs are an emerging technology and they still need to be improved, in our opinion they may be optimal in addressing the aforementioned challenges.

SOLUTIONS AND RECOMMENDATIONS

Solution to challenge 1: New formative and summative tests are being performed in order to evaluate the inherently emotionality of the environment. Due to the intrinsic variable nature of emotion, attention will be paid in choosing the right number of subjects to be involved in the experimental sessions. This is to avoid too few subjects for the formative tests and too many subjects for the summative tests. More experiments are being conducted in order to define a more refined set of rules for implementing the adaptability of the environment, starting from the recognition of the emotional user experience. This should give the chance of better reaching the intended emotional effects on each individual user.

Solution to challenge 2:

1. The migration to BCI 2000 is a key step, as it allowed us to adapt the helmet to our goals. The phase of signal pre-processing consists in cleaning up the signal

from any noise and reconstructing original brain activity. We are performing a set of experiments in order to compare exiting techniques for features extraction, in order to find the ones that best fit for real-time recognition of emotions.

2.   The main aim of this work is validate the hypothesis that a more natural and credible interaction is ensured by sacrificing the predictive accuracy in terms of performance, within a BCI-based emotion recognition system. Several experiments are being conducted to validate this hypothesis in different multimedia interactive applications.

Solution to challenge 3: In our initial phase of work, we logged salient gameplay events in the selected role-play game and corresponding emotional responses as recorded by the BCI to build "emotional" player profiles (clusters). Then we questioned users on such topical gameplay moments. Finally, we build a statistical inference model (i.e., a Bayesian Network) to correlate emotional clusters and questionnaire responses, in order to validate our overall approach. Several experiments are being conducted in order to provide experimental results in a heavily customized version of the role-playing game template, developed using the Microsoft's XNA toolkit.

REFERENCES

Allison, B. Z., Wolpaw, E. W., & Wolpaw, J. R. (2007). Brain-computer interface systems: Progress and prospects. *Expert Review of Medical Devices, 4*, 463–474. doi:10.1586/17434440.4.4.463

Arnold, M. B. (1960). *Emotion and personality*. New York: Columbia University Press.

Bickmore, T., & Giorgino, T. (2006). Health dialog systems for Patients and Consumers. *Journal of Biomedical Informatics, 39*(5), 556–571. doi:10.1016/j.jbi.2005.12.004

Birbaumer, N., Ghanayim, N., Hinterberger, T., Iversen, I., Kotchoubey, B., & Kubler, A. (1999). A spelling device for the paralysed. *Nature, 398*, 297–298. doi:10.1038/18581

Bowmann, D., Kruijf, E., La Viola, J., & Poupyrev, I. (2001). An introduction to 3-D user interface design. *Presence (Cambridge, Mass.), 10*(1), 96–108. doi:10.1162/105474601750182342

Bowmann, D., Kruijf, E., La Viola, J., & Poupyrev, I. (2005). *3D user interfaces: Theory and practice*. Boston: Addison-Wesley.

Bradley, M. M., & Lang, P. J. (1994). Measuring emotions: The self-assessment manikin and the semantic differential. *Journal of Behavior Therapy and Experimental Psychiatry, 25*(1), 49–59. doi:10.1016/0005-7916(94)90063-9

Carofiglio, V., De Rosis, F., & Novielli, N. (2009). Cognitive emotion modeling in natural language communication. In Tao, J. (Ed.), *Affective information processing* (pp. 23–44). London: Springer-Verlag. doi:10.1007/978-1-84800-306-4_3

Chanel, G., Kronegg, J., Grandjean, D., & Pun, T. (2005). *Emotion assessment: Arousal evaluation using EEG's and peripheral physiological signals.* Technical Report 05.02, Computer Vision Group, Computing Science Center, University of Geneva, Switzerland.

Choppin, A. (2000). *EEG-based human interface for disabled individuals: Emotion expression with neural networks.* (Master's thesis). Tokyo Institute of Technology, Japan.

Coan, J. A., Allen, J. J. B., & Harmon-Jones, E. (2002). Voluntary facial expression and hemispheric asymmetry over the frontal cortex. *Psychophysiology, 38*(6), 912–925. doi:10.1111/1469-8986.3860912

Dornhege, G., Millan, J. D. R., Hinterberger, T., McFarland, D. J., & Muller, K. R. (Eds.). (2007). *Towards brain-computing interfacing.* Cambridge, MA: MIT Press.

Ekman, P. (1999). Basic emotions. In Dalgleish, T., & Power, T. (Eds.), *The handbook of cognition and emotion* (pp. 45–60). Sussex, U.K.: John Wiley & Sons, Ltd.

Fasel, B., & Luettin, J. (2003). Automatic facial expression analysis: A survey. *Pattern Recognition, 36*, 259–275. doi:10.1016/S0031-3203(02)00052-3

Heller, W., Nitschke, J. B., & Lindsay, D. L. (1997). Neuropsychological correlates of arousal in self-reported emotion. *Neuroscience Letters, 11*(4), 383–402.

Izard, C. E. (1993). Four systems for emotion activation: Cognitive and non cognitive processes. *Psychological Review, 100*(1), 68–90. doi:10.1037/0033-295X.100.1.68

James, W. (1984). What is an emotion? *Mind, 9*, 188–205.

Kim, K. H., Bang, S. W., & Kim, S. R. (2004). Emotion recognition system using short term monitoring of physiological signals. *Medical & Biological Engineering & Computing, 42*, 419–427. doi:10.1007/BF02344719

Kostyunina, M. B., & Kulikov, M. A. (1996). Frequency characteristics of EEG spectra in the emotion. *Neuroscience and Behavioral Physiology, 26*(4), 340–343. doi:10.1007/BF02359037

Krepki, R., Blankertz, B., Curio, G., & Muller, K. R. (2007). The Berlin brain-computer interface (BBCI): Towards a new communication channel for online control in gaming applications. *Journal of Multimedia Tools Applications, 33,* 73–90. doi:10.1007/s11042-006-0094-3

Lazarus, R. S. (1991). *Emotion and adaptation.* New York: Oxford University Press.

Leeb, R., Lee, F., Keinrath, C., Scherer, R., Bischof, H., & Pfurtscheller, G. (2007). Brain- computer communication: Motivation, aim and impact of exploring a virtual apartment. *IEEE Transactions on Neural Systems and Rehabilitation Engineering, 15*(4), 473–482. doi:10.1109/TNSRE.2007.906956

Mandryk, R. L., & Atkins, M. S. (2007). A fuzzy physiological approach for continuously modeling emotion during interaction with play technologies. *International Journal of Human-Computer Studies, 65*(4), 329–347. doi:10.1016/j.ijhcs.2006.11.011

Millan, J. D. R., Galan, F., Vanhooydonck, D., Lew, E., Philips, J., & Nuttin, M. (2009). Asynchronous non-invasive brain-actuated control of an intelligent wheel-chair. In *Proceedings of the 31st Annual International Conference of the IEEE Engineering in Medicine and Biology Society.* Minneapolis, MN: IEEE.

Millan, J. D. R., Renkens, F., Mourino, J., & Gerstner, W. (2004). Non-invasive brain-actuated control of a mobile robot by human EEG. *IEEE Transactions on Bio-Medical Engineering, 51,* 1026–1033. doi:10.1109/TBME.2004.827086

Mugler, E., Bensch, M., Halder, S., Rosenstiel, W., Bogdan, M., Birbaumer, N., & Kubler, A. (2008). Control of an internet browser using the P300 event-related potential. *International Journal of Bioelectromagnetism, 10,* 56–63.

Murugappan, M., Rizon, M., Nagarajan, R., Yaacob, S., Zunaidi, I., & Hazry, D. (2007). EEG feature extraction for classifying emotions using FCM and FKM. *International Journal of Computer and Communications, 1,* 21–25.

Musha, T., Terasaki, Y., Haque, H. A., & Ivamitsky, G. A. (1997). Feature extraction from EEGs associated with emotions. *Artificial Life and Robotics, 1,* 15–19. doi:10.1007/BF02471106

Nijholt, A., Tan, D., Allison, B., Millan, J. D. R., Graimann, B., & Jackson, M. M. (2008). Brain- computer interfaces for HCI and games. In *Proceedings of the ACM CHI 2008* (pp. 3925-3928). New York, NY: ACM.

Obermaier, B., Muller, G. R., & Pfurtscheller, G. (2003). Virtual keyboard controlled by spontaneous EEG activity. *IEEE Transactions on Neural Systems and Rehabilitation Engineering*, *11*, 422–426. doi:10.1109/TNSRE.2003.816866

Ortony, A., Clore, G. L., & Collins, A. (1988). *The cognitive structure of emotions*. Cambridge University Press. doi:10.1017/CBO9780511571299

Plass-Oude Bos, D., Reuderink, B., van der Laar, B., Gurkok, H., Muhl, C., Nijholt, A., & Heylen, D. (2010). Brain-computer interfacing and games. In Tan, D. S., & Nijholt, A. (Eds.), *Brain-computer interfaces, human-computer interaction series* (pp. 149–178). London: Springer-Verlag.

Plutchik, R. (1980). A general psycho-evolutionary theory of emotion. In Plutchik, R., & Kellerman, H. (Eds.), *Emotion: Theory, research, and experiences* (pp. 3–33). New York: Academic press.

Russell, J. A. (2003). Core affect and the psychological construction of emotion. *Psychological Review*, *110*, 145–172. doi:10.1037/0033-295X.110.1.145

Russell, J. A., Weiss, A., & Mendelsohn, G. A. (1998). Affect grid: A single-item scale of pleasure and arousal. *Journal of Personality and Social Psychology*, *57*(3), 493–502. doi:10.1037/0022-3514.57.3.493

Salisbury, K., Conti, F., & Barbagli, F. (2004). Haptic rendering: Introductory concepts. *IEEE Computer Graphics and Applications*, *2*, 24–32. doi:10.1109/MCG.2004.1274058

van Gerven, M., Farquhar, J., Schaefer, R., Vlek, R., Geuze, J., & Nijholt, A. (2009). The brain-computer interface cycle. *Journal of Neural Engineering*, *6*(4), 041001. doi:10.1088/1741-2560/6/4/041001

Williamson, J., Murray-Smith, R., Blankertz, B., Krauledat, M., & Muller, K. R. (2009). Designing for uncertain, asymmetric control: Interaction design for brain-computer interfaces. *International Journal of Human-Computer Studies*, *67*, 827–841. doi:10.1016/j.ijhcs.2009.05.009

Wolpaw, J. R., Birbaumer, N., McFarland, D. J., Pfurtscheller, G., & Vaughan, T. M. (2002). Brain- computer interfaces for communication and control. *Clinical Neurophysiology*, *113*, 767–791. doi:10.1016/S1388-2457(02)00057-3

Zeng, Z., Pantic, M., Roisman, G. I., & Huang, T. S. (2007). A survey of affect recognition methods: Audio, visual and spontaneous expressions. In *Proceedings of the 9th international conference on Multimodal interfaces* (pp. 39-58). Minneapolis, MN: IEEE.

KEY TERMS AND DEFINITIONS

Affective Computing: Affective computing is human-computer interaction in which a device has the ability to detect and appropriately respond to its user's emotions and other stimuli.

Brain Computer Interface: A brain computer interface enables a direct communications pathway between the brain and a device that enables signals from the brain to direct some external activity, such as control of a device.

Human-Computer Interaction: Human-computer interaction is the study of how people interact with computers and to what extent computers are or are not developed for successful interaction with human beings.

Usability: Usability is the ease of use and learnability of a human-made object. The object of use can be a software application, website, book, tool, machine, process, or anything a human interacts with.

User Centered Design: User centered design is a design philosophy and a process in which the needs, wants, and limitations of end users of a product are given extensive attention at each stage of the design process. User-centered design can be characterized as a multi-stage problem solving process that not only requires designers to analyze and foresee how users are likely to use a product, but also to test the validity of their assumptions with regards to user behavior in real world tests with actual users.

User Experience: User experience is the way a person feels about using a product, system or service. It highlights the experiential, affective, meaningful and valuable aspects of human-computer interaction and product ownership, but it also includes a person's perceptions of the practical aspects such as utility, ease of use and efficiency of the system. User experience is subjective in nature, because it is about an individual's feelings and thoughts about the system. It is dynamic, because it changes over time as the circumstances change.

Virtual Environment: A virtual environment is a computer-based simulated environment where users interact with objects and/or other users via avatars. The environment, as well as the avatars, are usually represented in 2D or 3D graphics.

Chapter 14
Digital Heritage Systems:
The ARCO Evaluation

Stella Sylaiou
Hellenic Open University, Greece

Martin White
University of Sussex, UK

Fotis Liarokapis
Coventry University, UK

EXECUTIVE SUMMARY

This chapter describes the evaluation methods conducted for a digital heritage system, called ARCO (Augmented Representation of Cultural Objects), which examines the tools and methods used for its evaluation. The case study describes the knowledge acquired from several user requirement assessments, and further describes how to use this specific knowledge to provide a general framework for a holistic virtual museum evaluation. This approach will facilitate designers to determine the flaws of virtual museum environments, fill the gap between the technologies they use and those the users prefer and improve them in order to provide interactive and engaging virtual museums. The proposed model used not only quantitative, but also qualitative evaluation methods, and it is based on the extensive evaluations of the ARCO system by simple end-users, usability experts and domain experts. The main evaluation criteria were usability, presence, and learning.

DOI: 10.4018/978-1-4666-4046-7.ch014

ORGANIZATION BACKGROUND

The focus of this case study is the ARCO system, which was implemented through a research and development project that was partly funded by the European Union within the Information Societies Technology (IST) Programme, under Key Action 3, Multimedia, Content and Tools managed by the Information Society Directorate-General of the European Commission. The ARCO system was created by the ARCO Consortium organization — a mix of industrial and university partners across the European Union brought together for the purpose of executing the ARCO research and development project. The organization (or consortium) was comprised of the Centre for Computer Graphics at the University of Sussex, United Kingdom, who was also the project coordinator, the Poznan University of Economics, Poland, the Commissariat a l' Energie Atomique, France, the Giunti Editoral Group, Italy, the University of Bath, United Kingdom, the Sussex Archaeological Society and the Victoria and Albert Museum both in the U.K.

The project's research program was implemented over three years between 2001 and 2004, and was jointly financed by the European Union and the participants to the value of around 3.1 Million Euros. The research and development program was composed of several work packages including: WP1 Project Management, WP2 Requirements Specification, WP3 Object Modeller, WP4 Interactive Model Refinement, WP5 Database Management System, WP6 XML Metadata and Schemas, WP7 Augmented Reality Interface, WP8 System Integration and Evaluation and WP9 Exploitation, IPR and Dissemination. The results of WP5, WP6 and WP7 are the focus of the evaluation discussed in this chapter's 'case description,' while the IPR resulting from WP9 re exploited in a commercial product marketed by ARCO Centrum, see the section on 'current challenges facing the organization.'

SETTING THE STAGE

Quite early on, MacDonald and Alsford stated "… museums cannot remain aloof from technological trends if they wish to attract 21st century audiences" (MacDonald & Alsford, 1997). Since the 1990's Information and Communication Technologies become increasingly a critical factor for the success of cultural organisations, such as museums. "The present fiction in museums — that every visitor is equally motivated, equipped, and enabled 'to experience art directly'- should be abandoned. It is patronising, humiliating in practice, and inaccurate" as Wright (1989, p. 148) points out. Successful choices of ICT tools and methods can support personalised access to cultural information, entertain, educate, please (Silverstone, 1994, p. 165), and enhance the virtual museum experience. This changing perspective led museums to assist visitors to construct meaning about virtual museum exhibits, tell stories about the objects, and establish *connectedness* between the museum objects, various layers of information about their context and the virtual museum visitors (Hoptman, 1992). More and more museums use ICT technologies for the documentation, conservation, organisation and dissemination of their cultural data for extending themselves to new audiences around the world and on increasing visitors' participation, education and entertainment.

Virtual museums are digital collections that provide connectedness between various objects and their context using various ICT tools and methods, in order to provide an interactive and engaging experience to their users. Engagement is defined as the "quality of user experience that facilitates more enriching interactions with computer applications. It is defined by a core set of attributes: aesthetic appeal, novelty, involvement, focused attention, perceived usability, and endurability (willingness to use an application again or recommend it to others)" (O'Brien & McLean, 2009). The virtual museums concept has been introduced as a means to enhance user experience by Tsichritzis and Gibbs (1991), and also to overcome the limitations of brick-and-mortar museums. A key component of these virtual museum environments is 'Presence,' the sense of *being there* in a mediated environment, e.g. the degree to which the users feel that they are somewhere other than they physically are while experiencing a computer generated simulation (Shloerb, 1995; Stanney et al., 1998a; Ijsselsteijn et al., 2000). On the other hand Lee (2004) considers that Presence is also "a psychological state in which virtual objects are experienced as actual objects." Users can feel present in a virtual museum environment, or consider as being present the virtual objects in the real environment for the purpose of entertainment, learning, enjoyment, and subjective satisfaction.

CASE DESCRIPTION

Technology Concerns

In the context of technology choice for implementing a virtual museum exhibition, those technologies by themselves have no value. To have value, those technologies must be useable by real users (Dumas & Redish, 1999), which implies they must be fit for their purpose. Thus, the need for the evaluation of these technologies (in the context of a virtual museum) arises, and as such this has been widely recognised by the London Charter in the context of using three-dimensional (3D) visualisation in the research and communication of cultural heritage. The London Charter "established principles for the use of computer-based visualisation methods and outcomes in the research and communication of cultural heritage to ensure that computer-based visualisation processes and outcomes can be properly understood and evaluated by users and enabled computer-based visualisation authoritatively to contribute to the study, interpretation and management of cultural heritage assets." Evaluation of these technologies, that assess their efficiency and effectiveness and explore the information needs of virtual museum visitors, plays an important role in museum communication strategies (Marty, 2006; 2007). Over the years the objectives of system evaluation have changed significantly and started to examine higher-level aspects of user experiences and user needs relating to persuasion, fun, engagement, etc. (Markopoulos & Khan, 2011).

One of the significant problems of museums is that they hold archives of various-sized artefacts, which they cannot exhibit in an efficient and low cost manner (Liarokapis et al., 2008). A primary goal of ARCO was focused towards providing innovative, but simple to use technical solutions for digital cultural object creation, management and presentation in the context of a virtual museum exhibition, either online or in a museum kiosk scenario (White et al., 2004). A major concern for museums is the sheer scale and cost of creating digital objects (or digital representations of physical artefacts), meaning that not all artefacts can be digitised. However, ARCO aims to alleviate some of this cost by putting creation, management and presentation tools into the hands of museum staff, rather than technology specialists. This does not, however, preclude the need for value added services in any of these three processes.

To evaluate the ARCO system properly, i.e. ensure it is fit for museum use, the consortium included the Victoria and Albert Museum and the Sussex Archaeological Society (or SussexPast). The Victoria and Albert Museum represents museums at the national and international level, while SussexPast represented a regional perspective with its collection of small museums across Sussex including: Anne of Cleves House and Fishbourne Roman Palace. The Anne of Cleves house was built in the 16th century and formed part of Anne's divorce settlement from Henry VIII in 1541. It contains a wide range of collections such as Sussex pottery, for example. Fishbourne Roman Palace was accidentally discovered in the 1960's and it represented a military base at the time of the Roman invasion in AD 43 to a sumptuous Palace by the end of the first century. Objects from these two museums, as well as objects and Gallery spaces from the Victoria and Albert museum were digitised and input to the ARCO system for use in the evaluation phase — you can see some of these objects and a gallery space in Figure 2.

Technology Components

This chapter provides an overview of the technology components, methodologies and tools used for the evaluation of ARCO. We are evaluating the efficacy of the ARCO system, software and interface tools that allow museums to use them to build integrated Web3D, Virtual and Augmented Reality-based virtual museum exhibitions. The sense and level of engagement with virtual museum exhibitions that varies between visitor types, and which is activated by a range of factors, such as system usability, prior knowledge, technologies used, etc. will be explored. The issues discussed are related to the goals of human-centred system evaluation, the system apparatus and visual content, the evaluation criteria, the procedure followed and the research results. But first, this chapter outlines the ARCO system itself so that the reader can see what is being evaluated in this case study.

Figure 1 illustrates the ARCO architectural system overview and connectivity of constituent components from an abstract perspective. Before any ARCO components were designed and developed the ARCO project ran a series of early workshops with the museum pilot sites (Victoria and Albert Museum and SussexPast) where we experimented with various state-of-the-art tools for 3D object creation and implementation of virtual museums. These workshops helped to gather user requirements for the design and development of the ARCO system, and later workshops also helped to assess and evaluate the prototype system and technology components against user requirements at museum user trials.

Figure 1 defines the Data Digitization, Object Modelling and Object Refining that form the Content Production processes for ARCO. Content production is linked to the Content Management System (the ARCO Content Management Application — ACMA), which interfaces to both the ARCO database and the XML Data Exchange system. We can see from Figure 1 that the ARIF (Augmented Reality Interface) and X-VRML Server presents 'Data,' which is organised for presentation or visualisation by the 'Templates' as a collection of digital cultural objects within a virtual museum exhibition. The visualisation system, e.g. the Web or a museum kiosk, has the job of displaying the data in the context of a virtual museum exhibition. Threaded throughout the ARCO system are the XML technologies, notably the ARCO Metadata Element Set that is implemented as XML Schemas, and the XML Data Exchange Schema for interoperability and connectivity with other systems.

With ARCO, data acquisition or digitization can be achieved through many methods including the use of digital photogrammetry methods, which generally require some form of post processing to refine the resulting 3D model of an artefact. Artefacts, or digital cultural objects, then need to be managed in a way to produce

Figure 1. ARCO system architectural overview and connectivity of components

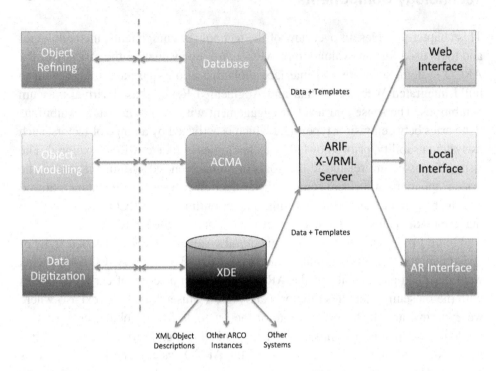

Figure 2. ARCO content production, management and visualisations systems

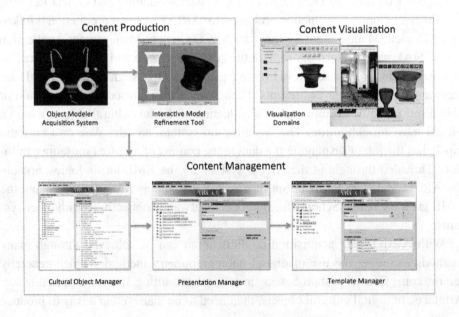

an archive for subsequent visualisation in the context of a virtual museum exhibition — a relational database system is used to store and manage these digital objects.

The architecture of the ARCO system can be broken into three main processes (See Figure 2): Content Production, Content Management, and Content Visualisation. Content production is responsible for the acquisition and digitisation of the museum artefacts. The content management process accounts for the storage and management of the digitised data, while content visualisation is in charge of the presentation of artefacts in virtual and augmented exhibitions.

A critical part of the ARCO system is its data model that consists of several related entities including the notion of four distinct object representations: 'cultural object,' 'acquired object,' 'refined object,' and 'media object.' A cultural object is defined as an abstract representation of a physical artefact where its sub-classes, the acquired object and the refined object are defined as non-abstract entities. The acquired object represents a digitisation of the physical artefact used in the system, while the refined object represents a refinement of an acquired object or another refined object. It is worth mentioning that there may be more than one refined object created from a single acquired object or refined object. Moreover, media objects are representations of the cultural object in a particular medium represented by some MIME type. Typical examples of media objects include 3D models and various types of images (e.g. static, panoramic) and description texts. Another key element of the ARCO system is the specification of an appropriate metadata element set to describe both the museum artefacts and the technical processes that transform the artefacts from the physical to the digital. For this purpose, an XML schema has been designed to implement the ARCO metadata element set; this is the ARCO Metadata Schema (AMS). AMS describes the cultural artefacts, their digital surrogates and specific data for creating virtual exhibitions.

Content Production

ARCO content production is primarily focused on two distinctive sets of technologies for manual and automatic 3D modelling of museum artefacts: the Object Modeller and the Interactive Model Refinement Tool. Figure 1 shows the Object Modeller System, which consists of both hardware and software. The purpose of the Object Modeller component is the digitisation of cultural objects using image-processing techniques. A textured 3D mesh is inferred from images of the artefacts. The first prototype of the Object Modeller was based on state-of-the art software, e.g. PhotoModeller, and use of a single DLSR camera — this system was tested at initial requirements gathering workshops to discover museum requirements. Therefore, with the first prototype, images are acquired using classical digital photography. No specific sensor being required, this prototype is a low-cost solution, which is particularly important for small local and regional museums. Moreover, this software can model objects of any size (as long as images cover the whole surface), whereas specific hardware solutions often impose constraints on the object size. For example, in the case of SussexPast it would be possible to digitally capture the building structure of one of their museums, which itself is of historical importance, as well as the artefacts contained inside.

The final Object Modeller system contains both hardware (for acquisition) and software (for 3D model generation). The main objective is the reduction of user interactions and thus speeds up the artefact modelling time. The system automatically generates a textured 3D model from stereoscopic images. The automation of the modelling task is made possible by using a dedicated image acquisition system based on a calibrated stereo rig and an LCD projector. The process starts with the acquisition of both specific images (using an LCD for structured light projection) for 3D shape recovery, and classical images for texture extraction.

From a stereoscopic acquisition, the user launches the automatic reconstruction process, which leads to the initial 3D mesh. This model is displayed and the operator is able to complete it by local modifications of the mesh, through basic tools (suppression of vertex/face, smoothing, etc.). The texture is automatically mapped onto the 3D mesh. A full reconstruction of an artefact is given by merging several meshes (results of stereo reconstruction). The stereo rig is moved around the object to cover the whole surface of the artefact. The merging operation is performed by registration of the stereo views combined with a refinement step based on the ICP algorithm (http://plum.eecs.jacobs-university.de/download/3dim2007/node2.html). The Object Modeller outputs an accurate 3D model; however, a refinement stage is still needed to fill any holes (as a consequence of light reflections), make the shape more regular, and the texture more homogenous. These tasks are performed with the Interactive Model Refinement tool, specifically with the Model Refinement Interface.

The Model Refinement Tool is based on the 3ds Max framework that complements the functionality of the Object Modeller tool. The content production also acquires other multimedia data such as images and movies, which are integrated into 'acquired object' or 'refined object' through the content management process. Specifically, typical operations required for refining Object Modeller output include: mesh removal (provide a means of removing overlapping faces, edges and points); mesh welding (zipping to joining meshes together); holes capping (provide a means of filling 'holes' in the object); texture re-mapping (provide a means of re-mapping textures at the sub-object level, i.e. faces); cleaning (remove erroneous surfaces); optimising (decimate meshes, i.e. reduce polygon count); smoothing (controllable smoothing of areas, which involve tessellation and displacement of vertices); tessellating (subdivide selected polygon areas or sub meshes); and re-meshing (to give a better overall smoothing process). Most of these operations are already present in

3ds Max, and some were implemented as a plug-in. The refinement tool was then simply created by reducing the complexity of the 3ds Max interface to give the museum user access to the controls needed, while at the same time providing a set of specific help tutorials to guide them through each refinement step (see Figure 4).

Other important features provided by the Model Refinement tool included: XML import and export from/to the XDE format; and database connectivity. Also, the creation of 3D cultural object models are only part of the process of creating digital surrogates of museum artefacts, as indicated in Figure 1, other data digitization is needed, e.g. metadata, to complete a digital cultural objects, including the acquisition of other multimedia data, such as images, image sequences (QuickTime VR or movie files) and audio files.

Content Management

The ARCO Content Management System (ACMS) is the central component of the ARCO architecture. It consists of two subcomponents: the ARCO database and ACMA – ARCO Content Management Application.

The ARCO database is the central repository used to store all persistent data produced and processed by all ARCO tools. ARCO data is comprised of digital representations of cultural artefacts including all multimedia objects, virtual exhibitions, 2D and 3D visualization templates, etc. Further, all objects stored in the ARCO database are described by XML-based metadata records. Data may be imported and exported from the ARCO database in various formats including XML for maximum interoperability with other museum systems.

The ARCO database is based on an Oracle ORDBMS, which is an advanced database management system needed to store all the data in the ARCO system with features for operating on that data, which otherwise would be either impossible or prohibitively difficult and expensive to implement. These features include:

- Remote and local access to data repository,
- Concurrent access of multiple users,
- Data consistency enforced by database structure,
- Access privileges for different users and groups,
- Fine-grained object access rights for users and groups,
- Backup and recovery of data,
- Advanced indexing and search capabilities including full text search on XML metadata records.

The ACMA tool enables efficient and user-friendly management of all data stored in the ARCO database. ACMA is composed of several data managers specialized in managing different types of data. Example managers are the Cultural Object Manager for managing virtual representations of cultural artefacts, the Presentation Manager for managing virtual exhibitions, the Template Manager for managing visualization templates, and the Template Object Manager for managing multimedia data. The ACMA tool itself is implemented in Java.

An important feature of the ARCO database and the ACMA tool is their extensibility, which allows users to extend the set of data types supported by the system and the structure of their metadata descriptions without modifying the database schema or the application code. This feature allows museums to customise the system for their specific needs both at the current time and in the future.

Data stored in the ARCO database may be automatically published on the Web via the ARIF and XVRML Servers in the form of 2D and 3D virtual galleries using the ACMA Presentation Manager. ACMA allows the publishing of virtual museum exhibitions on the Internet — a virtual museum exhibition includes the digital representation of cultural objects, their associated media objects, such as images, 3D models, texts, movies, sounds and relevant metadata (Mourkoussis et al., 2003), and any contextual virtual environment, e.g. a 3D model of a museum gallery space in which such digital objects reside online.

Content Visualisation

Museums require more cost-effective ways of creating virtual presentations of their archives that can be suitable both for museum curators and the public. Content visualization in ARCO is responsible for the interactive visualization of the digital representations of museum artefacts in real-time. This is performed by both virtual reality (VR) and augmented reality (AR) interfaces that combine a Web domain form of presentation of either VR or AR based virtual exhibitions. End-users (museum visitors) can navigate the contents stored in the database in a number of ways. This could be done either remotely through a web-browser, in a museum environment (i.e. museum kiosk), or by interacting with the virtual objects in an AR tabletop environment.

The Web Local and Web Remote domain visualizations offer options for interacting with digital cultural objects within a virtual museum exhibition. Additionally, ARCO's augmented reality interface (ARIF) is designed to provide the capability to switch between a Web domain based virtual museum and a table-top augmented reality system to further examine the museums digital cultural objects. ARCO's presentation or visualization framework can be adapted to different user interfaces and presentation domains. Examples of presentation domains include: (a) a Web Local domain used, for example when ARIF content is displayed on touch-screen displays in information kiosks located in the museum building, (b) a Web Remote

Figure 3. Content visualized in a Web browser (embedded) on the left and AR browser on the right

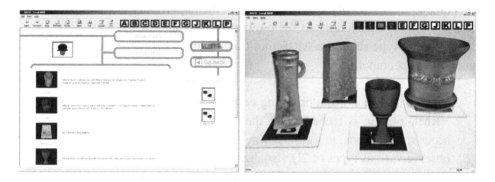

Figure 4. Reduction of 3ds max interface to a simpler format for the interactive object refinement tool

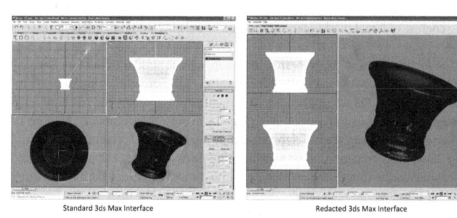

Standard 3ds Max Interface   Redacted 3ds Max Interface

domain, i.e. normal Internet access to a virtual museum exhibition and (c) a 3D Gallery domain appropriate for virtual exhibition spaces accessed remotely over the Internet.

Of particular interest is how ARIF can be utilized to display virtual museum exhibitions on a touch screen in the museum environment, utilizing table-top AR learning experiences, similar to the Magic Book concept (Billinghurst et al., 2001), which resembles a regular book including black and white markers in its pages where users can turn the pages, as they would do with a real book, to see AR contents. With the aid of a web camera, the AR browser overlays virtual objects upon video frames captured in real-time providing users with the impression that the virtual objects actually exist in the real environment, integrating both virtual and real objects together. When the users look at the computer screen, pictures pop out of the page and come to life as 3D objects, offering them the opportunity to examine selected cultural objects displayed in the AR browser from various viewing angles.

In this AR type setup the ARIF tool (See Figure 3) is composed of two main functional subcomponents:

- **Web Browser:** For the browsing component, a typical web browser with a VRML plug-in is embedded in the tool. This component allows a user to browse exhibitions, in a similar way as the end-user Web Local domain, and observe various types of 2D visualization of Cultural Objects, including pictures, textual descriptions, VRML scenes and movies. The ARIF X-VRML server dynamically generates all this content.
- **AR Browser:** This component allows a user to visualize in real time digital representations of Cultural Objects in an Augmented Reality environment containing real objects. The user can interact with the virtual models in the context of a real world scene composed of existing museum artefacts.

The functionality of the web browser component is similar to the functionality of a typical web browser such as Internet Explorer. The browser component is embedded directly in the AR application. The content presented by the AR browser is the same content as that presented in the Web local or Remote domains. The way of content presentation can be different depending on the applied presentation domain. Both 2D and 3D contents can be visualized in the Web browser. A user is offered typical navigation functionality. While a user is browsing virtual exhibitions using the Web browser, the main application continuously keeps track of the currently displayed objects and passes this information to the AR browser. At any time, a user can decide that the currently displayed Cultural Object should be visualized in the augmented reality environment. In such a case, a virtual object representing the Cultural Object is superimposed on a live video stream coming from a camera connected to the system (see Figure 3).

The ARCO Consortium, having now spent some 3.1 Million Euro on developing the ARCO system are faced with the challenge of evaluating this system—questions such as, does it work, is it fit for purpose, can museums (experts) use the system, can users (museum visitors) engage with virtual museum exhibition produced by the system?

These questions are answered through the implementation of an extensive usability evaluation program outlined in the next section.

ARCO Evaluation Setup

The components of the ARCO system (see Figure 1) that have been assessed include the Content Management component (ACMA) and the Content Visualisation component focused around the augmented reality interface (ARIF) that was discussed above (Wojciechowski et al., 2004). Thus, these components need to be made available for evaluation in an appropriate evaluation environment. At any particular evaluation stage, the components would be developed with certain functionality present. Thus, evaluation criteria based on a component user interface had to be developed. For an example, see the user-satisfaction evaluation questionnaire (Chin et al., 1988). These particular questionnaires focus on presence and usability of the two components under evaluation (ACMA and ARIF). These particular ARCO components (ACMA and ARIF) have been evaluated by utilizing a variety of methods (both empirical and expert-based) including presence and usability questionnaires, and cognitive walkthroughs, combining both quantitative and qualitative research methods (Sylaiou et al., 2004; Sylaiou et al., 2008). The main evaluation criteria to consider were: usability, presence, enjoyment and learning, which will be analysed further below.

For the setup of the evaluation it was necessary to consider both non-expert and expert user, approximately 30 and 6 respectively. Further, initial evaluation studies focused on the comparison of the assessments of two groups of expert evaluators, referred to as the domain experts. These were the cultural heritage experts with no direct knowledge of technological usability evaluations and the usability experts, who were aware of the usability aspects, yet acted as visitors of a virtual museum implemented utilizing the ARCO system (Karoulis et al., 2006a). Museum curators from the Victoria and Albert museum in London, UK participated in these experiments and provided invaluable feedback.

Two evaluation approaches have been employed: a questionnaire-based survey based on a modified QUIS questionnaire assessing user satisfaction related to interface and usability aspects of the system (Chin et al., 1988), and a Cognitive Walkthrough (Polson et al., 1992) session, both by museum curators as domain experts and usability experts. Specifically, the statistical elaboration of the quantitative data was performed that aimed to define the "accordance factor" (the degree to which the opinions of the curators were in accordance to those of the usability experts) and to determine whether the domain experts' experience with the system was similar with the usability experts' experience.

In summary, before evaluation begins you need to have ready for test and evaluation:

- A working system ready for testing by the chosen user group, in our case the ACMA and ARIF components

- A chosen user group, in our case a set of non-expert and experts w.r.t. domain under test, i.e. museum systems
- An evaluation approach, in our case appropriate questionnaires and cognitive walk-throughs (See Appendix I)

Once you have decided on the test and evaluation setup, you can begin to plan the evaluation techniques in more detail.

ARCO Evaluation Techniques

The ARCO project followed a participatory design approach that involved continual user observation (Greenbaum & Kyng, 1991; Namioka & Schuler, 1993). The evaluation of ARCO adopted the three key components of evaluation work: front-end, formative and summative (Borun & Korn, 1999; ICOM/CIDOC, 1996). The ARCO system design also followed an iterative user-centred development cycle. Each cycle unveiled various drawbacks and problematic areas that have been addressed and the system was accordingly improved. It should also be noted, that following improvements based on evaluations, etc. the ARCO system has now been commercialised through the ARCO Centrum (http://www.wirtualnemuzea.pl/pl) organization.

The system aspects that have been evaluated are the following:

1. *Technical usability* that refers to the perceptual and physical aspects of the human-computer interface,
2. *Domain suitability* that examines the appropriateness of the content of information and display presentations,
3. *User acceptability* that refers to the effectiveness of the system for supporting cognitive task requirements (Rasmussen and Goldstein 1998) and the satisfaction that provides.

Museum curators used two components of the ARCO system for evaluation, the ACMA and the ARIF interface, and completed a questionnaire while utilizing these components (Sylaiou et al., 2004; Karoulis et al., 2006; Sylaiou et al., 2006; Sylaiou et al., 2009; Sylaiou et al., 2012).

ACMA Evaluation: The usability evaluation of the ACMA interface, which is a module within the ARCO system used for the management of the virtual museum database that also provides tools for integrating 3D models into virtual museum exhibitions, was conducted through an expert-based approach (Sylaiou et al., 2008). The virtual museum implemented was based on an existing gallery in the Victoria and Albert Museum, London, UK.

Museum curators are in daily contact with museum domains; therefore, their feedback was invaluable towards conducting concrete system improvements. Recognizing the experience of domain experts when adopting an expert-based usability evaluation highlighted the need to incorporate feedback from museum curators who are not necessarily as familiar with computer systems as usability experts might be (Karoulis et al., 2006a), this is indicated by results obtained from adjusted QUIS questionnaires (Chin et al. 1988). The Questionnaire for User Interaction Satisfaction (QUIS) is a tool developed by the Human-Computer Interaction Lab (HCIL) at the University of Maryland and its aim was to assess users' subjective beliefs related to specific aspects of the human-computer interface tested. Here, study-specific parts of the QUIS were employed, but modified to address ARCO usability aspects. A statistical elaboration of the quantitative data was performed that aimed to define the "accordance factor" (i.e. the degree to which the opinions of the curators were in accordance to those of the usability experts) and to determine whether the domain experts' experience with the system was similar with the usability experts' experience.

The final conclusion of this study was that in complex interfaces, such as a virtual museum exhibition, both usability and domain experts should take part in usability studies for reliable and valid results.

Thus, another evaluation study, a combinatory evaluation involving museum curators as domain specialists and end-users representing the museum visitors, has been undertaken to investigate usability and educational efficacy of the interfaces to the ARCO components. Again, feedback was acquired through the administration of a usability questionnaire as well as through a cognitive walkthrough.

ARIF Evaluation: While the ACMA evaluation concerned testing the efficacy of the interface from a usability perspective through appropriate adapted questionnaires (QUIS), ARIF evaluation also involved a cognitive walkthrough. The cognitive walkthrough concerned the ARIF component in particular because the end product of the ARIF is a visualisation in some format (e.g. a virtual museum or AR presentation) of digitised artefacts. The scenario evaluated demonstrated how information about the virtual museum artefacts could be communicated in an interactive manner by the experimenters posing questions and resolving tasks while exposed to a virtual museum.

Data collected through the usability questionnaire and cognitive walkthrough was related to the clarity of terminology and documentation design, quality consistency and GUI interfaces issues. Both end-users and museum curators expressed frustration in relation to technological jargon utilized by the system developers, which they were not familiar with. This is a significant issue when designing systems for a non-technological context. Both the museum curators and the end users required higher resolution images in relation to the VRML artefact models' textures. System developers added a brief introduction to a quiz in the form of a video and provided simpler explanations concerning the scoring mechanism. They proposed the use of a clapping hand instead of a smiley face to indicate a correct answer with voice recognition of participants' responses being the most desirable attribute for future implementations (Karoulis et al., 2006b). The overall statistical elaboration of quantitative data indicated that museum curators and virtual museum visitors responded similarly. There was no statistically significant difference between the two groups' responses concerning the usability of the system interfaces.

In another study the preliminary evaluation studies mentioned above were extended by exploring the degree of perceived 'presence' during exposure to virtual museums implemented in ARCO, in an effort to acquire a 'top view' of the whole system rather than its components through perceived presence assessments (Sylaiou et al., 2008).

We now describe in more detail the elements of this evaluation case study in terms of usability, presence and learning in the context of a digital heritage system (ARCO) and its capability to create virtual museum exhibitions efficiently.

What Do We Mean by Usability?

Usability of a system is its ability to function effectively and efficiently, while providing subjective satisfaction to its users in a specified context of use (ISO 9241, 1998). Usability of an interface is usually associated with five parameters (ISO, 1998; Nielsen, 1993), derived from this definition, and we quote directly from Nielsen's 1993 paper:

- **Easy to learn:** The user can quickly go from not knowing the system to getting some work done with it.
- **Efficient to use:** Once the user has learned the system, a high level of productivity is possible.
- **Easy to remember:** The infrequent user is able to return to using the system after some period of not having used it, without having to learn everything all over.
- **Few errors:** Users do not make many errors during the use of the system, or if they do make errors they can easily recover from them. Also, no catastrophic errors should occur.
- **Pleasant to use:** Users are subjectively satisfied by using the system; they like it.

In essence, usability means user-friendly design of computer interfaces. It refers to the perceptual and physical aspects of the human–computer interface and examines, through feedback from the system users, whether it is user-friendly or not, understandable, interactive and satisfactory. Usability evaluation examines if the system tasks can be accomplished successfully.

Two important conceptions regarding the usability of an interface are "transparency" and "intuitiveness" (Nielsen, 1993; Preece et al., 1994). Transparency refers to the ability of the interface to fade out in the background, allowing the user to concentrate during his work on *what* he wants to do and not on *how* to do it, in our case not interfering with the learning procedure, while intuitiveness refers to its ability to guide the user through it by the use of proper metaphors and successful mapping to the real world, e.g., by providing him with the appropriate icons, correct labelling, exact phrasing, constructive feedback etc.

Usability Evaluation

Workshops and focus groups: As previously mentioned, the ARCO project, both before design and development work began, and during development, followed a participatory design approach and involved continual user observation. This was achieved through a series of workshops with focused user groups to gather requirements from the museum pilot sites on details such as the types of sites, monuments and objects that might be useful to capture in 3D, and how the museums contemplated the use of 3D and virtual museums to present their collections. Other information was gathered on the current state-of-the-art in content production, management and visualization tools and methods, including setting up experiments and tutorials for museum staff to use such tools. For example, this process led to the realization that 3D authoring tools such as 3ds max were, while in themselves very sophisticated, also capable of being reduced at the interface level to simpler formats allowing access to only the functionalities needed to do the job; and included the ability to add extra functionality through plug-ins. Thus, it was needless to develop an Interactive Object Refine Tool from scratch. Figure4 illustrates the re-configuration of the 3ds max interface to allow museums to use a more focused refinement strategy.

ACMA Domain Experts: Following on from the discussion on the ACMA Evaluation above, we consider the role of the domain expert in this evaluation. In this study museum curators from Victoria and Albert museum in London, UK examined and assessed the system and participated in interviews, providing valuable insight through the lens of their experience. The usability evaluation of ACMA, which is used to manage digital objects in the database together with their associated media objects (3D, images, video, etc.) and relevant metadata allowing the publishing of virtual museums on the Internet, was conducted through an expert-based approach.

The ACMA evaluation was focused on assessing the ease of management of the virtual museum database by museum curators using ACMA 'managers' to create a virtual museum (e.g. a virtual gallery) with artefacts already created as digital objects from a Victoria and Albert Museum collection. Evaluation methods such as heuristic evaluation and walkthroughs were employed in order to assess various components and interfaces of the system. The heuristic evaluation instrument was a specific questionnaire developed by the ARCO Consortium for the evaluation of the ACMA and ARIF components (ARCO Evaluation Report, 2004). The content of the ARCO system was evaluated in terms of information clarity. The evaluation also tested if the system is user-friendly, easy to understand and if the museum curators could find all the information required in an appropriate delivery format. The system's functionality of interaction, the consistency of design regarding the clear and accessible organisation of folders and objects and the effectiveness of managing access rights were measured. The evaluation also examined the export component of the system to test if the XDE format could be re-used, see Figure 1 — necessary because a key concept of ARCO is data interoperability with other museum systems. The system interface was assessed in terms of intuitiveness, predictability, aesthetic appeal and usability of the objects presented through VR and AR technologies. Usability was measured according to the ease of use, high user task performance, low user error rate, subjective user satisfaction and user retention over time (Nielsen, 1993; ISO, 1998). After the evaluation tasks were completed, an in-depth analysis taking into account the severity of the usability problems was undertaken, and user comments were classified into three main categories: positive comments, remarks/ suggestions and possible deficiencies. Typical user comments included:

Positive comments: The evaluation users liked the fact that the system functionalities were comprehensible, easy-to-use and straightforward. They consider the system as efficient in use and they characterized it as flexible and responsive to users' actions that allowed unhindered, quick, straightforward interaction. Finally, they considered as a clear system advantage the fact that ACMA was an attractive and exciting interface to use.

Remarks/suggestions: They asked for more control and customisation that allow them to control and customize the system interface. They suggested that a successful system must provide descriptive information concerning the various forms of access rights and the privileges related to them an advanced access control to the system to prevent unauthorized access, maintain data accuracy, ensure the appropriate use of information and protect users' privacy. Between the curators' suggestions was the need for system visibility. A virtual museum system should inform its users, when a task is accomplished through appropriate feedback using a progress indicator. Curators need accessibility to the virtual museum content, quick, easy and reliable system responsibility and access to information about the virtual exhibitions and the related tasks. Connected with the content accessibility is the system searching utility that must have advanced searching utilities. They also commented that the system must also be aesthetically pleasing and engaging. It shall also avoid negative statements that discourage the users.

Possible deficiencies: The problems that the curators faced were connected to the consistency and standards of GUI interfaces. More specifically, the system must take into account the prior knowledge and experience of the users. The users expected similar functions with the well-known operating system and consequently, they were dissatisfied when they had to interact with different system characteristics. The curators faced some problems connected to the system terminology and documentation. They claimed that the system terms 'are not self explanatory' and the system vocabulary must be comprehensible and familiar. Curators consider that users should be provided with recovery solutions from errors (e.g. the need for a back button either to retrace steps or to undo quickly an unwanted action). The users must control the navigation and need to know the point they are in the system and the route they have to follow for exploring other system parts. It is also essential to provide help in the users' navigation, because otherwise, there is the danger that they will feel frustration and abandon the effort of working with the system. The last two problems confronted by the curators were the functionality of graphic elements that mainly concern the contrast between body text and its background colour, and the quality of graphic elements that mainly were connected to the system limitations concerning storage and transmission speed of files over the Internet.

Given access to this range of user comments, the ACMA developers can now improve the design and functionality of the ACMA managers — Cultural Object, Presentation, and Template managers — refer to the section on Technology Components above.

ACMA and ARIF Domain and Usability Experts

In another evaluation study we focused on usability. Two groups of expert evaluators have participated; the cultural heritage experts who were museum curators who did not have any direct knowledge of technological usability evaluations, and the usability experts, which were aware of the usability aspects and acted as virtual museum visitors using the ARCO system (Karoulis et al., 2006). A Cognitive Walkthrough session was conducted not only by the museum curators as domain experts, but also by the usability experts (Polson et al., 1992). Furthermore, a questionnaire-based survey that used parts of the QUIS (Questionnaire for User Interaction Satisfaction) assessed the user satisfaction related to interface and usability aspects of the system (Chin et al., 1988). A statistical elaboration of the quantitative data was performed to define the degree to which the opinions of the curators were in accordance to those of the usability experts and to determine whether the domain experts' experience with the system was similar with the usability experts' experience.

The main result of the study was the fact that in order to acquire reliable and valid results by complex interfaces evaluations, such as those used in a virtual museum environment, both usability and domain experts should take part in usability studies. The curators' comments were valuable sources of information that helped to highlight the system's strengths and weaknesses and triggered a series of system refinements to enhance ease of navigation, add explanatory graphical elements and colours, etc.

What Do We Mean by Presence?

One of the key elements of the ARCO system is its ability to create a virtual museum exhibition, which by definition is a virtual environment. It seems reasonable then to evaluate how effective such a virtual museum is, when created by ARCO's ARIF component. But first, we discuss what 'presence' actually is.

There are several definitions of Presence, since it is considered as a multi-dimensional concept (Schuemie et al., 2001). Stanney et al. (1998b) stated that the sense of Presence is connected to the subjective impression of being immersed in and surrounded by a virtual world rather than the physical world the user is currently situated in. An '*illusion of non-mediation,*' as Presence is defined in the world of media and emergent technologies, such as videoconferencing, high definition television and home theatre (Lombard & Ditton, 1997; Freeman et al., 2000), occurs when the user fails to perceive the existence of a medium in his/her communication environment and reacts as if the medium were not there. The sense of Presence refers to the extent to which participants feel that they visited a place rather than viewed images generated by a computer (Slater, 1999) and they behave in the virtual environment (VE) as they do in the real world (Sanchez-Vives & Slater, 2005).

Often, a VE is populated by 3D objects in a 3D scene and, in this sense, subjective Presence also reflects the subjective experience of being co-located with a set of objects (Stevens et al., 2002). Presence can be considered as a psychological state in which virtual objects are experienced as actual objects in either sensory or cognitive ways (Lee, 2004). Perceived presence has been positively affected by stereo imagery, utilizing sound, large screen size and type of display such as a CAVE (Slater, 2004). However, presence is not consistently enhanced after exposure to photorealistic scenes as opposed to flat-shaded or lower fidelity 3D rendering. Slater and Wilbur (1997) distinguish between immersion and presence. They define immersion as a description of technology and presence as a person's subjective experience of 'being there' in a VE (Bystrom et al., 1999; Schubert et al., 1999). Researchers agree that acquiring subjective presence assessments is one of the main usability criteria of VE systems (Stanney, 2003).

Presence Evaluation

In another study the degree of perceived Presence and enjoyment after exposure to a virtual museum exhibition and its constituent artefacts implemented with ARCO's ARIF has been explored and an attempt to identify its relationship with previous ICT experience and enjoyment (Sylaiou et al., 2009) has been made. Sweetser et al. suggest "Player enjoyment is the single most important goal for computer games. If players do not enjoy the game, they will not play the game" (Sweetser & Wyeth, 2005, p.1). Based on this premise, the presence evaluation study's main aim was to acquire a 'top view' of the system rather than its components through perceived presence and enjoyment assessments. The Virtual Reality (VR) questionnaire (Slater, 1999) that was slightly modified, in order to specifically refer to a virtual museum scene, and the Augmented Reality (AR) Presence Questionnaire (Regenbrecht & Schubert, 2002) that measures the degree to which individuals experience the presence of virtual objects in a real environment, as well as the subjective impression they appear real, have been used for the evaluation.

This evaluation revealed interesting results. The previous computing users' experience was not significantly correlated with perceived presence or enjoyment. Thus, novice computer users could utilize virtual museums successfully as the level of their computing expertise would not influence their ability of feeling engaged with the virtual museum. There is a positive correlation (at a statistical level $p<0.01$) between VR presence and AR objects' presence. This indicates that the participants experienced similar locality with the cultural artefacts, therefore, perceiving they were sharing the same physical space as the synthetic objects. A significant positive correlation was revealed between enjoyment and both AR objects' presence and VR presence. As participants experience a rising sense of '*being there*' in the virtual museum, the more they experience enjoyment. Therefore, a high level of perceived presence is closely associated with satisfaction and enjoyment, which contribute towards a constructive experience while interacting with a virtual museum system. Enjoyment as well as presence, in this sense, could be invaluable system attributes, which could lead to user satisfaction while interacting with a particular interface.

What Do We Mean by Learning?

Another element of the ARCO system we wished to evaluate was its ability to provide a learning experience with its capability to create virtual museum exhibitions. A museum's effectiveness relies on the ability to convey information in an engaging way, communicate information about the museum artefacts and context, since Falk and Dierking (2000) define learning in terms of how users are able to comprehend the presented information. Digital technologies can have the potential to positively impact visitor meaning and consequently learning, because they provide to visitors the opportunity to customize their experiences and meet their personal needs and interests; they enhance the experience beyond the physical and temporal boundaries of the museum visit; and they layer multisensory elements within the experience, so as to enriching the quality of the physical context (Falk & Dierking, 2008, p.28). Learning is the situation in which the "individuals can be conceptualized as being involved in a continuous, contextually driven effort to make meaning in order to survive and prosper within the world, an effort that is best viewed as a never-ending dialogue between the individual and his or her physical and socio-cultural environment" (Gammon & Burch, 2008). Learning is driven by the interaction between visitors' external and internal conversation mediated by the changing context and by external shared media (Rudman et al., 2008). Museums can be considered as educational institutions that contribute to informal learning, as most people visit museums expecting to learn (Walker, 2008). The actions taken during play are closely connected to experiences of mastery and self-efficacy (Bandura, 1977; 1997). Many studies explored the potential and the contribution of the computer games to learning procedure (Kafai & Ching, 1996; Rieber, 1996; Gee, 2003; Squire & Barab, 2004).

In the past a number of AR games have been designed in different areas including education, learning, training, and enhanced entertainment. One of the earliest examples of educational applications was the MagicBook (Billinghurst et al., 2001), which shows how AR can be used in schools for educational purposes providing an interesting method of teaching. It enables users to read the book either like any traditional book or with a handheld display allowing the reader to see virtual 3D images popping out of the pages. Research led by the BBC identified how children aged five and six responded positively to AR learning. They argued that AR learning enables children to be more imaginative as children were observed to take over specific characters of the story in the process and make stories of their own. This enabled them to play as they naturally would and learn at the same time (Thomas, 2006). During the 'Earth, Sun and Moon' AR project children aged 10 years old could understand how the sun and earth interact together. This project showed the acceptance of learning via emerging technologies such as AR by children aged 10+ and also suggested it is a suitable teaching tool (Kerawalla et al., 2006).

In another study, the design and development of AR applications for educational purposes from the area of human medicine was presented (Nischelwitzer et al., 2007). Usability studies with children and the elderly showed that this technology has potential and can be of great benefit. Moreover, examples exist of AR educational applications used to support and simplify teaching and learning techniques currently applied in the higher education sector (Liarokapis, 2007) as well as on learning and performance (Holzinger et al., 2008). Additionally, the notion of 'immersion' itself is becoming considered as a central design tool as we move towards considering learning not only as knowledge construction, but also as socialization. Immersion is regarded as critical to good game design because it engages and motivates including components of interactivity, narrative, 'flow' and fidelity (Csikszentmihalyi, 1990; de Freitas & Liarokapis, 2011). The actions taken during play are closely connected to experiences of mastery and self-efficacy (Bandura, 1977; 1997). Players often take over a role, thus constructing a parallel reality that is the dominant one for the duration of the game. The users are in partial command of the events going on in the story; they receive immediate feedback on their actions and thus can respond to the effects they produce (Vorderer 2000; 2001). Interactivity can therefore not only enrich technological experiences (Steuer, 1992), but also increase the motivation to use a media setting because it makes exposure to learning entertaining as well as potentially making users feel successful. Such feelings of mastery may encourage users to maintain their engagement in learning actions within the media system and prevent them from exiting the exposure to learning situation, therefore enhancing engagement and concentration (Klimmt & Vorderer, 2003).

Learning Evaluation

The experimental AR game scenario included cultural information and required users to interactively answer a series of questions, as well as resolve tasks employing an AR game interface. The interactive game corresponds to learning by doing and to discovery learning, promoting user participation in an interactive experience in order to discover the correct answer (Hein, 1998). Designing games that support knowledge and skill acquisition has become a promising frontier for training, since games are able to capture concentration for long periods and can present users with compelling challenges (de Freitas & Liarokapis, 2011). Careful design of these technologies (i.e. AR and 3D in a virtual museum in the form of a game or a quiz) can disrupt a linear sequence of presenting information and thereby provides a more interesting way of discovering digital museum content. The technology, carefully engineered, makes the digital heritage object (artefacts) or collections more accessible and provides more interesting navigation solutions through that collection for all visitors irrespective of their age or abilities. Nowadays, we find that the new gaming paradigms may be supported by broader structures in which no clear winner exists aiming to achieve education or training objectives (Arnab et al., 2010). In this respect, the research community is challenged to investigate the factors that make such technologies effective, productive and engaging. Despite the number of AR applications in museums, the impact such 'virtual' exhibits have on the social ecology of exhibitions is largely unexplored (Reeves, 2004; Schmalstieg, 2005).

The evaluation study of the ARIF AR game used the ACMA-ARIF evaluation questionnaire and assessed the educational usefulness of the learning scenario embedded in an AR educational game implemented through the ARCO system, the quality of the presentation of questions in the AR environment, the ease of answering questions using double-sided markers, the quality of the integration of the Web and AR presentation as well as the scoring mechanism and the usefulness of audio accompanying the learning scenario.

A qualitative as well as a quantitative evaluation was conducted (Sylaiou et al., 2012). The qualitative evaluation was based on observation of problems encountered, while users were playing the AR game and provided very useful feedback complementing the quantitative elaboration of acquired user responses. The problems encountered and issues raised were grouped according to the functionality of the graphic elements, the quality of the graphics, the ease of navigation, the functionality of the AR elements, and the aesthetic issues in relation to the look and feel of the application as well as any general technological problems that needed to be addressed. According to the results feelings of defeat and failure may be caused by emergent media systems because their usage is, in many cases, experimental. As long as interactivity allows for experiences of control, mastery, and self-efficacy, it will intensify the pleasure of using the media product and thus increase the motivation to experience a strong sense of engagement. The advances of Augmented Reality (AR) and Serious Gaming technologies are predicted to rise exponentially and used on a range of mobile computing devices. Their effectiveness could be designed employing information about the human perceptual system and assessed from a human factors engineering point of view. The goal would be to understand the way humans perceive AR worlds across a range of displays and assess the effectiveness of such technologies for different applications.

By defining a situation as play, individuals establish a set of expectations that may differ from what should be expected in the real world. If users expect to enter a world with certain rules and peculiarities and are prepared to consider the media use as a playful action, they might feel a strong sense of engagement even in the presence of technical limitations. Such transportations to alternate realities are very appealing to children and adolescents because they enable them to expand their horizon of experience and possible activities by simulation. Their main motivation may be the need for diversion from real-world experience, a form of escapism as put forward by communication researchers (Katz & Foulkes, 1962; Henning & Vorderer, 2001). Therefore, media products such as highly interactive AR gaming applications for educational purposes that portray new and unusual environments may be more interesting to most individuals than simulations of real-world settings, increasing their motivation to feel a sense of engagement because it is fun to be there.

CURRENT CHALLENGES FACING THE ORGANIZATION

The main challenge facing the organization concerns how to effectively market and commercialise the ARCO system. Of the seven partners who participated in the ARCO project, only two partners (the University of Sussex and the University of Poznan) hold significant IP from a commercial perspective. The problem here is that neither University is particularly set up to market and exploit IP in terms of a product. This necessitated the setting up of the ARCO Centrum organization (a spinoff of the University of Poznan Informatics department) specifically for the purpose of continuing the development of ARCO, adding value to the system through services and selling the system itself to the intended market, i.e. museums. In this regard, we decided to setup ARCO Centrum in Poland, because the University of Poznan was in a better position to provide value added services to museums. Thus far, ARCO Centrum has necessarily focused on museums in Poland, with several successful sales, and so the current challenge is now to extend its customer base into the rest of Europe.

SOLUTIONS AND RECOMMENDATIONS

The ability to develop sophisticated and flexible web and mobile applications based on virtual and augmented reality and gaming engine technologies for application to museums is incredible taking into account the plethora of powerful tools and technologies for displaying such applications. In this respect, the research community is challenged to investigate the factors that make such technologies effective, productive and engaging for museum visitors. Our evaluations provide useful recommendations concerning improvement to the design of graphical elements in interfaces, as well as interactivity modes that are considered an important factor in determining an enhanced and engaging virtual museum experience. In the current chapter we presented the methods used for evaluation of a digital heritage system, in this case ARCO. Specific ARCO components have been evaluated by utilizing a variety of methods, both empirical and expert-based. The evaluation criteria proposed were Usability, Presence and Learning. The evaluation procedure involved simple end-users, as well as domain and usability experts.

The evaluation focused on showing that ARCO could provide a system that is easy-to-use, which can be used to build appealing and educational virtual museum environments that motivate the visitor. The ARCO components, themselves are functional and useable, and can be used effectively as an interactive tool with high educational impact. The virtual museum thus created with the ARCO system will trigger visitors to construct their knowledge through an enhanced virtual museum experience, and more specifically through 'learning-by-doing' and 'learning-by-exploring.'

ACKNOWLEDGMENT

This work has been funded by the Marie Curie Action on Human resources and Mobility, Marie Curie training site: Virtual Reality and Computer Graphics, project HPMTCT-2001-00326 and FP5 IST project ARCO. The authors would like to thank Katerina Mania, Assistant Professor, Department of Electronic and Computer Engineering, Technical University of Crete, for her comments that help improve the manuscript.

REFERENCES

ARCO Evaluation Report. (2004). Assessment and evaluation report on the ARCO system and its components. Retrieved July, 1, 2007, from http://www.arco-web.org/TextVersion/Documents/Deliverables/ARCO-D16-R-1.0-170904.pdf

Arnab, S., Protopsaltis, A., Minoi, J.L., Dunwell, I., & de Freitas, S. (2010). Promoting cross-cultural awareness through exposure in game-based Learning. *IEEE Learning Technology Newsletter,* January 2010 Edition.

Bandura, A. (1977). Self-efficacy: Toward a unifying theory of behavioral change. *Psychological Review, 84*(2), 191–215. doi:10.1037/0033-295X.84.2.191

Bandura, A. (1997). *Self-efficacy: The exercise of control.* New York, NY: Freeman.

Billinghurst, M., Kato, H., & Poupyrev, I. (2001). The MagicBook: A traditional AR interface. *Computer Graphics, 25,* 745–753. doi:10.1016/S0097-8493(01)00117-0

Borun, M., & Korn, R. (Eds.). (1999). *Introduction to museum evaluation. Committee on Audience Research and Evaluation, American Association of Museums, Professional Practice Series.* Washington, DC: AAM.

Bystrom, K. E., Barfield, W., & Hendrix, C. (1999). A conceptual model of the sense of presence in virtual environments. *Presence (Cambridge, Mass.), 8,* 241–244. doi:10.1162/105474699566107

Chin, J. P., Diehl, V. A., & Norman, L. K. (1988). Development of an instrument measuring user satisfaction of the human-computer interface. [New York: ACM/ SIGCHI.]. *Proceedings of the SIGCHI, 88,* 213–218.

Csikszentmihalyi, M. (1991). *Flow—The psychology of optimal experience.* New York, NY: Harper Collins.

de Freitas, S., & Liarokapis, F. (2011). (in press). Serious games: A new paradigm for education? *Serious Games and Edutainment Applications. Heisenberg: Springer.*

Dumas, J. F., & Redish, J. C. (1999). *A practical guide to usability testing.* Portland, OR: Intellect Ltd.

Falk, J. H., & Dierking, L. D. (2000). *Learning from museums: Visitor experiences and the making of meaning.* Walnut Creek: Altamira Press.

Falk, J. H., & Dierking, L. D. (2008). Enhancing visitor interaction and learning with mobile technologies. In Tallon, L., & Walker, K. (Eds.), *Digital technologies and the museum experience. Handheld guides and other media* (pp. 19–60). Walnut Creek: Altamira Press.

Freeman, J., Avons, S. E., Meddis, R., Pearson, D. E., & Ijsselsteijn, W. (2000). Using behavioural realism to estimate presence: A study of the utility of postural responses to motion-stimuli. *Presence (Cambridge, Mass.), 9,* 149–164. doi:10.1162/105474600566691

Gammon, B., & Burch, A. (2008). Designing mobile digital experiences. In Tallon, L., & Walker, K. (Eds.), *Digital technologies and the museum experience: Handheld guides and other media* (pp. 35–60). Lanham, MD: Rowan and Littlefield.

Gee, J. P. (2003). *What video games have to teach us about learning and literacy.* New York, NY: Palgrave Macmillan. doi:10.1145/950566.950595

Greenbaum, J., & Kyng, M. (Eds.). (1991). *Design at work: Cooperative design of computer systems.* Hillsdale, NJ: Lawrence Erlbaum.

Hein, G. E. (1998). *Learning in the museum.* London, UK: Routledge.

Henning, B., & Vorderer, P. (2001). Psychological escapism: Predicting the amount of television viewing by need for cognition. *The Journal of Communication, 51,* 100–120. doi:10.1111/j.1460-2466.2001.tb02874.x

Holzinger, A., Kickmeier-Rust, M., & Albert, D. (2008). Dynamic media in computer science education; content complexity and learning performance: Is less more? *Journal of Educational Technology & Society, 11*(1), 279–290.

Hoptman, G. H. (1992). *The virtual museum and related epistemological concerns* (pp. 141–159). Sociomedia. Multimedia, Hypermedia and the Social Construction of Knowledge.

ICOM/CIDOC. Multimedia working group. (1996). Introduction to multimedia in museums. Retrieved May 1, 2012, from http://www.willpowerinfo.myby.co.uk/cidoc/introtomultimediamuseums.pdf

Ijsselsteijn, W., deRidder, H., Freeman, J., & Avons, S. E. (2000). Presence: Concept, determinants and measurement. In *Proceedings of the SPIE, Human Vision and Electronic Imaging V* (pp. 3959-76).

ISO 9241-11. (1998). Ergonomic requirements for office work with visual display terminals – Part 11: Guidance on usability. Geneva: Switzerland: ISO.

Kafai, Y. B., & Ching, C. C. (1996). Meaningful contexts for mathematical learning: The potential of game making activities. In *Proceedings of the International Conference on Learning Sciences* (pp. 164-171).

Karoulis, A., Sylaiou, S., & White, M. (2006). Usability evaluation of a virtual museum interface. *Journal Informatica, 17*(3), IOS Press, 363-380.

Katz, E., & Foulkes, D. (1962). On the use of mass media for escape: Clarification of a concept. *Public Opinion Quarterly, 26*, 377–388. doi:10.1086/267111

Kerawalla, L., Luckin, R., Seljeflot, S., & Woolard, A. (2006). Making it real: Exploring the potential of augmented reality for teaching primary school science. *Virtual Reality (Waltham Cross), 10*(3), 163–174. doi:10.1007/s10055-006-0036-4

Klimmt, C., & Vorderer, P. (2003). Media psychology "is not yet there": Introducing theories on media entertainment to the presence debate. *Presence (Cambridge, Mass.), 12*(4), 346–359. doi:10.1162/105474603322391596

Lee, K. M. (2004). Presence, explicated. *Communication Theory, 14*(1), 27–50. doi:10.1111/j.1468-2885.2004.tb00302.x

Liarokapis, F., Sylaiou, S., & Mountain, D. (2008). Personalizing virtual and augmented reality for cultural heritage indoor and outdoor experiences. In *Proceedings of the 9th International Symposium on Virtual Reality, Archaeology and Cultural Heritage* (VAST '08) (pp. 55-62). Eurographics, Braga, Portugal.

Lombard, M., & Ditton, T. (1997). At the heart of it all: The concept of presence. *Journal of Computer-Mediated Communication, 3*(2).

London Charter. (2013). *London Charter for the use of 3-dimensional visualisation in the research and communication of cultural heritage*. Retrieved from http://www.londoncharter.org/

MacDonald, G. F., & Alsford, S. (1997). Towards the meta museum. In Jones-Garmil, K. (Ed.), *The wired museum: Emerging technology and changing paradigms*. Washington, DC: American Association of Museums.

Markopoulos, P., & Khan, V. (2011). Sampling and reconstructing user experience. [IJHCR]. *International Journal of Handheld Computing Research, 2*(3), 53–72. doi:10.4018/jhcr.2011070104

Marty, P. F. (2006). Meeting user needs in the modern museum: Profiles of the new museum information professional. *Library & Information Science Research, 28*(1), 128–144. doi:10.1016/j.lisr.2005.11.006

Marty, P. F. (2007). Museum websites and museum visitors: Before and after the museum visit. *Museum Management and Curatorship, 22*(4), 337–360. doi:10.1080/09647770701757708

Marty, P. F. (2011). *Museum informatics*. USA: Florida State University.

Mourkoussis, N., White, M., Patel, M., Chmielewski, J., & Walczak, K. (2003). AMS: Metadata for cultural exhibitions using virtual reality. In *DC-2003 Proceedings of the International DCMI Metadata Conference and Workshop* (pp. 135-144). University of Washington, Information School, Seattle, Washington, USA.

Namioka, A., & Schuler, D. (Eds.). (1993). *Participatory design. Principles and practices*. Hillsdale, NJ: Lawrence Erlbaum.

Nielsen, J. (1993). *Usability engineering*. San Diego, CA: Academic Press.

Nischelwitzer, A., Lenz, F.-J., Searle, G., & Holzinger, A. (2007). Some aspects of the development of low-cost augmented reality learning environments as examples for future interfaces in technology enhanced learning. In *Universal access to applications and services (LNCS 4556)* (pp. 728–737). New York: Springer. doi:10.1007/978-3-540-73283-9_79

O'Brien, H. L., & McLean, K. (2009). Measuring the user engagement experience. *Engagement by Design Pre-Conference Workshop, CHI 2009*. Digital Life New World, Boston, MA.

Polson, P. G., Lewis, C., Rieman, J., & Wharton, C. (1992). Cognitive walkthroughs: A method for theory- based evaluation of user interfaces. *International Journal of Man-Machine Studies, 36*, 741–773. doi:10.1016/0020-7373(92)90039-N

Preece, J. Y., Rogers, H., Sharp, D., & Benyon, S. Holland, & Carey, T. (1994). *Human-computer interaction*. Addison-Wesley.

Rasmussen, J., & Goodstein, L. P. (1988). Information technology and work. In M. Helander (Ed.), *Handbook of Human-Computer Interaction* (pp. 175-201). Elsevier Science Publishers BV (North Holland): New York.

Reeves, S. (2004). *Research techniques for augmented reality experiences*. Retrieved June 20, 2012, from http://www.mrl.nott.ac.uk/~str/doc/methods.pdf

Regenbrecht, H., & Schubert, T. (2002). Measuring presence in augmented reality environments: Design and a first test of a questionnaire. In *Proceedings of the 5th Annual International Workshop Presence 2002*. Porto, Portugal.

Rieber, L. P. (1996). Seriously considering play: Designing interactive learning environments based on the blending of microworlds, simulations, and games. *Educational Technology Research and Development, 44*(1), 43–58. doi:10.1007/BF02300540

Rudman, P., Sharples, M., & Lonsdale, P. (2008). Cross-context learning. In Tallon, L., & Walker, K. (Eds.), *Digital technologies and the museum experience. Handheld guides and other media* (pp. 147–166). Walnut Creek: Altamira Press.

Sanchez-Vives, M. V., & Slater, M. (2005). From presence to consciousness through virtual reality. *Nature Reviews. Neuroscience, 6*(4), 332–339. doi:10.1038/nrn1651

Schmalstieg, D. (2005). Augmented reality techniques in games. In *Proceedings of Fourth IEEE and ACM International Symposium on Mixed and Augmented Reality ISMAR05*.

Schubert, T. W., Friedmann, F., & Regenbrecht, H. (1999). Embodied presence in virtual environments. In Paton, R., & Neilson, I. (Eds.), *Visual representations and interpretations* (pp. 268–278). Springer-Verlag. doi:10.1007/978-1-4471-0563-3_30

Schuemie, M. J., van der Straaten, P., Krijn, M., & van der Mast, C. (2001). Research on presence in virtual reality: A survey. *CyberPsychology Behaviour, 4*(2), 183–201. doi:10.1089/109493101300117884

Schweibenz, W. (1991). The virtual museum: New perspectives for museums to present objects and information using the Internet as a knowledge base and communication system. In H. Zimmermann and H. Schramm (Eds.), *Proceedings of the 6th ISI Conference* (pp. 185-200). Prague, Konstanz, UKV.

Shloerb, D. W. (1995). A quantitative measure of telepresence. *Presence (Cambridge, Mass.), 4*(1), 64–80.

Silverstone, R. (1994). The medium is the museum. In Miles, R., & Zavala, L. (Eds.), *Towards the museum of the future* (pp. 161–176). London, New York: Routledge.

Slater, M. (1999). Measuring presence: A response to the Witmer and Singer Presence questionnaire. *Presence (Cambridge, Mass.)*, *8*(5), 560–565. doi:10.1162/105474699566477

Slater, M. (2004). How colourful was your day? Why questionnaires cannot assess presence in virtual environments. *Presence (Cambridge, Mass.)*, *13*(4), 484–493. doi:10.1162/1054746041944849

Slater, M., & Wilbur, S. (1997). A framework for immersive virtual environments (FIVE): Speculations on the role of presence in virtual environments. *Presence (Cambridge, Mass.)*, *6*, 603–616.

Squire, K., & Barab, S. (2004). Replaying history: Engaging urban underserved students in learning world history through computer simulation games. In *Proceedings of the 6th International Conference on Learning Sciences* (pp. 505-512). Santa Monica, CA: International Society of the Learning Sciences.

Stanney, K. M., Mourant, R. R., & Kennedy, R. S. (1998b). Human factors issues in virtual environments: A review of literature. *Presence (Cambridge, Mass.)*, *7*, 327–351. doi:10.1162/105474698565767

Stanney, K. M., Salvendy, G., Deisigner, J., DiZio, P., Ellis, S., & Ellison, E. (1998a). After effects and sense of presence in virtual environments: Formulation of a research and development agenda. Report sponsored by the Life Sciences Division at NASA Headquarters. *International Journal of Human-Computer Interaction*, *10*(2), 135–187. doi:10.1207/s15327590ijhc1002_3

Steuer, J. (1992). Defining virtual reality: Dimensions determining telepresence. *The Journal of Communication*, *42*(4), 73–93. doi:10.1111/j.1460-2466.1992.tb00812.x

Stevens, B., Jerrams-Smith, J., Heathcote, D., & Callear, D. (2002). Putting the virtual into reality: Assessing object presence with projection augmented models. *Presence (Cambridge, Mass.)*, *11*(1), 79–92. doi:10.1162/105474602317343677

Sussex Past (The Sussex Archaeological Society). (2013). Retrieved June 10, 2012, from http://www.sussexpast.co.uk/

Sweetser, P. M., & Wyeth, P. (2005). GameFlow: A model for evaluating player enjoyment in games. *ACM Computers in Entertainment*, *3*(3), 1–24. doi:10.1145/1077246.1077253

Sylaiou, S., Almosawi, A., Mania, K., & White, M. (2004). 'preliminary evaluation of the augmented representation of cultural objects system. In *Proceedings of the 10ᵗʰ International Conference on Virtual Systems and Multimedia, Hybrid Realities- Digital Partners, Explorations in Art, Heritage, Science and the Human Factor* (pp. 426-431). VSMM Conference, Softopia, Ogaki City, Japan.

Sylaiou, S., Economou, M., Karoulis, A., & White, M., (2008). The evaluation of ARCO: A lesson in curatorial competence and intuition with new technology. *ACM Computers in Entertainment, 6*(2).

Sylaiou, S., Mania, K., Karoulis, A., & White, M. (2009). Presence-centred usability evaluation of a virtual museum: Exploring the relationship between presence, previous user experience and enjoyment. [IJHCS]. *International Journal of Human-Computer Studies, 68*(5), 243–253. doi:10.1016/j.ijhcs.2009.11.002

Sylaiou, S., Mania, K., Liarokapis, F., & White, M. (2012). (Manuscript submitted for publication). Evaluation of an augmented reality educational game. *Journal of Cultural Heritage*.

Thomas, K. (2006). *Augmented reality: A new approach to learning*. FutureLab. Retrieved June 20, 2011, from http://www.futurelab.org.uk/resources/publications_reports_articles/web_articles/Web_Article496

Tsichritzis, D., & Gibbs, S. (1991). Virtual museums and virtual realities. In *Proceedings of InternationalConference on Hypermedia and Interactivity in Museums* (pp 17-25).

Victoria & Albert Museum (VAM). (2013). Website. Retrieved October 6, 2012, from http://www.vam.ac.uk/

Vorderer, P. (2000). Interactive entertainment and beyond. In Zillmann, D., & Vorderer, P. (Eds.), *Media entertainment: The psychology of its appeal* (pp. 21–36). Mahwah, NJ: Lawrence Erlbaum Associates.

Vorderer, P. (2001). It's all entertainment, sure. But what exactly is entertainment? Communication research, media psychology, and the explanation of entertainment experiences. *Poetics, 29*, 247–261. doi:10.1016/S0304-422X(01)00037-7

Walker, K. (2008). Structuring visitor participation. In Tallon, L., & Walker, K. (Eds.), *Digital technologies and the museum experience. Handheld guides and other media* (pp. 109–124). Walnut Creek: Altamira Press.

White, M., Mourkoussis, N., et al. (2004). ARCO-An architecture for digitization, management and presentation of virtual exhibitions. *IEEE Computer Society Conference, 22nd International Conference on Computer Graphics* (pp. 622-625).

Wojciechowski, R., Walczak, K., White, M., & Cellary, W. (2004). Building virtual and augmented reality museum exhibitions. In S. N. Spencer (Ed.), *Proceedings of the Web3D 2004 Symposium –the 9ᵗʰInternational Conference on 3D Web Technology* (pp. 135-144). ACM SIGGRAPH.

Wright, P. (1989). The quality of visitors' experiences in art museums. In Peter Vergo (Ed.), *The new museology* (pp. 119-148). London: Reaktion books.

KEY WORDS AND DEFINITIONS

Evaluation: Evaluation involves assessing the strengths and weaknesses of programs, policies, personnel, products, and organizations to improve their effectiveness (American Evaluation Association).

Learning: Learning is a situation in which an "individual can be conceptualized as being involved in a continuous, contextually driven effort to make meaning of that situation in order to survive and prosper within the world, an effort that is best viewed as a never-ending dialogue between the individual and his or her physical and sociocultural environment" (Gammon & Burch, 2008).

Museum Informatics: A subfield of Cultural Informatics, it is an interdisciplinary field of study that refers to the theory and application of informatics by museums (Marty, 2011).

Presence: Presence is defined as the sense of ''being there'' in a mediated environment, e.g. the degree to which the users feel that they are somewhere other than they physically are while experiencing a computer generated simulation (Shloerb, 1995; Stanney et al., 1998a; Ijsselsteijn et al., 2000).

Usability: Usability of a system is its ability to function effectively and efficiently, while providing subjective satisfaction to its users in a specified context of use (ISO 9241, 1998).

Virtual Museum: ". . .a logically related collection of digital objects composed in a variety of media, and, because of its capacity to provide connectedness and various points of access, it lends itself to transcending traditional methods of communicating and interacting with the visitors being flexible toward their needs and interests; it has no real place or space, its objects and the related information can be disseminated all over the world" (Schweibenz, 1991).

APPENDIX

Cognitive Walkthrough Evaluation

The evaluator executes the scenario and at each step of the interaction, answers the following questions:

- **Q1: Intention – Action:** Will the feasible and correct action be made sufficiently evident to the user and do the actions match with the intention as stated by the user?
- **Q2: Action – Form:** Will the user connect the correct action's description with what he/she trying to do?
- **Q3: Action Input – Feedback Output:** Will the user receive feedback in the same place and modality where he/she has performed his/her action?
- **Q4: Outcome – Form:** Will the user interpret the system's response to the chosen action correctly (i.e., will he/she know if he/she has made a right or wrong choice?)
- **Q5: Form – Assessment:** Will the user properly evaluate the results (i.e., will he/she be able to access if he/she got closer to his/her goal?)
- **Q6: Action/Outcome – Concern:** If the goal is wrong (or can be improved) will the user understand that the intention he/she is trying to fulfill cannot be accomplished with the current state of the world (or will he/she formulate alternative goals?)

Chapter 15
Usability Optimization of a Military Training System

Roberto K. Champney
Design Interactive, Inc., USA

Kay M. Stanney
Design Interactive, Inc., USA

Christina M. Kokini
Design Interactive, Inc., USA

Stephanie Lackey
*University of Central Florida,
Institute for Simulation and Training,
USA*

EXECUTIVE SUMMARY

While the application of usability engineering principles and methods is similar in commercial and military contexts, there are key requirements and challenges in military domains that must be addressed. The aim of this chapter is to describe the application of a combination of usability engineering methods in the development of a military training system. The case involves the research, design, and development of an instructional support system to help instructors and warfighters find and execute suitable training lessons that meet their training needs. Through the application of multiple methods (contextual task analysis, iterative designs, heuristic evaluations, formative and summative evaluations), the requirements for the system were identified, the system was then designed, developed, and iteratively improved to optimize key operational performance identified with the support of field stakeholders.

DOI: 10.4018/978-1-4666-4046-7.ch015

ORGANIZATION BACKGROUND

Design Interactive, Inc. (DI), based in Oviedo, Florida, is a leader in Humans-Systems Integration research and development. DI provides engineering services and consulting in human performance, training systems design and evaluation, cognitive readiness, and next-generation human-systems integration. Our vision is to provide serious solutions and diagnostics for human performance optimization. DI delivers interactive design and evaluation assistance throughout the development lifecycle. DI has an extensive history working and helping organizations achieve human performance optimization with their systems, having worked for research and defense agencies such as the Navy, Army, Air Force, Office of the Secretary of Defense, Department of Homeland Security, DARPA, IARPA, NASA, and Department of Transportation, as well as Fortune 500 Commercial Companies.

University of Central Florida Institute for Simulation and Training (IST), located in Orlando, Florida is an interdisciplinary research institute of the University of Central Florida (UCF) with an annual budget of $15+ M and a staff of 60 research faculty, a dozen research affiliates from other UCF departments and approximately 80 graduate and undergraduate students. IST performs leading edge basic and applied research in the art and science of simulation and actively supports the university's simulation education initiative. IST's research serves public and private human-in-the-loop simulation communities and advances the use of computer simulation for training, education and entertainment. The institute's vision is to be the premier academic research organization internationally recognized for creative, interdisciplinary contributions to the art and science of human-centric simulation. The institute conducts research for many government agencies but includes in its efforts the development of research projects with potential commercial applications and adaptation of military technology to civilian markets.

Lockheed Martin's Global Training and Logistics (GTL) business unit, based in Orlando, Florida, is a leading provider of training and logistics support to customers in more than 50 countries across the globe. From training pilots to fly the world's most advanced fighter jet to training troops to navigate a convoy through a hazardous urban environment, GTL offers decades of experience in helping customers achieve their missions. GTL's Advanced Simulation Center (ASC) in Burlington, Massachusetts provides simulation and training research and development services to a wide range of internal and external customers. With its origins in the United States Defense Advanced Research Projects Agency (DARPA) SIMNET program, ASC technology advances have impacted the entire modeling and simulation industry. These have included fundamental work in simulation networking protocols, semi-automated forces, immersive simulation, and augmented reality.

SETTING THE STAGE

Design Interactive, Inc. (DI) and the Institute for Simulation and Training (IST) were members of a multidisciplinary team involved in a science and technology project that sought to integrate pedagogical insights learned from science into innovative technology to satisfy the instructional field needs of the United States Marine Corps (USMC). The team was charged with conducting research on the latest pedagogical methods and on the instructional needs of Marines in the field. The findings of this research were to be integrated into the design and subsequent development of an instructional support system that Marines could use at their training locations. At the same time, budgetary pressures have forced the military services to "develop results-oriented performance metrics that can be used to evaluate the effectiveness of their training...initiatives" (US Government Accountability Office, 2011). This led the project sponsors to impose key performance criteria that the system should achieve in order to be acceptable for transition into the fleet's repertoire of tools.

Today's Marines take on more roles and master more knowledge, skills, and attitudes than ever before. This is compounded by the military's need to train troops with fewer resources. As a result, increases in efficiency and effectiveness are of key concern and priority. This has created a condition where every opportunity to train must be taken advantage of. At the same time, the budgetary pressures and the promises offered by simulation-based training have combined to produce a great number of training tools which have enabled warfighters to train new skills, maintain skills, and even rehearse missions at relatively low cost and at any time and place. The Deployable Virtual Training Environment (DVTE) is one of these instructional support tools that have been developed to address this challenge; it is comprised of a suite of laptop computers infused with a variety of training programs and simulation applications. Nonetheless, such proliferation of instructional tools has also resulted in a situation where finding and operating the tools is a challenge. Thus it was necessary to bridge this gap by providing a mechanism by which instructional needs and solutions could be matched; this was the premise by which the Instructional Support System (ISS) was conceived and commissioned to the team. The ISS was intended to support instruction conducted via the DVTE system.

At the same time it was important that any tool developed be done so in a manner that would improve conditions for Marines and not present an additional challenge. Thus usability was of utmost importance. The benefits of applying usability engineering methods in the design and development of interactive systems is unquestioned and continues to deliver benefits where applied (Mayhew, 1999; Bias & Mayhew, 2005). One challenge that still exists, though, is the alignment of design with operational performance criteria such that the usability return on investment (ROI) is assessed objectively and as part of the design strategy. Often usability criteria appear subjective to members of an interdisciplinary development team, thus making it difficult for usability engineering practitioners to justify design changes or recommendations. One approach that addresses this is the application of an Iterative Operational Assessment (IOA) approach, which utilizes various methods to objectively assess usability via measurable usability performance measures and align a system's design with operational performance to justify design recommendations. Traditionally, the iterative design process utilizes formative usability evaluations to identify usability issues to be addressed via redesign, while summative usability evaluations don't take place until a final design is ready (Kies, Williges, & Rosson, 1998). The IOA approach is similar, yet it makes use of "pre-summative" evaluations with prototypes to gauge a design's ability to support a desired performance goal. The term "pre-summative" is used to emphasize the empirical rigor by which the formative evaluations are carried through and to highlight the focus on human performance to evaluate the capabilities of a prototype system. The use of the IOA approach allows a design and development team to measure their designs against objective performance targets iteratively and address any deviation from the desired outcome via redesign. This process was applied to the design and development of a military instructional support system with great success. The process and outcomes are discussed next.

The Iterative Operational Assessment Approach

As the word implies, usability is concerned with the ease of use of an artifact. In other words, usability is the measure of how well an artifact can be used by its intended end-users to perform a specific task at a specific criterion (Lin, Choong, & Salvendy, 1997). In more formal and operational terms, usability can be determined by an artifact's ability to support its use in accomplishing a task *effectively, efficiently* and with *satisfaction* (ISO 9241-11, 1998). In order to design products with high levels of usability, a number of tools have been adapted or created that fall under three main groups: User Analysis Methods, Design Methods, and Usability Evaluation Methods (Hartson, Andre, & Williges, 2003; Lansdale & Ormerod, 1994; Kelkar, Khasawneh, Bowling, Gramopadye, Melloy, & Grimes, 2005; Nielsen, 1993; Gray & Salzman, 1998; Usability Net; usability.gov; Usability Professionals Association [UPA]). User Analysis Methods seek to learn and understand details about a product's users, their environment and the context under which the product will be utilized (e.g., focus groups, field observations, task analysis, surveys) (Dillon & Watson, 1996). Design Methods seek to guide the design of the product for better usability (e.g., human factors principles, Visualization and Gestalt principles) (Gillan & Bias, 2001). Usability Evaluation Methods seek to evaluation existing designs for their usability (e.g., heuristic evaluations, subjective usability evaluations, usability testing) (Whitefield, Wilson, & Dowell, 1991). In practice, each of these types of methods is distributed along a design and development timeline where each has a role and a particular type of output, yet it is still necessary to maintain a cohesive direction, particularly given the multiple disciplines that may be involved in the product design and development.

The design and development of interactive systems is a multi-disciplinary effort that must include the inputs and perspectives of a number of disciplines involved. This often involves considerable coordination between disciplines and sub-groups of a design and development team. At the same time, these varied inputs have implications in the usability of a system and thus must be subject to redesign as usability issues are identified. This often involves an iterative approach of design and evaluation where usability practitioners assess designs via subjective and empirical approaches utilizing end-user representatives to identify usability shortcomings (i.e., issues). Two types of evaluations often take place, formative evaluations (Hewett, 1986), which are diagnostic and aim to identify and address any observed usability shortcomings (Hartson, Andre, & Williges, 2001; Quesenbery, 2004), and summative evaluations which aim to quantify the usability performance of a system. The results of these evaluations are used to guide the design of a system in order to address observed usability shortcomings. While summative evaluation findings are usually not used for this purpose but rather to document the usability capabilities of a system, they do provide the means to fine-tune a system to achieve a desired usability performance. In addition summative-type evaluations also provide the means by which to justify design changes, particularly because of the many competing objectives under which a multidisciplinary development effort is constrained. This enables usability practitioners to add weight behind their evaluation reports such that they are not misunderstood as subjective assessments, which is key given that it is likely that software development and management members of the development team will be the ones who determine the validity and criticality of the usability findings (and not the usability practitioners) (Kneifel & Guerrero, 2003). While several useful approaches have been suggested by practitioners (e.g., report formatting guidelines, indoctrination of stakeholders) (Kneifel & Guerrero, 2003; Dumas & Redish, 1999; Redish, Bias, Bailey, Molich, Dumas, & Spool, 2002), they do have limitations. These approaches usually involve significant effort from non-usability members of the development team in participating alongside usability practitioners and thus are time and resource intensive. They also do not address the measurement of performance or support prioritization of observed issues, and may not provide sufficient insight to decision makers in the team (Champney, Kokini, & Stanney, 2011). In order to address these limitations, Champney et al. (2011) proposed the Iterative Operational Assessment (IOA) approach which is integrated in the iterative cycles that take place during the prototype design phase and utilizes both formative and summative-type evaluations iteratively to guide the design.

In contrast to a traditional iterative design and evaluation approaches where formative usability evaluations are performed on prototypes and summative evaluations are performed once the final design is ready, the IOA approach incorporates additional "pre-summative" evaluations on prototypes as illustrated in Figure 1. These "pre-summative" evaluations focus on assessing the human performance support capabilities of the prototype system, thus allowing one to measure the design's capabilities against a desired performance objective. This allows the development team to fine-tune the design in an iterative fashion where any deviation from a desired performance level is observed. Figure 2 presents an overview of the steps involves in executing the IOA approach as described in Champney et al. (2011)

CASE DESCRIPTION

The Team and the Process

As previously discussed, DI and IST were members of a multidisciplinary team involved in a science and technology project. A third member, Lockheed Martin (LM) comprised a group of software developers who, in addition to developing software, were also responsible for technical integration between the ISS, DVTE and

Figure 1. Application of Iterative Operational Assessment (IOA) approach

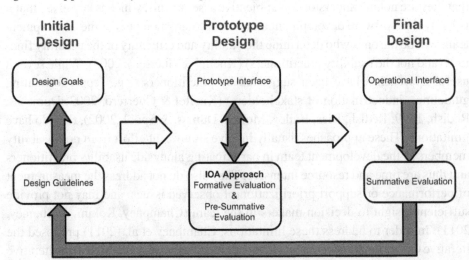

Figure 2. The IOA approach (adapted from Champney, et al. 2011)

the different simulation and software applications that the ISS would interact with. The team was organized such that DI was responsible for field research and design (i.e., conceptual and interface designs), IST was responsible for instructional design research, and LM was responsible for the technical integration and development. DI would conduct field research and develop the concept to fit within the needs of the target users and the research being conducted by IST. At the same time IST would conduct both literature-based and experimental research on instructional strategies which was fed to DI for integration into the ISS concept and design. DI would take the research provided and adapt it for operational use within the ISS design (e.g., change terminology, adjust its presentation, identify locations within system where findings would be applied, design mechanisms for application of research). Once DI had both the concept and system interface designs, these would be delivered to LM for development. The design document was very descriptive and was organized in a series of use cases to facilitate the development team's effort. Nonetheless this process would involve a series of meetings where DI and LM would discuss the design document and address questions or other concerns (e.g., schedule, resources, technology). This process was repeated multiple times over the course of three years.

Field Analysis and User Needs

Military instructors and warfighters have at their disposal a great number of simulation training tools that have been developed in support of their needs. However, this has produced many (sometimes overlapping) training tools which instructors and Marines must learn to identify and operate. This has resulted in unexpected challenges that need to be addressed via the development of the ISS. To this end this effort sought to first identify the field needs of the target population of users.

During this effort, the authors conducted a field and task analysis of the Marine training environment in order to gain insights from end users. To accomplish this, it was first necessary to identify and then locate the different types of end users who would utilize the system. While the team knew of the anecdotal challenges faced by instructors and Marines, it proved to be more challenging to characterize who these types of users were (e.g., only instructors, unit leaders, all Marines), and specifically identify who would utilize it (e.g., all instructors or just a subset). To address this, a series of interviews were conducted with subject matter experts (SMEs) who represented different locations where Marine training took place. This helped the team begin to characterize the environment, all potential training locations, and the key types of users. A select group of field sites were then identified, for which a series of field observations and on-site interviews with potential end-users took place. These interviews resulted in the characterization of 5 key user types: Instructors, Simulation Analysts, Simulation Facilitators, Marine Leaders, and Marines.

- Instructors are individuals who primarily conduct training at schoolhouses and who possess both domain task expertise and pedagogical expertise.
- Simulation Analysts are individuals who assist Instructors or Marine Leaders in creating simulation scenarios, or operating complex simulation applications while stationed on a base. They may also train other Marines to become Simulation Facilitators.
- Simulation Facilitators are Marines who have undergone specialized training to learn to operate the many simulation applications and training tools available to Marines in the field.
- Marine Leaders are the leadership within a group of Marines who have high domain task expertise and may take command of training while outside of the schoolhouse (e.g., while stationed overseas, in transit, or on base).
- Marines are the individuals who will undergo training with any of the instructional tools available.

Following the interviews and field observations, the data was utilized in meetings with stakeholders, including decision makers and the multi-disciplinary development team to share the results and to collectively define the high-level operational objectives for the project. Two objectives are presented here: 1) Enhance instructor efficiency and 2) Enhance instructional effectiveness. The data also allowed the team to uncover more specific field needs which were identified and organized in three key phases, following the phases of a training cycle: Pre-Training, During-Training, Post-Training. Each phase was characterized by specific sets of tasks and objectives.

Pre-Training

This phase is characterized by the preparatory activities that must take place in order to conduct training. In general terms this involves the identification of training needs (i.e., what needs to be trained) and the selection of training materials. Based on the field study, it was observed that this process was highly manual, non-standardized outside of schoolhouses, and lacked any automated support. This highlighted several challenges faced by the target users in this phase:

- **Training System Selection:** Currently users who conduct training (e.g., Instructors or Marine Leaders) have a wide choice of training tools from which to select. Nonetheless they must rely on their own knowledge to know which tools are available and which one to use; and even when a tool is known the user must still identify or create their own content. While "train-the-trainer" courses are available to develop Simulation Facilitators, who can then assist Instructors and Marine Leaders in developing relevant content, these individuals' proficiency is still affected by memory decay when they don't use the simulation application for long periods of time.

- **System Setup:** The preparation for conducting training and configuration of instructional tools is a manual process that may be cumbersome and lengthy for some types of training. Users who are familiarized with the technical "know-how" are still faced with a tedious set-up process where at times individual computers must be networked and applications initialized with the correct files and settings. This often requires considerable interaction, familiarization, and memorization of a system (e.g., a simulation application).

- **Scenario Selection:** This is a challenge given that there is no available reference to link existing scenarios with training objectives, and even when scenarios are available at one site, they are not necessarily shared with other sites. Of the existing training tools available, some contain pre-assembled curriculum while others serve as open-ended training platforms. With the latter ones, very few, if any, have distributed training materials and scenarios available from which to choose.

- **Scenario Creation:** In the absence of finding an existing suitable scenario, Instructors or Marine Leaders must develop new ones along with accompanying training content that supports a particular training objective either from 'scratch' or through adaptation of stored scenarios. While these users do possess the subject matter knowledge to develop and adapt scenarios on paper, the task does require technical skills to instantiate these ideas into a simulation application (e.g., from Simulation Facilitators or Simulation Analysts). In addition scenario design is a time-intensive and high workload task.

- **Pre-Training Materials:** In addition to having few scenarios to choose from there, is also a lack of availability and sharing of supporting instructional materials (e.g. maps, operational orders, etc.) and performance metrics associated with the scenarios.

During-Training

This phase is characterized by the execution of the training (e.g., a scenario), and by the assessment of trainee performance against a set of criteria (e.g., measures associated with training objectives). Based on the field study, two key challenges were observed:

- **Measures of Performance:** For instructional tools that serve as open-ended training platforms, there is a lack of integrated performance data collection that results from the user's (i.e. Instructor's) observational assessments. These assessments are made by the user and based on reference material sourced elsewhere (e.g., training manuals) or from domain knowledge (e.g., expertise). Thus the onus falls on the user conducting the training to maintain consistency and objectivity.
- **Training Adaptation:** It is often the case that a training scenario may need 'real-time' adaptation to ensure that key experiences within the simulation are encountered in order to drive a desired learning objective. In these situations, or when a training objective is not achieved, an instructor will intervene by querying the trainees or by adjusting the scenario to address key training point. These interventions often require technical expertise and lack any technical support by the instructional tools.

Post-Training

This phase is characterized by the after-action review activities that take place once a training exercise takes place (e.g., revisiting what occurred during training and providing guidance to the trainees). Based on the field study, two key challenges were observed:

- **Performance Diagnosis:** Due to the largely observation-based assessments, instructors tend to focus on outcome measures and tend to time their observations based on prior-knowledge of particular challenging portions of a task. While this may reveal the outcome of task, it does not provide the ability to identify root causes or error patterns of task failure during mission training (e.g., Why was a task failed? Who was responsible for the failure?). The lack of diagnostic tools available in the field results in reduced granularity of the feedback provided to trainees, which may impact training effectiveness.

- **Storage of Trainee Data:** While there is some record-keeping of required training progress and sustainment requirements, there is a lack of automated storage capabilities that not only capture event completion for trainees but also pattern data. When done manually, data recording and record-keeping results in additional workload for already busy leadership.

Together these findings resulted in a set of challenges that the system under development should attend to. The identified challenges not only affect those conducting the training but have implications regarding the trainee's performance; thus having an impact on overall training effectiveness.

System Design

Once the field challenges were identified, the team, together with project sponsors and field representative SMEs, collaborated to prioritize and identify those challenges that would be addressed within the scope of the ISS project. While the team determined that all challenges should be addressed, the effort required to attend to some of them was of such magnitude that scope limitations were set (e.g., scenario creation, training adaptation, performance diagnosis). As such, efforts for these would be limited to proof of concepts that would seek solution options to be implemented in subsequent efforts.

In order to address these needs, targeted capabilities were sought out for design and development. These capabilities focused on finding solutions to reduce or eliminate the difficulties faced by the target users. Within this case study, two key capabilities that addressed the pre-training challenges will be discussed in further detail: 1) the infrastructure to link training materials to operationally relevant training objectives, and 2) training launch and assessment support capabilities. The following are short descriptions of the system capabilities that were designed and developed.

Training Objective Link Infrastructure

As discussed earlier, three of the key pre-training challenges were training system selection, scenario selection, and pre-training materials, which implied that users had difficulty finding the right training materials and tools to suit their training needs. To this end, an infrastructure was devised within the ISS by which training materials, scenarios, and their necessary instructional tools could be linked to operational training objectives. This involved the design of a content library populated with training lessons (i.e., scenarios, instructor instructions, briefing materials and any other support materials) that were linked to operationally relevant training objectives (accompanied by relevant descriptions, and assessment metrics and criteria). During the field study, it was found that Marines utilize training manuals that prescribe specific tasks and conditions that trainees must be able to accomplish as part of their training, and therefore the system was designed such that the format and organization of these manuals could be integrated as the training objectives to which lessons were linked. This allows users to correctly identify training lessons by searching or browsing for key words or specific training objectives. Further, via the capability to define relationships between training objectives, the system made progress-tracking and future training recommendations possible.

Training Setup and Launching

In its present form, the process of setting up and beginning a training exercise with some of the instructional tools available is cumbersome and in some instances very time-consuming. The process requires specific technical skills and memorization, and the time and workload is greatly increased as the number of trainees taking part of the training increases. To address this, the capability to have the system automatically guide, store and automate some of these tasks was designed and developed in the ISS. The system was designed to contain pre-programmed set-up variables and other sub-capabilities that automate the training initiation tasks (e.g., an instructor can select a desired lesson and the system can launch it automatically).

Together these capabilities were designed to address the challenges encountered in the pre-training phase of a training cycle. While in general terms these capabilities were expected to address these challenges, a key factor that influences the success of these is the manner in which the functionalities are instantiated in an interactive system design. As such, the design of these capabilities evolved via an iterative approach; first through low fidelity mockups (e.g., Visio drawings) that were evaluated using heuristic methods (e.g., evaluated by a usability engineer not involved in the design of the system) and later through interactive prototypes from which user testing could be done.

Design Evaluation

As the design of the system took place, it was evaluated against the set of performance criteria identified and agreed upon with the project sponsors. This would ensure that the system design would be capable of accomplishing the desired performance goals. While utilizing design guidelines or other predictive modeling methods may guide a design or suggest a performance capability, it is not until a system is tested by target users that one can really evaluate its performance. To this end, a series of empirical evaluations were conducted. As illustrated in the IOA approach earlier, the nature of these evaluations was both formative and summative; i.e., the system was evaluated to identify both usability shortcomings and usability performance. Together the findings from these evaluations were used to guide the design further and enhance its usability.

Participants

A total of 56 Marines and SMEs (Simulation Analysts and Schoolhouse Instructors), about 93% male and ranging in age from 19-55 (mean = 25) years, were recruited to participate in the studies. About 83% were directly responsible for training Marines in some capacity. Given the availability of suitable participants, the number of participants per study varied from 9-16 individuals.

Method

The effort resulted in what could be described as a between-groups design in which each group of participants interacted with a different version of the system (V1 to V4), including a baseline condition (without the ISS). Throughout the project, after each version was completed, heuristic evaluations, formative user testing and pre-summative evaluations took place. The particular focus on this case study is on the pre-summative evaluations and on how these helped define and shape the design of the ISS.

In order to assess the systems performance in supporting the users tasks, task performance from representative tasks identified to be aligned with the challenges was collected for analysis. Given that the ISS would support any of the many instructional tools available, the team selected one system as the baseline condition with guidance from the project sponsors and SMEs. This baseline system would be used to represent the current conditions under which users operate. In this case, the baseline system was a set of simulation applications configured to operate together within a small network. Using the baseline system, each computer taking place in the simulation training must be configured individually every time a scenario is to be executed. The ISS was designed to be able to support this challenge and store configuration settings such that set-up could be executed remotely and with ease.

For the purposes of the pre-training challenges identified and addressed by the ISS design (the focus of this case study), two key tasks were used to represent the field tasks: 1) selecting a suitable scenario and 2) setting up a training operation. All participants were screened for familiarity with the baseline system, and only those familiar with the baseline system were allowed to participate in order to mitigate for familiarity bias. The following is a description of the tasks used for the evaluation:

- **Task 1:** This task involved finding a suitable scenario to match a given training objective. The scenario chosen for the evaluations was an existing scenario that is available in all versions of the baseline system. An SME was asked to map a training objective to this scenario such that a participant would be given this training objective and then asked to find a suitable scenario. Performance was measured by evaluating whether the participant selected the correct scenario.
- **Task 2:** This task involved selecting a specific scenario, configuring the application settings to execute the scenario, and launching it for a team of five imaginary trainees on their respective computers. Performance was measured by evaluating the time to launch the scenario for the team.

Results

Throughout the effort there were a variety of specific issues identified via the usability evaluations of each version of the ISS. These issues were then utilized to inform the design changes for the following versions. However, for the focus of this case study, the evolution of one particular screen within the ISS had a large impact on users' performance of the tasks described above. Within the flow of the tasks chosen for this case, one particular screen is required to make a selection for a lesson (Task 1), and is also part of the larger task of setting up a training exercise (Task 2).This screen, called "Select Lesson," experienced significant changes, helping to exemplify how the IOA was applied. The following is a presentation of how the evolution of the screen took place across versions.

- **ISS V1:** The first ISS design supporting these tasks was instantiated as a set of 'tabs' which supported the user in moving from one step to the next. This was intended to support the multiple steps that were required to accomplish the task of setting up a training exercise correctly and ensure that no steps were missed; it even included a status panel showing how many steps had been accomplished and which remained to be completed, as well as some diagnostic information of what was missing. Figure 4 shows a low fidelity diagram of the design approach. Usability results of this design showed that while it was better than baseline for both tasks, users often navigated back and forth between two of the tabs (i.e. Select Training Objective tab had to be completed before Select Lesson just to choose a lesson.). Though users seemed to be able to navigate through the screens, it was very inefficient. If a mistake or change needed to be made, they may have to go back to the previous tab, sometimes multiple times.

- **ISS V2:** Based on the usability evaluation of V1, a second iteration was designed to address the usability issued identified. In the V2 design, this particular screen integrated the functionality of two tabs in the V1 design (i.e., combined the Select Training Objective and Select Lesson tabs) among other design features (e.g., numbered labels to show order of functions, active next/back buttons). Figure 5 illustrates how the design changed. The usability evaluation showed that while efficiency (performance of Task 2) was greatly improved due to the reduced navigation, users had some difficulty with effectiveness (performance of Task 1). Further inquiry revealed that the increase in the amount of information on the screen made the screen too complex and consequently confusing to users. This resulted in a significant decrease in performance in terms of accurately choosing a relevant lesson to train to a particular training objective. Therefore, this version of the screen was efficient but not effective.

- **ISS V3:** The usability evaluation of V2 revealed the need for redesign in order to better support Task 1. The major design change made in an attempt to simplify the screen was to clearly display the selection method options, which were a key source of user confusion. Figure 6 illustrates the strategy utilized in which the selection options became radio buttons that were mutually exclusive and simply displayed. Users were less confused by this design since it reduced the amount of controls to only those relevant to the option selected. This also increased efficiency due to the clearer presentation of functions. Additionally, a keyword search option was added based on feedback that was repeatedly received by users. The usability evaluation of V3 revealed the efficacy of this design as performance on both tasks improved. It also revealed that the keyword search was a very popular option, being a search method that most users were familiar with, and consequently the performance of finding an appropriate lesson also increased. However, the keyword search in this version only searched words in the title of the lesson, limiting user performance because the correct lesson did not appear in the narrowed down list of lessons if the keyword they searched did not appear in the lesson title.

- **ISS V4:** Based on the usability findings of V3 a new iteration was created in V4. In this version the keyword search included words in the lesson title, training objective title, and lesson keywords defined by the lesson creator.

Figure 3. Training cycle

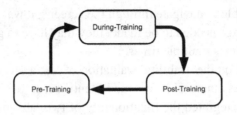

Figure 4. V1 of the ISS select lesson screen

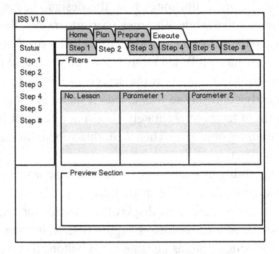

   The iterative evaluations supported the continuous improvement of the design. As may be observed in Figures 3 and 4, the findings from one evaluation yielded sufficient insight to continuously improve upon the system's usability performance. The evaluation results showed that a 98% and 79% improvement for Tasks 1 and 2 respectively could be achieved with the latest version of the ISS as compared to the baseline condition. One striking finding was the performance curve for Task 1 where performance decrease was found for V2. After careful review of the design, it was observed that the design enhancements implemented in V2 to support higher efficiencies in Task 2 had a negative effect on the performance of Task 1 (see Figures 7 and 8). Yet given the iterative approach used, these findings were used to address these limitations and achieve the positive results observed on Task 1 for subsequent versions.

Figure 5. V2 of the ISS select lesson screen

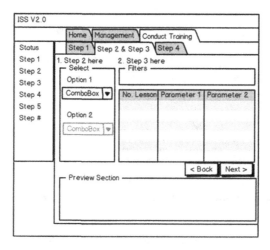

Figure 6. V3 of the ISS select lesson screen

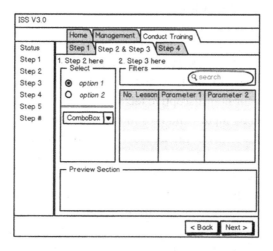

Figure 7. Task 1 performance across versions

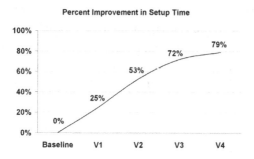

Figure 8. Task 2 performance across versions

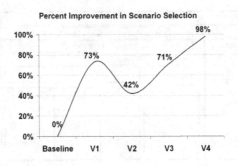

CHALLENGES FACED BY THE ORGANIZATION

Throughout the project, several challenges were encountered and addressed. What follows is a brief discussion of these challenges and how they were addressed.

Team and Process Challenges

The team had prior experience working on this type of project such that it was familiar with each other's capabilities. Nonetheless some challenges did exist. One challenge was the integration of field and science input given that the needs from the field often called for non-disruptive technologies that would allow the greatest flexibility while science input called for more strict conditions and requirements. This was understandable given the already heavy workloads placed on the target users whose processes may be disrupted by one more system. To address this challenge, the team adapted the research findings to meet the operational environment, for example by adjusting the terminology such that it was understood by them or providing options to utilize or not utilize the recommendations of the system. Another challenge was having remote teams. While both DI and IST are collocated in the same city in the southeast, the LM team was in the northeast part of the country. To address this challenge, the team relied on constant contact via weekly or biweekly teleconference calls, and in-person demonstration meetings every 6 months. A third challenge was having remote users. Target end users were located across the country and thus gaining access to them was a challenge. In order to reach users, DI would make field trips to meet groups of users at specific sites, and use other creative ways to get opportunities to get users in front of the system. In one instance even using remote-desktop and Voice Over IP software to allow a user in Iraq utilize the system.

Field Analysis Challenges

The length of the project (over 3 years) allowed the team sufficient time to explore and get to know the domain. Nonetheless this process had its challenges given the use of Marine users who have heavy workloads and limited accessibility. As described in the preceding section, initially the challenge was in identifying who exactly would be the most likely users of the ISS. Yet once this had been established, a challenge still remained in gaining access to individuals who fit that description and who were located in the continental US (i.e., not deployed to a war front, on transit on a ship, or on a remote base). To address this challenge, the team worked diligently with a Marine liaison to identify suitable locations and users; the team would then prepare and travel to a particular site on specific dates when users were available. Even then the team had to ensure that their inquiries or evaluations did little to disrupt Marine activities taking place and be aware that users were volunteers and could choose not to participate.

System Design Challenges

As with any design effort, a challenge always exists when a desired level of performance is required. Given that the link between a particular design and a desired performance level is not guaranteed due to the synergistic effect of the multiple design elements (e.g., organization, labels, terminology, context, etc.), this requires an iterative approach by which a design is tested for its performance. The team relied on the IOA approach and the use of pre-summative evaluations to assess the design against a desired level of performance and make design changes in order to specifically target the desired performance objectives.

Design Evaluation Challenges

During the evaluation of the ISS, the team was primarily challenged with the access to sufficient users to conduct the pre-summative evaluations. Given the additional quantitative rigor of the pre-summative evaluations, a higher number of users were necessary for the analysis. This additional requirement presented a challenge given the already difficult availability of participants. To address this, the team targeted locations and dates that coincided with opportunities when multiple users would be collocated for a particular event (e.g. a training course). This allowed the team access to multiple users during a short amount of time and in sufficient numbers.

Ongoing Challenges

During the course of this effort, a working version of the ISS was developed and optimized to meet specific human performance levels such that it could be transitioned and utilized by the fleet. As this process takes place the system is adopted by its end user community and it will take a life of its own. Given that it is a new product and not one replacement to an existing legacy system, new challenges are likely to emerge as new uses and types of users are encountered. Aside from these unpredictable challenges, there are operational challenges that its new user community will need to address such as creation, expansion and maintenance of its libraries, code update distributions, and the creation of specific security protocols to protect its data and use.

SOLUTIONS AND RECOMMENDATIONS

Given the very powerful effect in guiding the design of the ISS via the application of the IOA approach, it is believed that continued application of the method in ongoing refinement or expansion of the system should be maintained. Regardless of the team involved in the effort, the application of the approach should be sufficient to ensure that the system's capabilities to support human performance aligned with the identified objectives are maintained and enhanced.

ACKNOWLEDGMENT

This material is based upon work supported in part by the Office of Naval Research (ONR) under contract N00014-08-C-0186. Any opinions, findings and conclusions or recommendations expressed in this material are those of the authors and do not necessarily reflect the views or the endorsement of ONR.

REFERENCES

Bias, R. G., & Mayhew, D. J. (2005). *Cost-justifying usability*. San Francisco, CA: Morgan Kaufmann Publishers, Inc.

Champney, R., Kokini, C., & Stanney, K. (2011). Making the design process more usable: Aligning design with user performance. In *Proceedings of the Human Computer Interaction International Conference*. July 9-14. Orlando, Florida. USA.

Dillon, A., & Watson, C. (1996). User analysis in HCI: The historical lesson from individual differences research. *International Journal of Human-Computer Studies, 45*(6), 619–637. doi:10.1006/ijhc.1996.0071

Dumas, J. S., & Redish, J. C. (1999). *A practical guide to usability testing* (2nd ed.). Portland, OR: Intellect.

Gillan, D. J., & Bias, R. G. (2001). Usability science. I: Foundations. *International Journal of Human-Computer Interaction, 13*(4), 351–372. doi:10.1207/S15327590I-JHC1304_02

Gray, D. W., & Salzman, M. C. (1998). Damaged merchandise? A review of experiments that compare usability evaluation methods. *Human-Computer Interaction, 12*, 203–261. doi:10.1207/s15327051hci1303_2

Hartson, H. R., Andre, T. S., & Williges, R. C. (2001). Criteria for evaluating usability evaluation methods. *International Journal of Human-Computer Interaction, 13*(4), 373–410. doi:10.1207/S15327590IJHC1304_03

Hartson, H. R., Andre, T. S., & Williges, R. C. (2003). Criteria for evaluating usability evaluation methods. *International Journal of Human-Computer Interaction, 15*(1), 145–181. doi:10.1207/S15327590IJHC1501_13

Hewett, T. T. (1986). The role of iterative evaluation in designing systems for usability. In Harrison, M. D., & Monk, A. F. (Eds.), *People & computers: Designing for usability*. Cambridge: Cambridge University Press.

Kelkar, K., Khasawneh, M. T., Bowling, S. R., Gramopadye, A. K., Melloy, B. J., & Grimes, L. (2005). The added usefulness of process measures over performance measures in interface design. *International Journal of Human-Computer Interaction, 18*(1), 1–18. doi:10.1207/s15327590ijhc1801_1

Kies, J. K., Williges, R. C., & Rosson, M. B. (1998). Coordinating computer-supported cooperative work: A review of research issues and strategies. *Journal of the American Society for Information, 49*, 776–779.

Kneifel, A. A., & Guerrero, C. (2003). Using participatory inquiry in usability analysis to align a development team's mental model with its users' needs. In *Proceedings of the Society for Technical Communication 50th annual conference*. May 18-21, Dallas, Texas, USA.

Lansdale, M. W., & Ormerod, T. C. (1994). *Understanding interfaces: A handbook of human-computer dialogue*. San Diego, CA: Academic Press.

Lin, H. X., Choong, Y. Y., & Salvendy, G. (1997). A proposed index of usability: A method for comparing the relative usability of software systems. *Behaviour & Information Technology, 16*(4/5), 267–278. doi:10.1080/014492997119833

Mayhew, D. J. (1999). *The usability engineering lifecycle*. San Francisco, CA: Morgan Kaufmann Publishers, Inc.

Nielsen, J. (1993). *Usability engineering*. Boston: Academic Press.

Quesenbery, W. (2004). Defining a summative usability test for voting systems: A report from the UPA 2004 Workshop on Voting and Usability (Online). *Usability Professional's Association*. Retrieved January 20, 2008, from http://www.usability-professionals.org/upa_projects/voting_and_usability/documents/voting_summative_test.pdf

Redish, J., Bias, R. G., Bailey, R., Molich, R., Dumas, J., & Spool, J. M. (2002). Usability in practice: Formative usability evaluations – evolution and revolution. In *Proceedings of the Computer Human Interaction conference*. April 20-25. Minneapolis, Minnesota, USA.

Whitefield, A., Wilson, F., & Dowell, J. (1991). A framework for human factors evaluation. *Behaviour & Information Technology, 10*(1), 65–79. doi:10.1080/01449299108924272

KEY TERMS AND DEFINITIONS

Formative Evaluation: A form of usability evaluation that seeks to identify usability problems with a design prior to the release of a final design. The objective of this type of evaluation is to find usability issues such that they may be addressed via redesign in a next iteration of a design.

Iterative Operational Assessment (IOA) Approach: Is an approach to design and evaluate interactive systems that utilizes pre-summative evaluations in parallel with formative evaluations to adjust a design such that it is aligned with pre-set operational objectives of human performance. Further details of the approach are discussed in Champney, Kokini, and Stanney (2011).

Pre-Summative Evaluation: A form of usability evaluation that is less rigorous than a summative evaluation and conducted on a prototype version of the system. The goal of the pre-summative evaluation is of a formative nature where the primary objective is to assess the usability performance capability of the system and diagnose the source of any limitation on that performance. Based on the results of a pre-summative evaluation, a design is modified to address the observed level of human performance.

Stakeholders: Are those individuals or entities within or outside a development effort which have an impact or are impacted by the system under development. These may include those that are directly impacted by the usability of the system such as end-users or those indirectly affected by the use of the system, but they may also include others such as project sponsors or clients, marketing and sales individuals, team members. Given their various roles and relationships to the project stakeholders have varying degrees of influence in the direction of a development effort. As usability practitioners it is important to maintain a strong advocacy for those who are directly impacted by the system but may not have a direct manner with which to influence the design of system (i.e., its end-users).

Summative Evaluation: A form of usability evaluation that seeks to assess the efficacy of a final design in achieving the desired usability performance level. This type of evaluation is more rigorous than a formative as it requires quantitative assessments that may be utilized to compare one system against another. It is usually performed on a finished design and not on a prototype.

Usability: Is the construct that defines the ease of use of a system. It is strictly concerned with how usable a system is by its intended end-user community and traditionally composed of effectiveness (can the user's tasks be accomplished?), efficiency (how effortlessly and quickly can a task be accomplished?) and satisfaction (how satisfied are users with the manner in which the task is accomplished?) measures. While the more encompassing construct of User Experience (UX) has gained popularity recently, usability is still a key component of that experience that is focused and concerned with the optimization of use.

Usability Methods: Are approaches that are utilized to support the design of interactive systems and ensure high usability by its intended users. There are three types of Usability Methods: User Analysis, Design, and Evaluation. User Analysis methods seek to inform about who the design is form (its users). Design methods seek to inform the design based on best practices or design guidelines. Finally Evaluation methods seek to evaluate the design for its usability qualities and inform redesign.

Chapter 16
Pogo Chat

Rochelle Edwards
Electronic Arts Inc., USA

EXECUTIVE SUMMARY

Pogo.com, an Electronic Arts (EA) casual gaming website, has over 150 games. The older, timeless games, around 610 horizontal pixels, are neighbored by an online group chat window which allows players to communicate during gameplay. Newer games do not have the same size constraints, some as wide as 760 horizontal pixels. These newer games originally lacked a chat window; however, the feedback from Pogo users was clear – they wanted the ability to chat. This paper will focus on the iterative usability testing utilized in determining if and how chat should be added into these new games on Pogo. The chat solutions as well as some challenges faced in reaching these solutions are discussed. While players wanted a chat window in all games, they did not want it to interfere with their game play. There was a preference for multiple chat solutions depending on the size of the game brick.

ORGANIZATION BACKGROUND

Pogo.com, EA's casual gaming website, has been a steady place for players to play casual games including card games, word games, puzzle games, and more for over 12 years. Pogo, which was originally called the Total Entertainment Network (TEN), was acquired by EA in February 2001. The average player tends to be female and above the age of 35. Individuals who play at Pogo.com can play as a guest (where there is no barrier to entry), as a free player (where users sign up to create a user-

DOI: 10.4018/978-1-4666-4046-7.ch016

name which allows them to save their scores and more), or as a Club Pogo player (where a monthly or annual fee is paid, giving Club players access to added features and games). Free players and Club players have access to an online group chat window which is pinned to the right side of the vast majority of games (see Figure 1). For all games on Pogo, players manually select a chat room (or have the system choose one automatically to start a game faster). These chat rooms accommodate up to 60 players, and each chat room has its own group chat. Chatting takes place more commonly in slower-paced games such as *Pogo Bowl* or *Hog Heaven Slots*, where players may socialize while playing to enhance the gaming experience. In all games, players can chat during timed games by pausing them if they have been focusing on gameplay...or if their focus is more on socialization than game score or completion, players can always chat and let the timer run out. Players can also chat before games begin, once games end, and during intermissions (the latter being found for the free audience). In multiplayer games like *Spades*, *Canasta*, and *Dominoes*, the chat room is limited to the players at the table, and a player can then communicate with other teammates and/or opponents as well as individuals who are watching the game. The chat window also works to relay pertinent information, such as recent prize winners and achievement progress. In regard to the latter, Club Pogo players partake in daily and weekly challenges. For example, a weekly challenge may involve matching all four seasons in 10 games on *Mahjong Garden*. Players are able to see how far along they are in finishing a challenge by looking at the chat window – after a successful game, the window will reflect the progress (i.e. "All four seasons matched 3 of 7 times").

SETTING THE STAGE

Games without Chat

In order to appease current players and to pique the interest of new players, Pogo looks to bring fresh new games to its website. While there are some long-lived favorites that do not grow stale, players (including the loyal audience who has been with Pogo since its inception as well as a newer audience) seek novelty among the games. Some of these games are first featured on Facebook, and due to their popularity, are then brought over to Pogo.com. Pogo Games, a Facebook application, was introduced in 2010. It contains over 25 games, such as *SCRABBLE*, *Poppit!*, *BATTLESHIP*, *Pogo Bowl*, *MONOPOLY*, and *Rainy Day Spider Solitaire*. Many of the Pogo Games, such as the aforementioned titles, are already available on Pogo.

Figure 1. A game offered on Pogo.com, Poppit!, displaying a typical chat which is affixed to the right side of Pogo.com games. (© 2012, Electronic Arts Inc. used with permission)

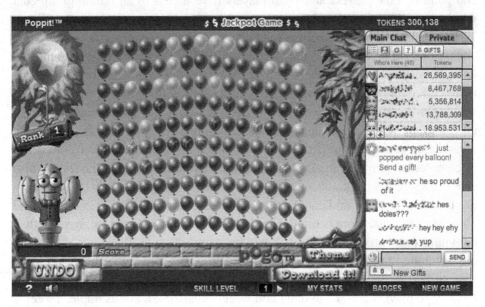

com; however, some titles (such as *Poppit! Sprint* and *Who Has the Biggest Brain*) were available first via Pogo Games, and it was deemed appropriate to bring them over to Pogo.com to increase the game library. Other games that were brought to Pogo.com from Facebook were developed by other EA subsidiaries, such as PopCap, including *Bejeweled 3*, *Plants vs. Zombies*, and *Zuma's Revenge*.

When playing games on the Pogo Games application on Facebook, the games that are carried over from Pogo.com have the same look and feel as they do on Pogo.com – the playing space does not fill the whole screen, and a chat window is embedded to the right of the game page. Additionally, the chat is filled with Pogo. com and Pogo Games gamers. However, the games that are brought to Pogo.com from Facebook, whether they came from Pogo Games or a PopCap game, have a different look and feel that is new to Pogo.com. Some of these games are larger because they were originally created for Facebook. Additionally, these games do not have an embedded chat area and are not compatible with the original Pogo chat from Figure 1 (see Figure 2). There is sufficient room on the page to shift the narrowest of games which has around 610 vertical pixels, creating enough white space to the right of the game for a chat window. This is not the case for all games. For example, wider games can have as much as 760 vertical pixels and do not have this extra

Figure 2. A newer game offered on Pogo.com, Bejeweled 3. This game lacked a chat window when it was first brought to the Pogo.com website. Of the newer games, this game is narrower, as there is white space to the right and left of the game brick. The game could be shifted left, making room for a chat window to the right of the game. (© 2012, Electronic Arts Inc. used with permission)

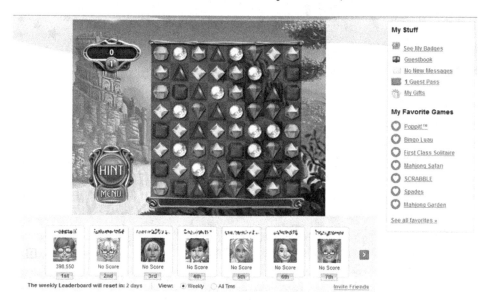

white space (see Figure 3). The right-hand panel where My Stuff and My Favorite Games are located is not even available real estate when considering the addition of a chat window for free players (see Figure 4). The designer had to consider a solution for all of these different scenarios – would a one-size-fits-all solution work best, or would each scenario require its own version for chat?

This chapter discusses the process and solution for chat windows across the various game widths. As the reader, you are welcome to put yourself into the shoes of the researcher or designer – what solutions do you see for these more complex scenarios? How would your approaches to designing and testing prototypes differ from that which is performed in the remainder of this chapter?

Why Add Chat?

The new games that lacked chat were introduced to Pogo.com starting in early 2011. Their initial response was quite positive. Marketing analysts on the team tracked performance from game to game using metrics such as daily or monthly active users (DAU or MAU), and it appeared that while most games on Pogo.com

Figure 3. A newer game offered on Pogo.com, Cirque du Flea. This game also lacked chat when it was first brought to Pogo.com. Unlike Bejeweled 3, this game is wider and there is no room to accommodate a chat window to the right side of the game. (© 2012, Electronic Arts Inc. used with permission)

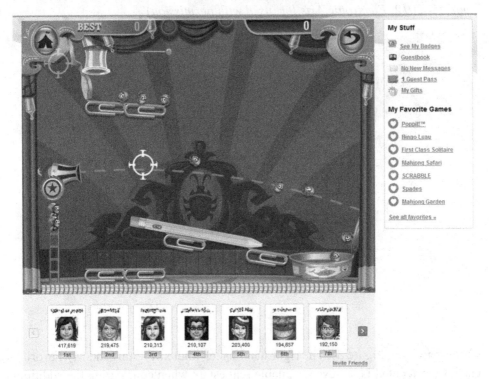

were steady, the new games were indicating a decline. The question, of course, was why? It was determined that chat was contributing to this decline from examination of player feedback. First, Pogo routinely collects quarterly feedback from close to 10,000 randomly-selected players. After release of these games, some players made specific mention to the fact that they could not chat in the newer games. Second, player comments were recorded from the Pogo forums. For example, one player stated, "Just played Bejeweled and there is no chat or a way to see my progress with getting the 33 Flames," indicating that without the chat window in *Bejeweled 3*, she could not chat or track her weekly badge progress, two key features for which players depend on the chat window. Third, during usability testing, the researcher asked users if they played some of the new games such as *Bejeweled 3* or *Zuma's Revenge*. Feedback from these users indicated that the lack of chat was seen as a missing feature and for some, deterred them from playing games that did not have chat. From these users' comments, a persona, or a fictional character could be created

Pogo Chat

Figure 4. Cirque du Flea as it appears for a free or guest player. In this case, there are advertisements. If a chat window were to be implemented, these advertisements cannot be moved and a chat window cannot cover them. (© 2012, Electronic Arts Inc. used with permission)

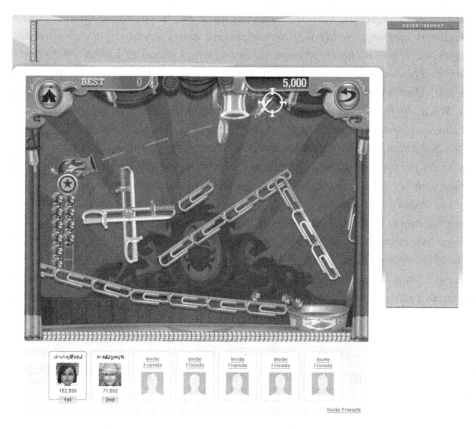

from observation or interviews with real customers demonstrating user wants and needs. This persona could help guide the development of chat in the new games to make sure that it would incorporate desires of players who regularly interface with the chat window. Such a persona is detailed below:

Sandy, a 43 year old housewife, sits down with her laptop in the kitchen at 8:30am once she has returned from dropping her daughter off at school. Coffee in hand, she is eager to start today's badge challenges. She boots up her computer, launches a browser, and selects Pogo from her favorites list. Last night, she and her daughter played on Pogo with her 12-year old niece, Jennifer. Jennifer lives 500 miles away, so the family enjoys their time online together. Jennifer always wants to play MONOPOLY The World Edition, which Sandy's daughter Leah loves, but Sandy isn't terribly fond of. Of course, she would never tell Leah and Jennifer that... They always go into the same chat room – "Shoe" – and they sit at a table together (along with two robot players). Once at the table, Sandy and Leah on one computer, and Jennifer on another, are free to chat about their lives and the game while they play for the next hour. Today, however, Sandy is following her morning routine. Every Wednesday morning, Sandy will devote several hours to playing the two weekly challenges. The first challenge required her to win 4 games of Euchre by 2 points or more. This was a game she had never played, and she didn't have the patience to learn. After several losses, she started chatting in the chat room to look for game tips. What she found was a partner who was willing to not only explain the game, but throw several matches to speed up the process so Sandy could earn her badge faster. She happily did the same in return, with very little effort, and she also added this sweet person, nicknamed "lilmissy218," to her friends list so she could play games with her in the future. The second challenge required her to pop 8400 balloons in Poppit! Sprint. After playing for several minutes, she noticed the absence of a chat room, which she relies upon to track her challenge progress. How can she see how many balloons she has popped? Beyond the challenge, how would she know if her friends came online? What if she wanted to talk to others about game strategy? Once Sandy finished the challenge, she went back to the Pogo homepage. She hadn't played that Poppit! Sprint game before, and thought it was fairly fun, but it just wasn't the same without having chat there. It just seemed...empty. With that, she went to play one of her favorite games, Hog Heaven Slots. She entered the same chat room as always, "Coffee Talk," and greeted the room as she started playing. She was instantly welcomed back by three online friends of hers, and they engaged in friendly conversation while they played...

From the persona, the deficit from the new chat was apparent, particularly for active players such as Sandy. Indeed, it seems that having the ability to chat while playing is a core feature to Pogo.com. A product manager (PM) worked to create a project starting in early 2012 to integrate chat into these newer games. As some users were avoiding the games solely due to their lack of chat, this was an issue with a clear resolution that could be fixed with a new design and iterative testing to confirm its performance.

Socialization in Games: Pogo.com is comprised of several different types of players who vary from Sandy, a player who typically chats. The Pogo gamer may play for various amounts of time. For example, there are retirees who play more than once a day for prolonged sessions as an outlet to pass time, which is starkly contrasted with players who have full-time jobs who may sneak the occasional quick game from their office computer. Players also vary in their desire to interact with others online. Some players only play 1-player games or games where they can play against a robot; others seek out socialization through multiplayer gameplay and use of the chat rooms. While this is a bit of a generalization and a single player may fall into many buckets depending on mood or other factors, it is a quick way to broadly capture the Pogo audience. As socialization increases through technology making it easier to communicate with friends through applications and games from Facebook and beyond, the growth to feed social outlets increases as well. Indeed, people enjoy being social while they play. During a talk at Game Developer's Conference in March of 2012, Zynga's chief operating officer (COO) offered some numbers on who plays *Words With Friends* (Nutt, 2012). Interestingly, 63% play with close friends and 43% play with relatives. Those who play strangers do not necessarily keep their distance – 74% of players indicated that they made new friends, and 1 in 10 met in real life. Not all games are built to be social or multiplayer; however, Moon and Kim (2001) indicated that it is important that users of websites find them to be useful and fun. The Pogo chat likely boosts both of these factors for players, as it allows players to receive game statistics at the end of a game, learn of players who may have achieved a goal or won a prize elsewhere on the website, and communicate with others to get immediate feedback. Additionally, the chat enhances the social medium, opening the door for communication during solo gameplay and facilitating gameplay in multiplayer games.

Within a games website like Pogo, it is not uncommon for fast-paced games to bear chat rooms that are quite silent (as the focus is on gameplay), while others are heavily trafficked with topics from weekend plans to casual flirting to health complaints. All of these rooms tend to be sprinkled with the occasional "good game!" or "way to go!," typically typed in abbreviations reserved for texting and chats (i.e. "gg" or "wtg," respectively). Different factors impact why someone would use a social tool such as social networking or chat. One such factor includes a perception of one's peer network. If a user believes other friends also use a particular social networking site, he or she is more likely to continue using it. For example, Lin and Lu (2011) located users of Facebook in Taiwan and received questionnaires from 402 users. The user's continued intention to use was strengthened not only when the user believes that he/she had friends in the network, but when he/she also perceived that more friends would be joining. In a study of instant messaging (IM), Li, Chau, and Lou (2005) found that the perception that more of one's friends were also on IM was positively associated with enjoyment and usefulness. Lin and Bhattacherjee (2009) gave a survey to 312 undergraduates in Taiwan to assess IM usage. It was found that if one's network was too small, social support was considered limited; therefore, users should seek to grow their network. From this study, the authors suggest that companies should enhance their tools to assist users in increasing their social networks. Additionally, it is implied that individuals seek social support through means such as IM.

In regard to social support, it can be obtained virtually (Walther & Boyd, 2002). It may come in the form of informational support, where individuals seek feedback or advice from others; emotional support, where individuals seek sympathy and affection; and esteem support, where individuals seek comments in regard to their skills and/or abilities. In regard to chat rooms in games, all three of these types of support can be accessed. Informational support may not only be in the more commonplace form, where users seek advice about an ailment or a relationship, but players may also seek help about the game that is being played. Esteem support can also cover both the personal and practical spectrum in a game chat room – users may want others to give them reinforcement beyond gaming, or they may just want to hear "great game!" after they win a tough round of *Canasta*. Emotional support is most likely just to lean toward the personal side. Indeed, many players will use the game chat rooms to discuss their personal lives and problems, and many do find solace from other players who are more than willing to listen...and share their woes. Individuals may turn to chat rooms to talk because their friends or family whom they would typically turn to in person happen to be unavailable (Leatham & Duck, 1990). The web, game websites, and online chat rooms are available 24 hours a day, and on a website like Pogo, there are always approximately 100,000 others online. While not everyone wants to chat, odds are, someone is willing to listen and strike up a conversation. At 3am on a Wednesday, this could be hard to do face-to-face. Walther & Boyd's research indicated access to be an important attribute for users who relied on computer-mediated communication, as they could both receive or give support any time of day. Related to this, on a gaming website, users are able to maintain a high degree of anonymity through use of a username in lieu of one's real name and through use of an avatar that does not need to resemble oneself. Walther & Boyd also found that the individuals who filled out their questionnaire cited anonymity as a key factor attracting them to computer-mediated communication. Chat rooms and web sites are considered to be a place to form weak-tie relationships, where people do not know each other face-to-face (Adelman, Parks, & Albrecht, 1987). Due to this distance, the anonymity provided allows individuals to disclose information that may be considered personal or embarrassing.

The Technology Acceptance Model (TAM) indicates additional factors for why a user would utilize chat. According to the TAM (Davis, 1989), individuals are likely to consider information technology based on two key variables: perceived usefulness and perceived ease of use. Perceived usefulness indicates whether or not a user believes information technology will help his/her job performance. Perceived ease of use has to do with how hard or easy the system is to use. Even if a system is useful, if it is too complex, it may be disregarded. These two factors correlate both with current and predicted future usage of technology. Li et al. (2005) investigated the facets of TAM and extended it to measure perceived enjoyment in a study on adoption of instant messaging. Intention to continue using IM was predicted by both perceived usefulness as well as perceived enjoyment. Looking at IM in the workplace, both perceived ease of use and usefulness impacted IM adoption (Glass & Li, 2010). Interestingly, age and gender did not have an impact on picking up instant messaging. Beyond research in the workplace, there appears to be a dearth of literature on the potential benefits of IM'ing in more casual settings.

Stickiness: If a chat window in a game is perceived as both useful and easy to use, it may work to increase the game's stickiness, or its ability to attract and retain customers. Gamers are hit with a plethora of game options when they come online to play. Therefore, a key factor to keep a game title successful is through stickiness. Zott, Amit, and Donlevy (2000) indicated that stickiness is created by rewarding loyal customers, allowing the service to be customizable or personalized to the user's experience (i.e. adding favorites), building virtual communities (most popular is through chat rooms), and establishing trust. Mantymaki and Riemer (2011) distributed an online survey to individuals who played on the German Habbo Hotel website. 844 usable questionnaires were analyzed. The vast majority of players were considered experienced, with more than 6 months of usage on the website. Players responded that they were more likely to continue using the website when they saw it as utilitarian (where players found it to help them interact socially) and hedonic (where players found it to be enjoyable), and when there was a strong social presence (where players had many added to their personal networks). The authors indicated that the key factors driving players to continue playing included factors one gets due to gameplay, such as spending time with friends and having fun. Wang (2009) distributed a questionnaire to online gamers in Taiwan, and 337 were analyzed. Gamers who were gratified from a trial experience and who experienced flow in the game were more motivated to continue playing; and that motivation was tied to stickiness (staying and playing longer/more frequently). Wu (2011) examined the factors from 318 Facebook users to determine what may impact stickiness. Social identity (to feel a sense of togetherness), perceived usefulness, perceived entertainment, and attitude were positively related to website stickiness. Social identity was related to perceived usefulness and perceived entertainment towards Facebook. Users' attitudes towards Facebook were impacted by perceived usefulness, perceived ease of use, and perceived entertainment. Walczuch, Verkuijlen, Geus, and Ronnen (2001) indicated that stickiness involves both visit duration and frequency. The authors indicated that related to chat, stickiness is boosted through community, where players can build relationships with others. This relationship is built through easy identification of other players, which is done through usernames and avatars and the ability to add friends to a friends list. From their research, community was deemed to be the stickiest, followed by categories such as information, e-mail, and entertainment. In the Pogo chat rooms, when a friend comes online, this is indicated and their messages stand out from non-friends when they are added to the chat. Additionally, Walczuch et al. indicate the importance of social control, where the user needs to feel safe, being able to block abusive comments and offensive users. Motivation is also mentioned, where users want to be recognized for their contributions. As this is a gaming platform, recognition comes after a milestone in the game has occurred. Finally, user-friendliness is listed. This is a consistent benchmark to be met and exceeded, and the point of this paper. As a new chat was being considered, to what degree was it considered not only acceptable, but usable, by the Pogo community?

CASE DESCRIPTION

Process

Three iterations of user testing were undertaken to insert and refine a chat window into the newer Pogo games that currently lacked chat. Within these iterations, there was one between subjects factor and one within subjects factor. The between sub-jects factor was Pogo status – Club or free. Free games have an advertisement on the right-hand panel which limits the real estate that would otherwise be available for a chat window, as is evident in Figure 4. For Club games, this space is filled with an area of My Stuff and My Favorite Games which lists a player's messages, gifts, and additional information (as in Figure 3). The within subjects factor is game width – narrower games such as those in Figure 2 versus wider games such as those in Figure 3.

It was important to see how the free and Club audiences reacted to the new features across the different versions of chat. Did the options need revision before release? Did one or both options have such a hindrance that they should not be released at all? Based on the needs for both a free and Club audience, users from both camps were recruited. It was important to capture players who differed in their chat usage as well.

Team Collaboration: While the researcher was able to recruit and perform test-ing, it took a strong team in order for the researcher to receive a solid prototype to utilize for testing and understand the product requirements. Without this compre-hension, the researcher would have been less able to create a structured test plan to capture the necessary feedback from the users to help guide the product along its fairly inflexible timeline to release. If the researcher fails to gather this information and the feedback handed over is off track from changes being made to the design or beyond the scope of engineering's capabilities, he/she runs the risk of missing the window of opportunity where changes can still be incorporated into the design.

For this project, the designer, artist, and PM were located in a satellite office and in different time zones than headquarters; therefore, the remainder of the team (research, engineering) collaborated with them remotely. The full team (PM, designer, researcher, engineer, and artist) spoke after the project kickoff to discuss what would be feasible for a new chat. The lead engineer was crucial in this meeting to guide the design – what factors were practical for not only the current release and its supporting features, but in consideration of future releases as well? The designer gathered feedback in regards to what should be created into a wireframe and the researcher learned key aspects that should be tested for usability.

Engineering: The lead engineer, with an understanding of how this chat was to work, divided the features of chat across her team members. An agile process was utilized such that the chat was meant to be released into production, and advanced features could then be built onto it via routine updates. Using this process, the team was able to speed up delivery of the new chat, and new features could be released not only for the new chat, but to the current chat, as well as to games that anticipated having a chat window several months down the road. Based on the wireframes and a comprehension of the chat workflow, a timeline was created within the engineering team. There were 7 iterations, each consisting of 2 week sprints. This 14-week project was considerably larger than previous projects, which tended to consist of coding and fixing current features (which were 2-4 weeks long in duration). This project, the creation of a new feature, was certainly longer, bringing with it exciting challenges.

Engineering was able to work on the back end before the design and art was finalized because the functions of chat were understood and concrete – it was just the user interface that was likely to change from testing. To work on this, the lead doled out tasks to three server engineers and two client engineers. In addition to these five fully-dedicated team members, additional support was relied upon as necessary for tasks such as troubleshooting and bug fixing. As the code was built, quality assurance (QA) tested it in a waterfall process. This indicated that a part of chat was built and passed through QA – if it was successful, it would move along. Otherwise, it would go back to the top to be fixed by the engineering team. Overseeing all of this was the development director (DD), who was making sure that everything met the project's as well as her own expectations and requirements, keeping to the project timeline.

Research: From the original conversation with the team, the researcher had gained enough information about the product and the goals for testing to put together a script. The script was being written to cover tasks that the designer, PM, and researcher thought were important to explore: How easy was it to find new and current features? How much did users like the new features or any changes to current features? Would they want to use the chat and these features in the future?

Did things behave as expected? A timeline was determined so the researcher could initiate recruitment, and the researcher and designer met regularly to make sure the prototypes would be on track for testing.

User Research: Overview

Formative Usability Testing: In industry, the researcher may be tasked to assess a product's usability concerns at many points during its lifecycle. When the researcher is brought on early when the product is still being developed, one typically starts with formative testing. This is a time of discovery where the researcher wants to find the large areas of concern or pain points. Unlike academia where large samples are the norm, perhaps due to very specific hypotheses and the anticipation of small effect sizes, industry is asking a much more basic question – is this product easy to use? (In some cases, is it fun? Is it safe?) One can answer this with far fewer participants – in the ball park of 4 to 10. Clear missteps in the product or user interface will surface immediately, and after only a handful of users, the feedback in regards to large errors will become redundant. At this point, the designer or engineer is able to iterate the product, testing can take place again, and this process can continue until the product functions well and users are satisfied (or until the team runs out of time, which is often the case in time-pressured industry).

Remote Testing: Remote usability testing is a method widely utilized across industry, particularly for computer systems where it is easy to share computer screens with a user. User researchers may select remote testing in order to access a broader demographic beyond those in their city limits. Additionally, while field testing may have its benefits, travel budgets are often restricted; therefore, remote testing allows researchers to reach individuals nationwide or worldwide without the need to exhaust a limited financial resource. Finally, not all users are keen on coming in to a laboratory or office to participate in testing – they may feel uneasy about the experience, or the times offered may not fit their schedule, particularly if extensive travel is involved. Once in the testing lab, the setup may be artificial, not replicating the user's own home environment. If software is being tested, is the user comfortable with the mouse and keyboard? Is the computer setup so much different (presumably newer) that the user does not get the same errors that he/she would at home? Is the screen resolution vastly different? For example, users may instantly notice a feature in the lab, but at home, where they use a small laptop and have far too many browser toolbars, that same feature may be found below the fold (indicating that it is out of sight when one is at the top of a web page and one must scroll down to see it) making it harder to discover.

In order to gain access to a wide array of current free and Club users, remote testing, in lieu of on-site testing, was selected in order to maximize the diversity

Figure 5. The game Plants vs. Zombies with a chat window affixed to the right side of the game as seen in the first iteration of testing. (© 2012, Electronic Arts Inc. used with permission)

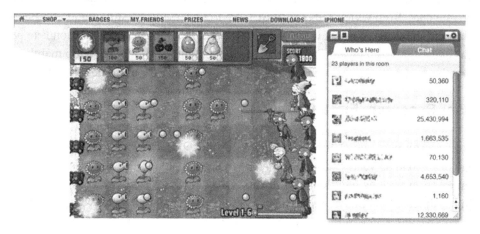

of the users and the comfort of their surroundings. With remote testing, users were able to perform tasks from their own homes. Screen sharing software was utilized so the users could view the prototypes from the researcher's computer, and the user and researcher communicated via telephone. Sessions were held one-on-one with the researcher, as typical game play on Pogo involves one user behind one computer. Additionally, this minimized the risk of group think or an overbearing personality, were multiple users to attend simultaneously. The researcher had to make remote testing work with prototypes that were lower in fidelity, as most areas of the chat prototypes were not clickable, and others had to be selected in a particular order to ensure that all features could be examined. For example, one could click in the area that read "Add your message here," and then the chat window would auto-populate with a message. After this message was sent, the user was able to explore more features such as adding someone in the chat room as a friend.

User Interface (UI): There were two different interfaces around which chat would be inserted. One UI was dedicated to the free Pogo audience, and the other, the Club Pogo members. The user researcher needed to understand the different game interfaces offered to the free and Club audiences. While the chat window looked markedly similar for the two groups, the game interface around which the chat window would be placed differed. For the free audience, advertising took up crucial real estate, challenging the placement for the chat window. For the Club audience, advertising was not a restriction. Additionally, the free and Club audiences had very different wants and needs to be taken into consideration. In regard to functional differences, the chat window has expanded features for Club players. They are able to use the emoticons (smiley faces), and they are granted access to the private chat, from which they can start 1-on-1 conversations with other Club Pogo players. There are also user differences. For example, the Club audience tends to be more resistant to change mostly due to the longer tenure with which Club members have been playing on the website and their high familiarity with the current UI.

User Research: First Iteration

From recruitment, which took two days, 4 free players and 4 Club players ranging in age from 30 to 65 years old were signed up to participate in a 30-minute study. They hailed from various locations in the United States, from as far west as California and as far east as Pennsylvania. The day before testing, a pilot study was performed to remove any kinks in the script or the protocol and to ensure that timing was on track. One free player failed to show up for her assigned time; therefore, only 3 free players (7 in total) participated in this iteration. The purpose of this iteration was to test the location and function of chat in games where the chat window would fit to the right side of the game brick (see Figure 5). Users were informed that the prototype was not fully functioning, meaning that some places the user may try to click on may not function (as is the nature with many prototypes). The researcher answered any questions the user may have had, and then proceeded to have the user walk through 6 tasks:

1. "How would you start playing the game (in this case, *Plants vs. Zombies*) from here?"
2. "What do you typically do when someone starts talking to you in chat?" This question was asked to get additional insight into users' different chat usage and behaviors.
3. "How would you say "hello" back to the person who is currently chatting with you?" When users navigated to the chat tab, a message appeared in the chat window from another online player that said "Hello!"
4. "How would you add this person to your friends list from here?"
5. "Is there anything that you dislike about the current Pogo chat?"
6. "Is anything missing from this chat window?"

Participants were also asked to rate the new chat compared to the current chat, on a scale from 1 (much worse) to 7 (much better), and their preferences were collected for certain features. At the end of testing, participants were thanked, the screen sharing was ended, and the researcher and user ended their phone call. Club players were given Pogo gems for their participation (a virtual currency utilized on Pogo that can be redeemed for items such as game episodes and badge albums) and free players were given an Amazon gift card. Select findings will be discussed below.

Focusing on the four Club players, all of them were able to locate the chat tab very easily, even with its location behind the Who's Here tab. This behavior was different from the current Pogo chat, where the chat window is located below the list of players in the chat room; however, in order to maximize space, this tabbed design was selected. All players were also able to quickly and easily locate the area for sending messages, which also looked visually different from the current Pogo chat. However, users had more trouble when it came to adding a friend. Half of the players wanted to look under Settings, one wanted to right-click the friend's name, and one wanted to navigate away from the Chat tab and to the Who's Here tab to add a friend from that section. Although this latter action would work, it was less efficient. A similar action is what is currently performed in chat; however, the new concept involved clicking on any player's name or message to reveal a drop-down menu directly on the chat instead of having to access this menu from Who's Here. Once users who could not find the menu were directed to it received it quite positively, with feedback such as, "Yeah, having that little arrow there makes it easier, makes it cleaner, it's a cleaner interface," and "Oh, that's a lot easier to mute somebody!" (Muting is an action whereby a player, typically an offensive player, can have his/her messages removed from view). It was definitely important to increase the visibility of the sub-menu accessible next to each player's message on the Chat tab so that more players would find it. Users were asked if they would prefer to see Who's Here or Chat as the default tab, and the feedback was split down the middle. Players who preferred Who's Here indicated they could first see who is in the chat, and then decide if they wanted to participate. Chat would also be less disruptive for those who did not typically chat. Players who preferred the Chat tab as a default indicated they wanted to see who was talking. Therefore, the answer to this question was not to be made solely by the researcher based on user feedback, but followed up with the full team to gather perspective from everyone.

Players were also asked to compare the new chat to the current Pogo chat. The mean rating was surprisingly high – with a rating of 5.79 ($SD = 1.73$), where 1 indicated "much worse" and 7 indicated "much better." Positive feedback was quite strong: "It makes the current one look about ten years old, that's so much more modern looking, cleaner," (Male, 42 years old). The negative feedback reflected the Club audience that is resistant to change – "Because I like the current chat. Cause I'm used to it probably," (Female, 65 years old). What did perform strongly was the location of the chat, as it was embedded to the right side of the game and had a similar feel to the current Pogo chat in that manner. Because there was nothing negative received in regards to the chat location, engineering was able to start moving forward producing this chat. Any small changes to features could always be inserted along the way and would not affect the building of the frame for the chat. However what remained unanswered was what chat should look like when it did not fit to the right side of a game. Additional research was necessary to help resolve this design question.

User Research: Second Iteration

For the second iteration, six users participated remotely in a similar fashion to the first iteration. It was indicated to the researcher that immediate feedback was needed to determine if the prototype was on track; therefore, participants who were already scheduled for another study were utilized for this iteration of testing. All six users were very dedicated Pogo players – one was a free player and five were Club players. Ages ranged from 27 to 63, and all six were females. This study was compiled with about one days' notice and the researcher had about 10 minutes to spend with each participant (as she was only able to utilize the spare time at the end of the primary study for which the participants were scheduled). Although this setup is somewhat nontraditional, it still allowed the researcher to surface informational feedback from the users which could be passed on to the designer to help guide the design process. The purpose of this iteration was to determine a preliminary location for chat in the wider games where chat cannot be placed to the right side of the games due to the width of the games removing any blank space between the end of the game brick and the beginning of the advertising real estate, which could not be removed or covered. If there is no room for chat to the right of games, how will users react? The version shown to participants had a line of chat fixed below the game brick (see Figure 6a); however, users could expand the chat window by clicking on "Show Chat." Doing so would bring up a moveable and resizable chat window (see Figure 6b). The expanded chat window would allow users to have the "feel" of the traditional chat, although it necessitated expansion from underneath the game and was not pinned to the side of the game. Again, the researcher explained that the prototype was not fully functioning, and then launched a prototype for the game Cirque du Flea. Users were asked questions such as:

1. "Do you see a way to chat in this game?"
2. "What would you do if you wanted to see more of the chat window?"
3. "What do you think of the location of the chat window?"

Figure 6. The game Cirque du Flea with: a) the minimized chat window below the game from the third iteration of testing; b) the chat window expanded from the third iteration of testing. (© 2012, Electronic Arts Inc. used with permission)

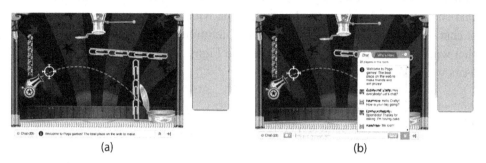

(a)   (b)

Regarding the first question, two of the six users did not immediately see the chat bar in this minimized state. One individual looked right past it, indicating "if you were going to have a chat, I think on the bottom would be best." All players noticed the "Show Chat" button, although one player thought the button needed an arrow or carat that she should click on. The largest concern involved the location of the expanded chat window. Upon clicking "Show Chat," the chat window opened on top of the game brick, as shown in Figure 6b. While players liked the functionality of this chat window compared to the current Pogo chat, in that it could be resized and its position altered, they did not like that it blocked the game. As one player stated, "it seems like it would be blocking, it would interfere with the game. Let me see if I can move it." This was a consistent theme with all players – although they would be opening up the chat window to chat, their first inclination would be to move the chat window out of the way, most likely, on top of the advertisement (which would not sit well with marketing). Because the advertisement cannot be blocked, the decision was made not to have the chat pop up over the advertisement in the first place. However, from testing it became clear that users would ultimately block the ad with the chat window, and by placing the chat window on top of the game, this added burden of being forced to move the chat window in order to multitask was moved onto the user. Indeed, this was not an optimal solution for chat in wider games. The designer worked toward a better solution which could be tested to see if it outperformed this type of chat option.

User Research: Third Iteration

For the third and final iteration, there were eleven participants – four Club players (all females ranging in age from 58-66), four free players (females aged 31-39), and three non-Pogo players (females aged 27-34). The non-Pogo players were recruited from a forum for another EA game, *Pet Society*. With this variety, it was possible to capture feedback from the many types of users who would come across chat – from first-time users to heavy users. The goal of this iteration was to finalize where chat should go and how it should look for the wider games. Users saw two styles of chat – a chat window similar to that from iteration 2 and a new design where the chat window was fixed below the game (see Figure 7). For both versions of chat, users were asked:

1. "Do you see a way to chat in this game?"
2. "How would you send someone a message?"

At the end of the study, users were also asked to compare the two different options – which did they like better and why? How do these chats compare to the current Pogo chat (if this applied) as well as other chat programs that the users may utilize? Regarding the first question for the expanding chat, which started off minimized as it did in iteration 2, five of 11 users did not notice the chat immediately. "I think because it's so small I didn't notice it, I didn't pay attention to looking at it." This performance was even worse than iteration 2, where 1/3 of users did not see the presence of a chat. However for the chat from Figure 7, all users noticed it. Also similar to iteration 2, users were unhappy with the expanding chat opening up on top of the game brick – "If you want to play the game and chat at the same

Figure 7. The game Cirque du Flea with the chat window displayed below the game from the third iteration of testing. (© 2012, Electronic Arts Inc. used with permission)

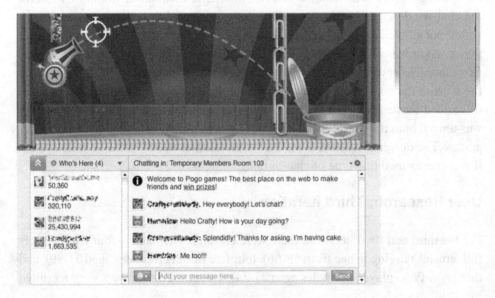

time, that's kind of like messing up your game. That's mostly what I'll do, play the game and chat at the same time."

The chat window below the game did not have this limitation; however, it had its own limitation – for players with a small monitor, the game brick would likely fill their monitor and players would have to scroll down to see the chat. Unlike the current Pogo chat, both playing and chatting could not happen simultaneously. Some players picked up on this – "It looks like I'd have to scroll to get to the bottom of the window and I'd have to scroll to type in a message, that would put me off." Others did not mind the fact that they may have to scroll – "I don't think that would bother me unless I was really interested in the game. Then I probably wouldn't worry about chatting anyway." Comparing the two different chat options, players unanimously preferred the chat below the game in lieu of the chat that popped up over the game. "The game's the most important thing. The chat is nice...I'll put it on the bottom definitely instead of a pop-up."

Players were also asked how they could minimize the chat below the game. Several players hit the Settings button (which was on the top right) instead of the minimize button (which was on the top left). From observation and user feedback, it became apparent that users expected the minimize button to be on the right side. While players seemed to prefer the chat below the game, they were hindered by this single aspect -- "I like that one much better. I like that it's not in front of your game. The only thing I don't like is there's a button on each side instead of just on the right side." It seemed to be an easy resolution to move the minimize button to conform to user expectations.

Finally, the Club Pogo players were also asked how important it was for their badge and challenge information to be tracked in the chat window. The badges and challenges work as a goal the player must achieve in the game in a certain amount of time, usually in one day, one week, or two weeks. For example, in *Poppit! Sprint*, a player may activate a badge challenge (i.e. collect 3111 coins in 2 weeks). After each round of the game, a player can traditionally see how well he or she is doing through informative text in the chat window. The chat also tells one of other players' achievements or prizes won in the game. There was unanimous desire to see this information in the chat for the new games. "Yes! I was frustrated in one of the dailies we just did...I had to keep clicking out of the game and going to the front screen...to see how far I got. So yes I was very aggravated that I couldn't see it [in the chat window]."

From this third iteration of testing, it was confirmed that users did not like for the chat window to open up on top of their game. Additionally, if the chat window starts off minimized, it is likely that many users will not even see it. While the chat window below the game had a limitation of requiring some users with smaller monitors to scroll in order to see both the game and chat in the same window, it was currently the best option available, as there was no real estate to place the chat to the side of the game, and if the chat were placed above the game, the same limitation would exist; however, the user would have to scroll down to see the game. Ultimately, Pogo is a games website; therefore, the game should always come first.

Next Steps

Based on the findings, a presentation was compiled for the PM, designers, and lead engineer after each iteration. During the meeting, video clips highlighting high and low points from testing were reviewed. For the areas that could use improvement, the team talked about whether the issues seemed problematic, and if so, what potential solutions could be. As a researcher, standing up for the user was paramount to support what was seen in testing. For example, the chat solution in iteration 2 did not test successfully because users did not like that the window popped up over the game brick. It was the researcher's job to emphasize this and make sure that the designer would go back to the drawing board to find a more optimal solution. Sharing negative user quotes, such as "the first thing I would do is move it over," gave the team insight into what player behavior would be if no change were made – users would open the game and be forced to make changes to their chat window each and every time as an initial action before they started playing or chatting. The designer was able to take this tangible feedback to help revise new iterations of the design, as was seen for the third iteration. From the user research presentation, many recommendations to improve the preliminary and subsequent versions of chat were generated, and the project moved forward into the hands of others. The design and engineering teams took the appropriate feedback from these presentations to move chat toward release.

Engineering was able to take the final design from the first iteration and incorporate it into the work that had already started for this new chat window. Challenges were faced early into the project due to staffing shortages, when engineers were moved to different efforts within EA due to a different studio's title needing immediate help. While such a challenge is commonplace, it leads to frustration not only due to the short-term understaffing, but due to the expected communication breakdown that occurs when one individual hands a project off to another. From this unexpected change in staffing, time on the project was certainly lost.

The team put the finalized product through rigorous testing and then opened the new chat up to a Pogo frag, or a time set aside for all colleagues with availability to log on to the development website and check out chat prior to its release. Any bugs or performance issues detected by employees at Pogo were passed on to the PM who routed them to the appropriate engineers for investigation. Once all issues with chat were solved, it was ready for release. Chat for narrower games (see Figure 8) was rolled out as a larger feature enhancement for the game *Bejeweled 3* on July 31, 2012, accompanying smaller changes to the website such as the addition of new episodes for hidden object games and the addition of new weekly badge challenges. The changes and features for wider games were tackled by engineering in a similar fashion to chat for narrower games. Due to the template created by the first iteration, engineering had a better grasp on the process behind this new chat window, so the chat for wider games was produced much faster from start to finish than the chat for narrower games.

Across the iterative design cycle for the wider games, an optimal design surfaced, and it was released for the first wide game, *Poppit! Sprint*, on August 28, 2012 (see Figure 9a). Iterative testing was able to inform design that players were less likely to notice the chat window in its minimized state and they did not respond well to a chat window that opened up on top of their game. However, they were satisfied with putting the full chat window below the game – it was better to have chat there than not to have chat at all. Further, for players who do not chat or for individuals who wish to focus on the leaderboard (where one can see friends' high scores compared to their own), the chat could be minimized, showing only the most current line (see Figure 9b).

Figure 8. The chat solution for narrow games such as Bejeweled 3 which could accommodate the chat window affixed to the right side of games. This is the chat as it is currently available on Pogo.com. (© 2012, Electronic Arts Inc. used with permission)

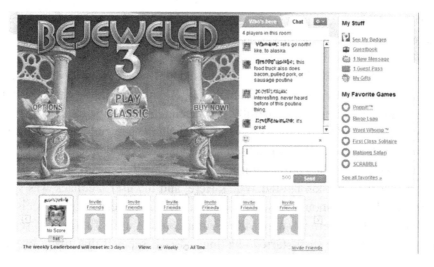

Figure 9. a) The chat solution for wider games such as Poppit! Sprint, as it is currently available on Pogo.com; b) how the chat solution for wider games appears when it is minimized. This figure also demonstrates text for badge progress. (© 2012, Electronic Arts Inc. used with permission)

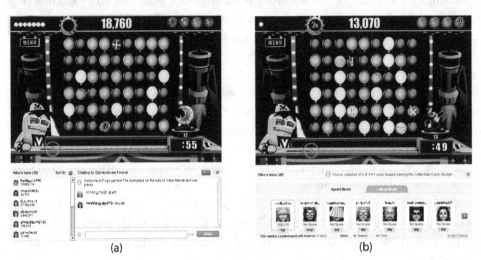

(a)   (b)

CURRENT CHALLENGES FACING THE ORGANIZATION

The new chat for *Bejeweled 3* was met with both praise as well as user confusion. Regarding the former, a brief article was written about it on a Pogo fan site called Badge Hungry. It indicated: "...this chat feature was sorely needed and wanted. Here's hoping they can roll it out to all of the other non-chat games in the near future" (Lura, 2012). There were several positive responses to this article, such as "This IS a good thing. Now we can play in the same room and chat instead of using a separate chat program. I'm looking forward to this:-)" and "Yay, Chat! I'm very happy they are FINALLY rolling this out in these games. Not sure I really like the design of it, but hey it's Chat – and with a little getting used to, I'm sure it will be fine." Comments also appeared in the player forums: "Yay! Thanks for adding chat! Definitely a step in the right direction. Hopefully private chat will later be implemented, and Jackpot Spin." While it is to be expected that the audience would adapt to a design that differed from what they were used to and that lacked identical features, what was unexpected was the confusion in finding the Chat tab. From testing, all users easily found the Chat tab behind Who's Here, and the user feedback was split in regards to which tab should be viewed as the default. The team made a decision to go with the Who's Here tab under the assumption that users first like to see who was in a room before they started chatting. Also, it seemed that many users did not utilize chat, and in this manner, chat could be out of sight as a default setting. The consequence of this decision was that many players using chat had a hard time locating chat or potentially did not notice the presence of a chat panel. In order to resolve this, the default tab was switched on Tuesday, September 4, 2012 so that the game now opened with the chat beside it instead of the list of who was in the chat.

A second feature that led to discontent was the lack of badge progress. From the third iteration of testing, it was very clear that users wanted to be able to track how far along they were in completing a badge challenge. However, in order to get the *Bejeweled 3* chat rolled out in time, this had not yet been integrated. Upon the release of chat for *Poppit! Sprint*, the badge progress was integrated into all new chat windows (see the text in the minimized chat window of Figure 9b). This feature is beneficial even for those who do not chat in the chat window, as many players partake in challenges and badges. One player noted, "Just also wanted to report that badge progress shows up in the chat now, too. I know that was a big complaint before… I'm in *Bejeweled 3* now, and it came up in chat saying 'so & so won the ____ badge.' " With the release of this feature and the soon-to-be updated default tab for *Bejeweled 3*, the behavior of the chat windows in the new games should be much closer to mirroring the current Pogo chat, removing any dissonance from the Pogo audience. This seemed to confirm the perceived usefulness aspect of Davis' (1989) Technology Acceptance Model – when the usefulness of chat was lacking, players were less satisfied. To date, the few negative comments around the *Poppit! Sprint* chat involves how one has to scroll down to see it, which was an anticipated negative to its design. "I do like how this chat shows both the names and the chat on one screen. What I don't like is that to see the chat, I have to scroll down below the game to see it… Other than that, I don't see anything wrong with it." Of course, the Pogo teams will keep a watchful eye on the forums and game performance statistics to determine if there is anything else negative in regards to the UI or engineering for chat that requires resolution. The new chat appeared in *Mahjongg Dimensions* on September 11, 2012; in *Zuma's Revenge*, *Plants vs. Zombies*, and *Slingo Ricochet* on September 25; and it will continue to roll out in the newer games until all games have a chat window.

SOLUTIONS AND RECOMMENDATIONS

User testing was able to bring pain points from users to the forefront to give justification to reworking a design or feature. This project relied largely on the feedback of users to steer the design direction of the chat windows. This spoke to the importance of selecting the appropriate users for such sessions who represented not only an end user of the product (i.e. a Pogo player), but who fit the needs for what was being tested (in this case, players who chat to varying degrees)? Had only heavy chat users been recruited, it was possible that feedback pertaining to the importance of minimizing the chat window would have been missed. Additionally, it was key to monitor user behavior once the product was released. Testing was performed on a low-fidelity prototype, and there may have been some items that stood out (i.e. chat affecting the page load) once the product was in production. While it is likely that QA teams would pick up on many issues, there are some things that cannot be anticipated until large numbers of users touch the product. For example, it was a split decision in regards to which tab should be made the default in the narrow chat window. Once it was released, the community forums indicated that users were confused. A solution was implemented (switch the default tab), and the confusion went away. If there is concern about the degree to which a new feature may impact users, one can utilize A|B testing. Here, half of the users would view the status quo and the other half would receive the new feature. Metrics can inform the team if performance (i.e. daily impressions) differs between the two groups. If so, a root cause can be determined and a decision can be made – should the new feature be removed, modified, or rolled out to all users?

The iterative testing cycle, utilized across research, design, and engineering, allowed the team to refine the product based on user needs and product requirements, giving way to a chat solution met with satisfaction across the Pogo population. This project demonstrated examples of testing across different user groups to gain and share feedback to speak for the user. Without this testing, it is possible that the new Pogo chat, particularly for wider games, could have been released with features which could have highly frustrated players. For gaming on Pogo, players are focused on the game first. A secondary aspect such as chat is not important enough to justify game interruption. User testing showed that this was the case even for very devoted players who were more likely to chat heavily. Consistent with the stickiness literature, players indicated they would be more likely to play certain games because chat was brought over to these games, holding a social and utilitarian purpose. Had the chat window interfered with gameplay, stickiness of these game titles would have declined due to a drop in ease of use. Continued tracking of user traffic with the rollout of chat to these new games is crucial to determine just how sticky these games are and the degree to which chat may increase stickiness in casual gaming.

REFERENCES

Adelman, M. B., Parks, M. R., & Albrecht, T. L. (1987). Beyond close relationships: Support in weak ties. In Albrecht, T. L., & Adelman, M. B. (Eds.), *Communicating social support* (pp. 126–147). Newbury Park, CA: Sage.

Davis, F. D. (1989). Perceived usefulness, perceived ease of use, and user acceptance of information technology. *Management Information Systems Quarterly, 13,* 319–340. doi:10.2307/249008

Glass, R., & Li, S. (2010). Social influence and instant messaging adoption. *Journal of Computer Information Systems, 51,* 24–30.

Leatham, G., & Duck, S. (1990). Conversations with friends and the dynamics of social support. In Duck, S. (Ed.), *Personal relationships and social support* (pp. 1–29). London: Sage.

Li, D., Chau, P. Y. K., & Lou, H. (2005). Understanding individual adoption of instant messaging: An empirical investigation. *Journal of the Association for Information Systems, 6,* 102–129.

Lin, C.-P., & Bhattacherjee, A. (2009). Understanding online social support and its antecedents: A socio-cognitive model. *The Social Science Journal, 46,* 724–737. doi:10.1016/j.soscij.2009.03.004

Lin, K.-Y., & Lu, H.-P. (2011). Why people use social networking sites: An empirical study integrating network externalities and motivation theory. *Computers in Human Behavior, 27,* 1152–1161. doi:10.1016/j.chb.2010.12.009

Lura. (2012). New! Bejeweled 3 has chat rooms. *BadgeHungry.* Retrieved July 31, 2012, from http://www.badgehungry.com/2012/07/31/new-bejeweled-3-has-chat-rooms/

Mantymaki, M., & Riemer, K. (2011). "Fun and friends and stuff." On the stickiness of social virtual worlds among teenagers. In P. Seltsikas, D. Bunker, L. Dawson, & M. Indulska (Eds.), *Proceedings of the Australasian Conference on Information Systems ACIS 2011* (paper 10). Sydney, Australia.

Moon, J. W., & Kim, Y. G. (2001). Extending the TAM for a world-wide-web context. *Information & Management, 38,* 217–230. doi:10.1016/S0378-7206(00)00061-6

Nutt, C. (2012). GDC 2012: Zynga's Schappert shares *Words with Friends* statistics. *Gamasutra.* Retrieved March 12, 3012, from http://www.gamasutra.com/view/news/165171/GDC_2012_Zyngas_Schappert_shares_Words_with_Friends_statistics.php

Walczuch, R., Verkuijlen, M., Geus, B., & Ronnen, U. (2001). *Stickiness of commercial virtual communities. MERIT – Infonomics Research Memorandum Series.* Maastricht, The Netherlands, MERIT.

Walther, J. B., & Boyd, S. (2002). Attraction to computer-mediated social support. In Lin, C. A., & Atkin, D. (Eds.), *Communication technology and society: Audience adoption and uses* (pp. 153–188). Cresskill, NJ: Hampton Press.

Wang, S.-C. (2009). Why do players stick to a specific online game? The uses and gratifications perspective. *Americas Conference on Information Systems AMCIS 2009 Proceedings* (paper 351). San Francisco, CA.

Wu, C.-M. (2011). What factors affect people's stickiness on the social network site? The case of Facebook in Taiwan. *Key Engineering Materials, 474-476*, 1573–1577. doi:10.4028/www.scientific.net/KEM.474-476.1573

Zott, C., Amit, R., & Donlevy, J. (2000). Strategies for value creation in e-commerce: Best practice in Europe. *European Management Journal, 18*, 463–475. doi:10.1016/S0263-2373(00)00036-0

KEY TERMS AND DEFINITIONS

Below the Fold: An item on a web page that one must scroll down to access because it does not fit in the viewable top portion of the screen. Heavily utilized features ought to be placed above the fold to guarantee that users can easily find them.

Casual Games: Simple games such as puzzle, word, or card games that tend to be quick to learn. Players are able to play for very short durations compared to other game genres such as adventure games or first-person shooters.

Iterative Design: A process to improve a product's usability through multiple steps that may include interaction design, prototyping, testing, and analysis. At each step, users interact with the product and feedback is utilized to refine the product for the next iteration.

Online Chat: A real-time conversation between two or more individuals using text communication.

Remote Testing: Usability testing that takes place where the participant and the moderator are in separate locations.

Stickiness: A term used in the marketing field to determine how many users visit a website or how much time users spend at a particular website.

User Research: The testing of a product, regardless of the design phase it may be in, to boost the understanding of what people want in order to make products and systems more effective and easier to use, as well as to guarantee that the users are satisfied. In regards to games, it is important that the players are having fun as well.

Compilation of References

Adelman, M. B., Parks, M. R., & Albrecht, T. L. (1987). Beyond close relationships: Support in weak ties. In Albrecht, T. L., & Adelman, M. B. (Eds.), *Communicating social support* (pp. 126–147). Newbury Park, CA: Sage.

Allison, B. Z., Wolpaw, E. W., & Wolpaw, J. R. (2007). Brain-computer interface systems: Progress and prospects. *Expert Review of Medical Devices*, *4*, 463–474. doi:10.1586/17434440.4.4.463

Andres, C. (1999). *Great Web Architecture*. Foster City, CA: IDG Books World Wide.

Anschuetz, L., Keirnan, T., & Rosenbaum, S. (2002). Combining usability research with documentation development for improved user support. In Proceedings of the SIGDOC. Toronto, Canada: The Association of Computing Machinery.

Applehans, W., Globe, A., & Laugero, G. (1999). *Managing Knowledge: A Practical web-based approach*. Boston, MA: Addison-Wesley.

ARCO Evaluation Report. (2004). Assessment and evaluation report on the ARCO system and its components. Retrieved July, 1, 2007, from http://www.arco-web.org/TextVersion/Documents/Deliverables/ARCO-D16-R-1.0-170904.pdf

Ariza Avila, C. (2006). *Application of a context model in context-aware mobile government services* (Unpublished doctoral dissertation). Universidade do Minho, Guimaraes, Portugal.

Arnab, S., Protopsaltis, A., Minoi, J.L., Dunwell, I., & de Freitas, S. (2010). Promoting cross-cultural awareness through exposure in game-based Learning. *IEEE Learning Technology Newsletter,* January 2010 Edition.

Arnold, M. B. (1960). *Emotion and personality*. New York: Columbia University Press.

Aurum, A., & Wohlin, C. (2005). Requirements engineering: Setting the context. In Aurum, A., & Wohlin, C. (Eds.), *Engineering and managing software requirements* (pp. 1–15). Heidelberg, Germany: Springer-Verlag. doi:10.1007/3-540-28244-0_1

Avison, D., & Fitzgerald, G. (2006). *Information systems development: Methodologies, techniques and tools* (4th ed.). Maidenhead: McGraw-Hill.

Baily, D., & Hinds, P. (2003). Out of sight, out of sync: Understanding conflict in distributed teams. *Organization Science, 14*, 615–632. doi:10.1287/orsc.14.6.615.24872

Bandura, A. (1977). Self-efficacy: Toward a unifying theory of behavioral change. *Psychological Review, 84*(2), 191–215. doi:10.1037/0033-295X.84.2.191

Bandura, A. (1997). *Self-efficacy: The exercise of control*. New York, NY: Freeman.

Bannon, L. (1992). From human factors to human actors: The role of psychology and human-computer interaction studies in system design. In *Design at work: Cooperative design of computer systems*. Hillsdale, NJ: L. Erlbaum Associates Inc.

Barendregt, W. (2006). Evaluating fun and usability in computer games with Children. In *Department of Industrial Design*. Eindhoven: Eindhoven University of Technology.

Bar-Ilan, J., & Belous, Y. (2007). Children as architects of web directories: An exploratory study. *Journal of the American Society for Information Science and Technology, 58*(6), 895–907. doi:10.1002/asi.20566

Barlach, A., & Simonsen, J. (2011). Innovation in partnership sourcing from a vendor's perspective. In Hertzum, M., & Jørgensen, C. (Eds.), *Balancing sourcing and innovation in information systems development* (pp. 193–212). Trondheim, NO: Tapir Academic Publishers.

Barlow, J., Keith, M. J., Wilson, D. W., Schuetzler, R. M., Lowry, P. B., Vance, A., & Giboney, J. S. (2011). Overview and guidance on agile development in large organizations. *Communications of AIS, 29*, 25–44.

Barnum, C. M. (2011). *Usability testing essentials: Ready, set--test*. Burlington, MA: Morgan Kaufmann.

Becker, S., & Mottay, F. (2001, January). A global perspective on website usability. *IEEE Software, 18*(1), 61–54. doi:10.1109/52.903167

Beldad, A., Van der Geest, T., De Jong, M., & Michaël, M. (2012). A cue or two and I'll trust you: Determinants of trust in government organizations in terms of their processing and usage of citizens' personal information disclosed online. *Government Information Quarterly, 29*(1), 41–49. doi:10.1016/j.giq.2011.05.003

Benedek, J., & Miner, T. (2002*). Measuring desirability: New methods for evaluating desirability in a usability lab setting*. Usability Professionals' Association, 2002 Conference Proceedings. Retrieved May 26, 2012 from http://www.microsoft.com/usability/uepostings/desirabilitytoolkit.doc

Bias, R. G., & Mayhew, D. J. (2005). *Cost-justifying usability*. San Francisco, CA: Morgan Kaufmann Publishers, Inc.

Bickmore, T., & Giorgino, T. (2006). Health dialog systems for Patients and Consumers. *Journal of Biomedical Informatics, 39*(5), 556–571. doi:10.1016/j.jbi.2005.12.004

Billinghurst, M., Kato, H., & Poupyrev, I. (2001). The MagicBook: A traditional AR interface. *Computer Graphics*, *25*, 745–753. doi:10.1016/S0097-8493(01)00117-0

Birbaumer, N., Ghanayim, N., Hinterberger, T., Iversen, I., Kotchoubey, B., & Kubler, A. (1999). A spelling device for the paralysed. *Nature*, *398*, 297–298. doi:10.1038/18581

Bock, G., & Qian, Z. (2005). An empirical study on measuring the success of knowledge repository systems. In Proceedings of the 39th Annual Hawaii International Conference on System Sciences. Kona, HI: Institute of Electrical and Electronics Engineers, Inc.

Bødker, K., Simonsen, J., & Kensing, F. (2009). *Participatory IT design: Designing for business and workplace realities*. Cambridge, MA: MIT.

Bolchini, D., Chatterji, R., & Speroni, M. (2009). Developing heuristics for the semiotics inspection of websites. In *Proc. of the 27th ACM international conference on Design of Communication (SIGDOC 2009)* (pp. 67-71). Indiana, USA: ACM Press. Retrieved from http://doi.acm.org/10.1145/1621995.1622009

Bolton, L. (2012). Enhancement of aircraft touchscreen HMI through use of haptic feedback. To appear in *the Proceedings of the HCI Aero 2012 conference*. Brussels.

Borgatti, P. (1998). Principles of questionnaire construction. *Analytic technologies*. Retrieved from http://www.analytictech.com/mb313/principl.htm

Borun, M., & Korn, R. (Eds.). (1999). *Introduction to museum evaluation. Committee on Audience Research and Evaluation, American Association of Museums, Professional Practice Series*. Washington, DC: AAM.

Bowmann, D., Kruijf, E., La Viola, J., & Poupyrev, I. (2001). An introduction to 3-D user interface design. *Presence (Cambridge, Mass.)*, *10*(1), 96–108. doi:10.1162/105474601750182342

Bowmann, D., Kruijf, E., La Viola, J., & Poupyrev, I. (2005). *3D user interfaces: Theory and practice*. Boston: Addison-Wesley.

Brace, I. (2008). *Questionnaire design: How to plan, structure, and write survey material for effective market research* (2nd ed.). London, England: Kogan Page Publishers.

Bradley, M. M., & Lang, P. J. (1994). Measuring emotions: The self-assessment manikin and the semantic differential. *Journal of Behavior Therapy and Experimental Psychiatry*, *25*(1), 49–59. doi:10.1016/0005-7916(94)90063-9

Brainard, L. A., & McNutt, J. G. (2010). Virtual government-citizen relations: Informational, transactional, or collaborative? *Administration & Society*, *42*(7), 836–858. doi:10.1177/0095399710386308

Brennan, S., Fussell, S., Kraut, R., & Siegel, J. (2002). *Understanding effects of proximity on collaboration: Implications for technologies to support remote collaborative work. Distributed work*. Cambridge, MA: MIT Press.

Bringula, R. P., & Basa, R. S. (2011). Factors affecting faculty web portal usability. *Journal of Educational Technology & Society*, *14*(4), 253–265.

Brooke, J. (1996). SUS: A quick and dirty usability scale. In Jordan, P., Thomas, B., Werdmaster, B., & McClelland, I. (Eds.), *Usability evaluation in industry* (pp. 1189–1194). London, UK: Taylor and Francis.

Brynskov, M., Christensen, B. G., Ludvigsen, M., Collins, A., & Grønbæk, K. (2005). Designing for nomadic play: A case study of participatory design with children. In *Proceedings of the 4th International Conference for Interaction Design and Children*.

Bystrom, K. E., Barfield, W., & Hendrix, C. (1999). A conceptual model of the sense of presence in virtual environments. *Presence (Cambridge, Mass.)*, *8*, 241–244. doi:10.1162/105474699566107

Cardosi, K. M., & Murphy, E.D. (1995). *Human factors checklist for the design and evaluation of air traffic control systems*. DOT/FAA/RD-95/3.1. Research funded by the Federal Aviation Administration's Office of the Chief Scientific and Technical Advisor for Human Factors (AAR-100).

Carofiglio, V., De Rosis, F., & Novielli, N. (2009). Cognitive emotion modeling in natural language communication. In Tao, J. (Ed.), *Affective information processing* (pp. 23–44). London: Springer-Verlag. doi:10.1007/978-1-84800-306-4_3

Carr, N. (2003). *Does IT Matter? Information Technology and the Corrosion of Competitive Advantage*. Boston, MA: Harvard Business School Press.

Cassidy, T. (2006). *Education management information systems (EMIS) in Latin America and the Caribbean: Lessons and challenges*. Inter-American Development Bank.

Champney, R., Kokini, C., & Stanney, K. (2011). Making the design process more usable: Aligning design with user performance. In *Proceedings of the Human Computer Interaction International Conference*. July 9-14. Orlando, Florida. USA.

Chandler, D. (2002). *Semiotics: The basics*. London, UK: Routledge. doi:10.4324/9780203166277

Chanel, G., Kronegg, J., Grandjean, D., & Pun, T. (2005). *Emotion assessment: Arousal evaluation using EEG's and peripheral physiological signals*. Technical Report 05.02, Computer Vision Group, Computing Science Center, University of Geneva, Switzerland.

Chellappa, R., & Gupta, A. (2002). Managing computing resources in active intranets. *International Journal of Network Management*, *12*(2), 117–128. doi:10.1002/nem.427

Chin, J. P., Diehl, V. A., & Norman, L. K. (1988). Development of an instrument measuring user satisfaction of the human-computer interface. [New York: ACM/SIGCHI.]. *Proceedings of the SIGCHI*, *88*, 213–218.

Chiuhsiang, J. L., Chi, N. L., Chin, J. C., & Hung, J. C. (2010). The performance of computer input devices in a vibration environment. *Ergonomics*, *53*(4), 478–490. doi:10.1080/00140130903528186

Choppin, A. (2000). *EEG-based human interface for disabled individuals: Emotion expression with neural networks*. (Master's thesis). Tokyo Institute of Technology, Japan.

Chudoba, K., & Maznevski, M. (2000). Bridging space over time: Global virtual team dynamics and effectiveness. *Organization Science*, *11*, 473–492. doi:10.1287/orsc.11.5.473.15200

Clarke, S. (1998). Organizational factors affecting the incident reporting of train drivers. *Work and Stress*, *12*(1), 6–16. doi:10.1080/02678379808256845

Compilation of References

Clutterbuck, P., Rowlands, T., & Seamons, O. (2009). A case study of SME web application development effectiveness via agile methods. *Electronic Journal of Information Systems Evaluation, 12*(1), 13–26.

Coan, J. A., Allen, J. J. B., & Harmon-Jones, E. (2002). Voluntary facial expression and hemispheric asymmetry over the frontal cortex. *Psychophysiology, 38*(6), 912–925. doi:10.1111/1469-8986.3860912

Cooper, A. (1999). *The inmates are running the asylum*. Indianapolis, IN: SAMS.

Costabile, M. (2001). Usability in the software life cycle. In Chang, S. K. (Ed.), *Handbook of software engineering and knowledge engineering* (pp. 179–192). City, NJ: World Scientific.

Courage, C., & Baxter, K. (2005). *Understanding your users: A practical guide to user requirements methods, tools, and techniques*. San Francisco, CA: Morgan Kaufmann.

Csikszentmihalyi, M. (1991). *Flow—The psychology of optimal experience*. New York, NY: Harper Collins.

Cui, Y., Honkala, M., Pihkala, K., Kinnunen, K., & Grassel, G. (2010). Linked Internet UI: A mobile user interface optimized for social networking. In *MobileHCI 2010* (pp. 45–54). Lisbon, Portugal: ACM Press. doi:10.1145/1851600.1851611

Danesi, M. (2007). *The quest for meaning: A guide to semiotic theory and practice*. Toronto: University of Toronto Press.

Dansky, H. K., Thompson, D., & Sanner, T. (2006). A framework for evaluating ehealth research. *Evaluation and Program Planning, 29*(4), 397–404. doi:10.1016/j.evalprogplan.2006.08.009

Davenport, T., & Prusak, L. (1997). *Information ecology: Mastering the information and knowledge environment*. New York: Oxford University Press.

Davis, A. M., Bersoff, E. H., & Comer, E. R. (1988). A strategy for comparing alternative software-development life-cycle models. *IEEE Transactions on Software Engineering, 14*(10), 1453–1461. doi:10.1109/32.6190

Davis, F. D. (1989). Perceived usefulness, perceived ease of use, and user acceptance of information technology. *Management Information Systems Quarterly, 13*, 319–340. doi:10.2307/249008

de Freitas, S., & Liarokapis, F. (2011). (in press). Serious games: A new paradigm for education? *Serious Games and Edutainment Applications. Heisenberg: Springer*.

De Saussure, F. (1965). *Course in general linguistics* (Baskin, W., Trans.). New York, NY: McGraw-Hill.

de Souza, C. S., & Cypher, A. (2008). Semiotic engineering in practice: Redesigning the CoScripter interface. In *Proceedings of the working conference on Advanced Visual Interfaces (AVI 2008)* (pp. 165-172). Napoli, Italy: ACM Press. Retrieved from http://doi.acm.org/10.1145/1385569.1385597

de Souza, C. S., Leitão, C. F., Prates, R. O., & da Silva, E. J. (2006). The semiotic inspection method. In *Proc. of VII Brazilian symposium on Human Factors in Computing Systems (IHC 2006)*, (pp. 148-157). Natal, RN, Brazil: ACM Press. Retrieved from http://doi.acm.org/10.1145/1298023.1298044

de Souze, C. S. (2005). *The semiotic engineering of human-computer interaction*. Cambridge, MA: The MIT Press.

Dey, A., & Abowd, G. (2000). Towards a better understanding of context and context awareness. In *Proceedings of the Workshop on the What, Who, Where, When and How of Context-Awareness, Affiliated with the CHI 2000 Conference on Human Factors in Computer Systems*. New York, NY: ACM Press.

Dillman, R. W. (2012). Tutorial: Signs and language. Retrieved May, 2012 from http://www.rdillman.com/HFCL/TUTOR/Semiotics/sem1.html

Dillon, A., & Watson, C. (1996). User analysis in HCI: The historical lesson from individual differences research. *International Journal of Human-Computer Studies, 45*(6), 619–637. doi:10.1006/ijhc.1996.0071

Dingsoyr, T., & Royrvik, E. (2003). An empirical study of an informal knowledge repository in a medium-sized software consulting company. In Proceedings of the International Conference on Software Engineering. Portland, OR: Institute of Electrical and Electronics Engineers, Inc.

Dix, A., Finlay, J., Abowd, G., & Beale, R. (1998). *Human-computer interaction* (2nd ed.). Hertfordshire, UK: Prentice Hall.

Dornhege, G., Millan, J. D. R., Hinterberger, T., McFarland, D. J., & Muller, K. R. (Eds.). (2007). *Towards brain-computing interfacing.* Cambridge, MA: MIT Press.

Dougherty, D. (2001, 26 January). *LAMP: The open source web platform.* Retrieved from http://onlamp.com/pub/a/onlamp/2001/01/25/lamp.html

Dourish, P. (2004). What we talk about when we talk about context. *Personal and Ubiquitous Computing, 8*(1), 19–30. doi:10.1007/s00779-003-0253-8

Druin, A., Bederson, B., Boltman, A., Miura, A., Knotts-Callahan, D., & Platt, M. (1999). Children as our technology design partners. In Druin, A. (Ed.), *The design of children's technology* (pp. 51–72). San Francisco, CA: Morgan Kaufmann Publishers.

Dumas, J. S., Molich, R., & Jeffries, R. (2004, July/August). Describing usability problems: Are we sending the right message? *Interactions - All Systems Go: How Wall Street Will Benefit from User-centered Design, 11*(4), 24-29. doi: 10.1145/1005261.1005274

Dumas, J. F., & Redish, J. C. (1999). *A practical guide to usability testing.* Portland, OR: Intellect Ltd.

Durrani, Q., & Qureshi, S. (2012). Usability engineering practices in SDLC. *ICCIT: 1st Taibah University International Conference on Computing and Information Technology.* Al-Madinah Al-Munawwarah, Saudi Arabia. Retrieved from http://www.taibahu.edu.sa/iccit/allICCITpapers/pdf/p319-durrani.pdf

Dzida, W., Herda, S., & Itzfelt, W. (1978). User-perceived quality of interactive systems. *IEEE Transactions on Software Engineering, SE-4*(4), 270–276. doi:10.1109/TSE.1978.231511

Ekman, P. (1999). Basic emotions. In Dalgleish, T., & Power, T. (Eds.), *The handbook of cognition and emotion* (pp. 45–60). Sussex, U.K.: John Wiley & Sons, Ltd.

Falk, J. H., & Dierking, L. D. (2000). *Learning from museums: Visitor experiences and the making of meaning.* Walnut Creek: Altamira Press.

Compilation of References

Falk, J. H., & Dierking, L. D. (2008). Enhancing visitor interaction and learning with mobile technologies. In Tallon, L., & Walker, K. (Eds.), *Digital technologies and the museum experience. Handheld guides and other media* (pp. 19–60). Walnut Creek: Altamira Press.

Fasel, B., & Luettin, J. (2003). Automatic facial expression analysis: A survey. *Pattern Recognition*, *36*, 259–275. doi:10.1016/S0031-3203(02)00052-3

Faulkner, L. (2003). Beyond the five-user assumption: Benefits of increased sample sizes in usability testing. *Behavior Research Methods, Instruments, & Computers*, *35*(3), 379–383. doi:10.3758/BF03195514

Faulkner, X. (2000). *Usability engineering*. Basingstoke: Macmillan Press.

Finstad, K. (2010). Response interpolation and scale sensitivity: Evidence against 5-point scales. *Journal of Usability Studies*, *5*(3), 104–110.

Floyd, C. (1984). A systematic look at prototyping. In R. Budde, K. Kuhlenkamp, L. Mathiassen, & L. Zullighoven (Eds.), *Approaches to prototyping: Proceedings on the working conference on prototyping* (pp. 1-18). Heidelberg: Springer Verlag.

Ford, G., & Gelderblom, H. (2003). The effects of culture on performance achieved through the use of human computer interaction. In *Proceedings of the 2003 annual research conference of the South African institute of computer scientists and information technologists on Enablement through technology* (SAICSIT 2003) (pp. 218-230). Republic of South Africa.

Fowler, M., & Kendall, S. (1999). *UML distilled*. Addison-Wesley Professional.

France, D. J., Cartwright, J., Jones, V., Thompson, V., & Whitlock, J. A. (2004). Improving pediatric chemotherapy safety through voluntary incident reporting: Lessons from the field. *Journal of Pediatric Oncology Nursing*, *21*(4), 200–206. doi:10.1177/1043454204265907

Freeman, J., Avons, S. E., Meddis, R., Pearson, D. E., & Ijsselsteijn, W. (2000). Using behavioural realism to estimate presence: A study of the utility of postural responses to motion-stimuli. *Presence (Cambridge, Mass.)*, *9*, 149–164. doi:10.1162/105474600566691

Gabbard, J., Swan, J., Hix, D., Lanzagorta, M., Livingston, M., Brown, D., & Julier, S. (2002). Usability engineering: Domain analysis activities for augmented reality systems. In A. J. Woods, J. O. Merritt, S. A. Benton, & M. T. Bolas (Eds.) *Stereoscopic displays and virtual reality systems IX* (pp. 445–457). San Jose, CA: Photonics West, Electronic Imaging conference.

Gammon, B., & Burch, A. (2008). Designing mobile digital experiences. In Tallon, L., & Walker, K. (Eds.), *Digital technologies and the museum experience: Handheld guides and other media* (pp. 35–60). Lanham, MD: Rowan and Littlefield.

Gee, J. P. (2003). *What video games have to teach us about learning and literacy*. New York, NY: Palgrave Macmillan. doi:10.1145/950566.950595

Gillan, D. J., & Bias, R. G. (2001). Usability science. I: Foundations. *International Journal of Human-Computer Interaction*, *13*(4), 351–372. doi:10.1207/S15327590IJHC1304_02

Gilutz, S., & Nielsen, J. (2002). Usability of websites for children: 70 design guidelines. *Nielsen Norman Group*, pp. 117-121. Retrieved from http://www.nngroup.com/reports/kids/

Gilutz, S., & Bekker, M. (2003). Children's online interfaces: Is usability testing worthwhile? *IDC, 7*(3), 143–145.

Glass, R., & Li, S. (2010). Social influence and instant messaging adoption. *Journal of Computer Information Systems, 51*, 24–30.

Gould, J. D., & Lewis, C. H. (1985). Designing for usability: Key principles and what designers think. *Communications of the ACM, 28*(3), 300–311. doi:10.1145/3166.3170

Gray, D. W., & Salzman, M. C. (1998). Damaged merchandise? A review of experiments that compare usability evaluation methods. *Human-Computer Interaction, 12*, 203–261. doi:10.1207/s15327051hci1303_2

Greenbaum, J., & Kyng, M. (Eds.). (1991). *Design at work: Cooperative design of computer systems*. Hillsdale, NJ: Lawrence Erlbaum.

Greenberg, S., & Buxton, B. (2008). Usability evaluation considered harmful (some of the time). In *ACM Conference on Human Factors in Computing Systems (CHI 2008)* (pp. 111-120). Florence, Italy: ACM Press.

Grudin, J. (2006). Enterprise knowledge management and emerging technologies. In Proceedings of the 39th Annual Hawaii International Conference on System Sciences. Kona, HI: Institute of Electrical and Electronics Engineers, Inc.

Gulati, A., & Dubey, S. (2012). Critical analysis on usability evaluation techniques. *International Journal of Engineering Science and Technology, 4*(3), 990–997.

Guntamukkala, V., Wen, H. J., & Tarn, J. M. (2006). An empirical study of selecting software development life cycle models. *Human Systems Management, 25*(4), 265–278.

Hainey, T. (2007). Information systems development methodologies, techniques & tools (4th ed.). *International Journal of Information Management, 27*(1), 58-59. doi: doi:10.1016/j.ijinfomgt.2006.09.002

Häkkilä, J., & Mäntyjärvi, J. (2005). Collaboration in context-aware mobile phone applications. In *Proceedings of the 38th Hawaii International Conference on System Sciences*. HI, USA.

Häkkilä, J., & Mäntyjärvi, J. (2006, October 25–27) Developing design guidelines for context-aware mobile applications. In *Proceedings of the 3rd International Conference on Mobile Technology, Applications & Systems (Bangkok, Thailand, October 25 - 27, 2006). Mobility '06, vol. 270*. ACM, New York, NY.

Hanna, L., Risden, K., & Alexander, K. (1997). Guidelines for usability testing with children. *Interaction, 4*(5), 9–14. doi:10.1145/264044.264045

Hanna, L., Risden, K., Czerwinski, K., & Alexander, K. (1998). The role of usability research in designing children's computer products. In Druin, A. (Ed.), *The design of children's technology*. San Francisco, CA: Morgan Kaufmann Publishers.

Harding, M., Storz, O., Nigel, D., & Friday, A. (2009). Planning ahead: Techniques for simplifying mobile service use. In *HotMobile 2009*. Santa Cruz, CA, USA: ACM Press. doi:10.1145/1514411.1514422

Harris, D. (2011). *Human performance on the flight deck*. Farnham, England: Ashgate.

Hart, S. G., & Staveland, L. E. (1988). Development of NASA-TLX (Task Load Index) - Results of empirical and theoretical research. In Hancock, P. A., & Meshkati, N. (Eds.), *Human mental workload*. Elsevier Science Publisher B.V.doi:10.1016/S0166-4115(08)62386-9

Compilation of References

Hartson, H. R., Andre, T. S., & Williges, R. C. (2001). Criteria for evaluating usability evaluation methods. *International Journal of Human-Computer Interaction, 13*(4), 373–410. doi:10.1207/S15327590IJHC1304_03

Hartson, H. R., Andre, T. S., & Williges, R. C. (2003). Criteria for evaluating usability evaluation methods. *International Journal of Human-Computer Interaction, 15*(1), 145–181. doi:10.1207/S15327590IJHC1501_13

Hein, G. E. (1998). *Learning in the museum.* London, UK: Routledge.

Heller, W., Nitschke, J. B., & Lindsay, D. L. (1997). Neuropsychological correlates of arousal in self-reported emotion. *Neuroscience Letters, 11*(4), 383–402.

Henning, B., & Vorderer, P. (2001). Psychological escapism: Predicting the amount of television viewing by need for cognition. *The Journal of Communication, 51*, 100–120. doi:10.1111/j.1460-2466.2001.tb02874.x

Hertzum, M., Bansler, J. P., Havn, E. C., & Simonsen, J. (2012). Pilot implementation: Learning from field tests in IS development. *Communications of the Association for Information Systems, 30*(1), 313–328.

Hertzum, M., & Jacobsen, N. E. (2003). The evaluator effect: A chilling fact about usability evaluation methods. *International Journal of Human-Computer Interaction, 15*(1), 183–204. doi:10.1207/S15327590IJHC1501_14

Hewett, T. T., Baecker, R., Card, S., Carey, T., Gasen, J., Mantei, M., et al. (1996). *ACM SIGCHI Curricula for human-computer interaction.* Retrieved October 13, 2009, from http://www.acm.org/sigchi/cdg/cdg2.html

Hewett, T. T. (1986). The role of iterative evaluation in designing systems for usability. In Harrison, M. D., & Monk, A. F. (Eds.), *People & computers: Designing for usability.* Cambridge: Cambridge University Press.

Holtzblatt, K., & Jones, S. (1993). Contextual inquiry: Aa participatory technique for system design. In Schuler, D., & Namioka, A. (Eds.), *Participatory design: Principles and practices* (pp. 177–210). Mahwah, NJ: Lawrence Erlbaum.

Holzinger, A., Kickmeier-Rust, M., & Albert, D. (2008). Dynamic media in computer science education; content complexity and learning performance: Is less more? *Journal of Educational Technology & Society, 11*(1), 279–290.

Hoptman, G. H. (1992). *The virtual museum and related epistemological concerns* (pp. 141–159). Sociomedia. Multimedia, Hypermedia and the Social Construction of Knowledge.

Hornbæk, K. (2010). Dogmas in the assessment of usability of evaluation methods. *Behaviour & Information Technology, 29*(1), 97–111. doi:10.1080/01449290801939400

Hubona, G., & Shirah, G. (2004). The gender factor performing visualization tasks on computer media. In *Proceedings of the 37th Hawaii International Conference on System Sciences.* HI, USA.

Ibrahim, A., & Salim, S. (2004). Designing software for child users: A case study of a web page construction kit for children. *Malaysian Journal of Computer Science, 17*(1), 32–41.

ICOM/CIDOC. Multimedia working group. (1996). Introduction to multimedia in museums. Retrieved May 1, 2012, from http://www.willpowerinfo.myby.co.uk/cidoc/introtomultimediamuseums.pdf

Ijsselsteijn, W., deRidder, H., Freeman, J., & Avons, S. E. (2000). Presence: Concept, determinants and measurement. In *Proceedings of the SPIE, Human Vision and Electronic Imaging V* (pp. 3959-76).

International Business Machines (IBM). (2007). User-centered design. *IBM Design: UCD Process.* Retrieved September 17, 2012, from http://www-01.ibm.com/software/ucd/ucd.html

International Institute for Educational Planning. (2010). *Guidebook for planning education in emergencies and reconstruction.* UNESCO.

Islam, M. N. (2011). A semiotics perspective to web usability: An empirical case study. In *Proc. of IADIS International Conference on Interface and Human Computer Interaction (IHCI 2011)* (pp. 19-28). Rome, Italy: IADIS.

Islam, M. N. (2011). Beyond users' inaccurate interpretations of web interface signs: A semiotic perception. In *Proc. of the IFIP 13th International Conference on Informatics and Semiotics in Organizations (ICISO 2011)* (pp. 31-40). Leeuwarden, The Netherlands: Fryske Akademy.

Islam, M. N. (2012). Towards designing users' intuitive web interface. In *Proc. of the 6th International Conference on Complex, Intelligent, and Software Intensive Systems (CISIS-2012)* (pp.513-518). Palermo, Italy: IEEE CS.

Islam, M. N., Tetard, F., Reijonen, P., & Tarkkanen, K. (2012). Integrating semiotics perception in usability testing: A light-weighted experiment on an e-health application. In *Proc. of IADIS International Conference on Interface and Human Computer Interaction (IHCI 2012)* (pp. 141-148). Lisbon, Portugal: IADIS.

Islam, M.N. (2008). Semiotics of the web interface: Analysis and guidelines. *Journal of Computer Science and Technology (JCS&T),* 8(3), 166-167.

Islam, M. N. (2012). Semiotics perception towards designing users' intuitive web user interface: A Study on web sign redesign. In Hakkikur, (Eds.), *Knowledge and technologies in innovative information systems* (pp. 139–155). Berlin, Germany: Springer Verlag. doi:10.1007/978-3-642-33244-9_10

Islam, M. N. (2013). *A systematic literature review of semiotics perception in user interfaces. Accepted to be published in Journal of Systems and Information Technology (JSIT),* 15(1). UK: Emerald Publishers.

Islam, M. N., Ali, M., Al-Mamun, A., & Islam, M. (2010). Semiotics explorations on designing the information intensive web interfaces. *International Arab Journal of Information Technology,* 7(1), 45–54.

ISO 13406-1:1999 (2007). Ergonomic requirements for work with visual displays based on flat panels. ISO.

ISO 9241 -11. (1998). Guidance on usability standards. Retrieved September, 2012 from http://www.iso.org/iso/iso_catalogue/Catalogue _tc/catalogue_detail.htm?csnumber=16883

ISO 9241-11. (1998). Ergonomic requirements for office work with visual display terminals – Part 11: Guidance on usability. Geneva: Switzerland: ISO.

ISO International Organization for Standardization. (1998). International ISO standard 9241-11, ergonomic requirements for office work with visual display terminals (VDTs) - Part 11: Guidance on usability (1st ed.). Switzerland.

Izard, C. E. (1993). Four systems for emotion activation: Cognitive and non cognitive processes. *Psychological Review*, *100*(1), 68–90. doi:10.1037/0033-295X.100.1.68

James, W. (1984). What is an emotion? *Mind*, *9*, 188–205.

Janeiro, J., Barbosa, S. D., Springer, T., & Schill, A. (2009). Enhancing user interface design patterns with design rationale structures. In *Proceedings of the 27th ACM international conference on Design of communication (SIGDOC 2009)* (pp. 9-16). Indiana, USA: ACM Press.

Janhager, J. (2005). *User consideration in early stages of product development: Theories and methods* (Unpublished doctoral dissertation). Royal Institute of Technology, Stockholm, Sweden.

Jansson, L., Handest, P., Nielsen, J., Saebye, D., & Parnas, J. (2002). Exploring boundaries of schizophrenia: A comparison of ICD-10 with other diagnostic systems in first-admitted patients. *World Psychiatry; Official Journal of the World Psychiatric Association (WPA)*, *1*(2), 109–114.

Jeng, J. (2005). Usability assessment of academic digital libraries: Effectiveness, efficiency, satisfaction, and learnability. Libri. *International Journal of Libraries and Information Services*, *55*(2/3), 96–121.

Johnson, C. W. (2003). How will we get the data and what will we do with it then? Issues in the reporting of adverse healthcare events. *Quality & Safety in Health Care*, *12*(2), 64–67. doi:10.1136/qhc.12.suppl_2.ii64

Joly, A. V., Pemberton, L., & Griffiths, R. (2009). *Card sorting activates with preschool children* (pp. 204–213). HCL.

Jung, Y., Anttila, A., & Blom, J. (2008). Designing for the evolution of mobile contacts application. In *MobileHCI 2008* (pp. 449–452). Amsterdam, the Netherlands: ACM Press. doi:10.1145/1409240.1409311

Jureta, I. J., Faulkner, S., & Schobbens, P. Y. (2008). Clear justification of modeling decisions for goal-oriented requirements engineering. *Requirements Engineering*, *13*(2), 87–115. doi:10.1007/s00766-007-0056-y

Kafai, Y. B., & Ching, C. C. (1996). Meaningful contexts for mathematical learning: The potential of game making activities. In *Proceedings of the International Conference on Learning Sciences* (pp. 164-171).

Kamishlian, C. C., & Albert, B. (2011). You need an outlet and a browser: How children understand and use the Internet. *User Experience*, *10*(1), 12–15.

Karoulis, A., Sylaiou, S., & White, M. (2006). Usability evaluation of a virtual museum interface. *Journal Informatica, 17*(3), IOS Press, 363-380.

Karvonen, K. (2000). The beauty of simplicity. In Proceedings of the ACM Conference on Universal Usability. Arlington, VA: The Association of Computing Machinery.

Katz, E., & Foulkes, D. (1962). On the use of mass media for escape: Clarification of a concept. *Public Opinion Quarterly*, *26*, 377–388. doi:10.1086/267111

Kelkar, K., Khasawneh, M. T., Bowling, S. R., Gramopadye, A. K., Melloy, B. J., & Grimes, L. (2005). The added usefulness of process measures over performance measures in interface design. *International Journal of Human-Computer Interaction*, *18*(1), 1–18. doi:10.1207/s15327590ijhc1801_1

Kerawalla, L., Luckin, R., Seljeflot, S., & Woolard, A. (2006). Making it real: Exploring the potential of augmented reality for teaching primary school science. *Virtual Reality (Waltham Cross)*, *10*(3), 163–174. doi:10.1007/s10055-006-0036-4

Kies, J. K., Williges, R. C., & Rosson, M. B. (1998). Coordinating computer-supported cooperative work: A review of research issues and strategies. *Journal of the American Society for Information*, *49*, 776–779.

Kim, K. H., Bang, S. W., & Kim, S. R. (2004). Emotion recognition system using short term monitoring of physiological signals. *Medical & Biological Engineering & Computing*, *42*, 419–427. doi:10.1007/BF02344719

Kim, K. L. (1996). *Caged in our own signs: A book about semiotics*. Berkeley, CA: Greenwood.

Klimmt, C., & Vorderer, P. (2003). Media psychology "is not yet there": Introducing theories on media entertainment to the presence debate. *Presence (Cambridge, Mass.)*, *12*(4), 346–359. doi:10.1162/105474603322391596

Kneifel, A. A., & Guerrero, C. (2003). Using participatory inquiry in usability analysis to align a development team's mental model with its users' needs. In *Proceedings of the Society for Technical Communication 50ᵗʰ annual conference*. May 18-21, Dallas, Texas, USA.

Kostyunina, M. B., & Kulikov, M. A. (1996). Frequency characteristics of EEG spectra in the emotion. *Neuroscience and Behavioral Physiology*, *26*(4), 340–343. doi:10.1007/BF02359037

Krepki, R., Blankertz, B., Curio, G., & Muller, K. R. (2007). The Berlin brain-computer interface (BBCI): Towards a new communication channel for online control in gaming applications. *Journal of Multimedia Tools Applications*, *33*, 73–90. doi:10.1007/s11042-006-0094-3

Kreuger, R. A., & Casey, M. A. (2009). *Focus groups: A practical guide for applied research* (5th ed.). Thousand Oaks, CA: Sage Publishers.

Krug, S. (2000). *Don't make me think*. Indianapolis, IN: New Riders Publishing.

Krug, S. (2010). *Rocket surgery made easy: The do-it-yourself guide to finding and fixing usability problems*. Berkeley, CA: New Riders.

Kuen Seong Su, D., & Siew Yen Yee, V. (2007). Designing usable interface for navigating mobile chat messages. In *OZCHI '07* (pp. 291–294). Adelaide, Australia: ACM Press. doi:10.1145/1324892.1324953

Kuniavsky, M. *Observing the user experience: A practitioner's guide to user research*. San Francisco, CA: Morgan Kaufmann.

Lansdale, M. W., & Ormerod, T. C. (1994). *Understanding interfaces: A handbook of human-computer dialogue*. San Diego, CA: Academic Press.

Laster, S., Stitz, T., Bove, F. J., & Wise, C. (2011). Transitioning from marketing-oriented design to user-oriented design: A case study. *Journal of Web Librarianship*, *5*(4), 299–321. doi:10.1080/19322909.2011.623517

Compilation of References

Law, J. (1987). On the social explanation of technical change: The case of Portuguese maritime expansion. *Technology and Culture*, *28*, 227–252. doi:10.2307/3105566

Lazarus, R. S. (1991). *Emotion and adaptation*. New York: Oxford University Press.

Leatham, G., & Duck, S. (1990). Conversations with friends and the dynamics of social support. In Duck, S. (Ed.), *Personal relationships and social support* (pp. 1–29). London: Sage.

Lecerof, A., & Paterno, F. (1998). Automatic support for usability evaluation. *IEEE Transactions on Software Engineering*, *24*(10), 863–888. doi:10.1109/32.729686

Leeb, R., Lee, F., Keinrath, C., Scherer, R., Bischof, H., & Pfurtscheller, G. (2007). Brain-computer communication: Motivation, aim and impact of exploring a virtual apartment. *IEEE Transactions on Neural Systems and Rehabilitation Engineering*, *15*(4), 473–482. doi:10.1109/TNSRE.2007.906956

Lee, K. M. (2004). Presence, explicated. *Communication Theory*, *14*(1), 27–50. doi:10.1111/j.1468-2885.2004.tb00302.x

Lehrer, J. (2012). Groupthink: The brainstorming myth. *New Yorker*. Retrieved from http://www.newyorker.com/reporting/2012/01/30/120130fa_fact_lehrer?currentPage=all

Lewis, C. (1982). *Using the thinking-aloud method in cognitive interface design. IBM Research Report RC 9265*. NY: Yorktown Heights.

Lewis, R. J. (1995). IBM computer usability satisfaction questionnaires: Psychometric evaluation and instructions for use. *International Journal of Human-Computer Interaction*, *1*(7), 57–78. doi:10.1080/10447319509526110

Liarokapis, F., Sylaiou, S., & Mountain, D. (2008). Personalizing virtual and augmented reality for cultural heritage indoor and outdoor experiences. In *Proceedings of the 9th International Symposium on Virtual Reality, Archaeology and Cultural Heritage* (VAST '08) (pp. 55-62). Eurographics, Braga, Portugal.

Li, D., Chau, P. Y. K., & Lou, H. (2005). Understanding individual adoption of instant messaging: An empirical investigation. *Journal of the Association for Information Systems*, *6*, 102–129.

Lidwell, W., Holden, K., & Butler, J. (2003). *Universal principles of design*. Beverly, MA: Rockport Publishers.

Lin, C.-P., & Bhattacherjee, A. (2009). Understanding online social support and its antecedents: A socio-cognitive model. *The Social Science Journal*, *46*, 724–737. doi:10.1016/j.soscij.2009.03.004

Lin, H. X., Choong, Y. Y., & Salvendy, G. (1997). A proposed index of usability: A method for comparing the relative usability of software systems. *Behaviour & Information Technology*, *16*(4/5), 267–278. doi:10.1080/014492997119833

Lin, K.-Y., & Lu, H.-P. (2011). Why people use social networking sites: An empirical study integrating network externalities and motivation theory. *Computers in Human Behavior*, *27*, 1152–1161. doi:10.1016/j.chb.2010.12.009

Liu, Y., Osvalder, A., & Karlsson, M. (2010). Considering the importance of user profiles in interface design. In Matrai, R. (Ed.), *User interfaces* (pp. 61–80). Vukovar, Croatia: InTech Publishing. doi:10.5772/8903

Lombard, M., & Ditton, T. (1997). At the heart of it all: The concept of presence. *Journal of Computer-Mediated Communication, 3*(2).

London Charter. (2013). *London Charter for the use of 3-dimensional visualisation in the research and communication of cultural heritage.* Retrieved from http://www.londoncharter.org/

Lura. (2012). New! Bejeweled 3 has chat rooms. *BadgeHungry.* Retrieved July 31, 2012, from http://www.badgehungry.com/2012/07/31/new-bejeweled-3-has-chat-rooms/

Lynch, P., & Horton, S. (2009). *Web style guide: Basic design principles for creating web sites* (3rd ed.). New Haven, CT: Yale University Press.

MacDonald, G. F., & Alsford, S. (1997). Towards the meta museum. In Jones-Garmil, K. (Ed.), *The wired museum: Emerging technology and changing paradigms.* Washington, DC: American Association of Museums.

Madill, J. J. (1998). Marketing in government. *Optimum, the Journal of Public Sector Management, 24*(4), 11-18.

Magaña Echeverría, M. A., Santana-Mancilla, P. C., & Rocha, V. M. (2012). An educational management information system to support. *International conference on New Horizons in Education.* Prague.

Mandryk, R. L., & Atkins, M. S. (2007). A fuzzy physiological approach for continuously modeling emotion during interaction with play technologies. *International Journal of Human-Computer Studies, 65*(4), 329–347. doi:10.1016/j.ijhcs.2006.11.011

Mantymaki, M., & Riemer, K. (2011). "Fun and friends and stuff." On the stickiness of social virtual worlds among teenagers. In P. Seltsikas, D. Bunker, L. Dawson, & M. Indulska (Eds.), *Proceedings of the Australasian Conference on Information Systems ACIS 2011* (paper 10). Sydney, Australia.

Markopoulos, P., & Bekker, M. (2003). On the assessment of usability testing methods for children. *Interacting with Computers, 15,* 227–243. doi:10.1016/S0953-5438(03)00009-2

Markopoulos, P., & Khan, V. (2011). Sampling and reconstructing user experience. [IJHCR]. *International Journal of Handheld Computing Research, 2*(3), 53–72. doi:10.4018/jhcr.2011070104

Martin, S. K., Etchegaray, J. M., Simmons, D., Belt, W. T., & Clark, K. (2005). Development and implementation of the University of Texas close call reporting system. *Advances in Patient Safety, 2,* 149–160.

Marty, P. F. (2006). Meeting user needs in the modern museum: Profiles of the new museum information professional. *Library & Information Science Research, 28*(1), 128–144. doi:10.1016/j.lisr.2005.11.006

Marty, P. F. (2007). Museum websites and museum visitors: Before and after the museum visit. *Museum Management and Curatorship, 22*(4), 337–360. doi:10.1080/09647770701757708

Marty, P. F. (2011). *Museum informatics.* USA: Florida State University.

Mateus, M., Salvador, T., Scholz, J., & Sorensen, D. (1996). *Proceedings from CHI: Engineering Ethnography in the Home.* New York: ACM Press.

Mayhew, D. J. (2002). Usability testing: You get what you pay for. *Deborah J. Mayhew & Associates - Software and Web Usability Engineering Consultants.* Retrieved September 16, 2012, from http://drdeb.vineyard.net/index.php?loc=17

Mayhew, D. (1992). *Principles and guidelines in user interface design.* Englewood Cliffs, NJ: Prentice-Hall.

Mayhew, D. (1999). *The usability engineering lifecycle: A practitioner's handbook for user interface design.* San Francisco, CA: Morgan Kauffman.

McNay, & Heather, E. (2000). Corporate Intranets: Building communities with data. IEEE Technology & Teamwork, pp. 197-201.

Mendoza-González, R., Vargas Martin, M., & Rodríguez Martínez, L. (2011). *Identifying the Essential Design Requirements for Usable E-Health Communities in Mobile Devices, E-Health Communities and Online Self-Help Groups-Applications and Usage* (Smedberg, Å., & Global, I. G. I., Eds.).

Millan, J. D. R., Galan, F., Vanhooydonck, D., Lew, E., Philips, J., & Nuttin, M. (2009). Asynchronous non-invasive brain-actuated control of an intelligent wheelchair. In *Proceedings of the 31st Annual International Conference of the IEEE Engineering in Medicine and Biology Society.* Minneapolis, MN: IEEE.

Millan, J. D. R., Renkens, F., Mourino, J., & Gerstner, W. (2004). Non-invasive brain-actuated control of a mobile robot by human EEG. *IEEE Transactions on Bio-Medical Engineering, 51*, 1026–1033. doi:10.1109/TBME.2004.827086

Millard, D., & Ross, M. (2006). Blogs, wikis & rss: Web 2.0: Hypertext by any other name? In Proceedings of the seventeenth conference on Hypertext and hypermedia. Odense, Denmark: The Association of Computing Machinery.

Millet, B., & Patterson, P. (2012). User centered design. In *Design and designing.* Oxford, UK: Berg Publishers.

Mohammad Nasir Uddin, M., & Paul Janecek, P. (2007). Faceted classification in web information architecture: A framework for using semantic web tools. *The Electronic Library, 25*(2), 219–233. doi:10.1108/02640470710741340

Moon, J. W., & Kim, Y. G. (2001). Extending the TAM for a world-wide-web context. *Information & Management, 38*, 217–230. doi:10.1016/S0378-7206(00)00061-6

Moore, G. (1965). Cramming more components onto integrated circuits. *Electronics, 38*(8).

Morris, C. (1938). Foundations of the theory of signs. R. Carnap et al. (Eds.), *International Encyclopedia of Unified Science, 2*:1. Chicago: The University of Chicago Press.

Mostéfaoui, G., Pasquier-Rocha, J., & Brézillon, P. (2004). Context-aware computing: A guide for pervasive computing community. *IEEE/ACS Proceedings of the International Conference on Pervasive Services,* Beirut, Lebanon, 39–48.

Mourkoussis, N., White, M., Patel, M., Chmielewski, J., & Walczak, K. (2003). AMS: Metadata for cultural exhibitions using virtual reality. In *DC-2003 Proceedings of the International DCMI Metadata Conference and Workshop* (pp. 135-144). University of Washington, Information School, Seattle, Washington, USA.

Mugler, E., Bensch, M., Halder, S., Rosenstiel, W., Bogdan, M., Birbaumer, N., & Kubler, A. (2008). Control of an internet browser using the P300 event-related potential. *International Journal of Bioelectromagnetism, 10*, 56–63.

Murugappan, M., Rizon, M., Nagarajan, R., Yaacob, S., Zunaidi, I., & Hazry, D. (2007). EEG feature extraction for classifying emotions using FCM and FKM. *International Journal of Computer and Communications, 1*, 21–25.

Musha, T., Terasaki, Y., Haque, H. A., & Ivamitsky, G. A. (1997). Feature extraction from EEGs associated with emotions. *Artificial Life and Robotics, 1*, 15–19. doi:10.1007/BF02471106

Nakhimovsky, Y., Eckle, D., & Riegelsberger, J. (2009). Mobile user experience research: Challenges, methods & tools. In *Workshop on Human-Computer Interaction and Security Systems, ACM CHI 2009* (pp. 4795-4798). Boston, Massachusetts, USA: ACM Press.

Namioka, A., & Schuler, D. (Eds.). (1993). *Participatory design. Principles and practices*. Hillsdale, NJ: Lawrence Erlbaum.

Naranjo-bock, C. (2011, March 7). Approaches to user research when designing for children. *UXmatters*. Retrieved from http://www.uxmatters.com/mt/archives/2011/03/approaches-to-user-research-when-designing-for-children.php

Neilson, J. (1993). *Usability engineering*. San Diego: Academic Press.

Nguyen, V. T., & Oh, H. A. (2010). Users' needs for social tagging and sharing on mobile contacts. In *MobileHCI 2010* (pp. 387–388). Lisbon, Portugal: ACM Press.

Nielsen, J. (1998). Introduction to web design. In Proceedings of the SIGCHI on Human Factors in Computing Systems. Los Angeles, CA: Association for Computing Machinery.

Nielsen, J. (2000). Why you only need to test with 5 users. Retrieved May 26, 2012 from http://www.useit.com/articles/five_second_test/

Nielsen, J. (2005). Heuristic evaluation. Technical Report. UseIt, ISSN 1548-5552, 2005. Retrieved February 1, 2012 from http://www.useit.com/papers/heuristic/

Nielsen, J. (2010, September 13). *Children's websites: Usability issues in designing for kids*. Retrieved from http://www.useit.com/alertbox/children.html

Nielsen, J., & Landauer, T. K. (1993). A mathematical model of the finding of usability problems. In *Proceedings ACM/IFIP INTERCHI'93 Conference* (pp. 206-213). Amsterdam, The Netherlands.

Nielsen, J., & Molich, R. (1990). Heuristic evaluation of user interfaces. In *CHI '90 Proceedings of the SIGCHI Conference on Human Factors in Computing* (pp. 249-256). New York: ACM.

Nielsen, J. (1993). *Usability engineering*. San Francisco, CA: Morgan Kaufmann.

Compilation of References

Nielsen, J. (1994). Guerrilla HCI: Using discount usability engineering to penetrate the intimidation barrier. In Bias, R. G., & Mayhew, D. S. (Eds.), *Cost-justifying usability* (pp. 245–272). Boston, MA: Academic Press.

Nielsen, J. (2000). *Designing web usability.* Indianapolis, IN: New Riders Publishing.

Nielsen, J., & Mack, R. L. (1994). *Usability inspection methods.* New York: John Wiley & Sons.

Nielsen, J., & Tahir, M. (2002). *Homepage Usability: 50 websites deconstructed.* Indianapolis, IN: New Riders Publishing.

Nijholt, A., Tan, D., Allison, B., Millan, J. D. R., Graimann, B., & Jackson, M. M. (2008). Brain-computer interfaces for HCI and games. In *Proceedings of the ACM CHI 2008* (pp. 3925-3928). New York, NY: ACM.

Nischelwitzer, A., Lenz, F.-J., Searle, G., & Holzinger, A. (2007). Some aspects of the development of low-cost augmented reality learning environments as examples for future interfaces in technology enhanced learning. In *Universal access to applications and services (LNCS 4556)* (pp. 728–737). New York: Springer. doi:10.1007/978-3-540-73283-9_79

Norman, D. (2005). Human-centered design considered harmful. *Interactions. Communications of the ACM, 12*(4), 14–19.

Norman, D. A. (1998). *The design of everyday things.* Cambridge, MA: MIT Press.

Norman, D. A. (2002). *The design of everyday things.* New York: Basic Books.

Norman, D. A. (2011). *Living with Complexity.* Cambridge, MA: MIT Press.

Nutt, C. (2012). GDC 2012: Zynga's Schappert shares *Words with Friends* statistics. *Gamasutra.* Retrieved March 12, 3012, from http://www.gamasutra.com/view/news/165171/GDC_2012_Zyngas_Schappert_shares_Words_with_Friends_statistics.php

O'Brien, H. L., & McLean, K. (2009). Measuring the user engagement experience. *Engagement by Design Pre-Conference Workshop, CHI 2009.* Digital Life New World, Boston, MA.

O'Reilly, T. (2005). What Is Web 2.0: Design patterns and business models for the next generation of software. Retrieved July 17, 2006 from http://www.oreillynet.com/pub/a/oreilly/tim/news/2005/09/30/what-is-web-20.html.

Obermaier, B., Muller, G. R., & Pfurtscheller, G. (2003). Virtual keyboard controlled by spontaneous EEG activity. *IEEE Transactions on Neural Systems and Rehabilitation Engineering, 11*, 422–426. doi:10.1109/TNSRE.2003.816866

Oktem, U. G. (2002). Near-miss: A tool for integrated safety, health, environmental and security management. (Unpublished manuscript). The Wharton School, University of Pennsylvania, Risk Management and Decision Processes Center.

Ontario Ministry of Municipal Affairs and Housing. (2011, July 25). Section 2: An overview of local government. *Local Government.* Retrieved October 12, 2012, from http://www.mah.gov.on.ca/Page8391.aspx

Ortony, A., Clore, G. L., & Collins, A. (1988). *The cognitive structure of emotions.* Cambridge University Press. doi:10.1017/CBO9780511571299

Paavilainen, J. (2010). Critical review on video game evaluation heuristics: Social games perspective. In *ACM Future Play 2010* (pp. 56–65). Vancouver, BC, Canada: ACM Press. doi:10.1145/1920778.1920787

Pabllo, C., Soto, R., & Campos, J. (2008). Mobile medication administration system: Application and architecture. In *EATIS'08*. Aracaju, Sergipe, Brazil: ACM Press. doi:10.1145/1621087.1621128

Papadomichelaki, X., & Mentzas, G. (2012). E-GovQual: A multiple-item scale for assessing e-government service quality. *Government Information Quarterly*, 29(1), 98–109. doi:10.1016/j.giq.2011.08.011

Parhi, P., Karlson, A. K., & Bederson, B. B. (2006). Target size study for one-handed thumb use on small touchscreen devices. In *Proceedings of the 8th conference on Human-computer interaction with mobile devices and services*. New York, NY, USA.

Pearrow, M. (2000). *Web site usability handbook*. Independence, KY: Charles River Media.

Peirce, C. S. (1932-52). *Collected writings (8 Vols.)*. Charles Hartshorne, Paul Weiss & Arthur Burks (Eds.). Harvard University Press.

Perfetti, C. (2005). 5 second tests: Measuring your site's content pages. Retrieved May 26, 2012 from http://www.uie.com/articles/five_second_test/

Persson, A., Långh, M., & Nilsson, J. (2010). Usability testing and redesign of library web pages at Lund University, Faculty of Engineering: A case study applying a two-phase, systematic quality approach. *Information Research, 15*(2).

Peryer, G., Noyes, J., Pleydell-Pearce, C. W., & Lieven, N. (2010). Auditory alert characteristics: A survey of pilot views. *The International Journal of Aviation Psychology, 15*(3), 233–250. doi:10.1207/s15327108ijap1503_2

Phimister, J. R., Oktem, U. G., Kleindorfer, P. R., & Kunreuther, H. (2000). Near-miss system analysis: Phase I. (Unpublished manuscript). The Wharton School, University of Pennsylvania Risk Management and Decision Processes Center.

Plass-Oude Bos, D., Reuderink, B., van der Laar, B., Gurkok, H., Muhl, C., Nijholt, A., & Heylen, D. (2010). Brain-computer interfacing and games. In Tan, D. S., & Nijholt, A. (Eds.), *Brain-computer interfaces, human-computer interaction series* (pp. 149–178). London: Springer-Verlag.

Plutchik, R. (1980). A general psycho-evolutionary theory of emotion. In Plutchik, R., & Kellerman, H. (Eds.), *Emotion: Theory, research, and experiences* (pp. 3–33). New York: Academic press.

Polson, P. G., Lewis, C., Rieman, J., & Wharton, C. (1992). Cognitive walkthroughs: A method for theory- based evaluation of user interfaces. *International Journal of Man-Machine Studies, 36*, 741–773. doi:10.1016/0020-7373(92)90039-N

Preece, J. Y., Rogers, H., Sharp, D., & Benyon, S. Holland, & Carey, T. (1994). *Human-computer interaction*. Addison-Wesley.

Preece, J., Rogers, Y., & Sharp, H. (2002). *Interaction design: Beyond human-computer interaction*. New York: John Wiley & Sons.

Pruitt, J., & Adlin, T. (2006). *The persona lifecycle: Keeping people in mind throughout product design*. San Francisco, CA: Morgan Kaufmann.

Compilation of References

Quesenbery, W. (2004). Defining a summative usability test for voting systems: A report from the UPA 2004 Workshop on Voting and Usability (Online). *Usability Professional's Association*. Retrieved January 20, 2008, from http://www.usabilityprofessionals.org/upa_projects/voting_and_usability/documents/voting_summative_test.pdf

Rasmussen, J., & Goodstein, L. P. (1988). Information technology and work. In M. Helander (Ed.), *Handbook of Human-Computer Interaction* (pp. 175-201). Elsevier Science Publishers BV (North Holland): New York.

Rasmussen, J., Pejtersen, A.-L. M., & Goodstein, L. P. (1994). *Cognitive systems engineering*. Wiley.

Ravden, S., & Jonhson, G. (1989). *Evaluating usability of human-computer interfaces*. Chichester, UK: Ellis Horwood Limited.

Read, J. C. (2011). Mess days: Working with children to design and deliver worthwhile mobile experiences. *User Experience, 10*(1), 4–6.

Redish, J., Bias, R. G., Bailey, R., Molich, R., Dumas, J., & Spool, J. M. (2002). Usability in practice: Formative usability evaluations – evolution and revolution. In *Proceedings of the Computer Human Interaction conference*. April 20-25. Minneapolis, Minnesota, USA.

Reeves, S. (2004). *Research techniques for augmented reality experiences*. Retrieved June 20, 2012, from http://www.mrl.nott.ac.uk/~str/doc/methods.pdf

Regenbrecht, H., & Schubert, T. (2002). Measuring presence in augmented reality environments: Design and a first test of a questionnaire. In *Proceedings of the 5th Annual International Workshop Presence 2002*. Porto, Portugal.

Region, N. J. C. (2011). IT strategy 2014. [Aalborg Oest.]. *Niels Bohrs Vej, 30*, 9220.

Rieber, L. P. (1996). Seriously considering play: Designing interactive learning environments based on the blending of microworlds, simulations, and games. *Educational Technology Research and Development, 44*(1), 43–58. doi:10.1007/BF02300540

Robert, S., Robert, B., & Sandy, F. L. (1992). *New vocabularies in film semiotics: Structuralism, post-structuralism and beyond*. London: Routledge, Taylor & Francis.

Rosenthal, J., & Booth, M. (2005). Maximizing the use of state adverse event data to improve patient safety. Retrieved from http://www.premierinc.org/quality/tools-services/safety/safety-share/03-06-downloads/01-patient-safety-gnl61.pdf

Rosson, M. B., & Carroll, J. M. (2002). *Usability engineering: Scenario-based development of human-computer interaction*. San Francisco: Morgan Kaufmann.

Royce, W. W. (1987). *Managing the development of large software systems: Concepts and techniques*. Paper presented at the Proceedings of the 9th international conference on Software Engineering. Monterey, California, United States.

Rubin, J., & Chisnell, D. (2008). *Handbook of usability testing: How to plan, design, and conduct effective tests*. Indianapolis, IN: Wiley Publishers.

Rudd, J., Stern, K., & Iseness, S. (1996). Low versus high fidelity debate. *Interaction, 3*(1), 76–85. doi:10.1145/223500.223514

Rudman, P., Sharples, M., & Lonsdale, P. (2008). Cross-context learning. In Tallon, L., & Walker, K. (Eds.), *Digital technologies and the museum experience. Handheld guides and other media* (pp. 147–166). Walnut Creek: Altamira Press.

Ruggles, R. (1997). *Knowledge Management Tools*. Boston, MA: Butterworth-Heinemann.

Russell, J. A. (2003). Core affect and the psychological construction of emotion. *Psychological Review, 110*, 145–172. doi:10.1037/0033-295X.110.1.145

Russell, J. A., Weiss, A., & Mendelsohn, G. A. (1998). Affect grid: A single-item scale of pleasure and arousal. *Journal of Personality and Social Psychology, 57*(3), 493–502. doi:10.1037/0022-3514.57.3.493

Saddler, H. J. (2001). Design: Understanding design representations. *Interaction, 8*(4), 17–24. doi:10.1145/379537.379542

Saffer, D. (2008). *Designing gestural interfaces*. Sebastopol, CA: O'Reilly Media.

Salgado, L. C. d-C, de Souza, C.S., & Leitão, C. F. (2009). *A semiotic inspection of ICDL*. Monografias em Ciência da Computação, No. 31/09. ISSN: 0103-9741.

Salisbury, K., Conti, F., & Barbagli, F. (2004). Haptic rendering: Introductory concepts. *IEEE Computer Graphics and Applications, 2*, 24–32. doi:10.1109/MCG.2004.1274058

Sanchez-Vives, M. V., & Slater, M. (2005). From presence to consciousness through virtual reality. *Nature Reviews. Neuroscience, 6*(4), 332–339. doi:10.1038/nrn1651

Sanders, J., & Curran, E. (1994). *Software quality*. Addison-Wesley.

Sauro, J. (2011, February 2). Measuring usability with the system usability scale (SUS). In *Measuring usability*. Retrieved September 29, 2012, from http://www.measuringusability.com/sus.php.

Scanlon, T., Schroeder, W., Snyder, C., & Spool, J. (1998). Websites that work: Designing with your eyes open. In Proceedings of the SIGCHI on Human Factors in Computing Systems. Los Angeles, CA: Association for Computing Machinery.

Schmalstieg, D. (2005). Augmented reality techniques in games. In *Proceedings of Fourth IEEE and ACM International Symposium on Mixed and Augmented Reality* ISMAR05.

Schroeder, W., Brittan, D., & Spool, J. M. (2005). *Recruiting without fear: How to find first-rate participants for design studies* (Rep.). User Interface Engineering. Retrieved from http://www.uie.com/reports

Schubert, T. W., Friedmann, F., & Regenbrecht, H. (1999). Embodied presence in virtual environments. In Paton, R., & Neilson, I. (Eds.), *Visual representations and interpretations* (pp. 268–278). Springer-Verlag. doi:10.1007/978-1-4471-0563-3_30

Schuemie, M. J., van der Straaten, P., Krijn, M., & van der Mast, C. (2001). Research on presence in virtual reality: A survey. *CyberPsychology Behaviour, 4*(2), 183–201. doi:10.1089/109493101300117884

Schuler, D., & Namioka, A. (Eds.). (1993). *Participatory design: Principles and practices*. Mahwah, NJ: Lawrence Erlbaum.

Schusteritsch, R., Wei, C. Y., & LaRosa, M. (2007). Towards the perfect infrastructure for usability testing on mobile devices. *In Proceedings of CHI 2007* (pp. 1839-1844). San Jose, CA, USA. ACM Press.

Schwaber, K., & Beedle, M. (2002). *Agile software development with scrum*. Upper Saddle River, NJ: Prentice Hall.

Schweibenz, W. (1991). The virtual museum: New perspectives for museums to present objects and information using the Internet as a knowledge base and communication system. In H. Zimmermann and H. Schramm (Eds.), *Proceedings of the 6th ISI Conference* (pp. 185-200). Prague, Konstanz, UKV.

Seffah, A., Gulliksen, J., & Desmarais, A. (2005). An introduction to human-centered software engineering: Integrating usability in the development process. In Seffah, A., Gulliksen, J., & Desmarais, A. (Eds.), *Human-centered software engineering: Integrating usability in the software development lifecycle* (pp. 3–14). Dordrecht, The Netherlands: Springer. doi:10.1007/1-4020-4113-6_1

Sewry, D., & Sunassee, N. (2003). A theoretical framework for knowledge management implementation. In Proceedings of the 2002 annual research conference of the South African institute of computer scientists and information technologists on Enablement through technology. Port Elizabeth, South Africa: The Association of Computing Machinery.

Shloerb, D. W. (1995). A quantitative measure of telepresence. *Presence (Cambridge, Mass.)*, 4(1), 64–80.

Shneiderman, B. (2000). Universal usability. *Communications of the ACM*, 43(5), 84–89. doi:10.1145/332833.332843

Silver, M. (2005). *Exploring interface design*. Clifton Park, NY: Delmar Learning.

Silverstone, R. (1994). The medium is the museum. In Miles, R., & Zavala, L. (Eds.), *Towards the museum of the future* (pp. 161–176). London, New York: Routledge.

Simonsen, J., Hertzum, M., & Barlach, A. (2011). Experiences with effects specifications. In Hertzum, M., & Jørgensen, C. (Eds.), *Balancing sourcing and innovation in information systems development* (pp. 145–163). Trondheim, NO: Tapir Academic Publishers.

Singh, A., & Wesson, J. (2009). Evaluation criteria for assessing the usability of ERP Systems systems. In Proceedings of the 2009 Annual Conference of the South African Institute of Computer Scientists and Information Technologists. Vaal River, South Africa: The Association of Computing Machinery.

Slater, M. (1999). Measuring presence: A response to the Witmer and Singer Presence questionnaire. *Presence (Cambridge, Mass.)*, 8(5), 560–565. doi:10.1162/105474699566477

Slater, M. (2004). How colourful was your day? Why questionnaires cannot assess presence in virtual environments. *Presence (Cambridge, Mass.)*, 13(4), 484–493. doi:10.1162/1054746041944849

Slater, M., & Wilbur, S. (1997). A framework for immersive virtual environments (FIVE): Speculations on the role of presence in virtual environments. *Presence (Cambridge, Mass.)*, 6, 603–616.

Smiley, L., & Millet, B. (2011). Near miss reporting systems: Best practices and development guidelines. In *Proceedings of the International Society for Occupational Ergonomics and Safety*. Baltimore, MD.

Smith, D., & Valdes, R. (2005). Web 2.0: Get ready for the next old thing. Gartner Research Paper. Stamford, CT.

Smith, S., & Mosicr, J. (1986). *Guidelines for designing user interface software*. Bedford, MA: MITRE Corporation.

Snyder, C. (2003). *Paper prototyping: The fast and easy way to design and refine user interfaces*. San Francisco, CA: Morgan Kaufman Publishers.

Sousa, K., & Furtado, E. (2005). From usability tasks to usable user interfaces. In *Proceedings of the 4th international workshop on Task models and diagrams (TAMODIA 2005)* (pp.103 – 110).Gdansk, Poland: ACM Press.

Speroni, M. (2006). *Mastering the semiotics of information-intensive web interfaces*. (Unpublished doctoral dissertation). Faculty of Communication Sciences, University of Lugano, Switzerland.

Squire, K., & Barab, S. (2004). Replaying history: Engaging urban underserved students in learning world history through computer simulation games. In *Proceedings of the 6th International Conference on Learning Sciences* (pp. 505-512). Santa Monica, CA: International Society of the Learning Sciences.

Stacey, M., & Eckert, C. (2003). Against ambiguity. [CSCW]. *Computer Supported Cooperative Work*, 12(2), 153–183. doi:10.1023/A:1023924110279

Staggers, N. (1994). The staggers nursing computer experience questionnaire. Clinical method. *Applied Nursing Research*, 7(2), 97–106. doi:10.1016/0897-1897(94)90040-X

Stanney, K. M., Mourant, R. R., & Kennedy, R. S. (1998). Human factors issues in virtual environments: A review of literature. *Presence (Cambridge, Mass.)*, 7, 327–351. doi:10.1162/105474698565767

Stanney, K. M., Salvendy, G., Deisigner, J., DiZio, P., Ellis, S., & Ellison, E. (1998). After effects and sense of presence in virtual environments: Formulation of a research and development agenda. Report sponsored by the Life Sciences Division at NASA Headquarters. *International Journal of Human-Computer Interaction*, 10(2), 135–187. doi:10.1207/s15327590ijhc1002_3

Stanton, N. (Ed.). (2004). *The handbook of human factors and ergonomics methods*. Boca Raton, FL: CRC Press. doi:10.1201/9780203489925

Stapleton, J. (1998). *DSDM* (Repr. ed.). Harlow: Addison-Wesley.

Steuer, J. (1992). Defining virtual reality: Dimensions determining telepresence. *The Journal of Communication*, 42(4), 73–93. doi:10.1111/j.1460-2466.1992.tb00812.x

Stevens, B., Jerrams-Smith, J., Heathcote, D., & Callear, D. (2002). Putting the virtual into reality: Assessing object presence with projection augmented models. *Presence (Cambridge, Mass.)*, 11(1), 79–92. doi:10.1162/105474602317343677

Stewart, T. (2009). Usability evaluation. *Behaviour & Information Technology*, 28(2), 99–100. doi:10.1080/01449290902786510

Sun, S.-T., Pospisil, E., Muslukhov, I., Dindar, N., Hawkey, K., & Beznosov, K. (2011, July). *What makes users refuse web single sign-on? An empirical investigation of OpenID* (pp. 1–20). Pittsburgh, PA, USA: SOUPS. doi:10.1145/2078827.2078833

Sussex Past (The Sussex Archaeological Society). (2013). Retrieved June 10, 2012, from http://www.sussexpast.co.uk/

Compilation of References

Sweetser, P. M., & Wyeth, P. (2005). Game-Flow: A model for evaluating player enjoyment in games. *ACM Computers in Entertainment, 3*(3), 1–24. doi:10.1145/1077246.1077253

Sylaiou, S., Almosawi, A., Mania, K., & White, M. (2004). ˙preliminary evaluation of the augmented representation of cultural objects system. In *Proceedings of the 10th International Conference on Virtual Systems and Multimedia, Hybrid Realities-Digital Partners, Explorations in Art, Heritage, Science and the Human Factor* (pp. 426-431). VSMM Conference, Softopia, Ogaki City, Japan.

Sylaiou, S., Economou, M., Karoulis, A., & White, M., (2008). The evaluation of ARCO: A lesson in curatorial competence and intuition with new technology. *ACM Computers in Entertainment, 6*(2).

Sylaiou, S., Mania, K., Karoulis, A., & White, M. (2009). Presence-centred usability evaluation of a virtual museum: Exploring the relationship between presence, previous user experience and enjoyment. [IJHCS]. *International Journal of Human-Computer Studies, 68*(5), 243–253. doi:10.1016/j.ijhcs.2009.11.002

Sylaiou, S., Mania, K., Liarokapis, F., & White, M. (2012). (Manuscript submitted for publication). Evaluation of an augmented reality educational game. *Journal of Cultural Heritage.*

Teoh, C. (2012).User interviews – a basic introduction. Retrieved May 3, 2012, from http://www.webcredible.co.uk/user-friendly-resources/web-usability/user-interviews.shtml

Thomas, K. (2006). *Augmented reality: A new approach to learning.* FutureLab. Retrieved June 20, 2011, from http://www.futurelab.org.uk/resources/publications_reports_articles/web_articles/Web_Article496

Thompson, D., Canada, A., Bhatt, R., Davis, J., Plesko, L., & Baranowski, T. (2006). eHealth recruitment challenges. *Evaluation and Program Planning, 29*(4), 433–440. doi:10.1016/j.evalprogplan.2006.08.004

Thurnher, B. (2004). *Usability engineering.* TU Wien, Institute of Software Technology and Interactive Systems (IFS). Retrieved from http://qse.ifs.tuwien.ac.at/courses/Usability/downloads_05/Usability_Engineering_20040920b.pdf

Tian, L., Ahn, J., Cheng, H., Xing, X., Liang, L., Han, R., et al. (2012). Demo – MVChat: Flasher detection for mobile video chat. In *MobiSys 2012* (p 457). Low Wood Bay, Lake District, UK.

Tolbert, C. J., & Mossberger, K. (2006). The effects of e-government on trust and confidence in government. *Public Administration Review, 66*(3), 354–369. doi:10.1111/j.1540-6210.2006.00594.x

Tsichritzis, D., & Gibbs, S. (1991). Virtual museums and virtual realities. In *Proceedings of International Conference on Hypermedia and Interactivity in Museums* (pp 17-25).

Tsichritzis, D., & Klug, A. (1978). ANSI-X3-SPARC DBMS framework - report of study-group on database management-systems. *Information Systems, 3*(3), 173–191. doi:10.1016/0306-4379(78)90001-7

Tullis, T. S., & Stetson, J. (2004). *A comparison of questionnaires for assessing website usability*. Paper presented at the Usability Professionals Association Conference. Minneapolis, Minnesota.

Ulep, S. K., & Moran, S. L. (2005). Ten considerations for easing the transition to a web-based patient safety reporting system. In K. Henriksen, J.B. Battles, E.S., & D.I. Lewin (Eds.), *Advances in patient safety: From research to implementation*. Rockville, MD: Agency for Healthcare Research and Quality.

Universidad de Granada. Spain. (2013). *Mobile devices*. Retrieved May 23, 2012 from http://leo.ugr.es/J2ME/INTRO/intro_4.htm

Usability first. (2012). Website. Retrieved March, 2012 from http://www.usabilityfirst.com/glossary/learnability/

van Gerven, M., Farquhar, J., Schaefer, R., Vlek, R., Geuze, J., & Nijholt, A. (2009). The brain-computer interface cycle. *Journal of Neural Engineering*, *6*(4), 041001. doi:10.1088/1741-2560/6/4/041001

Veen, J. (2000). *The Art and Science of Web Design*. Indianapolis, IN: New Riders Publishing.

Venkatesh, V. (1985). Determinants of perceived ease of use: Integrating control, intrinsic motivation, and emotion into the technology acceptance model. *Information Systems Research*, *11*(4), 342–365. doi:10.1287/isre.11.4.342.11872

Venkatesh, V., Morris, M. G., Davis, G. B., & Davis, F. D. (2003). User acceptance of information technology: Toward a unified view. *Management Information Systems Quarterly*, *27*(3), 425–478.

Vicente, K. J. (1999). *Cognitive work analysis: Towards safe, productive, and healthy computer-based work*. Lawrence Erlbaum Associates, Inc.

Victoria & Albert Museum (VAM). (2013). Website. Retrieved October 6, 2012, from http://www.vam.ac.uk/

Vidgen, R., Avison, D., Wood, B., & Wood-Harper, T. (2002). *Developing web information systems: From strategy to implementation*. London: Butterworth-Heinemann.

von Niman, B., Rodríguez-Ascaso, A., Brown, S., & Sund, T. (2007). User experience design guidelines for telecare (e-health) services. *Interaction*, *14*(5), 36–40. doi:10.1145/1288515.1288537

Vorderer, P. (2000). Interactive entertainment and beyond. In Zillmann, D., & Vorderer, P. (Eds.), *Media entertainment: The psychology of its appeal* (pp. 21–36). Mahwah, NJ: Lawrence Erlbaum Associates.

Vorderer, P. (2001). It's all entertainment, sure. But what exactly is entertainment? Communication research, media psychology, and the explanation of entertainment experiences. *Poetics*, *29*, 247–261. doi:10.1016/S0304-422X(01)00037-7

Vronay, D., Smith, M., & Drucker, S. (1999). Alternative interfaces for chat. *UIST'99 CHI Letters*, *1*(1), 19-26.

Wagner, L. M., Capezuti, E., & Ouslander, J. G. (2006). Reporting near-miss events in nursing homes. *Nursing Outlook*, *54*, 85–93. doi:10.1016/j.outlook.2006.01.003

Wagner, L. M., Capezuti, E., Taylor, J. A., Sattin, R. W., & Ouslander, J. G. (2005). Impact of a falls menu-driven incident-reporting system on documentation and quality improvement in nursing homes. *The Gerontologist, 45*(6), 835–842. doi:10.1093/geront/45.6.835

Wagner, R., & Sternberg, R. (1985). Practical intelligence in real-world pursuits: The role of tacit knowledge. *Journal of Personality and Social Psychology, 49*(2), 436–458. doi:10.1037/0022-3514.49.2.436

Walczuch, R., Verkuijlen, M., Geus, B., & Ronnen, U. (2001). *Stickiness of commercial virtual communities. MERIT – Infonomics Research Memorandum Series*. Maastricht, The Netherlands, MERIT.

Walker, K. (2008). Structuring visitor participation. In Tallon, L., & Walker, K. (Eds.), *Digital technologies and the museum experience. Handheld guides and other media* (pp. 109–124). Walnut Creek: Altamira Press.

Walther, J. B., & Boyd, S. (2002). Attraction to computer-mediated social support. In Lin, C. A., & Atkin, D. (Eds.), *Communication technology and society: Audience adoption and uses* (pp. 153–188). Cresskill, NJ: Hampton Press.

Wang, S.-C. (2009). Why do players stick to a specific online game? The uses and gratifications perspective. *Americas Conference on Information Systems AMCIS 2009 Proceedings* (paper 351). San Francisco, CA.

Warell, A. (2001). *Design syntactics: A functional approach to visual product form – Theory, models, and methods* (Unpublished doctoral dissertation). Chalmers University of Technology, Gothenburg, Sweden.

Weiss, A. (2005). The power of collective intelligence. *netWorker, 9*(3), 16–23. doi:10.1145/1086762.1086763

White, M., Mourkoussis, N., et al. (2004). ARCO-An architecture for digitization, management and presentation of virtual exhibitions. *IEEE Computer Society Conference, 22nd International Conference on Computer Graphics* (pp. 622-625).

Whitefield, A., Wilson, F., & Dowell, J. (1991). A framework for human factors evaluation. *Behaviour & Information Technology, 10*(1), 65–79. doi:10.1080/01449299108924272

Williamson, J., Murray-Smith, R., Blankertz, B., Krauledat, M., & Muller, K. R. (2009). Designing for uncertain, asymmetric control: Interaction design for brain-computer interfaces. *International Journal of Human-Computer Studies, 67*, 827–841. doi:10.1016/j.ijhcs.2009.05.009

Wilson, C. (Ed.). (2010). *User experience re-mastered: Your guide to getting the right design*. Burlington, MA: Morgan Kaufmann.

Wojciechowski, R., Walczak, K., White, M., & Cellary, W. (2004). Building virtual and augmented reality museum exhibitions. In S. N. Spencer (Ed.), *Proceedings of the Web3D 2004 Symposium –the 9th International Conference on 3D Web Technology* (pp. 135-144). ACM SIGGRAPH.

Wolpaw, J. R., Birbaumer, N., McFarland, D. J., Pfurtscheller, G., & Vaughan, T. M. (2002). Brain- computer interfaces for communication and control. *Clinical Neurophysiology, 113*, 767–791. doi:10.1016/S1388-2457(02)00057-3

Wright, P. (1989). The quality of visitors' experiences in art museums. In Peter Vergo (Ed.), *The new museology* (pp. 119-148). London: Reaktion books.

Wu, A. W., Pronovost, P., & Morlock, L. (2002). ICU incident reporting systems. *Journal of Critical Care, 17*(2), 86–94. doi:10.1053/jcrc.2002.35100

Wu, C.-M. (2011). What factors affect people's stickiness on the social network site? The case of Facebook in Taiwan. *Key Engineering Materials*, *474-476*, 1573–1577. doi:10.4028/www.scientific.net/KEM.474-476.1573

Yandziak, J. J., De Lima, O., Verboonen, M., Gomes, J. O., & Guerlain, S. (2006). Critical review and redesign of a petroleum industry accident/incident reporting system. In Michael DeVore (Ed.), *Proceedings of the 2006 IEEE Systems and Information Engineering Design Symposium* (pp. 222-227).

Zeng, Z., Pantic, M., Roisman, G. I., & Huang, T. S. (2007). A survey of affect recognition methods: Audio, visual and spontaneous expressions. In *Proceedings of the 9th international conference on Multimodal interfaces* (pp. 39-58). Minneapolis, MN: IEEE.

Zhao, J. J., Zhao, S. Y., & Zhao, S. Y. (2009). Opportunities and threats: A security assessment of state e-government websites. *Government Information Quarterly*. doi:doi:10.1016/j.giq.2009.07.004

Zott, C., Amit, R., & Donlevy, J. (2000). Strategies for value creation in e-commerce: Best practice in Europe. *European Management Journal*, *18*, 463–475. doi:10.1016/S0263-2373(00)00036-0

About the Contributors

Miguel A. Garcia-Ruiz graduated in Computer Systems engineering and obtained his MSc in Computer Science from the University of Colima, Mexico. He received his PhD in Computer Science and Artificial Intelligence at the University of Sussex, UK. Miguel took a virtual reality course at Salford University, UK, and a graphics techniques internship at the Madrid Polytechnic University, Spain. Miguel is an Assistant Professor with the Department of Computer Science and Mathematics, Algoma University, Canada. He has published scientific papers in major journals, book chapters and three books, and directed a video documentary on virtual reality. His research interests include educational virtual environments and usability of multimodal human-computer interfaces.

* * *

Fabio Abbattista is an associate professor at the Department of Informatica, University of Bari, Italy. In the past years, his research activity has been mainly devoted to computational intelligence, and in particular evolutionary algorithms and classifier systems. He is actually involved in studying the application of computational intelligence techniques and methods to the development of adaptive computer games, with a focus on dynamic content generation. To this aim, recently, he started a research program for analyzing and evaluating brain-computer interfaces as a tool to detect mental states of players involved in a game experience.

Ana C. Ahumada graduated as Software Engineer from the Universidad de Colima at Mexico and is a specialist in Human-Computer Interaction (HCI). She is member of the IHCLab of the Universidad de Colima. Currently, she is finishing her thesis about a usability study made to the e-planea platform of the Universidad de Colima. Her research interests are User Experience, Usability and Human-Computer Interaction. She is planning to study a Master Degree in User Centered Interactive Systems. She is aiming at working in the usability and user experience sector.

Hana Al-Nuaim is an associate professor in Computer Science and the Dean of King Abdulaziz University Women's Campuses, Jeddah, Saudi Arabia. She received her Bachelor's in CS from the University of Texas at Austin and Masters and DSc in Computer Science from George Washington University, USA. She was a former CS Department head and as the Vice Dean of e-Learning and Distance Education helped launch the first e-learning program in the kingdom for women. She has extensive faculty training background and referred papers for publications in HCI, user-centered design, usability, multimedia, e-learning, e- government and knowledge cities and has been involved in many Web-based research projects.

Francisco Javier Álvarez is a professor in Computer Science at Universidad Autónoma de Aguascalientes. He holds a Ph.D. in Engineering (UNAM, México, 2004), He has a number of collaborations with very important researches in prestigious universities around the world. Dr. Álvarez Rodriguez has reported his work in journals, book chapters, conference papers, and technical reports, and so far has supervised almost 40 students at the graduate and undergraduate level. His current research interests include software engineering (methodologies, metrics, among others), and distance education (educational Internet technologies, learning environments, learning objects, among others).

Anders Barlach is a Ph.D-fellow with the department Computer Science at Roskilde University, and a research fellow with the CSC (Computer Sciences Corp.). He is employed by the CSC on an industry research grant from the Danish Government in collaboration with Roskilde University. His research interests include Nursing Informatics, Patient Empowerment, Effects Driven IT Development and Participatory IT Design. Currently empirical work is concentrated around Pilot-Implementation and application of Evaluation methods in commercial contexts.

Joshua Boelter is a Software Architect in the PC Client Group where he leads the development of consumer focused software and the technology that makes consumer experiences possible. He holds a BS in Computer Science and a MS in Software Engineering. Josh joined Intel in 1999 and has worked on a number of consumer focused products including leading the team that developed the Intel® Pair & Share experience and the underlying cross-device connectivity technology. He has been a champion of interdisciplinary teams and applying agile development practices to the entire software development lifecycle. Josh strives to build products that his mom would use while pushing the boundaries of the technology that enables them.

Stefano Bonelli works as a Human Factors and Usability expert. He obtained a master degree (2008), with specialisation in Human-Computer Interaction. He has been involved in evaluation with end-users, HMI assessment and design, and dissemination activities in EU funded projects such as FLYSAFE (2005-2009), ALICIA (2009-2013) and EUROCONTROL funded projects such as CRISTAL MED (2005-2009).

Julie Buelow began her journey into web design at a Toronto studio called "Toronto Image Works" in the year 2000 when CSS was in its infancy and tables were in their glory. Her passion for usability was sparked in 2004 after attending a presentation, "The Secret Strategies of Highly Successful Websites" by Jared Spool and Christine Perfetti. To learn more, Julie took the Certificate in Information Design at the iSchool Institute at the University of Toronto. Courses included Usability Evaluation, Information Architecture, Web Analytics, and Business Analysis, which enabled her to lead over 28 usability projects and conduct over 120 testing sessions. This experience has led to the collaborative usability methods and insights described in her chapter. To date her focus has been usability in local government, primarily public health websites and campaigns. Further interests include inclusive design and sustainable design. Julie holds an Honors B.A. in Criminology and Economics from the University of Toronto, St. Michael's College.

John Busvine is a Curriculum Manager at The Open University, where he manages the development and delivery of a suite of modules in the Undergraduate Computing & Information Technology programme, largely in an online e-learning environment. Before joining the Open University, John worked in publishing, principally in business information services, where he managed editorial content and helped to develop a bespoke online publishing system. John's undergraduate study was at Cardiff University where he gained a BA in Philosophy.

Ginger Butcher is an award-winning Science Writer and accomplished Education product developer with over 15 years experience working for *NASA Headquarters* and *NASA Goddard Space Flight Center*. Ginger has over a decade of experience creating unique education products that teach NASA science concepts to young children. This includes an extensive background translating complex scientific concepts for students, educators and the general public through various media such as videos, interactive displays, books, brochures, and websites. Her undergraduate work focused on remote sensing and cartography. Ginger's work on her Masters in

Instructional Systems Design involved exploring techniques to teach kindergartens abstract concepts involved in satellite data interpretation. She translated this work into various interactive websites for K-4 students for NASA. Ginger continues her work developing education and outreach experiences for NASA's Aura satellite mission.

Valeria Carofiglio is assistant professor at the Department of Informatica, University of Bari, Italy. In the last years, her research activity has been devoted to the analysis and the synthesis of human factors in the field of human-computer interaction, with particular interest in computational models of emotions. She is actually experimenting with the use of brain-computer interfaces for monitoring mental states, off-line as well as in real-time applications.

Roberto K. Champney is a Senior Research Associate at Design Interactive Inc. He has had significant experience in systems design and evaluation having served as lead analyst and designer in several system designs. His work focuses on Task Analysis, design and evaluation of Training Environments and Interactive Systems, Human Performance Assessments and Training Management tools and conduction of Training Effectiveness Evaluations. His research has focused on human performance and training in military domains, design and assessment of interactive systems, usability and user experience involving human emotions. He researched and developed methods for emotional design now in use in industry, co-developed manuscripts for publication and technical reports to inform designers and developers on design recommendations. He has worked on several multidisciplinary teams where he has developed an expertise in capturing the Voice Of the Customer (VOC) for transformation into design requirements and specifications. Roberto poses in-depth understanding of usability engineering, human computer interaction, human factors, and ergonomics principles to help guide the design process. He holds a PhD in Human Engineering and Ergonomics, from the University of Central Florida.

Rochelle Evans Edwards works at Electronic Arts as the usability research manager for Pogo.com, a casual games website. She holds a Ph.D. in Human Factors/Human Computer Interaction from Rice University in Houston, Texas in the United States. For her dissertation, she assessed subjective ratings of flow and affect to determine why users who like a product may rate it higher in quality. In her current role, she ensures that Pogo's gaming experience and site navigation is entertaining and user-friendly. She works to integrate the measures of flow and affect with traditional satisfaction metrics in industry to assess user enjoyment. Most recently, she has published in Proceedings of the Human Factors and Ergonomics Society and Interacting with Computers.

Morten Hertzum, PhD, is an associate professor of Computer Science at Roskilde University, Denmark. His research interests include user-centered design, usability evaluation methods, achieving benefit from IT, and information seeking and visualization. Currently his empirical work concerns IT in healthcare. He has published articles in journals such as Information Processing & Management, International Journal of Human-Computer Interaction, International Journal of Human-Computer Studies, Communications of the AIS, and Information & Organization.

Muhammad Nazrul Islam, MSc, is a PhD student at Department of Information Technologies at Åbo Akademi University, Finland. He is also a faculty member at Department of Computer Science and Engineering, Khulna University of Engineering & Technology (KUET), Bangladesh. His research interests are focused on Human-Computer Interaction, Information Systems Usability, User Experience, and Computer Semiotics. He is the author of 23 peer-reviewed publications in journals and conferences.

Colleen Kaiser is an accomplished, results-oriented User Experience Architect who enjoys creating interactive websites and applications for desktop and mobile devices. Her focus over the past 15 years has been on improving productivity and satisfaction by delivering engaging products that are designed with the user in mind. With a 360-degree view of the product lifecycle, she is skilled at turning initial concepts into finished products with measured evaluation steps along the way. She has extensive experience doing user research and usability testing with users of all ages. Her passion for exploring new testing tools and pushing existing methodologies in new directions results in collecting rich data and insights that work to continually refine the user experience.

Cynthia Kaschub joined Intel in 2008 after completing her PhD in Cognitive Psychology. Prior to joining Intel, she has been active in research in a variety of domains including emotion and attention, psychophysiology, medical education and decision-support tool development for the Navy. Cynthia spent her first few years as at Intel as a Human Factors Engineer embedded within a software development team within the PC Client Group. In this group she worked within an interdisciplinary team developing and evaluating the user experience from product inception to release. Currently, Cynthia joined the Perceptual Computing Group within Intel where she leads a team of UX practitioners chartered with developing experiences that integrate human senses into Intel's computing platforms. Regardless of group and role, Cynthia is an active advocate of the user and their role in shaping the experience they desire and Intel aims to deliver.

Karen Kear is a senior lecturer at the UK Open University, where she designs and teaches module on Information Technology, and carries out research in e-learning. Karen joined the Open University as an educational software designer, having worked for many years as a software developer for British Petroleum, and prior to that as a theoretical physicist in the nuclear energy industry. Karen's undergraduate study was at Cambridge University UK, where she gained a BA in theoretical physics. She also has an MSc in Information Technology from Keele University UK, and a PhD from the UK Open University. Karen is a fellow of the UK's Higher Education Academy.

Christina Kokini is a Research Associate at Design Interactive, Inc., and has been involved in design, development and evaluation of virtual training tools for the Office of Naval Research, and the Army Research Laboratory. Her work focuses on training system design, development, and usability, including designing functionality into products to support user requirements, as well as conducting usability and training effectiveness evaluations. She holds a Master's degree from Penn State University in Industrial Engineering with a Human Factors Option, where her research focused on the direct effect of contextual characteristics on the perceived usability of a product. She also has a Bachelor's degree from Purdue University in Industrial Engineering.

Stephanie Lackey earned her Master's and Ph.D. degrees in Industrial Engineering and Management Systems with a specialization in simulation, modeling and analysis at the University of Central Florida. Dr. Lackey conducted high-risk research and development aimed at rapid transition of virtual communications capabilities to the Field and Fleet as a computer engineer with the United States Naval Air Warfare Center Training Systems Division (NAWC TSD). She joined the University of Central Florida (UCF) Institute for Simulation and Training's (IST) Applied Cognition and Training in Immersive Virtual Environments (ACTIVE) Lab in 2008, and assumed the role of Lab Director in 2010. Dr. Lackey leverages her experience in advanced predictive modeling to the field of human performance in order to develop methods for improving human performance in simulation-based and immersive training environments and human-robot interfaces.

Fotis Liarokapis is the director of Interactive Worlds Applied Research Group (iWARG) at Coventry University and a research fellow at the Serious Games. He has contributed to more than 65 refereed publications and has more than 450 citations. He has been invited more than 40 times to become member of international conference committees and has chaired 11 sessions in 7 international conferences. Moreover, he has secured around £150,000 from a number of research projects. In addition, he is a member of IEEE, IET, ACM, BCS and Eurographics. Finally, he is on the editorial advisory board of The Open Virtual Reality Journal published by Bentham and the editor-in-chief of the International Journal of Interactive Worlds (IJIW) published by IBIMA.

Martha A. Magaña is a professor in Educational Planning and Management at the School of Pedagogy of the Universidad de Colima, Mexico. She is currently pursuing a PhD in Leadership and Management of Higher Education Institutions at the Universidad Anáhuac and she received a Masters degree in Educational Research at Universidad de Colima, Mexico in 2000. Her research interests are on Training and Educational Research. Professor Magaña currently is the head of the Department of Institutional Planning and Development of the Universidad de Colima.

Ian Martin is a senior lecturer and course leader in Business Information Technology at Leeds Metropolitan University, UK. Ian's research interests include spatial and temporal perspectives on the sociology and history of computing work. Ian has a PhD from the University of Manchester, UK. His PhD thesis, 'Centring the computer in the business of banking: Barclays Bank and Technological Change, 1954-1974', is a labor history of early computing work.

Ricardo Mendoza-González is a Researcher/Professor at Instituto Tecnológico de Aguascalientes (Mexico). He holds a Ph.D. in Computer Science (Universidad Autónoma de Aguascalientes, México, 2009), a Master's degree in Computer Science (Universidad Autónoma de Aguascalientes, México, 2007), and a Bachelor of Computer Science (Instituto Tecnológico de Aguascalientes, México, 2004). Dr. Mendoza-González has reported his work in prestigious journals and international conferences. He collaborates with researchers of the University of Ontario Institute of Technology (UOIT), and Universidad Autónoma de Aguascalientes (México). His current research interests include several topics on: human-computer interaction, information security, usability, artificial intelligence, and software engineering. He is member of the National System of Researchers (SNI) in Mexico.

Barbara Millet was an assistant professor at Texas Tech University. She is currently a principal user experience researcher at Motorola Solutions, Inc. She provides human factors and user research leadership for the company's worldwide radio solutions and mobile computing products. She received her PhD in industrial engineering from the University of Miami and has more than 15 years of research and industry experience in human factors and product design. Her interest areas include user interface design, human factors, performance measurement, and quantitative measures in usability.

Jaime Muñoz Arteaga is a Professor in Computer Science at the Universidad Autónoma de Aguascalientes, Mexico. He holds a Ph.D. in Computer Science, Human-Computer Interaction (University Toulouse 1 (UT1), Toulouse, France, 2000). He has a number of collaborations with very important researches in prestigious universities around the world. Dr. Muñoz Arteaga has reported his work in journals, book chapters, conference papers, and technical reports, and so far has supervised over 45 students at the graduate and undergraduate level. His current research interests include several topics on human-computer Interaction, mobile technologies, software engineering, and artificial intelligence.

Linda Napoletano holds a Ph.D. in Human Computer Interaction. She has 8 years experience on EU co-funded projects aiming at designing and validate humans' integration into technology innovation processes. She has been involved as human factors, validation and training expert in EU, EUROCONTROL and ENAV funded projects, among others Caats2 (2006-2009), ALICIA (2009-2013), BEMOSA (2009-2012) and VIRTUAL LIFE (2009-2011), and training on HF fundamentals for the IANS. Linda is san Associate Researcher in HCI at the University of Sassari and Siena, Italy.

Pedro C. Santana is a professor in Human-Computer Interaction (HCI) and Software Engineering at the School of Telematics Engineering of the Universidad de Colima at Mexico. He is currently pursuing a PhD in Telematics at the Universidad de Vigo and he received a Masters degree (with honors) in Computer Science at Universidad Autónoma de Baja California (UABC), Mexico in 2005. His research interests are on Human Computer Interaction, Learning Technology, Software Engineering and Ubiquitous Computing. Professor Santana was recognized with the 2012 IBM Faculty Award to support his research on "Ambient Intelligence and Natural Interactions in the Mexican Classrooms."

Jesper Simonsen is Professor of Design Studies at Roskilde University, Denmark. Since 1991 he has conducted research in collaboration with industry on Participatory Design developing theories and methods for IT design in an organizational context. His publications include Participatory IT Design: Designing for Business and Workplace Realities (MIT Press, 2004), Design Research: Synergies from Interdisciplinary Perspectives (Routledge, 2010), and Routledge International Handbook of Participatory Design (Routledge, 2012).

Neil K. Simpkins was a technology consultant to the European Commission for a number of years, later working on concentration of effort and resources across a large programme of European language processing projects. He was also a project leader developing sophisticated reporting and trading applications for large organisations in the financial sector. He has worked at several UK universities, including Southampton and Oxford Brookes before being appointed as a lecturer in web application development at the Open University where he has developed a range of successful courses and pursues his research interests in internet technology focusing on server-side aspects.

Kay M. Stanney is President and Founder of Design Interactive, Inc., a dynamic startup company in the Human-Systems Integration field, working for the Department of Defense, various Federal agencies, and Fortune 500 corporations. Dr Stanney received a B.S. in Industrial Engineering from SUNY Buffalo, after which time she spent three years working at Intel Corporation. She received her Masters and Ph.D. in Industrial/Human Factors Engineering, from Purdue University, after which time she spent 15 years as an Industrial Engineering professor at the University of Central Florida.

R. Todd Stephens is the Sr. Technical Architect of the Evolving Technologies for the AT&T Corporation. Todd is responsible for setting the corporate strategy and architecture for the development and implementation of the enterprise collaborative and social solutions. Todd has over 135 professional and academic publications including 8 patents in the field of technology innovation. Todd holds degrees in Mathematics and Computer Science from Columbus State University, an MBA degree from Georgia State University, and a Ph.D. in Information Systems from Nova Southeastern University.

Stella Sylaiou has a B.Sc. in History and Archaeology a M.A. in Museology and a Ph.D. degree from Inter-departmental Postgraduate Program, Protection, Conservation and Restoration of Cultural Monuments, part of which was funded by the Marie Curie Scholarship for the Transfer of Knowledge in the Centre of VLSI and Computer Graphics, University of Sussex, UK., a M.Sc. degree in Archaeological Computing (University of Southampton, UK) and a Diploma in Open and Distance

Learning (Hellenic Open University). She worked in Ephorates and Museums, in the Hellenic Archaeological Cadastre and taught at the Fine Art and Art Sciences Department, Univ. of Ioannina, Greece, the Visual and Applied Arts Department, Univ. of Western Macedonia, Greece. She participated in twelve research projects, she has contributed to forty refereed publications. She currently works as a Post-doctoral research fellow in the Aristotle University of Thessaloniki and as Adjunct Faculty and tutor for the Hellenic Open University (MSc. in Cultural Organizations' Management).

Franck Tétard, PhD, is a Senior Lecturer at Department of Informatics and Media, at Uppsala University, Sweden, and a Research Fellow at the Institute for Advanced Management Systems Research, Åbo Akademi University, Finland. He is also a Docent in Information Systems Usability at Åbo Akademi University. His research interests include mobile technology adoption, mobile usability and mobile learning. He is the author of 35 peer-reviewed publications in journals and conferences.

Martin White holds a BSc (Hons) in Computer Systems Engineering and a PhD in Computer Science (3D Computer Graphics) from the University of Sussex, where he is currently a Reader in Computer Science. Martin is currently working with American Express investigating how social media can connect virtual communities to the digital economy through micropayments and rewards mechanisms. Martin is a Member of the British Computer Society (MBCS) and the Institute of Engineering and Technology (IET). He has published 170 articles in the fields of computer graphics hardware and software, more recently focusing on digital heritage and motion sensing systems. His current research interests include digital heritage, motion capture, and mobile apps exploiting payment, rewards and social media in the digital economy. Martin has project managed on many EU and UK funded research projects, the most recent collaborating with industry on the UK's Technology Strategy Board calls within the UK's digital economy research theme.

Index